An Introduction to
SECONDARY DATA
ANALYSIS with IBM SPSS STATISTICS

SAGE was founded in 1965 by Sara Miller McCune to support the dissemination of usable knowledge by publishing innovative and high-quality research and teaching content. Today, we publish over 900 journals, including those of more than 400 learned societies, more than 800 new books per year, and a growing range of library products including archives, data, case studies, reports, and video. SAGE remains majority-owned by our founder, and after Sara's lifetime will become owned by a charitable trust that secures our continued independence.

Los Angeles | London | New Delhi | Singapore | Washington DC | Melbourne

An Introduction to
SECONDARY DATA ANALYSIS with **IBM SPSS STATISTICS**

John MacInnes

SAGE

Los Angeles | London | New Delhi
Singapore | Washington DC | Melbourne

Los Angeles | London | New Delhi
Singapore | Washington DC | Melbourne

SAGE Publications Ltd
1 Oliver's Yard
55 City Road
London EC1Y 1SP

SAGE Publications Inc.
2455 Teller Road
Thousand Oaks, California 91320

SAGE Publications India Pvt Ltd
B 1/I 1 Mohan Cooperative Industrial Area
Mathura Road
New Delhi 110 044

SAGE Publications Asia-Pacific Pte Ltd
3 Church Street
#10-04 Samsung Hub
Singapore 049483

Editor: Mila Steele
Assistant editor: John Nightingale
Production editor: Ian Antcliff
Copyeditor: Richard Leigh
Proofreader: Thea Watson
Marketing manager: Sally Ransom
Cover designer: Shaun Mercier
Typeset by: C&M Digitals (P) Ltd, Chennai, India
Printed and bound by CPI Group (UK) Ltd,
Croydon, CR0 4YY

Library of Congress Control Number: 2016944792

British Library Cataloguing in Publication data

A catalogue record for this book is available from
the British Library

ISBN 978-1-4462-8576-3
ISBN 978-1-4462-8577-0 (pbk)

For Jana

CONTENTS

COMPANION WEBSITE

An Introduction to Secondary Data Analysis with IBM SPSS Statistics is more than just a book. You'll see that throughout, I urge you to get on and do analysis as the best way to learn about it. To help you do that, the book is supported by a wealth of online material to help you become a proficient secondary data analyst. Visit the SAGE companion website at **https://study.sagepub.com/macinnes** to find a range of free tools and resources that will enhance your learning experience.

These include:

- A series of step-by-step video-tutorials, in which I show you exactly how to use the IBM SPSS software to prepare and analyse secondary data. These videos correspond to the data analysis techniques covered in the book, so it's really helpful to use the book and the website together
- A Microsoft Excel file containing a 'confidence interval calculator', a helpful tool you can use with SPSS to find the margin of error of sample data
- SPSS syntax files which will enable you to perform the analytical techniques covered in the book and help you to answer the exercises at the end of each chapter
- Weblinks to all sorts of other useful SPSS learning resources, such as videos on all the main commands available in SPSS, and guides to a range of useful data sources from national data archives and international organisations such as the UN, the World Bank, the OECD, Eurostat and many others

When you come across this icon 🐾 in the book, it means there's a resource on the companion website to help you with the corresponding aspect of secondary data analysis in the text.

So, when you see 🐾, go straight to https://study.sagepub.com/macinnes to help you get started with secondary data analysis. There is a world of data out there for you to explore, and with the data analysis skills you'll learn using the book and the companion website, that world will soon become a less daunting and more fascinating and exciting place to be.

Good luck!

John MacInnes

ABOUT THE AUTHOR

John MacInnes is Professor of Sociology at the University of Edinburgh. He has been teaching students quantitative methods and data analysis for 30 years. He has been Strategic Advisor to the UK Economic and Social Research Council on Quantitative Methods Training and currently advises the British Academy on quantitative skills, the UK Q-Step programme on statistics pedagogy and researches on statistics anxiety for the ESRC National Centre for Research Methods. He is a Fellow of the Academy of Social Sciences and the Royal Statistical Society. His own research and publications range over population ageing and demographic change, gender identity, national identity and the sociology of industry.

ACKNOWLEDGEMENTS

Individual authors might write books, but they come from the collective effort of many people. My first debt is to my students who have taught me what works well or not so well in teaching and learning data analysis. My second debt is to my colleagues at the University of Edinburgh. It's unfair to single out individuals, but I will: Lindsay Paterson has been a constant source of enlightenment and encouragement. My third debt is to all those who have been busy trying to improve the standard of quantitative skills in UK social science over the last decade. The Nuffield Foundation, Economic and Social Research Council, and Higher Education Funding Council for England, and the passionate commitment of Linda Alebon, Sarah Lock, Rachel Tyrrell, Sharon Witherspoon and others who made Q-Step possible. I've had a wonderful editorial and production team at Sage: Ian Antcliff, Katie Metzler, John Nightingale, Alysha Owen, Mila Steele and their colleagues. Their professionalism has been exceeded only by their patience. I tell students that mistakes are fine when they are learning data analysis, the trick is to learn from them. There are probably a few still lurking in this book. If you find one, do let me know.

SECONDARY DATA ANALYSIS

The Evidence Is Out There

━━━━━━━ **introduction** ━━━━━━━

There is a vast and ever growing amount of easily accessible data available for analysis on almost any topic in the social sciences. It can be used to get some sense of the dimension of an issue, or for a more thorough and careful analysis that will take a good deal more preparation and time.

The internet has made secondary data analysis much easier, and the basic skills needed to get started are simple. However, there also are all kinds of challenges to getting the most out of empirical evidence, so that there will always be new and more powerful data analysis skills to learn.

1 ● 1   WHAT IS 'SECONDARY' DATA ANALYSIS?

A simple philosophy lies behind this book: that data analysis is something best learned by doing it. Curiosity and a capacity to be intrigued by empirical evidence are your most important resources. You'll build up your knowledge and expertise as exploring the data leads you to ask new questions and discover the technical skills you need to answer them.

Secondary data analysis simply means using evidence, usually quantitative, that someone else has collected and compiled. Many people imagine that secondary data analysis requires technical expertise that they don't have, that it takes time and skill to discover and access the relevant data or that the potential results don't justify the time invested in obtaining them. All these notions may once have had some truth in them, but the development of the internet, computing power and software, alongside a tremendous rise in the number and diversity of social surveys, has revolutionised not only the amount and range of data available, but also how easy it is to access and use. You can now become a secondary data analyst, and access useful and powerful data, in a matter of minutes, as I invite you to do in Chapter 3.

These skills are fundamental ones for all social scientists, because without such skills they are rather like a traveller who cannot read a map. The mapless tourist may happen upon interesting features of a landscape but they can get no real sense of how they might fit into the wider geography of the land they explore. The social sciences' only claim to be scientific rests on the way they use empirical evidence. Given the sheer scale of contemporary society, most of that evidence has to be quantitative. This is no criticism of qualitative work: it's just that without some quantitative context even the most perceptive ethnography is of limited use. Unfortunately, the social sciences tend to be heavy on theory and light on evidence. Theories are expounded more often than they are tested against the evidence. This is not a sustainable position for credible scientific work. Moreover, it is not necessary: the range and quality of secondary data available for social scientists to work with and use to test and elaborate their theory are growing all the time.

Collecting sound quantitative evidence is resource-intensive, technical, skilled work. It is best done by government statistical institutes, survey organisations, and consortia of experienced academics who know not only the theory but also the practice of doing it well, and who've got the resources to do so. That helps explain why most high-quality social survey research is of recent origin. There are remarkably few high-quality surveys from the period before the 1970s. It is only in the last forty years that we've seen the explosion of good survey data, together with the development of data archives to store and catalogue it, and only in the last decade has this been followed, thanks to the internet, with truly easy access to that data, access that enables everyone, with a minimum of expertise, to use it in powerful ways. There is now a wealth of high-quality data that allows anyone to map the social world around them in unprecedented detail, so that no one unable to do this can really claim to be a social scientist.

The term 'secondary data analysis' is an unfortunate one as it implies that such analysis is somehow second best. The term is a hangover from an era in which an individual or team of social scientists themselves designed the surveys and sometimes also collected much of the data that they worked with. Surveys would usually be bespoke affairs, designed to collect data relevant to a specific study. The scientists' analysis of the results was the 'primary' activity. However, were others to discover another use for the same data and use it for this different purpose, it became 'secondary' data analysis. While the days of the bespoke survey are not over, most surveys are now omnibus affairs, collecting data on a range of subjects and explicitly designed for 'secondary' use by others. Governments who need to collect data for all kinds of purposes now feel obliged, rightly, to make data that has been collected with public resources available for others to use and explore. In a sense almost all data analysis now is 'secondary'.

As well as social surveys based on face-to-face, telephone or self-completion interviews, new sources of data, whether captured through administrative processes, social media or other methods, are growing in importance. The volume of data is growing exponentially. It has been claimed that the world now creates as much new data every two years as existed in all previous history. Like many such claims this is almost certainly an exaggeration (for example, much of that 'data' comprises spam email) and impossible to verify, but it does capture the phenomenal rate of growth of data available to contemporary social scientists if they have the imagination, energy and skill to use it.

Secondary data analysis is relatively easy; the survey designers and data collectors have done most of the hard and difficult work. However, like any skill, it takes a little effort to learn to do it well. Above all, it takes a little time to develop the experience needed to use data critically. Paradoxically, one of the most important skills a researcher can develop is not technical expertise in the location, management and analysis of data – important though that is – but the ability to keep a good grasp of its limitations. Even the best map is a drastic simplification of the terrain it represents. So it is with data. The best analysts develop a good sense of what the data does not, and cannot, reveal. They also keep in mind the data that is *not* there. That enables them to make much more powerful use of what the evidence can genuinely support.

1 ○ 2 QUICK AND DIRTY OR CAREFUL AND CAUTIOUS?

In some ways secondary data analysis is *too* easy. You can rustle up some basic information based on secondary data on almost any topic in a few minutes. This is the quantitative equivalent of looking up *Wikipedia*: it's enough to give you a rough idea of what knowledge might be out there, and if it's worth pursuing the investigation further. I am a fan of 'quick and dirty'. One of the most useful skills you can develop is to quickly scan a data source either to see if it contains the kind of information you are after and is therefore worth investigating in more depth, or to get a quick sense of whether a rough idea 'flies' and could be developed further. It is also a wonderful way to reality-check more abstract and theoretical ideas in social science. If the theory is accurate, what kind of empirical data would be consistent or inconsistent with it? Do we find any such patterns? Be sceptical of theories which do not or cannot suggest empirical results or make broad predictions. Perhaps not every theory can be tested empirically, but if it cannot be so tested then it also has to be admitted that the theory is not really a theory but something else. Of course there is ample room for discussion about what constitutes testing. A good habit to develop is to ask of any piece of work: what is its evidence base?

Quick and dirty is fine for a first and very preliminary look. It is, however, only the very first stage of a scientific approach; the latter stages are more likely to take ten weeks than ten minutes. The difference lies in the care taken with every stage of the process, from the formulation of an exact research question, to the design of an empirical exploration or test of that question, a review of the possible data sources, careful attention to the measurement of the relevant variables, and consideration of how best to summarise and present the results.

Thorough secondary analysis takes time. Even the execution of a simple idea can require extensive data preparation and management that must be done carefully and checked for errors. Checking definitions may require you to delve deep into the data documentation, including original questionnaires and interviewer protocols, to make sure that a variable in a dataset is actually measuring what you hope it is measuring. You may need to review the sampling procedures to check that the weights supplied in the dataset are appropriate for the analysis you want to undertake, or consider whether any high-profile political events during the fieldwork period might have affected interviewees' responses.

For example, you might be interested in whether there is a relationship between age and religious belief. In ten minutes you could go to the European Social Survey website, and, using Nesstar, calculate the correlation coefficient between age and respondents' answers to the question 'How religious are you?' that were measured on a scale from 1 to 10 for the latest wave of the survey in 2012. If you did so you'd find that Pearson's r comes out at 0.14 across the 50,000 responses from the thirty-odd countries covered by that survey. You would thus have some preliminary rough evidence that older people *are* more likely to rate themselves as more religious, but that the relationship is not a particularly strong one.

However, this would be only the very beginning of a more thorough analysis. First, you might be interested in how the concept 'religious belief' ought to be defined and operationalised. Is it best thought of as a categorical question (either one believes in religion or one does not) or a matter of degrees of belief? If it is the latter, what might such 'degrees' comprise and what survey questions might uncover them? Would we want some corroboration of claims to belief in terms of action: declaring that one belongs to a particular religion, for example, or going to religious services, or praying? One might want to go even further and think about evidence of how far or in what ways religious belief influences a person's life: do they make decisions based on scripture, ritual or prayer, for example, or follow other ways of thinking and decision making? In other words, is their religious belief central to their social action, or, even in the case of the fervently devout, actually rather marginal to it?

Rather than focusing exclusively on the characteristics of 'believers', you would want to make *comparisons* between people with different degrees of belief or none at all, in terms of other variables such as their marital status, ethnicity, where they live, what jobs (if any) they do or their social attitudes. One might expect a range of factors other than age are correlated with religious belief. This might lead you to reduce your estimate of the impact of age itself in so far as it was correlated with these other factors. Comparison is the bread and butter of much quantitative research, since it most closely approaches the experimental method. Except in rare situations, experiments are rarely either possible or ethical in the social sciences, so that we substitute systematic observation. The basis of all systematic observation is the comparison of groups defined by the variable of interest, such as religious belief.

While many 'omnibus' surveys will have a few basic questions on religion (such as asking a person's denomination and how frequently they attend services), delving more deeply into religious belief and its correlates would probably require identifying surveys with modules on religion. For each survey it will be important to know such information as who was covered by the survey or its target population (whether children or adolescents were included, for example) and the way the questions were asked (in what order, how 'don't know' responses were dealt with, whether it was a self-completion questionnaire or an interview, whether interviewers prompted or probed). We would almost certainly want to take some account of the impact of the history of religious institutions in different countries through some kind of comparative analysis.

1 ● 3   DATA EXPLORATION AND THEORY TESTING

Finally, the researcher may have two similar but conceptually completely distinct aims for the research. The research may be *exploratory*: reviewing promising patterns in the data with no clearly established theoretical model or hypothesis guiding that exploration. Catherine Marsh (1988) argued that this aspect of research was akin to detectives looking for evidence or clues. The aim is to collect a range of evidence that may be relevant to the subject under investigation. Alternatively, the research might have a clearly defined *hypothesis* to test. Just as a trial in a courtroom, with lawyers for prosecution and defence, uses evidence to reach a judgement about whether one particular event happened or not 'beyond reasonable doubt', to use Marsh's analogy, so too does a test of a hypothesis either fail or, provisionally, succeed. Most research involves both exploration and hypothesis testing.

What is rarely sufficiently appreciated is the danger of relying on the same data to do both activities. We can think of any dataset as a mixture of signal and noise. The signal comprises the true but invisible values of the variables we want to measure. The noise comprises all the error that gets mixed in with these true values in the process of data construction. There is no 'noise-free' data, since it is always compromised to some extent by the challenges of measurement, sampling and response. It follows that any pattern in the data consistent with a given hypothesis could be there *either* because of the signal *or* because of the noise. For example, it might just have been the case that the sample drawn for the European Social Survey in 2012 happened to contain more older religious respondents than there are in the population of Europe overall, or perhaps something in the survey instrument encouraged older people to emphasise their religiosity, or older religious people were more likely to respond than their less religious peers. The only way to deal with this is either to use one set of data for exploration, and another set for hypothesis testing, or to adopt a much higher standard of test before hypotheses are accepted. Otherwise the commendable process of data exploration can degenerate into the undesirable habit of 'data snooping'. I discuss this issue in Chapter 4 when describing significance testing and its many weaknesses if used indiscriminately.

1 ● 4   THE SOCIAL CONSTRUCTION OF DATA

Any careful and comprehensive analysis starts out from understanding how the data it works with has been produced or, to use a popular term, 'socially constructed'. All data is produced in this way. Surveys neither harvest facts nor automatically produce 'objective knowledge', let alone 'the truth'. However, this does not mean that the results of secondary data analysis are merely a function of the outlook or standpoint of the analyst, who has cherry-picked some 'results' that happen to fit with a pre-established theory. A good theory or claim about some aspect of how societies operate (such as a claim that religious belief is stronger or more widespread among its older members) can be compared with the evidence. Moreover, every stage of how that claim has been tested against the evidence is open to scrutiny by peers, who can replicate the analysis and debate whether the way the data was used, concepts were defined or operationalised and so on was adequate.

None of this means that secondary data analysis produces only 'superficial' knowledge. There are three main objections that have been raised against quantitative data analysis in general and secondary data analysis in particular. The first is that the way in which quantitative analysis collects data 'fragments' the inevitable complexity of social reality into discrete pieces of data, which once torn from their social context cannot reveal the texture of social life. It measures only what it is possible to measure, not what is really important. It seems to me that, on the contrary, it is this criticism that is 'superficial'.

Can something that cannot be measured be said to exist? The most basic 'measurement' that is possible of any phenomenon is categorisation and classification: whether something is an example of a wider class of objects. If something can be classified then its correlates can be measured too. There are undoubtedly social phenomena that comprise many variables and very few cases. But this is a challenge to be taken up by the refinement and elaboration of concepts in such a way that more cases can be brought into the analysis, not by retreating from the axioms of a scientific approach. Most science begins with careful description. Description inevitably requires categorisation and quantification. It degenerates into the regurgitation of trivial 'facts' only if done in the absence of some theoretical framework that establishes its potential relevance. 'Fragmentation' of data is actually a basic foundation of social scientific knowledge of any sort. Only once the data has been reduced to its constituent elements can patterns and structures within it be identified that would be invisible to a casual observer. This is the whole point of social science research.

The second objection sometimes made is that the collection of data requires an undesirable power relationship between the investigator and their respondents. There is indeed a power relationship, but how far it is undesirable is a question of the nature and purposes of the research. The power relationship is an inevitable part of the scientific process. If the scientist is not in control of this process, or responsible for it, it ceases to be scientific, no matter how positive the process might be in other ways. However, this is also a power relationship to which the interviewee gives what ought to be their informed consent, and from which they can withdraw. Social scientists, like any others, have the obligation to conduct research in an ethical way, and subject to peer review. Another, rather bizarre, variant of this argument is the proposition that structured interviewing of the kind that produces quantitative data is inherently 'masculine'. Its proponents seem blissfully unaware of the implications of the logic of this argument: the profoundly anti-feminist idea that men have a natural facility with numbers. Nor is it clear that non-quantitative forms of research escape power relationships in research, rather than reformulate them in a less formal or visible way.

The third criticism sometimes made is that quantitative data is better at answering 'what' questions rather than 'why'. It can describe social structure or regular patterns of belief or behaviour and so on, but is less able to generate evidence about the origin of such structures or *why* such patterns of behaviour exist. Again I'm sceptical about this criticism. There is long debate in the philosophy of social science literature about the nature of knowledge, empirical evidence and processes of causation and correlation. However, the idea that quantitative evidence cannot answer 'why' questions is just wrong. There are many 'why' questions it can and does answer, often by using precisely the kind of knowledge that emerges from fragmenting social experience into discrete measurements and collecting these from respondents in highly structured ways.

Let me cite one 'why' question as an example. Why is global fertility falling? Because we have very good data on births (almost every state attempts to keep track of how many new citizens are born each year, and many link this to, for example, data about the parents) we can answer this question in great detail, comparing the strength of the impact in different countries of such factors as trends in infant perinatal and older age mortality, better women's education and employment opportunities, parents' aspirations for the education of their children, the cost of rearing children, work–life balance policies that facilitate the reconciliation of the conflicting demands of parenting and employment, progress in public health provision and the availability of and knowledge about contraception and abortion, belief that 'planning' a family is a genuine alternative to receiving 'God's will' and so on. All these are factors that can be, and have been, estimated from survey data.

1 ● 5 THE STRUCTURE OF THIS BOOK

The focus of this book is on how to locate, access and manage data in order to analyse it effectively. It is neither a primer on social statistics, nor an introduction to SPSS as statistical software, nor a book about sampling and survey methods, nor a comprehensive guide to data analysis, but rather brings together aspects of all of these topics in order to give you the skills needed to do secondary data analysis. While it assumes no prior knowledge, it will be easier to understand if you already have some familiarity with what quantitative data is, with elementary descriptive statistics or with software packages such as Excel or SPSS, and can remember at least a little of school maths. However, it also aims to be a useful reference handbook for those more experienced in secondary data analysis that can be consulted as need be, hence the organisation of the chapters.

1 ● 6 THE CHAPTERS

Chapter 2 is a brief introduction to surveys, quantitative methods and descriptive statistics. If you're already knowledgeable about these areas, skip this chapter. Conversely, if you know nothing about any of these topics you'll find this chapter a steep learning curve on its own; you may find it best to supplement it with some of the other reading listed at the end of the chapter. It is best used as a refresher if you have already studied these topics, or as a point of reference to remind you of the meaning of key terms or procedures as you work through the rest of the book.

Chapter 3 is an introduction to the panorama of some of the best secondary data that can be used with nothing more than a web browser. It introduces Nesstar, a web-based analysis platform that anyone can master in a couple of hours, and which is used by many data providers. It also presents some basic secondary data skills and rules of good practice to follow when accessing, analysing and presenting secondary data.

Chapter 4 introduces you to the SPSS program as a means of storing, managing, analysing and reporting on data. It does so by looking at attitudes to homosexuality in Europe, and at gender and employment. Although we start with its menu-driven interface, and using a 'practice' dataset, we move on to learning and using syntax as a quicker and more effective way of working. The chapter includes 'step by step' instructions for producing summary descriptive and inferential statistics, tables and graphics and exporting them to other applications. It also covers recoding variables and selecting subsets of data for analysis.

Datasets usually come with extensive documentation, often thousands of pages long. It is therefore important to learn how to navigate your way around such documents quickly to get to the information you need to work with a dataset, or to answer a problem you encounter when doing so. Chapter 5 suggests a dozen questions that you should know the answers to in order to analyse any dataset effectively. We then move on to using the full dataset from Round 6 (2012) of the European Social Survey. We get some practice in searching data documentation to answer some of the puzzles that secondary data analysis often throws up by looking at the correlates of depression as measured by a Depression Scale (CES-D 8) constructed from the answers to a series of questions in one of the modules of the survey. Finally we download a data extract from the US General Social Survey to look at how attitudes to mothers' working have shifted over time in the United States and discover how to make a 'codebook' for your secondary data analysis projects.

An excellent way to develop your skills in secondary data analysis is to take some published work based on a publicly available dataset and attempt to replicate the analyses contained in it. We do this with two articles in Chapter 6, on religion, ethnicity and national identity (using the UK Home Office Citizenship Survey) and on helping behaviour and attitudes (using the European Social Survey Round 3). You'll find that doing so gives you a much deeper understanding of the analytical choices faced by the original authors and the decisions they made. It also allows you to explore what the impact of making different choices would have been on the analysis, or to explore other ways of analysing the same data. Such an approach delivers a much sharper critical insight into the articles that even the closest reading of the article text could ever do.

Chapters 7 and 8 deal with data management. By this point in the book you will have come to understand how important this is. Paradoxically, the 'analysis' part of secondary data analysis takes relatively little time and effort, although it is important to choose the right kind of analysis and interpret it correctly. Rather you will find that the more challenging and time-consuming aspect lies in managing and preparing your data so that it is in a format that can be analysed in the way you want. This means more than just selecting cases or variables for analysis. Often you need to deal with weights and missing values, construct new variables using the information from several existing variables together, assemble your dataset from more than one source of data, create a new dataset out of an existing one, or merge a dataset with another one. We look at all these operations and when they need to be undertaken. We use the World Bank site to download data and build an SPSS data file that we'll use in Chapter 9. Then we look at how to handle household roster information and the 'hierarchical' nature of some of the data that you'll encounter. Finally, I stress the importance of keeping an accurate record of your work.

Chapter 9 covers ordinary least squares multiple linear regression: a long name for an analysis technique that is much less intimidating than its name implies and allows us to set up powerful 'control' conditions in observational analysis that are usually as close as social scientists can get to mimicking experimental control. We look at infant mortality and fertility across the world, and how transforming variables (e.g. by taking their logarithm) often allows us to model associations where we are more interested in relative change than in absolute numbers, and how to deal with categorical variables by producing sets of dummies. We also look at causation and correlation, and why good evidence of the latter is not necessarily evidence of the former. Finally, we look at a range of diagnostic tests that help us to decide if a model we build of some social relationship or process using linear regression is any good.

Chapter 10 looks at one of the most widely used techniques in secondary data analysis, binary logistic regression, where the dependent variable takes only two values. I look at how such regression can be understood as a further development both of the analysis of contingency tables and of linear regression. When analysing the social attitudes or behaviour of individuals, as opposed to institutions or countries, most of the variables we deal with are categorical rather than continuous, which makes logistic regression necessary. First we look at odds, odds ratios and probabilities so that we have a clear understanding of what we are doing, and then work through the components of a logistic regression analysis and its results. Finally, in Chapters 11 and 12, we bring all our skills together to look at political activity and the 'Arab Spring' using data from the World Values Survey and completing our replication of two journal articles that we started in Chapter 6.

Chapter 13 takes stock of what you've learnt in the book, and emphasises perhaps the most important skill a secondary data analyst can nurture: healthy scepticism about the value and quality of the data they work with. As the Polish economist Kalecki once said: 'The most foolish thing to do is not to calculate. The next most foolish is to follow blindly the results of your calculations.' This does not mean that statistics are merely 'damned lies' but rather that if the social production and analysis of data are to be done well they must always be done critically, that is to say, with a sober assessment of the real difficulties of the measurement of social phenomena and a sound understanding of both the potential and inevitable limitations of the kinds of analysis we can carry out on the results of these measurements.

The book is linked to a website which has videos demonstrating all the procedures described in each of the chapters and other resources to help you develop your skills, including further practice exercises, examples of SPSS syntax, practice datasets and links to various other learning and data resources. At the end of each chapter you'll find a summary of the key concepts and skills covered in it. You may find this helps to check that you've understood the most important points from each chapter. However, you'll find that by far the best way to use this book is alongside a computer. The only good way to learn about data analysis is to do it. You could read a library of books about art, but that would be of little help in learning to draw or paint: only practice would develop the skills you need. So it is with data analysis. Like any skill that takes a little time to develop, the rewards grow as you become more proficient, but I hope you'll soon find that becoming a data explorer is just as interesting as investigating unknown corners of the earth. Don't worry about taking wrong turnings or making mistakes. Playing around with data is an excellent way to learn all about it.

A note on presentation

Throughout the text **Helvetica Neue LT Std Medium font** is used to refer to SPSS commands, menus and syntax. Bold typeface is used when referring to **variable names,** while italics are used for *emphasis*.

2

UNDERSTANDING THE BASICS OF STATISTICS

This chapter gives a brief introduction to social surveys, data analysis and statistics, showing that understanding statistics is more about having a set of logical rules than dealing with mountains of numbers.

- Statistics is about logical rules for collecting and interpreting evidence, because 'seeing is not believing' in social processes
- Societies are large and complex, so that numbers are an inevitable and valuable tool in making sense of them
- Numbers can be used well or badly: condemning all numbers is just as mistaken as having a naive faith in them
- Statistics comprises five key ideas: measurement, variation, association, models and uncertainty
- Statistics comprises a set of logical rules, but this does not mean that no subjective judgement is required
- Statistical analysis is inherently subversive because it submits all received wisdom to an empirical test that is beyond the control of the scientist

2.1 WHAT IS STATISTICS?

Everyone can do statistics. Statistics is mostly *not* about numbers, formulae, calculation and maths you can't understand. Statistics is about using evidence to understand the world better, evidence that usually takes the form of data. That 'world' includes everything from your personal lifestyle (such as the risks or benefits of different diets or the chances of finding a taxi) to fundamental questions about the nature of the physical world (such as whether the Higgs boson exists or global warming is taking place). We continually use evidence to refine our understanding of the world or to solve problems within it without even being very conscious of it. For example, we can pick up clues about another person's emotional state by looking at their facial expression without any conscious effort on our part. You might look out of the window in the morning to see what the weather is like before deciding what to wear or how to travel somewhere. You'll almost certainly interpret that evidence in some way by using other information too. Thus your evidence is about the weather now, but your interest may really be in knowing what the weather will be like when you set out or return. You might well draw upon your experience of what the weather has done on similar days in the past to predict how it will behave. Unless you live somewhere with very settled weather patterns, you'll also accept that your prediction is not totally reliable.

Statistics is essentially a formalisation of this kind of process: collecting information, or data, about the world in order to describe and understand it, and sometimes to make predictions about how it might behave that can be compared with how it actually does behave. Without necessarily being aware of it you use the products of statistical knowledge all the time, for the simple reason that virtually all our sound knowledge of society is statistical. At its simplest level this comprises counting people and what they do or think. Such measurement is often more difficult than it might appear to be (for a start, people move around, are born and die, may have other priorities in life than responding to censuses or surveys, and when they do respond may neither understand a question in the way the survey designer expected, nor be disposed to tell the whole truth). However, it is proof of both the power and ubiquity of statistics that we usually take it for granted that a vast amount of information is readily available to us about almost any subject. Every piece of that information has its origin in surveys, census and administrative records based upon statistics.

'Big data' means we have revolutionary opportunities to understand the world that simply didn't exist a few years ago, *if* we can make sense of the evidence in the data. Big is almost unimaginably big. The world now produces and captures more data in one year than it did from the invention of writing until the invention of the computer. However, the techniques needed to understand and use 'big' data are much the same as those for 'small' or indeed any data.

2.2 WHY STATISTICS?

Statistics is a science. Science is unique because it produces knowledge that is more than personal opinion. It requires proof, it requires others to be able to replicate it and it requires us to change our minds when new evidence comes along. Without the scientific attitude we would lose far more than modern technology, we would lose the freedom to let our curiosity take us where convention or dogma ordains we should not go. There are few things more exciting than new insights that topple old pillars of wisdom.

Statistics is fundamental to almost all science because it helps correct what Kahneman (2011) calls 'cognitive illusions'. These are analogous to visual illusions that you may be familiar with, but are about how we think rather than how we see. It looks as if our brains are wired to process information in a particular way. One of the results of this is that we are very good at retro-fitting plausible causal narratives to the barest minimum of evidence. We can 'explain' things to our own satisfaction without really understanding them. Worse, we are then excellent at collecting snippets of ideas that fit with our initial explanation in order to reassure ourselves that we are right. In other words, we are good at seeing what we are looking for or want to see, and missing other relevant evidence that might actually give us a very different view. Statistics is about developing rules for collecting and analysing evidence that corrects these biases.

Statistics can also be used to confuse, befuddle, hoodwink or lie to the unwary. Statistics that are irrelevant, misleading or just plain wrong can be used to dress up a limp argument and give it a spurious aura of expert credibility. It is remarkable how easily a good grasp of the basic principles of statistics – knowledge anyone can acquire – helps you to distinguish a sound argument from one that just sounds good. A good test of using statistics well is whether the focus is on the numbers themselves, or on the story that they are used to tell. Good statistics tell a sound story. If there is too much emphasis on the numbers themselves, it is usually because they have not been adequately understood and interpreted, or because they have been added for decoration: to dress up an otherwise unwarranted argument in order to make it look 'scientific'.

2.3 STATISTICS ANXIETY

Most people approach statistics with all the pleasure and anticipation of a visit to the dentist, but with the difference that at least at the dentist's it's the dentist who does the work. This is especially true for those who see themselves as a 'language' rather than a 'number' person, or who think they are 'number phobic'. There are *some* good reasons for this dread. Statistics *does* have its traps for the unwary. Unlike the discussion and evaluation of arguments in an essay, where there is rarely a definitive 'wrong' answer, and precisely what is being said and how is open to a great variety of interpretation, there *are* parts of statistics where there is a definitely correct and incorrect way to do things. Worse, when using a computer it is sometimes easy to get only one step wrong and, try as you might, what you are attempting to do just does not work out for a reason that you cannot fathom.

However, these are hardly features that set statistics apart from other skills. There is a definitely right and wrong way to drive a car, for example, and it involves both learning and following simple rules (drive on the left or right, stop at red lights, obey speed limits, look in your mirror) and developing skills that involve some judgement and are improved with a bit of practice (stopping, starting and changing gear smoothly, calculating overtaking distances, etc). Actually, statistics is easier today than it has ever been before, because calculators or statistics packages on computers, such as Excel, IBM SPSS Statistics software and R, do virtually all the numerical calculations for you. In fact a good grasp of statistics is possible without much reliance on numbers. Rather statistics is about learning good rules for collecting, interpreting and presenting empirical evidence with some kind of quantitative component.

If you think about your own experience, you are *very* unlikely to be a purely language person, or number phobic. Without even noticing it, you use numbers all the time. You know how old you are and your date of birth, or how many months there are in a year or days in a week. You can tell the time from a watch or clock. You understand fractions or proportions, so that if someone tells you it is 'quarter past eleven' you know they mean '11.15'. You probably have a fair idea of your height, weight, waist and chest measurements, your shoe size, your postcode and your telephone number(s), and if you are a bit of a nerd, you might even be able to recount your bank account or passport number. You will have a more or less accurate idea of how much time you spend on different things each week, and how much money you have in the bank, or the size of your overdraft. You could tell me the difference between the approximate cost of a textbook and a bus fare, and compare how much bigger the former is.

Even if you think *you* don't use numbers, plenty of powerful people and institutions who influence your life certainly *do*. Take any newspaper (whether it is a sober broadsheet title, a tabloid or free giveaway) and count the number of articles that contain a number as an important part of the story. Then count how many refer to a survey, poll or market research. Not for nothing did George Orwell make the title of his dystopian novel and the subject of its first sentence a number (*Nineteen Eighty-Four*; 'The clock struck thirteen.'). He was well aware of the way in which those seeking to claim authority for their arguments turned to *numbers* to give them justification. Numbers can be used well or badly. As Orwell was aware, numbers are often used very badly indeed. Usually this is because the important thing is the argument, policy or belief being put forward, and the numbers are simply selected, twisted or cited out of context in order to legitimise it.

There are two things you can do about this. One is to denounce all numbers as rubbish or the work of the devil ('lies, damned lies and statistics') and decide to have as little to do with them as the dentist. The trouble is that, just as ignoring the dentist is likely to give you toothache, ignoring numbers actually leaves you at their mercy. If *all* numbers are rubbish, how do you make informed choices between alternative ones? How do we generate, summarise and interpret evidence about anything other than our own very personal experience? Unless *you* can make *your own* judgements about numbers, you end up being entirely dependent on what 'experts' claim the numbers mean, when many 'experts', much of the time, almost certainly have a reason for wanting to select and interpret the numbers in *their* particular way. If you want it to be your own life you lead, rather than one other people and institutions control by careful selection and presentation of the 'evidence', then a little number knowledge goes a long way. In any area of management or business life, in the public, private or voluntary sectors, being able to assess the quality of the evidence in reports of all kinds will be fundamental to your work. A solid command of a few key statistical ideas will equip you with the ability to tell worthwhile evidence from spin.

2 ● 4 PROBLEM SOLVING AND THE STATISTICAL IMAGINATION

For many people statistics conjures up the idea of 'number crunching', processing vast amounts of numerical data with at best a tenuous relation to real life in order to produce a distorted or partial view of reality. Statistics can be, and often are, misused in that way. However, good statistics have nothing to do with this. The historical development of statistics has always been rooted in the search for the solution to practical problems. An important feature of its early history was its link to astronomy: more accurate measurements of the movement of the moon and stars could enable ships, including warships, to navigate more effectively. The idea of using random samples to measure the characteristics of a population came in part from the study of crops and how to make agriculture more efficient. Warfare and the demands of the military contributed to the development of statistics. Florence Nightingale not only used statistics to improve the treatment of military hospital patients, but also pioneered graphical presentation of those statistics in the form of pie charts in order to convey the results of her statistical inquiries vividly to the politicians she had to persuade. She thus used statistics not only to tackle a practical problem (revolutionising the survival rates for patients in military hospitals), but also to *present* her arguments in a convincing way to those with no grasp of numbers at all.

The word 'statistics' comes from the word 'state', and originally developed to describe the information-gathering activities of modern governments, as from the early nineteenth century onwards they became interested in developing more accurate knowledge about their populations. Only as it came to be grasped that there were certain mathematical techniques that were common to solving problems in scientific investigation, measurement and description did a separate discipline of statistics emerge. As the rigour and complexity of scientific knowledge increased, so too did the range of specialist statistical techniques develop to cope with this. However, the statistical knowledge necessary to develop a critical understanding of the kinds of numbers used in much medical, social and natural science, in everyday policy debates or in business, is fairly straightforward. A principle that is worth keeping in mind is that while knowledge of this or that statistical technique is useful, what is more important is the ability to see when a piece of evidence or argument can be subjected to statistical reasoning and interpretation. This requires imagination – a statistical imagination – which can see how numbers can be used well, together with some practical skills in finding the numbers – the data – that you need. This book will help you to develop both.

2 ● 5 FIVE KEY DIMENSIONS OF STATISTICS

You can think of statistics and the methods used to produce it as *quantitative evidence*. Quantitative evidence does use numbers, but they are only a means to more important ends. I find it helpful to think of statistics as based around five key concepts: measurement, variation, association, models and probability.

2●5●1 Measurement and classification

The first idea is that of *measurement*. We may want to know how big, or hot, or long, or old, or fast, or frequent something is. Did it rain today? Where? How much? Constant or showers? More or less than elsewhere? How long do people live? Has this changed over time? Is it influenced by where people live, the resources they have or education they've received? How many people believe in religion? Do their beliefs differ from those who do not? What proportion of a population are employed? Is unemployment rising or falling? Are some people at greater risk of unemployment than others? How safe is the neighbourhood I live in? What sort of crime occurs there? How does this compare with other areas, or the same area in past periods?

To measure or count phenomena we first need to classify or define them, so that we don't measure the wrong thing. It is no good counting sheep if what you need to know is how many goats there are. While some definitions are clear and simple, others are anything but. Measurement thus requires classification: the sorting of things into coherent categories that have some logical rationale. We need to know what it is we are measuring, what units that measurement can be expressed in, and what we are applying the measure to. For example, if we wanted to know how many people were employed in Germany in 2010, we would need definitions of the categories 'Germany' and 'employee'. By 'Germany' we might mean the contemporary Federal Republic of Germany. But if we wished to make comparisons with the period before 1989 we'd need to take account of the fact that before unification there were two states (the Federal Republic of Germany and German Democratic Republic) which each collected data on employment. 'Employment' too needs a precise definition. Do we include self-employed workers? What about those on 'zero-hours' contracts? Do we want to distinguish between part-time and full-time or temporary and permanent employees? What about those who 'normally' work but were on maternity leave, on holiday or temporarily sick? What about those with more than one job: do we count jobs or people? How we answer these questions will depend on what the focus of our interest is, but they will have a substantial impact on the number we arrive at for employment. In Germany in mid 2015 just under 40 million people aged 15 or over were employed. Just under 4 million of these workers were self-employed, just under 5 million were on temporary contracts and just over 11 million were working part-time; 2 million had more than one job and 1.6 million took parental leave that year. We could use these numbers to arrive at very different estimates of the volume employment, depending on how we wanted to define it. The key point is that our definitions have to be comprehensive and clear. This might appear to be stating the obvious, but often we'll find that we need to define and classify carefully, or our attempts to measure things will go awry. Often this is because what we *can* measure is not the same as what we *want* to measure.

Measuring inanimate objects is usually straightforward (although the technology needed to do it may be highly complex). Measuring people or social institutions or processes is more of a challenge. Most of the things we want to measure are invisible or intangible (such as attitudes, beliefs or concepts). They can change unpredictably over time. There may be ethical or political issues involved in collecting information. Those being measured may not wish to disclose the information, might wish to alter or distort it in some way (to give what they imagine is a socially acceptable answer), or simply might not have one: people are not necessarily aware of every aspect of their emotional, mental or physical state! Unlike the natural sciences, in the social sciences it is rarely possible to set up *experiments* in which some parts of a process are manipulated or controlled, so we have to rely on *observation*. In part because we cannot use experiments, we may be interested in trying to measure a great many different things at once.

Measurement wriggles around in many curious ways. For example, not all your shoes are the 'same' size. A size 7 in one brand may be more like an 8 in another. Different countries use different standards. An 8 in the USA may be a 7 in the UK, and a 42 in Europe. How long is a metre? That seems a silly question until you think a bit more about it. It's no use saying 'a metre is what my ruler says is a metre', because that begs the question of how the length of the ruler was decided! (Originally 1 metre was intended to be one ten millionth of the distance from the earth's equator to the pole. It was 'defined' by the length of a metal bar stored at the International Bureau of Weights and Measures. It is now defined as the distance light travels in a vacuum in 1/299,792,458th of a second!)

The numerical data produced by measuring not only depends upon such definition and classification of the units of measurement, but also has to be collected. However, 'collection' gives too passive a sense of the process. Data does not grow on trees to be harvested by diligent data harvesters. Rather it depends upon the use of methods of data production, such as laboratory experiments, censuses or surveys, interviews, and administrative records. Quantitative evidence is *always*, even in the natural sciences, *socially constructed* to some degree. These methods of data production may work very well for some measures, and less well for others. However, a very good first question to ask about any number you ever come across is *where does it come from?* The answers often yield surprises.

The great advantage of secondary data analysis is that all the work of data production has already been done for you. Moreover, it will usually have been done to a high professional standard, using measurement techniques that have been tested and refined. However, this comes with two drawbacks. The most obvious one is that you are limited by what the original investigators decided was worth measuring. They may not have collected all the information that your study requires. A less obvious but just as important drawback is that when the data has been assembled in a dataset it is too easy to project an aura of absolute authenticity on to it, as if it constituted 'the truth', and forget its social, and therefore always less than perfect, origins. You should always try to keep in mind how it was produced, and the imperfect, fallible means by which it was collected. A good rule of thumb to follow is that almost any data is better than no data at all, but that all data comes with some measurement error, and that this has to be remembered. The truth may be out there, but not always captured faithfully in your data.

2•5•2 Levels of measurement

Different kinds of things can be measured in different ways or have different *levels of measurement*. Some things, like the height, weight, income or age of a person, the temperature of a room, the price of a commodity, or the time spent doing something, are continuously variable and can take *a directly meaningful numerical value* in some unit of measurement: centimetres, kilograms, euros, years, degrees Celsius, seconds and so on. Because the units in which they are measured can be subdivided infinitely, units always take the form of *intervals*. Thus if we describe something as being 10 centimetres long, we usually mean not that it is exactly this length (i.e. 10.00000... cm) but rather that it lies somewhere on an *interval* between 9.5 and 10.5 cm long. This level of measurement is therefore called the *interval* level of measurement. Some such measurements have a 'real' zero. For example, if someone is 20 years old we can say that they are twice as old as someone 10 years old, because the concept of being zero years old makes sense. However, if the temperature in a room is 20 degrees Celsius we cannot say that it is twice as hot as one with a temperature of 10 degrees, because a temperature of 0 degrees is not a real zero but only a convention. It is the point at which water freezes, but it is not a point of 'zero' temperature. Were we to measure the temperature on a different scale (Fahrenheit, Kelvin) the numbers would all change. Where we have 'real' zeros we talk of *ratio* levels of measurement (since ratios calculated from any two measurements are directly meaningful).

Other phenomena can often be measured *only* by classification. It is not possible to be more or less pregnant, or more or less dead, in the way in which one can be shorter or taller. A woman is either pregnant or not. A person is either employed or not (although we might make different *definitions* of what constitutes employment). A person can only be born in one place. When classification can only be done by putting different cases or observations into different categories, and *naming* them, then we have the *nominal* level of measurement. This is a common level of measurement in the social sciences. If we want to describe someone's religion, or their occupation, the party they voted for, what country they live in, whether they support the idea of capital punishment or how they travel to work, we can only classify their characteristics into different categories, such as Protestant, atheist, Muslim, or sales rep, academic, lorry driver and so on. Classification systems need two characteristics: the categories must be *mutually exclusive*, so that no observation can be put into more than one category, and they must be *comprehensive*, so that every imaginable observation can be covered. For example, in the UK Labour Force Survey the data on 'place of birth' includes not only every country in the world, but the category 'at sea or in the air'. Around five in every million births take place there. This second characteristic accounts for the frequent use of the response 'other' in questionnaires and surveys: it's a useful catch-all.

Sometimes when there are a number of categories that all measure the same thing, these categories can be put into a meaningful *order*. We might want to measure what attitudes people take to an issue and classify them into groups of 'strongly agree', 'agree', 'no opinion', 'disagree' and 'strongly disagree'. Each successive class indicates *less* agreement with the issue. However, note that the classes we have here are *not* intervals in the sense we saw above. It would make no sense, for example, to say that people who 'agreed' were half as much in agreement as those who 'strongly agreed'. This is the *ordinal* level of measurement. Other examples include someone's highest educational qualification, subjective estimation of health (e.g. good, fair, poor) or social class. Just like measurement, classification is always a *social* process, both in the natural as well as social sciences, even though almost all good classification systems have some form of 'objective' referent. We can think of measurement and classification together as *empirical description*.

2•5•3 Reliability and validity

Empirical description, measurement and classification always involve *error*. In statistics error usually doesn't mean 'mistake'. Rather it refers to inevitable inaccuracies that creep into any system of measurement. This can be because the measuring instrument is imperfect. If I weigh myself on a set of scales, the scales might be poorly set up so that they systematically under- or over-record my actual weight. However, even if they are perfectly calibrated they will only show my weight to a certain degree of accuracy (perhaps the nearest 10 grams) and my precise weight will be a little above or below that figure. My weight will probably vary over the course of the day as I eat or drink or visit the toilet, or as the atmospheric pressure changes, so that there is no 'perfect' measurement of my weight. This doesn't mean that measuring my weight is pointless, only that it will contain a margin of error.

Sometimes 'errors' can be conceptual, rather than caused by the measuring instrument. I might be interested in investigating smoking behaviour, and design a questionnaire for a survey. If I am careless about how precisely I define 'smoking', there might be room for doubt about whether someone is classified as a smoker or not. Does any form of tobacco use count or only cigarettes? Do I define as a smoker someone who might take an occasional puff of someone else's cigarette? How about those who used to smoke but (say they) no longer do so? Finally, some error arises because any kind of measurement, surveying or recording is done by fallible human beings who can make mistakes in the recording process.

We can assess measurement and classification in terms of *validity* (are we really measuring exactly what we want to measure, or something a little different?) and *reliability* (does the measurement system give us the same results in the same situations?). An example of a measure with high reliability and low validity would be school league tables. Since the tables are based on published exam performances it is a highly reliable measure, in the specific sense that where pupil examination performance is similar, the score obtained by the school will be similar. It does not depend, for example, on some subjective evaluation of how good or bad the school is according to range of criteria. However, it is a measure with questionable validity. It may measure the 'performance' of parents, the home and family background of pupils, or the cost of housing in a school catchment area, rather than how well the school is actually doing.

2•5•4 Variation: variables, values and cases

Measurement and comparison are necessary and possible because things *vary*. Empirical description tries to capture the nature of this *variation*, or the *distribution* of people, companies or whatever the object of our analysis is, across this variation. To keep things clear, we refer to the objects of our measurements as *cases* or *observations*. What we are measuring, because it varies, we refer to as a *variable*. The result of the measurement of a variable that we take for any given case we refer to as its *value*.

Almost everything in the universe varies. Individual examples of the same object differ and/or the characteristics of that object can change over time. This infant is a girl, that infant is a boy. She is 80 cm tall today, he is 78 cm. In a year's time their heights will have changed. People are different heights or earn different amounts, work in different occupations (or perhaps do no paid work) or live in different areas. Companies have large or small turnovers, make grand profits or dreadful losses, grow or decline, make different products, have their head offices in different countries and so on. The population size of countries or the size of their economies changes over time. Indeed, it is easier to see variation than to think of things that do *not* vary or change. There are some 'constants', mostly in the physical world. The speed of light is one. So far as we know, it travels at the same speed (in a vacuum) everywhere in the universe. Capturing all this change and variation requires some clear rules to make systematic measurement possible.

A first step is to think of the world in terms of objects and events. Objects include animate objects such as people as well as things like a litre of water. Some objects exist because we choose to imagine and describe them, such as happiness; others exist only because of social institutions that make them possible, such as the interest on bank deposits, or the rate of unemployment. Others exist quite independently of whether we think about them (e.g. a government), even if *how* we think of them is a product of language or other social processes. We can describe any object in terms of some of its characteristics at a point in time. This person is 24 years old, female, works as a bus driver and lives with her partner. Ten years from now she may be 34 (if she is still alive), manage the bus company and live alone. That person is 70, male, retired and widowed.

Events happen to objects. A person dies. A coin flipped in the air lands heads up. An unemployed person finds a job. Someone is stopped and searched by the police. Just as the characteristics of objects vary, and we may be interested in capturing and describing that variation, so can the frequency of events. We can define an event and then determine if and when, or how often, it occurred over the course of a period of time. The bus driver moved in with her partner in 2002, was promoted in 2003 and 2007, and got divorced in 2010.

We can think of each example of an object or event that we measure as a case or observation. We can think of the characteristic that we want to measure because it changes or varies, including the frequency of events, as a variable. We refer to the result of a measurement that we observe for an individual case as its value. For each case, each variable has one, and only one, value. Thus when we measure something we *observe* the value that each case takes for a variable. We call the pattern of variation in a variable its *distribution*, because it describes how the cases are distributed across the different values the variable takes. Variables, values and cases are the holy trinity of statistics. Once you are able to see the world in terms of variables, values and cases you are ready to measure it and do statistics. At first this can seem a confusing process, and it is easy to get values and variables mixed up. The best way to get the distinction clear is practice.

Think of the two infants we mentioned above. Each of them is a case. One of the variable characteristics of infants is their sex. For the variable **sex** we found that one took the value 'boy' and the other took the value 'girl'. Another variable characteristic is their height. For the variable **height**, one took the value 78 cm, the other the value 80 cm. Here we had two cases (the two infants) and two variables (**sex** and **height**) and each of the two variables took two values (one for each case). Our **height** variable is an interval variable (height varies continuously) while **sex** is nominal (babies are male or female).

Here is another example, drawn from the Millennium Cohort Study, carried out in the UK since the year 2000 to follow the fortunes of a sample of children born in that year. Let our variable be the weight of the babies when they were born, measured in pounds and ounces. Each baby in the study is a case, and the value observed for each case is the weight of that baby at birth. There were over 16,000 babies in the study, so it would be tedious to list each of the

Table 2.1 Babies' birth weights, UK Millennium Cohort Study, 2000

Weight at birth	Number	%
under 3 lb	101	0.6
3 lb 0 oz – 3 lb 15 oz	141	0.9
4 lb 0 oz – 4 lb 15 oz	338	2.1
5 lb 0 oz – 5 lb 15 oz	1,192	7.4
6 lb 0 oz – 6 lb 15 oz	3,588	22.3
7 lb 0 oz – 7 lb 15 oz	5,466	33.9
8 lb 0 oz – 8 lb 15 oz	3,734	23.2
9 lb 0 oz – 9 lb 15 oz	1,277	7.9
10 lb 0 oz – 10 lb 15 oz	238	1.5
11 lb and over	27	0.2
All weights	16,102	100

Source: University of London, Institute of Education, Centre for Longitudinal Studies (2012) *Millennium Cohort Study: First Survey, 2001–2003* [data collection], 11th edition. UK Data Service. SN: 4683.

values for weight individually. Instead we can group them into ranges, or intervals, of weights, and so Table 2.1 shows how many babies were born weighing from 3 to 4 lb, from 4 to 5 lb and so on. Thus if a baby was 5 lb 6 ounces when it was born it would be counted in the row of the table for '5 lb 0 oz – 5 lb 15 oz'. (We'll see how to access Millennium Cohort Study data and produce this table in Chapter 4.)

Let's consider these measurements briefly. In this example we can obviously see variation. A few babies are born very small, others can be three or four times heavier than the lightest, but most babies seem to be between about 6 and 9 lb at birth. The baby's weight at birth is an interval variable. Here we have just over 16,000 cases: each baby in the study. The value for each case is that baby's weight in pounds and ounces at birth. Individual values are not shown in this table, but we can see from the table how many cases took each range of values of the variable. Thus, for example, there were 338 babies with a value for the variable from 4 lb 0 oz to 4 lb 15 oz. Because this table shows the *frequency* or number of cases (the babies) that take each range of values (their weights) on a single variable (weight of babies at birth) it is called a *frequency table*. Dealing with raw numbers is often clumsy so we *standardise* the table using percentages in the final column. Thus, for example, the 238 babies born with weights between 10 and 11 lb accounted for 1.5% of all 16,102 babies with weights recorded in pounds and ounces in the study. Taken as a whole the frequency table shows the *distribution* of all the values for the variable **weight**.

Note that there are two sources of 'error' in our table. Although neither is very important, it is good practice to get used to thinking about error. One is the recording of babies' weights. Since it was done by fallible human beings we cannot be sure that no mistakes were made in the course of this record taking: for example, a figure '1' might occasionally have been misread for a '7'. However, we can at least see that the range of weights shown seems plausible. Babies with weights under 3 lb at birth would be rare, as would those weighing 11 lb or more.

The other source of 'error' lies in the way I have presented the results. By grouping the babies into the ranges of weights in the table we have sacrificed some accuracy for ease of presentation: we cannot tell the precise weight of each baby from the table, only the number of babies within ranges of weights that are 1 lb wide.

When we look at the distribution of the number of babies across the weight categories we can see a pattern in the distribution. Most babies are in the middle of the weight range: around 6–9 lb. Conversely babies over 11 lb or under 3 lb are quite rare. This distribution, where the value of the variable for most cases is near the middle, and the number of cases declines as we go further from it, is one that crops up quite often. It has a special name – the *normal* or *Gaussian* distribution – and some very useful qualities.

When dealing with variation we often want to find succinct ways of describing it, in order to avoid long lists of numbers. When dealing with variables at the interval level of measurement there are four numbers that prove to be especially useful: the *mean*, the *median*, the *variance* and the *standard deviation*. You're almost certainly already familiar with the first one as 'the average' of a set of numbers. We could summarise the 16,102 weights by their mean value, obtained by adding together each value for babies' weight and dividing by the total number of babies. The result would be 7lb 8 oz. Of course, this doesn't mean that every baby weighed that amount, or even that most of them do. However it gives us a good guide to the approximate weight of most babies: it tells us that they neither weigh a few ounces or a half a ton.

The usefulness of the mean in describing variation would clearly be greater if we also had some measure of the spread of babies weights around this mean value. This is what the *standard deviation* does. We could make a list of the differences between each baby's weight and the mean (a number known as the *residual*) and take the mean of these numbers. Here we hit a snag. If we do this, the result must be zero, since weights below and above the mean simply cancel each other out. To circumvent this we first square the residuals (i.e. multiply each number by itself) so that negative numbers become positive, before we sum them, and *then* divide by the number of babies. This number is called the *variance*. You can think of it as expressing the amount of variation in any variable. To undo the effect of squaring the residuals we then take the square root of this number, and the result is the *standard deviation*. You can think of this as the 'average' distance between the weight of any baby and the mean value for all babies. It tells us how spread out the weights are. Were you to do these calculations you'd find that the standard deviation for the weights of our babies is 1lb 5oz. For any variable, the larger the value of the standard deviation relative to the mean, the more spread out are the values of that variable.

The *median* is another way of expressing the 'average' value for a variable. Sometimes the distribution of values for a variable is skewed: there may be many more high values than low values, or *vice versa*. Individual wealth is a good example. There are a small number of enormously wealthy billionaires in the world. At the other end of the scale a substantial proportion of the earth's population own almost nothing. If we calculated a mean for wealth we'd get a value that was well above the amount of wealth that most people have, because the value of the mean would be dragged upwards by the small number of exceptionally wealthy people. We get a better summary measure by ranking each person according to their individual wealth, from the poorest to the richest, and taking the wealth of the person in the middle. This *median* value would be below the value we'd get for the mean. Conversely, because the distribution of babies' weights was *not* skewed, we'd find that the median, or the weight of the 'middle' baby, was the same as the value for the mean.

Let's take another example of variation. In the same study the main carer for the baby (usually the mother) was asked if they smoked, or had done so in the past. This nominal variable (describing the smoking behaviour of the baby's main carer) could thus take one of three values (mutually exclusive categories defined by the researchers) for each case (each main carer): smokes now; no longer smokes; never smoked. Again we can show the results as a frequency table (Table 2.2).

Table 2.2   Carer's smoking habits, UK Millennium Cohort Study, 2000

	N	%
Currently smokes	5,621	30.3
No longer smokes	3,188	17.2
Never smoked	9,719	52.4
Total	18,538	100

Source: University of London, Institute of Education, Centre for Longitudinal Studies (2012) *Millennium Cohort Study: First Survey, 2001–2003* [data collection], 11th edition. UK Data Service. SN: 4683.

Table 2.2 shows the distribution of these three values across all the cases. Alongside the actual number of cases, in each row of the table is shown the percentage this number represents of all the cases in the table. For example, 3,188/18,538 = 17.2%. This makes it easier to describe the distribution: we can quickly see that about half of the people surveyed had never smoked, a sixth had once smoked but given up, and about three in ten still smoked.

Because things vary we can also make comparisons. Actually we are usually more interested in such comparisons than in the absolute values of the measurement itself. Are there more men than women in an occupational group? How do their earnings compare to their male peers? What percentage of votes did the Republicans win in that state? How did it compare with the Democrats? How did it compare with the previous election in the same state or elections in other states? Is the rate of return on one investment higher or lower than the alternatives? Is it riskier or safer? In fact, almost all of statistics involves making precise comparisons that enable us to answer questions or solve practical problems. The art of statistics usually lies in identifying the most useful and appropriate comparisons to make.

In social sciences the workhorse of comparison making is the *contingency table*. While frequency tables show the distribution of values for one variable, contingency tables show the distribution of values for one variable, *contingent upon* or conditional upon the values of a second variable. They are sometimes referred to as 'cross-tabulations', or 'crosstabs' for short. Earlier we saw the frequency distribution of smoking behaviour for the main carers for a sample of babies born in 2000. We might expect smoking behaviour to vary by sex. The *Health Survey for England 2012* (HSE) also asked adults about whether they currently smoke cigarettes regularly, or have done so in the past. The results *comparing* men and women are in Table 2.3.

It's clear that men are more likely than women either to be a current smoker (24% compared to 17%), or have been a regular smoker in the past (28% compared to 23%). You probably did not have to think too much about how to interpret this table, but it is worthwhile pausing to review its contents in detail, since understanding crosstabs is an essential building block of data analysis and presentation.

Table 2.3 Smoking status, adults, England, 2012

	Men	Women	Total
Current cigarette smoker (%)	24.0	17.3	20.6
Ex-regular cigarette smoker (%)	27.8	23.0	25.3
Never regular cigarette smoker (%)	48.2	59.7	54.1
Total (%)	100	100	100
N (weighted)	4,265	4,514	8,780

Source: NatCen Social Research, University College London, Department of Epidemiology and Public Health (2014). *Health Survey for England, 2012* [data collection]. UK Data Service. SN: 7480.

First note that the main body of the crosstab comprises two frequency tables side by side, one for 'men' and one for 'women', each describing the distribution of the variable **smoking status**. Because these frequency distributions have been standardised, by using percentages, the number of men and women compared does not affect the result. There could have been 40,000 women or 400 men and this would have made no difference to our interpretation of the result. There are two further frequency distributions displayed in the table: one for each of the variables in it. Under the column headed 'Total' we have a frequency table for the variable **smoking status** based on all observations in the survey, regardless of the sex of the respondent. Along the row headed '*N* weighted' we have a frequency table for the variable **sex**: there were 4,265 men and 4,514 women for whom we had data on smoking status. The variable **sex**, displayed across the columns of the table, is in what is called the table *header*, while the variable **smoking status**, displayed down the rows of the table, is in what is called the *stub*. The frequency distributions for each individual variable (**sex** and **smoking status**) are in the *margins* of the table. Because the percentages have been standardised down the columns of the table they are referred to as 'column percentages'. When you compared men and women, you compared the distribution of the values of **smoking status** according to the values taken by **sex**: you scanned the column percentages along the row, to see whether they changed or not. Because this distribution changed, you could conclude that there was an association between **sex** and **smoking status**. Were there *no* relationship between **sex** and **smoking status** we would have got a result like the one shown in Table 2.4, where comparing column percentages along the row shows little change.

Table 2.4 Smoking status, adults, England, 2012

	Men	Women	Total
Current cigarette smoker (%)	20.4	20.7	20.6
Ex-regular cigarette smoker (%)	25.5	25.1	25.3
Never regular cigarette smoker (%)	54.0	54.1	54.1
Total (%)	100	100	100
N (weighted)	4,265	4,514	8,780

Source: fictional data produced for illustrative purposes only.

You may find it useful to think in terms of *dependent* and *independent* variables, where the former are hypothesised to be influenced in some way by the independent variable, perhaps by some kind of causal relationship. In this example we would be hard pressed to imagine that smoking influences a person's sex. However, we might well imagine that their sex might influence their propensity to smoke – not because biological sex itself is responsible, but because it might be strongly associated with other social factors that influence smoking. When we examined the possible relationship between the two variables we looked to see whether the distribution of the dependent variable changed according to the values taken by the independent variable. Note that this relationship is not an 'all or nothing' affair: it can be stronger or weaker. It is clearly not the case that all men smoke and no women do. Rather it looks as if sex may be one of a number of variables that might help account for who is or is not a smoker.

Note that the position of the variables in the table is unimportant. Had we switched the variables we would have produced Table 2.5, using row percentages rather than column percentages.

Table 2.5   Smoking status, adults, England, 2012

	Current cigarette smoker	Ex-regular cigarette smoker	Never regular cigarette smoker	Total	*N* (weighted)
Men	24.0	27.8	48.2	100	4,265
Women	17.3	23.0	59.7	100	4,514
Total	20.6	25.3	54.1	100	8,780

Source: NatCen Social Research, University College London, Department of Epidemiology and Public Health (2014) *Health Survey for England*, 2012 [data collection]. UK Data Service. SN: 7480.

We could also have standardised Table 2.5 by producing column percentages. However, these would have been less useful, since they would have given us the proportion of smokers who were men and women rather than the proportion of men and women who were smokers.

Frequency and contingency tables are usually the simplest and best ways of summarising the distribution of values for one or a pair of variables. They are a simple but powerful way of describing the variation that exists in the world around us. Being able to understand them directly, rather than relying on the commentary that accompanies them, is one of the most important skills you can master.

2•5•5 Association: relationships, patterns and correlation

The world is full of patterns, structures, relationships and regularities. We have just seen one: that men are a little more likely than women to smoke. Another way of thinking about this is that (at least some) variation is not random, but comes from the way in which different parts of the natural and social worlds are somehow connected. Voting patterns may be understandable in terms of variables such as income, occupation, property ownership, religion or gender. Social mobility might be linked to education, economic change or ethnicity, and so on. Once we think of features of the world in terms of variation, it is hard to avoid our next concept: *association*. Perhaps the distribution of one variable is *associated* in some way with the distribution of another variable.

When variation in one object or process is associated with variation in another one, we have association, also called *correlation* or a *relationship*. The amount of association can vary. Occasionally the association is perfect. Suppose we measured the length of a metal bar and its temperature. We'd find a *perfect* association: indeed, if we did this carefully and accurately enough, we'd discover that knowing the value of one thing would allow us to perfectly predict the other. (That's how thermometers work, where the metal in question may be a column of mercury in a tube.) By contrast, where there is no association at all, where the distribution of values for one variable has no connection to the distribution of values for the other variable across the cases we are considering, we can describe two phenomena as *independent* of each other. For example had a survey of smoking behaviour produced the results shown in Table 2.4 we could have concluded that there was no association between sex and smoking because there was no difference in the distribution of the smoking status variable when we compared men and women. Whether a respondent was a man or woman had no influence on the likelihood of them smoking.

One of the most powerful uses of quantitative evidence is to examine such associations. Do attitudes to cohabitation vary with age? If so, is this because people's attitudes change across the life course or are influenced by their generation or perhaps are mainly affected by the times in which they live? Do people with higher education qualifications earn more? If so, how much more? Is this true for everyone? We will look at ways of describing association and correlation below, in terms of correlation coefficients and in terms of conditional probability. But for the moment, let us just note one feature that we'll return to. Evidence of correlation is *necessary* for there to be a causal link between two variables, but it is not *sufficient*: there may be no causal link at all. Correlation is *not* causation. Think of the following (real) example. There is a well-known correlation, demonstrable for different countries or areas within them, between ice-cream sales and property crime (theft and robbery). Would banning ice-cream reduce crime? The correlation is produced by two other, genuinely causal relationships. Hot weather increases both the opportunities for property crime (more people out and about in the streets and parks to rob, pleasanter conditions for housebreaking) and also the demand for ice-cream.

As Karl Marx once said: 'Philosophers have only interpreted the world, the point is to change it.' Much of the time we are interested not only in understanding or describing some aspect of the world but also in *intervening* to *change* it in some way: to reduce unemployment or poverty, mitigate climate change or just sell more product or pass more exams. Any intervention requires some theory of *cause and effect* (to get result X, we need to do Y, and so on). In later chapters we'll look at how to detect attractive but fallacious forms of reasoning about cause and effect: a vital weapon in good decision making.

2•5•6 Models and summary statements

A model is a simplified, often smaller-scale, version of reality; a summary statement that includes the essential aspects we are interested in and leaves out the extraneous detail. We make models: they do not spring automatically from the natural or social world. A good model focuses on what we want to investigate, and discards other features that are not relevant.

Think of model aeroplanes. A simple plastic toy may simply be smaller than the real thing, but look like it because it preserves its shape or colour. Another model might be made of light material and have an elastic band and propeller that enables it to make a short flight. Such a model will not preserve the shape of any real aeroplane – if it did it wouldn't fly – but instead will highlight another aspect of a plane: that with the right kind of design of wings and propulsion system it can gain lift and stay in the air longer than if it were a mere projectile, such as a stone thrown into the air. The two different models focus on two different features.

We use models all the time, although we rarely realise it. We classify all kinds of things as similar in some way, so that even if we meet a particular example for the first time, we expect it to behave in a similar way to other examples. No two apples are exactly alike, but we expect them to have a familiar taste and texture, and are rarely disappointed: we carry round a 'model' in our heads of what an apple is like. A map is another example of a model. It cannot possibly reproduce everything in the area that it covers, and would be of little use if it did, but instead gives us a scaled-down summary of the most important information we need to orient ourselves or find a particular location.

A précis or abstract of a piece of writing tries to produce a brief summary of the essence of what is being said, stripping out illustration, extraneous detail or more subtle elaboration or qualification of the argument to concentrate on one or more important elements. Similarly, summary statements or models attempt to reduce a large volume of data to a few key characteristics. In this sense, a statistical model is rather like a poem. A novel might run to several hundred pages, while a poem might be only three or four lines long. The poem reduces a set of ideas to their bare essentials, yet in a way that suggests links to much wider cultural references. Similarly, a good statistical model reduces the story told by thousands or millions of measurements to the essence of what seem to be the most relevant measurements or comparisons that make sense of the problem we have in hand and what we or others already know about it.

As we shall see, models can be produced by simplifying or abstracting from reality, as in the examples above. However, we can also produce purely hypothetical models that have a particular feature we are interested in, and then compare this model to what happens in the world. Very often the 'model' we want to test is that something doesn't happen, or has no effect, or that two variables are not associated. If we find that such a model is *not* a good representation of reality then, paradoxically, we may have some useful evidence that the effect or relationship that we are interested in does in fact exist.

We can think of the crosstabs we examined earlier in terms of models. The table did not try to show every potential factor that might influence whether a person smokes. It focused on one only: sex. It did not try to describe the tremendous variety of smoking behaviour that might occur, from an occasional draw on a pipe, to chain-smoking cigarettes, but instead divided respondents into those who were currently, had in the past or had never been 'regular smokers'. However, it gave us a useful model of smoking, showing that sex is a relevant factor in smoking behaviour. One of the ways it did this was by showing how far our actual data diverged from the data we would have expected had there been no link between sex and smoking, shown in Table 2.4. We were able to conclude this because we compared two models.

2●5●7 Uncertainty, probability and randomness

You already have an intuitive grasp of probability and doubtless use this idea many times in the course of the day. 'I'll finish work by about five o'clock' could mean I will *probably* be done some time between half past four and half past five. 'I think it is going to rain' means you are not absolutely certain, but estimate that it is more likely to rain than not. If you have ever thrown a dice, tossed a coin, played cards, placed a bet or bought a lottery ticket you've dealt in probability. It might come as some surprise to learn, then, that the understanding of probability in scientific terms is relatively recent (the last couple of centuries), came in part from the analysis of gambling and is still the subject of intense debate and argument.

Until the seventeenth century, people assumed that probability was a question of *fortuna* or fate and could not be analysed systematically or scientifically. In the course of that century the basics of the mathematics of probability started to be understood. However it was still assumed that probability described situations where it was impossible to measure every possible cause of an event. The French philosopher Laplace imagined that an intellect possessed of perfect knowledge of the universe would have no need of probability since the present would perfectly determine the future. In the course of the nineteenth century this understanding came to be reversed, reaching its climax in the development of quantum mechanics which came to understand the behaviour of sub-atomic particles in terms of the probabilities of their location at any point in time. Contemporary physicists' understanding of the world is thoroughly probabilistic or 'stochastic'. (The fascinating story of these developments is told by Hacking (1990), Porter (1986) and others.) However, this does not mean that we live in a world of meaningless randomness. We can often make surprisingly precise predictions about how 'chance' will turn out. This is why betting companies employ statisticians, rather than just sporting experts, to calculate what odds to offer their clients.

Probability is at the core of statistics for two reasons. Statistics sets out to measure the world, but as we have already seen, even the best measurements are imperfect, and we can use probability to estimate just how imperfect they are likely to be. There is one basic obstacle to our aim of measuring almost any aspect of the world. It is far, far too big. One of the key tasks of the United Nations Population Division (UNPD) is to measure world population. However, it would be a quite impossible task to actually count each of the 7 billion people on the planet, if for no other reason than around 270 babies are born each minute and a rather smaller number of people die (*UN World Population Prospects* 2015 edition available at http://esa.un.org/unpd/wpp). Imagine we devised a simple questionnaire that took 1 hour to administer. Working 24 hours a day, it would take 1,000 interviewers just under 80 years to interview everyone, by which time, of course, the majority of respondents would already be dead. Even though many countries carry out population censuses every 10 years or so, the UNPD has to construct estimates based on collating information collected in many different ways from the world's governments and assessing its accuracy and reliability. Thus although the population estimates it produces are the best possible, given the information available, they are rather like my prediction of when I'll finish work: they will contain a margin of error. We can use probability to describe how large that error is likely to be.

A better way of dealing with this problem of measurement is to take *samples* of the world: very small pieces of it that we use to represent all of the rest. This poses two problems that we can use an understanding of probability to solve. The first is how to select our sample. We might assume that the bigger the sample is the better, but this is not the case. What matters is *how our sample is selected*. If we can arrange for everything that we want to measure to have a known *probability* of being included in the sample (as if we had put everything in a large bag and drawn out examples blindfold) then we can make extremely good estimates about very large populations from very small samples indeed. Such samples are called *random samples*. Better still, we can also use probability to work out how accurate these estimates are likely to be: how much *error* they are likely to contain. In my view, random sampling and the laws of inferential statistics deduced from it rank as one of the very greatest scientific inventions. Without such inference we'd simply not have any of the knowledge we do possess about the modern world.

The second use of probability in statistics concerns the future. When we want to solve a problem we are thinking about the future, about doing something new or differently from how it has been tackled before. Or we may simply want to know the probability of some future event occurring: will it rain tomorrow, will an asteroid collide with the earth, will interest rates rise or fall, how many children will need a primary school place in 10 years' time? No one can foretell the future. But some predictions are better than others. We can use probability not only to make better predictions, but also to estimate how good any prediction is likely to be. Conversely, prediction can often be used as a tool to increase or test our understanding. We may have a theory about how two or more variables operate. We can sometimes set up a test of the kind 'given our knowledge of these variables, we predict that if variable 1 takes value *X*, then variable 2 will take value *Y*'. We can then gather evidence to see if our prediction is realised or not. *Experiments* are a systematic way of establishing and testing predictions, and in the social sciences we can often use observation to establish similar forms of predictive tests.

Clearly the natural or social world is not so simple as to be reducible to a handful of easily observed or measured variables, but a current issue in economics illustrates the kind of debate that can occur. In the aftermath of the crash of 2008, many governments increased the money supply very substantially via 'quantitative easing' (QE). Some economists argued that such an increase must lead fairly quickly to increased inflation. Others argued that because economies were below capacity and interest rates were near zero, there was little risk of inflation. These predictions came from alternative models of how economies work. Many governments continued with substantial QE, and none suffered significant inflation. This is at least provisional evidence that the second economic model was superior, because it made a better prediction.

Randomness is an important idea within probability, and again you almost certainly have a fair intuitive idea of what it comprises. Randomness refers to the lack of order or structure and the dominance of chance, luck or indeterminate variation. If I say 'the disease struck at random' I'd be suggesting that there was no way of predicting who or where it would strike next. A randomly drawn lottery ticket is one where every ticket has an equal chance of being drawn and there is no way to determine in advance which is the best one to buy. However, randomness often doesn't look random. A good, simple random process is tossing a coin. Whether it lands on heads or tails is a random, unpredictable outcome. However if you toss a coin 5 times, you have a 25% chance of getting three heads one after the other at some point in the series of tosses. It might not look random, but it is. Nasser Hussain, the cricket captain, famously lost the toss 14 times in consecutive matches. There was no fix. The process was still random. At some point, some team captain, somewhere, playing in one of tens of thousands of matches around the world was going to come up with that unlucky record. Conversely processes that are not random can look as if they are. This is why 'poorly performing' or even murderous doctors (such as the infamous Harold Shipman) are so difficult to detect. It is very difficult to distinguish a bad doctor from an unlucky one, or one with a higher than average proportion of gravely ill patients.

Randomness is double-edged. It plagues all experimental data, especially when only small numbers of subjects or amounts of material can be experimented with; it is fiendishly difficult to distinguish the experimental effect from the effects of randomness or chance variation. However, randomness also makes random sampling possible. With random sampling we can make reliable statements about vast target populations of natural or social phenomena based on examining very much smaller amounts of data. A useful way to think about this, as suggested by Ian Hacking (2002), is how statistics enables us to make informed but 'risky' statements about the world. All statements or descriptions of the world are actually true or false, but we are rarely in a position where the evidence lets us know definitively which is the case. We thus want to be able to make provisional statements that are *probably* true (but open to disproof, contradiction and revision in the face of new evidence) and to be able to estimate how high or low that probability is. Because they are open to revision they are *falsifiable*. Think back to my earlier remarks about science and authority. Statistics invites us to substitute a careful assessment of what our best provisional statement is, and how confident we are about it, for authoritative pronouncements about how the natural or social world *must* be, whether the basis of that authority is scripture, a philosopher king or just common sense.

2 ● 6 THE LOGIC OF QUANTITATIVE EVIDENCE

While we use numbers to measure and describe the world, the numbers themselves, and the calculations we use them for, are much less important than the *logic* of what we do with them. This logic is based on rules for handling evidence. If our rules are good ones and we follow them properly, then the conclusions we draw from our evidence are likely to be sound. However, rather like the proceedings in a court of law, following and applying these rules always depend upon making good judgements. They can never, ever, produce results that are definitively correct, a guarantee of the truth or not subject to debate, challenge, contradiction or improvement. Just because evidence is quantitative, it does not mean that it is any more or less 'scientific' than other sources of knowledge.

Studying and learning secondary data analysis and statistics is a rather different activity than reading humanities or social science theory or articles or books about substantive topics in the social sciences, in which you read the material and then weigh up the merits of different arguments or approaches in an essay or a seminar group discussion. This is because at the heart of statistics lies a set of precisely stated, abstract, logical rules. Unlike substantive social science arguments or theories, these rules have no empirical content whatsoever, and they are, ultimately, 'true' by definition. It is not a question of different theories having different strengths or weaknesses, or fitting different aspects of empirical evidence better or worse. These rules simply have to be followed to get correct results.

This does not mean that data analysis has no use for judgement. On the contrary, I hope that by the end of this book you will appreciate that it is precisely by having a good grasp of basic statistical rules that you will have a better feel for just how much the robust use of quantitative evidence depends upon making judgement calls at every stage of the process, and that it is by evaluating the judgements made that we can appreciate whether any piece of quantitative evidence is worthwhile or not. None of this makes data analysis or statistics especially difficult. Rather they use a slightly different skill set than that involved in, for example, essay writing.

They are made considerably easier by the fact that you will probably find that you already know the great majority of the rules we study. Many of them are rooted in common sense and experience, as we shall see. However, unlike common sense, statistical rules are formulated in a logically tighter manner, and produce some highly counter-intuitive (and extremely useful) results that common sense or experience alone could never have produced.

2 7 THEORY AND PRACTICE

Secondary data analysis can neither be usefully learnt by rote, nor absorbed by careful study. In my experience, the only way to get a good grasp of it is by doing it: working through practical examples. Data analysis can be deceptive because it is often easy to study a new argument or technique and come away with the feeling that you have understood it, when in fact you have not truly grasped important details. The best, indeed the *only*, way to discover if this is the case, is to try the new technique yourself. It is only then that you discover whether your understanding was as sound as you imagined it to be. For that reason this book has many exercises and empirical examples. Partly this is to ensure that at least some of the examples cover material you may have some familiarity with because of the discipline you come from. But mostly it is so that you can try as many different examples/exercises on a topic as you find you need in order to get a sound understanding of it. While you do not need to work through every example, resist the temptation to skip them. You will find that it is a much more effective use of your time to work through a couple of examples than trying to 'learn' the material by memorising formulae or rules. My experience is that if you understand what you are doing and why, and can do a few examples successfully on your own without having to check too often that you are on the right track, then the formulae and so on will take care of themselves.

2 8 A LITTLE KNOWLEDGE IS A DANGEROUS THING

There is a well-known saying, 'a little knowledge is a dangerous thing'. I rather like the ambiguity of this expression. A little knowledge can be dangerous when we presume we have more knowledge than we actually do. Too naive a faith in evidence that has not been properly scrutinised or robustly tested, risks misleading us. For example, the mass media routinely report different health scares or advice about lifestyles, diets or behaviours that are said to lower or raise the risk of illness or death. Most of these reports, on closer scrutiny, vastly exaggerate the risks or benefits involved because they misread or misreport the true risks. However, media exaggeration is certainly not the only route into misplaced faith in numbers. Once it has been collected and organised into tables and put in a research report or newspaper article, quantitative evidence inexorably accumulates an aura of truth. The 'facts' appear to 'speak for themselves'. We are so busy analysing what results they might deliver that we can easily overlook or forget all the different processes that make the data or other evidence we work with less powerful or less accurate than we wish it to be. There is no substitute for getting to know your data sources well, and in an era when the standard of data documentation has improved greatly, no excuse for not doing so.

Paradoxically, the more we are aware of the *limitations* of our knowledge, the more *useful* it is to us. This is always the case with quantitative evidence. All our attempts to measure the world, whether that is the natural or social world, are always prone to some margin of *error*. Error in itself is not bad. It does not mean 'mistake'. Rather it is a way of thinking about the inevitable difference between the knowledge we might ideally like to have and what we can practically collect, or what we can boil down into convenient summaries. Error has five main sources, which we need to be aware of when analysing secondary data. If we keep these in mind, we can keep a sense of perspective about how useful and how precise our knowledge is.

sources of error

1   The world is *too big* to measure. There is simply far too much potential data to collect, even if we could. We almost always depend on smaller samples of the world. But what is true of our sample may not be true of the world from which it has been drawn, and it is this world that we really want to know about. Sampling is a powerful technique. Almost all of our knowledge of the world depends upon it. However, it does introduce a margin of error into our estimates that we must always stay alert to.

2   We can only measure the *present* (and aspects of the past). However, usually we want to know about the *future*, or how to intervene in the future to make some change. We measure the patient's temperature so that we might deal with their fever. We measure the rate of unemployment to judge whether the economy is depressed or overheating. The past may well be a useful guide to the future, especially in the natural world where, so far as we know, the laws governing the behaviour of matter or energy do not change over time. However, although there may be some universal and unchanging patterns in human society, we also know that we can both anticipate the future (and alter our behaviour accordingly) and not only remember the past but also learn from it. This makes the past at best an uncertain guide to the future in the social sciences. In addition, any successful intervention needs a good model of causal processes rather than simple correlation. We may think we have evidence of a cause and effect, so that we can bring about effects we want (a normal body temperature, a stable economy), but such evidence is more difficult to obtain than our own cognitive systems (which seem to be wired to produce causal narratives at the drop of a hat) often lead us to imagine.

3   We may not have measured, or observed, what we need to measure, so that our measurements may not be *valid*. Much of the time quantitative evidence is about establishing links or associations between different variables. We are often interested in these associations because they may be evidence of a causal connection, and thus a new way to intervene in the world. An association between the money supply and economic activity may guide economists about how best to manage an economy. However, if we are dealing with *observational* rather than *experimental* data (as we often are, since many experiments are impossible) we always run two risks. The first is that our chosen way of measuring the variable(s) we are interested in has poor *validity*, so that while we imagine we are measuring one phenomenon in fact we may be measuring something else. For example, in an election study we might ask respondents how they voted in a previous election. However, we would be ill-advised to take the resulting measurement as an accurate factual description of voting in that election, since we know from many studies that respondents over-report voting for the successful party or candidate, and under-report voting for others. The second risk is that we do not measure all the relevant important variables, so that any association we observe might be the product of *unobserved* phenomena. For example, we could only know that the substantial association between ice-cream sales and rates of theft is really a function of the weather if we had also collected data on the weather!

4   Although valid, our measuring instruments may be *unreliable*. We often assume that those who collect data or evidence go out with tools that, if measuring the same item repeatedly, will produce the same result each time. This is relatively easy to arrange and test in the physical world, but less so in the ever evolving social world. The meanings of the words in questions may change gradually over time. Old categories become outdated and are replaced with new ones. One need only look at early examples of population census questions, striking in their quaintness, to see how quickly societies change. The same concept may be understood very differently in different cultures. For example, in the World Values Survey a question is fielded that asks respondents whether it is ever justified for 'a man to beat his wife'. In societies where patriarchy is still strong we might expect respondents to interpret this question very differently from those where greater progress has been made against sexual inequality and 'wife beating' would be more likely to be seen as (unlawful) sexual violence rather than the exercise of some form of domestic authority.

5   Finally, even if we have perfect instruments, a good sample, observe everything we need to and examine a process that we can be sure will operate in the future in the same way as it has done in the past, we are still not safe! We may just be unlucky. The world is full of random variation that has, and can have, no comprehensive explanation. While we might prefer to imagine that 'in principle' all things are knowable, so that with perfect information we could work out the cause and consequence of everything, such a deterministic universe is a myth. Randomness is everywhere, and one of the forms it can take is apparently meaningful patterns in our data that are only the product of chance and coincidence. There is an entertaining website ✎ at http://www.tylervigen.com/spurious-correlations that records examples of unlikely (and ultimately meaningless) patterns. However, statistics allows us not only to tame the effects of randomness, luck or chance, but also put it to effective use.

'A little knowledge is a dangerous thing' has a second meaning. Even a little knowledge is far better than faith, superstition, or ignorance. Sometimes even a simple and straightforward piece of data can yield an insight or make people aware of something that they might otherwise overlook or forget. In 1854 John Snow plotted the cases of cholera in an outbreak in Soho, London, in which some 600 people died (Figure 2.1). By showing that the cases were concentrated near a particular water pump, he was able to show that cholera might be a water-borne disease, overturning the theory that it was bad air that brought it, and paving the way for more effective prevention and ultimately treatment of the disease. (The latter took some decades, since many 'experts' were scornful of the empirical evidence Snow produced. *The Lancet* dismissed his conclusions but was outdone by *The Times*: 'we prefer to take our chance with cholera ... than be bullied into health ... It is a positive fact that many have died of a good washing ... no longer protected by dirt' (cited in Norton, 2012: 113).) In 2011, the *Guardian* published the information that *News of The World* journalists had hacked the phone of a murdered youngster: one single piece of data that changed the entire relationship between politics and the press in the UK.

Knowledge, especially scientific knowledge obtained in a rigorous way, such that we can claim that it goes beyond our personal opinion or conviction, can be power. Indeed, one might argue that the scientific method, and, at the heart of that, statistical ways of processing knowledge, have been at the core of the most amazing human progress from the Enlightenment onwards. Statistics is about developing a critical but scientific attitude to the evidence and data that is always all around us. Good statistics are, by definition, subversive. If they change our knowledge, they subvert what we thought was the established order of things before we had

Figure 2.1 John Snow's map of fatal cholera cases in Soho, 1854

that knowledge. (There is a good review of this kind of argument in Berthold Brecht's play, *The Life of Galileo*, available in many editions.)

2.9 EXPERIMENTS

Experiments are procedures designed to produce knowledge independently of the views of the observer, or to test one or more of these views in an objective way, in the sense of producing evidence that not only the observer but also others would accept as being consistent with the view, or 'hypothesis', being tested. The core logic of an experiment is as follows. That part of the world in which we are interested in is described and measured in terms of *variables*. A *hypothesis* is produced about the effect of one variable – the *explanatory* or *independent* variable – upon one or more *response* or *dependent* variables. The values of all other variables are held constant, while the values of the explanatory variable are *manipulated*. If the values of the *response* variable(s) change then it can only have been the change in the value of the *explanatory* variable that *caused* this to happen. We have *provisional* evidence that this variable causes changes in the values of one or more other variables. The evidence is provisional, since further experiments may refine or refute it.

Experiments are usually *replicated*, to check that the findings of the original experiment can be produced as before, and cannot be attributed to confirmation bias on the part of the experimenter: our tendency to find what we are looking for or confirm our convictions. Confirmation bias can be unconscious and profound, as best illustrated by the story of a horse. 'Clever Hans' was a horse that performed impressive feats of mental arithmetic. However, the psychologist Oskar Pfungst was able to show that what the horse was actually doing was responding to cues from his trainer and audience that neither was actually aware of. The trainer genuinely believed he'd taught the horse to count, as did the audience. Moreover, their belief was quite consistent with the evidence before them. What they failed to investigate, but Pfungst did, was whether *other* explanations were possible, including ones that did not depend upon assuming equine mathematical skills.

Many kinds of political and sociological processes are difficult to reduce to experiments, although occasionally 'natural' experiments occur because of the way events fall out. Psychological processes are easier to investigate this way as they are easier to reproduce in the lab in a way that might be reasonably extrapolated to life beyond the lab. For example, Pfungst performed a series of tests on Hans, one of which was to control for whether the questioner knew the correct answer to a question. Pfungst discovered that Hans was almost always wrong when the questioner was unaware of the right answer. This set Pfungst on the path of investigating non-verbal clues as a possible explanation of Hans's behaviour. Thus Pfungst treated 'questioner's knowledge of the answer' as an explanatory variable and 'whether Hans is correct' as response. By manipulating the first, he was able to establish a direct causal relationship with the second.

The key point about this knowledge is that, although it was Pfungst as an experimenter who 'produced' it, the knowledge he produced was quite independent of his own beliefs *because it could be reproduced (or challenged) by others*. In this sense it was 'objective'. He might have started with a hunch or conviction about how the world works that was quite personal, but was able to transform this into something more substantial and public by setting up an experiment to test it.

So far, so simple. However, experiments are not as straightforward as this account might make them appear. There may be doubt or debate about what the relevant variables are and how they can be detected or measured. Holding other variables constant may not be easy. Results may vary from experiment to experiment for reasons that are difficult to discover.

Most important of all, experiments involving *people* face several problems. People cannot just be hauled off into a laboratory and 'measured' as if the laboratory setting itself did not influence them. There are all sorts of 'variables' describing people which cannot be either held constant (people continuously grow older and there is no way to stop this!) or manipulated (we cannot change someone's sex, or the school they went to, or their beliefs). Unlike atoms, people can think, and think ahead, and even anticipate the results of an experiment, or its implications. Finally, most experiments would simply be unethical. Imagine we were interested in the effect of child poverty on life chances. We could hardly take a group of children and consign them to an impoverished upbringing in order to compare their eventual biographies with those of more fortunate peers!

Some experiments with people are possible, for example in the field of epidemiology: the study of disease and its treatments. The Salk vaccine trial, described by Freedman et al. (2007: 3), is one such example. Here the explanatory variable was whether or not children received a vaccine against polio. The response variable was whether or not they contracted the disease. Polio epidemics varied in virulence from year to year, so it was important to control (or hold constant) the many other factors that might affect a child's exposure either to the disease itself or factors that gave the child resistance to it. Children were thus randomly allocated either to a *treatment* group (and given the vaccine) or a *control* group (and given a placebo – an injection of salt dissolved in water). If the vaccine was effective, the children in the treatment group could be expected to develop fewer cases of polio than those in the control group. Doctors who would diagnose cases of polio were not told which children had been vaccinated, lest this affect their judgement in diagnosing cases of polio.

The incidence of polio is not high (only a very small proportion of children might contract it in any one year), so that the study had to be extremely large: over 400,000 children randomly allocated to the vaccine and the placebo. By the end of the study 28 per 100,000 children who had received the vaccine had contracted polio, compared to 71 per 100,000 in the 'control' group: clear evidence that the vaccine was effective because it was much larger than any difference we might expect by random variation. Even so, there was still work to do to ensure that everyone who would benefit from it was vaccinated. A young singer called Elvis Presley was used to popularise its uptake in adolescents.

Work on the vaccine continued to improve. The bar chart in Figure 2.2 records the number of polio cases in the UK since 1950, with the height of the bars proportional to the number of cases. Polio rapidly became a very rare disease in the UK as effective vaccination became standard. Note how before the development of the vaccine, incidence of the disease varied from year to year, depending on the virulence of epidemics. Today polio continues to be endemic in only two countries, Pakistan and Afghanistan, with Nigeria, the last country in sub-Saharan Africa to eradicate the disease, recording no cases since 2014.

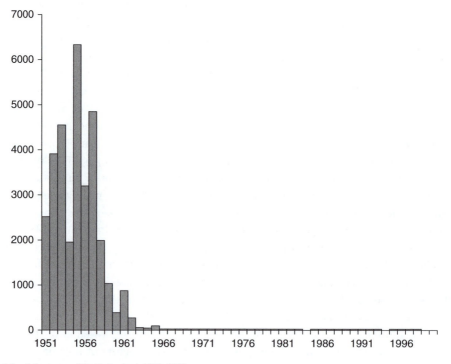

Figure 2.2   Polio cases notified in England, 1950–2000

Source: http://www.post-polio.org/ir-eng.html

Although the Salk vaccine trial was not conducted in a laboratory, it was an experiment in the sense that the investigators manipulated the explanatory variable. It took two values: *vaccine* and *placebo*. The response variable also took two values: *contracted polio* and *polio-free*. They could not hold the other variables constant. (That would have been impossible – imagine controlling exactly what hundreds of thousands of children did for a year!) However, they used another technique that achieves the same result: *random selection*. Children were allocated randomly to the two groups: each child had an equal chance of being assigned to the vaccine or placebo, as if a coin had been tossed to decide their fate. In a large enough group this process ensures that in each of the two experimental conditions, vaccine and placebo, the other characteristics of the children would have a high probability of having a similar distribution: for example, the proportion of children from rich or poor backgrounds, from different ethnic groups, from rural or urban areas, with good or poor health records, over- or underweight would be similar in each group. Because the trial selected children into the vaccine and placebo groups on a random basis, and measured the treatment group (who received the vaccine) against a control group (who did not) the Salk study was an example of a *randomised controlled experiment*. The scientists could be sure that any difference between the control and treatment groups at the end of the study *must* have been produced by the unique variable that differed between them: the variable describing whether or not they had been vaccinated.

2●10 OBSERVATIONAL STUDIES

Medical interventions such as use of a drug or vaccine are not too difficult to run as an experiment. But many other things we'd like to measure present more of a problem. We cannot, for example, raise or lower the temperature of the planet and see what happens. Nor can we split the planet in two and compare what happens if the temperature of one half is raised! Thus rather than laboratory experiments, much of our knowledge comes from *observational* studies where we observe patterns in nature or society – *correlations* or *associations* between variables – and from this observation make inferences about possible causal links. The underlying logic is the same as with the experiment: we measure the explanatory and response variables to see if they are correlated. However, because we cannot manipulate the explanatory variable, merely observe the different values that it takes, we also need to observe and measure other variables that are also correlated with it.

The key difference between observational studies and randomised controlled experiments, such as the Salk vaccine trial, is that since the explanatory variable cannot be manipulated, neither can it be *controlled*. For example, imagine we were studying the effect of living in a deprived neighbourhood on children's school performance. We could not just uproot and relocate children from one area to another and then see how they progressed at school. Not only would this be unethical, it would be methodologically nonsensical: the process of putting these children into a 'control' group would itself probably have an effect upon the outcome. We could, however, observe the school performance of children living in different areas, some of which were deprived and others not. Of course, as well as being different in terms of where they lived, these two groups of children would very likely *also* differ systematically in other ways: attendance at nursery school, the occupations or ages or incomes of their parents, time spent reading or studying outside the classroom, facilities for study at home, and so on. In an observational study it is difficult, but not impossible, to overcome the drawback that many variables, not only the experimental one, will affect the response variable of interest. We look briefly at how to do this later on in the book when we consider regression and *conditional probability*.

2.11 SURVEYS

At first sight a social survey does not look much like a laboratory experiment, but at heart they follow the same logic. Just as the experimenter cannot know the results of an experiment before it takes place, neither can the survey researcher know what the responses of the interviewees will be. Just as the designers of the Salk vaccine trial randomised children to receive the vaccine or a placebo, so the sample of people chosen for a survey will be based on random sampling, so that they will be representative of the target population from which they have been drawn. Just as analysis of the vaccine trial was based on the comparison of the probabilities of contracting polio conditional upon receiving the vaccine or placebo, so too does most survey analysis comprise comparison of the probabilities of observing respondents to possess some characteristic, conditional upon their being observed to possess another.

This might sound like a complicated procedure, but it is one that you already practice intuitively in your daily life without even consciously thinking about it. If you are on campus and noticing those around you, you can probably divide the people you see into staff and students without knowing which category they belong to, by virtue of how old they look. The probability that a person is a lecturer, librarian or administrator, *conditional upon their being older*, is higher than that they are a student. You intuitively use conditional probabilities to make the association between age and status. However, enough theory! In the next chapter we'll look at data online, and see how you can use this form of logic to think of associations between variables, and quickly access useful evidence from the internet.

what you have learned

We have covered a good deal of material in this chapter. Review the summary points below to check whether you have picked up the key arguments it has made.

- Numbers in themselves are neither good nor bad: what matters is how they are used
- We often take measurement for granted, because it is so ubiquitous, but even simple measurements are often very hard to achieve
- The first and most important question to ask of any number is where it came from
- Things vary in different ways so that there are levels of measurement: interval (ratio), ordinal and nominal
- Good measurements are reliable and valid
- Variation is captured by variables, values and cases or observations
- We are usually interested in the distribution of values for a variable
- Distributions can be displayed visually by graphics or in a frequency table, or summarised by descriptive statistics of level (central tendency), spread, and shape

- Standardisation of various kinds enables us to compare different distributions
- Comparison is fundamental to observation, so that contingency tables or 'crosstabs' are very useful
- We usually focus our interest in a dependent variable and observe ways in which independent variables may be associated with it
- Correlation is necessary but insufficient evidence of causation
- Probability measures uncertainty, including how likely it is that data from a sample will resemble that from a target population, were it possible to measure that population
- Error is everywhere. Our aim is to reduce it to manageable proportions. It is better to be approximately right than precisely wrong!
- Experiments are unusual in the social sciences, where we must usually rely on observation and statistical control. This increases the risk of confirmation bias, but can be countered by replication

DOING SECONDARY DATA ANALYSIS IN FIVE MINUTES

━━━━━━━━━ **introduction** ━━━━━━━━━

You do not need any special software to begin secondary data analysis. Many sites on the web allow you to explore data, producing frequency and contingency tables or summary statistics. Many use Nesstar, an online data analysis program.

- All that is required to do secondary data analysis is a web browser
- Many excellent sites allow you to do simple analyses online
- You'll learn how to produce frequency and contingency tables, bar charts and other output using dialog boxes
- You'll learn how to deal with missing values
- You'll learn good table manners

All you need to get going with secondary data analysis is a computer and an internet connection. Many data sources have websites associated with them that allow you to examine the data online, creating tables or graphs without any software of your own. The number of such sites is growing all the time, so that what follows is not meant as comprehensive guide, but rather a selection of the kind of resources that are out there to be discovered and some basic techniques to make best use of them. You can do some simple but powerful secondary data analysis in a few minutes. Here's how.

3 ● 1   GAPMINDER

The Gapminder website is a good place to start if you have never explored the power of secondary data before. Led by Hans Rosling, it has a range of data on countries of the world from 1800 onwards. Most of the social sciences are built on some core ideas about the revolutionary social, political and economic changes that have taken place across the globe over the last couple of centuries, based around the growth of individualism, the spread of markets, rationalisation and bureaucratisation, the rising power of the modern state, the decline of patriarchy and the power of science and technology that has driven unprecedented increases in living standards. This is a complex story, but we can grasp some of its essence by looking at some key variables.

There is a companion website for this book at https://study.sagepub.com/macinnes. Here you will find web links cited in the book, copies of IBM SPSS Statistics software syntax files, exercises and answers to them, as well as a range of other material. Where there is further information on the website you'll see this symbol 🐾 in the text.

Go to 🐾 http://www.gapminder.org and click on the heading **GAPMINDER WORLD**. This will load a graphic entitled 'Wealth and Health of Nations' (Figure 3.1). The horizontal axis of the graph (X-axis) displays the gross domestic product (the value of all goods and services produced in a year) per person of countries of the world in 'purchasing power parity' inflation-adjusted dollars. That is, it gives us an estimate of the income per person in the equivalent of today's

US dollars for the countries of the world for as far back as data is available. The axis is on a *logarithmic* scale. This makes it easier to see changes in income levels over time, since travelling the same distance along the axis represents the same *relative* change in income. Thus, for example, the distance from $200 to $400 is the same as that from $20,000 to $40,000. Were we to use a linear scale that tracked absolute differences we wouldn't be able to see much difference between countries with low incomes on a scale small enough to capture the income levels of high-income countries. (Logarithms are explained in more detail in the appendix to Chapter 4.) Income per person for a country tells us nothing about the distribution of income within that country, but it gives us a rough and ready indicator of the general standard of living. It is approximate because adjusting for changes in prices over long periods of time cannot take full account of the impact of technological change. The world in 1850 had no electric light, electronics, cars, antibiotics and so on at *any* price. The world in 2016 has little use for steam engines or gas lighting. Thus although adjusting for inflation probably underestimates the degree of change that has taken place, as long as we are interested in orders of magnitude rather than precise comparisons, this measurement will serve us well enough.

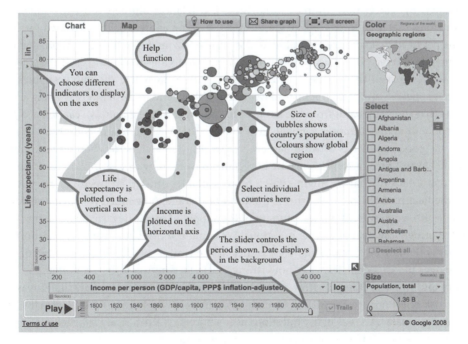

Figure 3.1 Gapminder Wealth and Health of Nations webpage

Average life expectancy at birth in years is shown on the vertical scale (*Y*-axis) of the graph. Life expectancy is a useful measure of people's health. Like inflation-adjusted GDP per person, it is a summary measure that does not tell us about the range of life expectancies in a country at a point in time. Women tend to live slightly longer than men. Particularly in earlier periods, life expectancy was heavily influenced by infant and child mortality. Until the development of vaccination for infectious diseases and better public health, water supplies and sanitation, epidemics or poor harvests decimated the recently born, reducing average life expectancies.

Thus an average life expectancy of 30 years does not mean that most people died aged 30, but that so many people died at earlier ages that few would survive to reach the 70 or 80 years that we would regard as normal now.

The *bubbles* plotted on the graph represent individual countries. Their colour represents global geographic regions, and their size is proportional to the country population size. The graph shown on the webpage is for the most recent data available, mostly around the year 2013. If you place your cursor over any bubble it will show the name of the country and the data for GDP per person and average life expectancy in that country. The slider at the bottom of the graph below the *X*-axis controls which year the graph displays, but for now let us concentrate on the most recent year.

3 ● 2 UNDERSTANDING THE GAPMINDER ANIMATION

It looks as if Luxembourg has the highest standard of living, while Andorra has the highest life expectancy. There is a clear, but by no means perfect, *correlation* between income and life expectancy. By 'correlation' we mean that there is a relationship between two *variables*. The two variables that are plotted on the graph we are looking at are **wealth** (measured by average income per head in a country) and plotted along the horizontal *X*-axis of the graph, and **health** (measured by average life expectancy at birth of people living in a country). If there were no relationship between these variables we'd find no pattern in where the bubbles representing countries appeared on the graph. Instead we find that they tend to cluster loosely along an invisible line that slopes upwards from the left towards the right of the graph. We can tell at a glance that people in richer countries generally live longer. However, the relationship is far from perfect. Some poorer countries with similar levels of wealth do much better than others on health: compare North Korea or Nepal, with life expectancies over 70, with Lesotho (48) or Papua New Guinea (60). This is what we might expect. Many variables other than wealth alone will determine the health of a population: the distribution of income, how much resource is devoted to public health, good water supplies, sanitation, the supply of medical services and so on.

We routinely use data to answer questions. We could use this data to answer questions such as 'what is the range of wealth across countries of the world?' or 'do people in India or China have longer life expectancies?', or 'how strong is the link between the economic power of a country and life expectancy?'. However, just as important in secondary data analysis is using data to *ask* questions, to stimulate our curiosity and delve deeper into a subject. This graph, like any good data, raises as many questions as it answers. We've already touched on one: how accurate is the data – does it measure what we really want it to?

We might want to check the sources from which the data came. If it was supplied by national agencies, can we be sure that North Korea can be relied upon to honestly report economic output or life expectancy? (It might wish to exaggerate to support its propaganda battle against South Korea; or it might wish to *underestimate* to strengthen its case for international aid.) How good is the data quality for countries where subsistence farming is the basis of most livelihoods, there is only a limited rural cash economy, and nothing like the resources available to richer countries for national statistical agencies to collect even basic information about their populations? This is a question you should remember to ask yourself about any data. In their excellent book *The Tiger That Isn't*, Blastland and Dilnot (2008: 15) make a fundamental point about all quantitative data that is easy to overlook: 'we can establish a simple rule: if it has been counted, it has been defined, and that will almost always have meant using force to squeeze reality into boxes that don't fit'. Of course that doesn't mean that we shouldn't count! But it does mean that we always need to keep in mind that reducing the world to numerical measurements always simplifies to some extent from a world that is much more complex. Good measurements simplify that world in a useful and powerful way, such as the data we're using here, but that never means that the data tells us the whole story, or possibly even the most adequate one. The Gapminder site allows you to check on the source of the data it uses (go to the **DATA** tab on the homepage) and usually has links to the sites of the data providers.

A second question that the graph might raise for us is the global spread of wealth and health. One world region stands out: sub-Saharan Africa. None of the countries on the mainland there have an average life expectancy above 70, and in many countries it is below 60, despite the fact that income per person ranges from below $1,000 to over $10,000. Only one country outside sub-Saharan Africa has such a low life expectancy: Afghanistan. One reason for this, aside from slower economic development, may have been the impact of the HIV epidemic in sub-Saharan Africa.

3 ● 3 TWO CENTURIES OF WORLD HISTORY IN TWO MINUTES

A third question the graph might raise is how all these countries arrived at their current position. The slider at the bottom allows you to select different years, while the **Play** tab at the bottom right allows you to generate an animation that shows the evolution of health and wealth in countries over time. Here it is especially important to keep in mind the issue of data quality. When you play the animation you'll see that the country bubbles bounce around rather erratically, especially in earlier years. While some of this represents real change – in earlier periods a run of bad harvests could ruin a country's economy – it also represents changes in the quality, accuracy and sources of the data available. Drag the slider at the bottom of the graph to '1800'. Not all countries have data for this period, but there are more than enough to get a general picture. Only in Iceland is life expectancy above 40 and in many countries it is under 30. Only very few countries have wealth that is substantially greater than the poorest ones, and the UK and Netherlands – countries which led the industrial revolution – stand out as somewhat richer than the rest. Note too how small the bubbles were. World population in 1800 is estimated to have been around 1 billion. At the time of the end of the Black Death around 1350, it was a little more than one third of a billion. It would take more than a century to reach 2 billion in the 1920s. It took less than 40 years to double from 3 billion around 1960 to around 6 billion towards the end of the 1990s.

Adjust the small scale to the right of the **Play** tab to slow down the speed of the animation, and click on **Play**. You will see the evolution of global health and wealth over two centuries. Let the animation play and pause it around 1860. You can see how many countries in Europe, together with some of their current and former colonial settlements (such as the USA, Canada and Australia) are pulling away in terms of wealth, and although there now appears to be a clearer relationship between health and wealth, it is easier to see progress in the latter than the former. Pause again around 1900. There is now a much greater difference between the industrialised areas of Europe and North America and most of Asia and Africa, where neither living standards nor health have changed much over the century. As you restart the anima-tion look carefully at the period 1917 to 1919. The impact of the First World War and the flu pandemic that followed it causes both living standards and life expectancy to plunge dramati-cally, but then the upward progress continues. By the 1920s some industrialised countries have achieved life expectancies in the low sixties, while in many poorer ones it stays below half that level. There is now a very strong link between health and wealth, which gets even stronger as we move into the 1950s, the era in which the term 'Third World' was coined to describe the now yawning gulf between the prosperity of the industrialised North and much of Asia and Africa. As you pass 1929 notice the impact of the great crash, and that of the Second World War in the early 1940s. In the early 1960s you can see the disastrous impact of the economic dislocation and famine produced by Mao's 'Great Leap Forward' in China. However, as we move through the later 1960s onwards more countries start to join the affluent group with relatively high life expectancies, and by the 1990s the world's two most populous countries, India and China, both start to make real economic progress, reaching levels of life expectancy enjoyed only in rich countries a few decades earlier. It is no longer possible to see a clearly distinct 'Third World', although sub-Saharan Africa continues to lag well behind the rest of the world.

There is much more data on the Gapminder site that you can display on the graph, and many more ways to display it. The site has an online and hard copy guide, as well as videos and other resources, and allows you to search and download all the original data that drives the visualisations. The best way to discover its many features is to explore it using your curi-osity as a guide. The videos are excellent, especially on 'myths' about population, poverty and development in what used to be called the 'Third World', and all are based on data from the site, giving you some sense of its many applications. The video *The Joy of Stats* is a wonderful introduction to quantitative analysis if you have not already seen it. Any data site with a tab entitled **IGNORANCE** is surely worth exploring (click on it and surprise yourself).

3 ● 4   THEORY AND EMPIRICAL DATA

Gapminder is a fun site but it has a truly serious purpose that lies at the core of secondary data analysis. If you are a social science student you've doubtless encountered concepts such as 'modernisation', 'growth', 'capitalism', 'education' and 'imperialism'. However, we often have a much weaker grasp of the empirical dimensions of these concepts than we imagine. I doubt, for example, if many are aware that life expectancy in developing countries almost doubled in the second half of the twentieth century. When they do not have enough empirical content, concepts easily slip from our control and it becomes all too easy to use them to make almost any argu-ment appear convincing. Unfortunately, too many prestigious academic careers have been built on doing just that. There is a simple way to avoid this. For any concept ask 'how can it be measured?' and then ask 'what's the empirical evidence?'. If a concept cannot be measured, no matter how imperfectly, then what use is it? If we don't have some empirical evidence about it, what can we possibly know about it? These critical questions are two of the most powerful you can ask about almost any topic, and you can set about answering them using secondary data.

There is also a complementary danger to be avoided, however. Society comprises more than a collection of empirical 'facts'. Staring at the Gapminder visualisations or studying the data behind them cannot tell you much about global society and its development unless you have some prior idea about what you are looking for. Churning through large amounts of data without some provisional sense of what you are looking for is sometimes called 'data dredging' or 'data-driven analysis': fishing haphazardly for ideas. You need to organise the data using concepts and theories to make sense of it. This is usually an iterative process, so that is useful to think in terms of *data exploration* and *theory testing*. Concepts and theories ultimately arise from empirical evidence and our attempts to make sense of it and order it. To do that we need to *explore* the data, driven by our curiosity: we look for patterns, connections, paradoxes, unusual cases and so on. However, just as 'facts never speak for themselves', exploration eventually has to lead to concepts, theories, models, summaries or other attempts to describe and understand the data. *We* project patterns and structures onto the data: the data doesn't do it for us. Once we've developed these ideas, we can then check their consistency with the empirical evidence we have: we *test* them. If they don't end up fitting the data well, we can improve or abandon them.

3 ● 5 THE US GENERAL SOCIAL SURVEY

Gapminder is an example of a site that provides *aggregate* data: data that has already been assembled for presentation in particular ways (such as time series data on an indicator for countries of the world). The US General Social Survey (GSS), by contrast, provides direct access to *microdata*. Microdata is data that is in its original format as a set of variables, cases and values

Figure 3.2   The US General Social Survey webpage

that the individual researcher can explore and assemble in the way that best suits the analysis they want to carry out. The GSS has been running since 1972 based at NORC at the University of Chicago. As well as a core of questions that are repeated every year, it runs modules on various topics and claims to be 'the most frequently analyzed source of information in the social sciences'. Its homepage is at ✆ www.gss.norc.org (Figure 3.2).

GSS data has a complex structure, as the sampling methods have changed over time, and different subsets of respondents are asked different sets of questions. We will look at the GSS in greater detail later, but in this chapter we'll look at two of the online tools that allow you to explore the data. We will focus first on the SDA platform hosted by the University of California, Berkeley. It is quick and straightforward to use, and also has a YouTube channel with brief 'How to' videos at ✆ https://www.youtube.com/user/sdatutorials.

3 ● 6   ANALYSING GSS DATA ON ATTITUDES TO GENDER ROLES USING THE SDA

To access the SDA, first click on **GSS Data Set** under **Quick Links** to the right of the GSS homepage (Figure 3.2). In the next page that opens, click on the hyperlink to **SDA** at the end of the text under **Download the Data**. This takes you to the SDA archive page ✆ (http://sda.berkeley.edu/archive.htm) with a list of hyperlinks to different surveys that it can be used to explore. The first item in this list, under the heading **General Social Surveys (GSS)** is entitled **General Social Survey (GSS) Cumulative Datafile 1972-2014 - release 2 (SDA 4.0)**. Click on this link and the page shown at Figure 3.3 will appear.

On the left-hand side is a list of variables from the GSS organised into folders by subject area. Since there are more than 5,000 variables we'll need to use the search function to help us find what we are looking for. In several years GSS has asked respondents about male breadwinner ideology by asking whether they agreed or disagreed with the following statement: 'It is much better for everyone involved if the man is the achiever outside the home and the woman takes care of the home and family.'

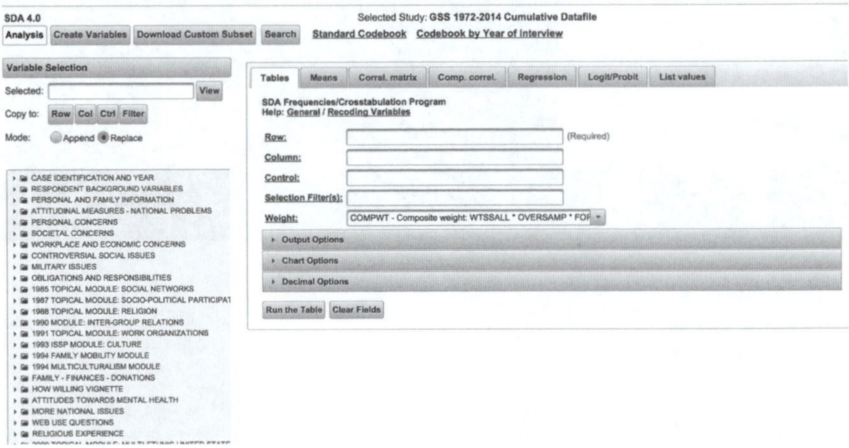

Figure 3.3   The General Social Survey

We want to find the variable created from this question. Click on the **Search** tab at the head of the page and enter the terms 'woman' and 'home' in the search box. This should return half a dozen questions that used both these terms. Click on the view button next to **FEFAM**, which is the name of the variable we are after. This gives us a quick description of the variable and responses to it. There are about 26,000 valid responses, so we know the question must have been fielded in several years.

Click on the **analysis** tab at the top left of the screen. Under **Variable Selection** enter the name of our variable – **FEFAM** – in the **Selected** box. Ensure that **Append** is checked, next to **Mode**. Click the **Col** button next to **Copy to:** and you'll see that the variable now gets posted

Table 3.1 Male Breadwinner ideology, USA, 1977–2014

Frequency distribution

FEFAM

Cells contain row percentages	1 Strongly agree	2 Agree	3 Disagree	4 Strongly disagree	Row total
1977	19.0	47.0	28.2	5.9	100
1985	9.7	38.7	39.3	12.3	100
1986	8.8	38.3	40.1	12.8	100
1988	9.0	32.0	43.3	15.8	100
1989	9.6	30.6	43.1	16.7	100
1990	6.6	32.5	46.5	14.4	100
1991	7.6	33.3	42.0	17.1	100
1993	5.5	29.4	47.5	17.6	100
1994	6.4	27.7	47.9	18.1	100
1996	7.4	30.5	44.6	17.4	100
1998	6.8	27.2	47.2	18.7	100
2000	11.1	28.9	40.7	19.3	100
2002	10.3	28.8	42.9	18.0	100
2004	8.7	28.0	45.9	17.5	100
2006	9.1	26.2	47.4	17.3	100
2008	8.2	27.0	47.2	17.5	100
2010	6.8	28.6	43.5	21.2	100
2012	6.5	25.2	48.3	20.0	100
2014	6.3	24.7	48.1	20.9	100
Col. total	8.6	30.6	43.9	16.9	100

to the **Column** box in the **Tables** tab on the right-hand side of the screen. In the variable list on the left of the screen click on the arrow icon next to the first folder labelled **CASE IDENTIFICATION AND YEAR**. This will reveal a list of three variables. We want the second one **YEAR – GSS YEAR FOR THIS RESPONDENT**. Click on this and it will be posted to the **Selected** box above. Now click the **Row** button underneath to add this variable to the rows of the table we are going to create. In the right-hand pane beneath where our two variables appear you'll see an **Output Options** tab. Click on this to reveal a variety of options for creating our table. You'll see that the default option for calculating the percentages in tables is for column percentages. Uncheck this and choose **Row percentages** instead. Uncheck **Color coding** under **Other options** too. We've now told SDA to produce a contingency table or crosstab with the variable **YEAR** displayed in the rows of the table, and the variable **FEFAM** in the columns, and with the percentages in the table running along the rows so that they show the distribution of responses to the gender roles question from all respondents in different years. Finally, click the **Run the Table** button at the bottom and you should create Table 3.1.

3 ● 7 INTERPRETING THE RESULTS IN A CONTINGENCY TABLE

Our table shows the results for the variable **FEFAM** for all adults for each year in which the question was fielded in the survey. We therefore have two variables in our table. In the *columns* of the table we have the responses that survey respondents could give to the statement about the roles of men and women. In the *rows* of the table we have the variable for the year in which the survey took place and the question was asked. In each *cell* of the table we have the percentage of all respondents from that year who chose that response. In each row of the table we have the frequency distribution for the variable **FEFAM** standardised to percentages for the year in question. Thus, for example, we can see that 19% of all respondents in 1977 said that they 'strongly agreed' with the statement, and 47% said they 'agreed' with it. Since the same question was asked over a period of almost four decades, scanning the table can give us a good idea of how gender role attitudes have changed over this period in the USA. In 1977 about twice as many people agreed with the statement as disagreed with it, whereas the reverse is now true.

Studying the table reveals some other patterns. Notice that although there is a fairly steady trend towards more disagreement with the statement over time, this trend seems to be interrupted in 2000. There are three possible explanations for this that might lead us to explore further. One is that public attitudes did shift in this way around this time. Perhaps some high-profile event or other dramatic social or political change caused the longer-run trend in attitudes to stall. A second possibility is that the way attitudes were measured changed in some way, undermining the reliability of the measure. Perhaps the question wording was altered, or the order in which the question appeared in the survey changed, or a new sampling or field-work procedure changed the characteristics of the sample drawn. This could be checked if need be by consulting the survey documentation available on its website, something we discuss further in Chapter 5. A third possibility is that there was no underlying change in the way attitudes were shifting in the population and the change shown in the data results from sampling fluctuation. Any estimate from a sample contains a margin of error, usually of the order of a couple of percentage points (we discuss this further in Chapter 4). It could be that such error is responsible for the blip in our long-run trend.

Note too that SDA also generates a bar chart based on your table. Often graphics are a good way to spot patterns and trends in the data more easily. Each bar in the chart represents one row of your table, with colours in the bar representing different values of the column variable, and the length of each coloured section of the bar proportional to the percentages in that row of the table.

3 ● 8 RECODING VARIABLES

We could make our table simpler, however, by collapsing together the responses 'strongly agree' and 'agree' and doing the same with 'disagree' and 'strongly disagree'. Then we can carry out some further analysis with our new version of the **FEFAM** variable. Go back to the SDA main page (your browser will have opened a new page to display the table we created). To the right of the **Analysis** tab, click the one entitled **Create Variables**. You'll see the right-hand pane of the window changes to a **Recode** dialog box. A *dialog box* is a common means of inputting information or commands to analysis packages. (As we'll see in Chapter 4, SPSS makes widespread use of them.) First we're asked for a name for the new variable to be created. This can be almost any name that makes sense and will act as a reminder of what is in our variable. Since we're creating it out of **FEFAM** we might call it **FEFAM2**. Our label for the new variable (a longer description of it) could be the question wording that created it, or a shorter summary of it. Click on the red

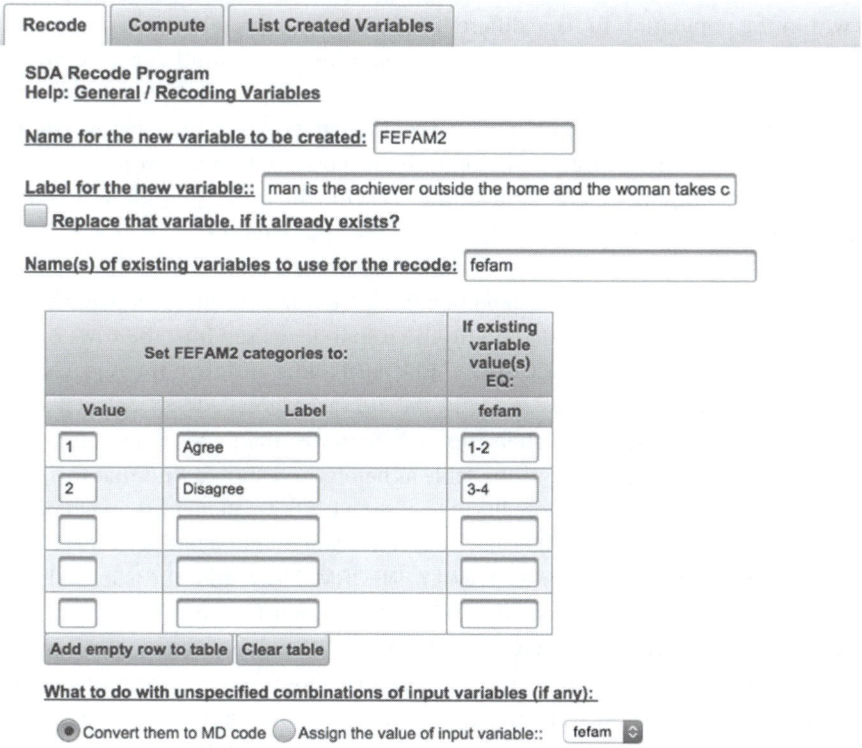

Recode	Compute	List Created Variables

SDA Recode Program
Help: General / Recoding Variables

Name for the new variable to be created: FEFAM2

Label for the new variable:: man is the achiever outside the home and the woman takes c

☐ Replace that variable, if it already exists?

Name(s) of existing variables to use for the recode: fefam

Set FEFAM2 categories to:		If existing variable value(s) EQ:
Value	Label	fefam
1	Agree	1-2
2	Disagree	3-4

| Add empty row to table | Clear table |

What to do with unspecified combinations of input variables (if any):

◉ Convert them to MD code ◯ Assign the value of input variable:: [fefam ⬥]

Figure 3.4 Creating new variables in the GSS

text which now appears, and we get another dialog box which asks us for values and labels for the new variable. We want the existing values 1 (strongly agree) and 2 (agree) to be put together as a single agree category, and we could give this the numerical code 1. Similarly, we want the existing values 3 (disagree) and 4 (strongly disagree) to be put together as a single disagree category, and we could give this the numerical code 2. To carry this out we'd fill in the dialog box as shown in Figure 3.4.

As you may have noticed when we examined the variable, **FEFAM** could also take other values (e.g. if the question was not asked or if the respondent did not give an answer). We can safely ignore these responses just now, by treating them as missing, and we'll accept the default option **Convert them to MD code**. *Missing values* are values recorded for cases on a variable where we do not have a value for what we are trying to measure. Typically we discard such cases before doing our analysis. We'll deal with missing values in more depth in Chapter 4. We can now click the **Start Recoding** button at the bottom of the dialog box. The system then gives us a summary of the new variable we've created and how we created it. We now have a version of the variable that makes it easy to quickly compare the proportions of people who agreed or disagreed with the 'male breadwinner' statement whether or not their (dis)agreement was 'strong'.

3.9 EXPLORING SOME CORRELATES OF MALE BREADWINNER IDEOLOGY

We've seen that views of adults as a whole have changed over time. But we might expect different groups within the population to have different attitudes. One hypothesis we might investigate is whether men and women have different views about this issue. Another is whether there is a correlation with political views. Those who see themselves as conservative might be more likely to agree with the statement. Yet another is whether there is a correlation between age and views on this issue: perhaps older people are more likely to subscribe to male breadwinner ideology. We can begin by pooling the results from all the years in which the question was fielded. If we wish we can focus our interest down to shorter time periods later on.

Click on the **Analysis** tab to take us back to the **Tables** dialog box. We can write in the name of our new variable **FEFAM2** in the **column** box. Let's see how attitudes compare by sex. To do this we want to place the variable describing the respondent's sex into the rows of the table. Click on the **RESPONDENT BACKGROUND VARIABLES** folder and then the **Age, Gender, Race and Ethnicity** sub-folder. Respondents' sex is the second variable, called **SEX**. Select it and change the **Mode** selection to **Replace**, and then copy to the **row** of the table in the right-hand pane. Again choose row percentages and run the table as before. You should find that it is indeed the case that over this period men are more likely to agree with the statement than women, but the difference is perhaps less than we might have expected: a matter of a few percentage points.

Go to the folder **PERSONAL AND FAMILY INFORMATION** and the sub-folder **VOTING PATTERNS** where you'll find the variable **POLVIEWS** near the end of the list (caution: do not select either **POLVIEWY** or **POLVIEWX** – these are different variables). Replace **SEX** with **POLVIEWS** and run the table again. As we might expect, those who rate themselves as conservative are more likely to agree with the statement than those who describe themselves as liberal.

What about age? As before, we can replace the variable **POLVIEWS** with the variable **AGE** (the first variable in the **Age, Gender, Race and Ethnicity** sub-folder) in the rows of the table.

When you do this you'll see that age does indeed have an impact, with younger respondents less likely to agree with the statement than older ones. However, since age is recorded as a single year of age, it would make sense to recode this variable to make its presentation simpler. Use the same steps as before to create a new variable **AGEGROUP** taking the values 18–29, 30–44, 45–59, 60–74 and 75–89 (or any other division that makes sense to you). Note that you have to assign a numerical value for your new variable corresponding to each range of values of the original **AGE** variable that you want to collect together, as shown in Table 3.2.

Table 3.2   Values for age group recode

Value code	Age group
1	18–29
2	30–44
3	45–59
4	60–74
5	75–89

Note that the GSS records the age of all those aged 89 and over as 89. One reason for this is to maintain the anonymity of respondents. It could theoretically be possible (although in practice very difficult) for someone to identify a single respondent with an unusually high age living in a particular geographical area.

3 ● 10 USING A THIRD VARIABLE IN A CONTINGENCY TABLE

Keep in mind that the results we've looked at in the last few crosstabs pool all the surveys in which the question was asked since 1977. We might want to compare what has happened over time by creating a three-way crosstab using a *control* variable. This gives us what you can think of as a three-dimensional table, which is reproduced on the page by presenting different 'slices' of the table, one for each value of the control variable.

Using the same procedures as before, recode the **YEAR** variable to create a variable that describes the decade the survey was fielded in (since the question was only fielded once in the 1970s, put 1977 in with the 1980s so that your categories are up to 1989, 1990–1999, 2000–2009 and 2010–2014. Put the new variable you create into the **control** box and run the table, so that you now have results describing the relationship between age and views on gender roles for four successive time periods. What do you find?

Now that you've equipped yourself with the basic skills needed to use the SDA platform you can explore the GSS data to discover some of the riches that lie buried within it. There are many more variables on gender role attitudes, so you might want to see if they undergo a similar change over time to that we've found with **FEFAM**. Or you might want to look at the impact of ethnicity or race, or level of education on people's attitudes or their geographical distribution (hint: use the variable **REGION** which divides the USA into nine main regions). Is there a difference in attitudes towards gender roles between the southern states in the USA and elsewhere?

You might want to explore respondents' attitudes to the death penalty or gun control, or some of the other issues covered by GSS over the years.

3 ● 11 USING GSS DATA EXPLORER TO ANALYSE THE GSS

One of the weaknesses of SDA is that it is not easy to export results from it. Although you can copy and paste what is on your webpage (including any charts) to Excel or other packages, it is not a very satisfactory solution. If you want to be able to download tables or charts that you create, you can use an alternative platform called GSS Data Explorer. You must register to use this, but it takes only a minute to do so. You proceed by adding variables to a cart, as if you were buying something online, and then creating a project, which is just some operation you carry out on the data, such as producing a table.

Follow these steps to re-create the table of gender role attitudes by year that we built using SDA. Go to the GSS homepage **Data Explorer:**

🔖 https://gssdataexplorer.norc.org/

Then click on the tab **EXPLORE GSS DATA** and you'll see the **Search Data** page shown in Figure 3.5. Clicking on the **Features** tab at the top of the page takes you to a very brief review of how it works. The **Search Data** page lists the variables created by the GSS over the years and the questions that produced them. Since there are over 5,000 variables, you need to be able to search them, which you can do by a **keyword** or **subject** search. If you did not know the name of the variable you are searching for you could click on the **Choose Subjects** box and check 'Women', near the end of the list, and then click the orange **SEARCH** tab on the right-hand side at the top of the page. This brings up a list of variables concerned with women and gender roles.

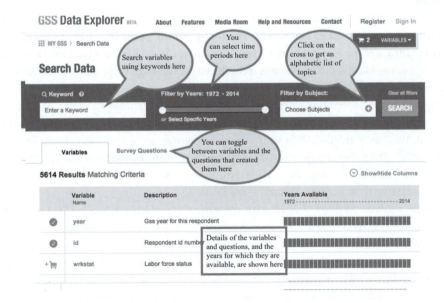

Figure 3.5 The GSS Data Explorer homepage

However, since we already know that the variable we want is called **FEFAM** from our work with SDA, you can locate it by typing this in the **Keyword Search** box. The variable **YEAR** is preloaded to your cart. Once you have the **FEFAM** variable in your cart, choose **Analyse data** from the **Actions** tab at the top right of the screen and in the screen that follows choose **Cross Tabulation** and click **Next.** You will probably find that the **YEAR** variable has already been inserted in the table as a column variable. We want it in the rows of the table, so click the small cross at the top right of the variable box to dismiss it. Then drag the variable year to the **Row Variable** box, and the variable **FEFAM** to the **Column Variable** box. Make sure you check **Exclude Missing Values** at the bottom of the dialog box and click **Create Analysis.** The default presentation is to show raw counts for the table cells, but you can change this to row percentages using the **Display Options** dialog box above the table. Use the **print** icon 🖶 or **EXPORT** button to print your table or export it as a PDF or Excel file. As with SDA, you can create new variables or do other kinds of analysis.

3 ● 12 THE WORLD VALUES SURVEY

The World Values Survey (WVS) has been running since 1981. It started with only 10 countries, but that last wave (2010–2014) covered no less than 60. Individual teams of academics led by a principal investigator field the survey in different countries using a questionnaire developed by the Executive Committee which also looks after the data archiving. Its homepage is at

🔌 http://www.worldvaluessurvey.org/wvs.jsp

Click on the **Data & Documentation** tab under the list of **Site Sections** to the left of the page. Then choose **Online Analysis** from the sub-menu on the **Data and Documentation** page. This produces a map of the world with tabs for each of the six WVS waves. Choose the latest wave, **2010-2014.** You can then select which countries to examine. Although you can select as many as you like, it is best to limit your choice to half a dozen or so at a time, as larger numbers make reading the table or graphs produced more difficult. In the examples below I've chosen Algeria, China, Egypt, Hong Kong, India, Malaysia, Pakistan, and Singapore. Finally, you can select a survey question to examine by clicking on the **Survey questions** tab, which brings up the page shown in Figure 3.6.

You can either view a list of questions, or by clicking the **Show tree** button, see a hierarchy of folders with questions for different subsections of the questionnaire. Then all you need do is select a question and click the **Show** button next to it to view the results from the countries you have chosen. We can follow up the issue of gender roles that we looked at in the USA. There is no direct equivalent in the WVS to the question on male breadwinner ideology asked in the GSS, nor would it necessarily be appropriate or useful. Not all countries have gone through the development of varieties of the male breadwinner system common in Europe and North America in the decades after the Second World War. However, there are questions that tap into similar issues. One is **V45**, which asks respondents whether they agree with the statement 'When jobs are scarce men should have more right to a job than women'.

Click **Show** and you'll see a frequency table of results for each country. Above the table you can choose the option **Show Column % (excluding DK/NA)** to discard missing cases (that

Figure 3.6 The World Values Survey homepage

is respondents who did not have an answer to the question or did not want to give one). In Algeria, India, Malaysia, Pakistan and Egypt there is strong support for the idea, but much less so in China, Hong Kong and Singapore. By clicking on the **Time Series** tab you can compare the results from earlier waves of the WVS, if the country took part and the relevant question was asked. While we saw a clear time trend in the US data, it is not so obvious here. There is some evidence of a shift in attitudes in Egypt, whereas they appear to have shifted in the other direction in India. Compare these results with those for **V53**, 'On the whole men make better business executives than women do'. Do you find similar patterns of attitudes? If you wish to save any of the tables you run, clicking on the Excel ☒ or PDF 🖶 icon to the right of the **Responses** tab will download a copy of any table you have produced. As with GSS, there are many variables you can follow up to examine the contrasting patterns of beliefs and attitudes in different regions of the world. There are some suggestions to get you started in the exercises at the end of this chapter.

3 ● 13 USING NESSTAR TO EXPLORE DATA FROM THE INTERNATIONAL SOCIAL SURVEY PROGRAMME

Nesstar is on online data analysis platform that is used by many data providers, including the UK Data Service, the European Social Survey, European Values Survey and Eurobarometer. It was developed by Norwegian Social Science Data Services (NSD). It allows you to create simple tables and graphs from datasets, and export them in a variety of formats, and to explore the dataset description and its documentation without having to download the data itself. It is thus a convenient way to check out if a dataset contains the information you want and is worth downloading to work on using the more powerful analysis features available in SPSS. Although we'll cover all the basics that you will need to get started here, a complete user guide for Nesstar is available at

🖱 http://www.nesstar.com/help/4.0/webview/index.html

The ZACAT – GESIS portal at the Leibniz Institute for the Social Sciences hosts several collections of European data that can be explored and analysed online. Go to the homepage at

🖱 http://zacat.gesis.org/webview/

You need to register to use the portal, but you are prompted to do this when you start to use the data. All you need do is supply your email contact details, a password is sent to you, and you can then log in. As usual, you must agree to the terms and conditions, which you should read and check that you understand. A question mark icon ❓ at the right of the grey toolbar in the page header offers a help function if you need it.

On the left of the homepage is a pane with the list of the dataset collections in the catalogue. Next to the title of each collection is an icon with a plus sign in it ⊞. Clicking on this icon expands the selection next to it. When you do so the box changes to a minus sign ⊟. Clicking on this collapses the selection back to the original heading. This allows you to navigate among the datasets and their contents in the catalogue. Click on **ISSP**, the first collection in the catalogue. This presents a general description of the International Social Survey Programme in the right-hand pane, which also tells you how to access more detailed information about the ISSP and its component surveys, including the codebooks for the survey and the original questionnaires. The description includes a note about weights that you can safely ignore for just now. We deal with weights later on in Chapter 4.

In the left-hand pane click on **by Module Topic** which takes you to a list of the topics that ISSP has covered in different years. ISSP repeats modules on some topics regularly, making it possible to look at change over time. Click on the topic **Family and Changing Gender Roles** and you'll see that this module has been fielded four times between 1988 and 2012. Click on the title of the 2012 module and two new headings appear, **Metadata** and **Variable Description**. Click on **Metadata** and a brief description of the survey is displayed in the right-hand pane, including the countries in which the survey was fielded, when the fieldwork was carried out, its target population (which in most but not all countries was adults aged 18 or over), links to the questionnaires used in different countries and a brief description of the topics in the module and other variables included in the dataset. We look at using data documentation in more detail in Chapter 5.

Now click on **Variable Description** and a list of groups of different variables within the dataset appears in both panes of the window. Click on **Substantial Variables** to display a list of the main variables recorded in the survey. Clicking on a variable in the list displays some basic information about that variable, including the wording from the questionnaire that produced the variable, the values it takes and labels for those values, and the number of valid and missing cases. You may notice that each variable has two versions. This is because the version of the survey fielded in Spain used a slightly different way of asking some of the questions in the module. For now we can ignore Spain and look at results from other countries. Click on the first version of the variable **Q2b Men's job earn money, women's job look after home**. This will display some details about the variable. It was produced by asking respondents how far they agreed with the statement 'A man's job is to earn money; a woman's job is to look after the home and family'. Let's explore this variable, which is very similar to the **FEFAM** variable we looked at in the US GSS. Click on the **TABULATION** tab in the grey toolbar and the display in the right-hand pane will change to an empty table that you can now populate. Select the variable **Q2b** in the left-hand pane and you'll find that this opens a small dialog box with four options. Click on the second one: **Add to column**. Your window should now look similar to the one shown in Figure 3.7.

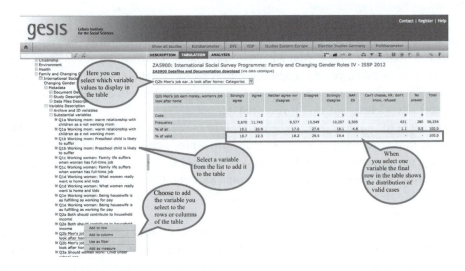

Figure 3.7 The GESIS ISSP page using Nesstar

Since we want to compare different countries we can add the variable for country to the rows of the table. In the left-hand pane click on **Archive and ID variables**, then select the fifth variable in the list, **Country ISO 3166 Code**, and add it to the rows of the table. We now need to edit what is shown in the table. You will see that above the table are three drop-down menus that allow you to do this. The right-hand menu controls what appears in the cells of the table. Since we want to look at the distribution of views about gender roles within each country in order to compare them, select **Row percentage** in this menu. This will produce the crosstab we require. You may find that some or all of the missing values are displayed for one or both variables. If you find this, click the small arrow to the right of the variable name displayed above the table itself, and in the sub-menu that appears, choose **Change selection**. This displays a dialog box that determines which values for the variable are to be displayed. Uncheck any missing values in the value list and then click **OK** at the top of the dialog box. We can now compare how respondents answered in different countries. However, we have dozens of countries in the table, and five possible responses for the gender role variable, so that our table is rather unwieldy and difficult to understand. We can make it easier to understand if we rank the countries by the pattern of the responses to the variable. Click on the heading **Agree** at the top of the table and you'll see that a small pair of arrows appears ⬍ . Click this icon, which allows you to sort the rows of the table by the proportion of responses taking this value for each country. Choose **sort**

descending. This makes it much easier to interpret the table. It becomes clear that while male breadwinner gender roles still command some support in Latin America and developing countries, they have little support in most European countries or North America.

A visual display is often better than a table of numbers for getting a feel for the data. In the grey toolbar above the right-hand pane you'll see an icon for charts ▥. Click the third icon down for **horizontal bar charts** and your table will be converted into a barchart with five colours for the different answer options.

3 ⬤ 14 USING NESSTAR TO RECODE VARIABLES

However, our graphic still isn't as straightforward to interpret as we might like. One problem is that respondents had four options to choose from, since they could 'strongly' agree or disagree. As we did with the GSS, we can put the *strongly agree* and *agree* responses together, and do the same for *strongly disagree* and *disagree*. Another problem is that the proportion of respondents saying *don't know* varies across different countries. We'd be better to treat these responses as *missing* to be able to directly compare views on gender roles. We can do this by recoding the gender role variable using Nesstar, using a similar procedure to that we used on the SDA platform for the US GSS.

Click on the **Compute** icon in the toolbar **Σ** to bring up its dialog box. In the dropdown menu under **Create** select the last option: **Recode**. You will then be asked to choose which variable you wish to recode. Click on the gender roles variable (be sure to choose the first, not second version) and click on the **Recode** tab that appears when you do so. This opens a Recode dialog box which asks you to assign the existing values that the variable takes to new values, along with labels for those values. We want to set the old 1s and 2s (strongly agree and agree) to the same new value, and the old 4s and 5s (strongly disagree and disagree) to another single new value. You can always check on the original variable's values and labels for them in the description of the variable that appears under the Recode dialog box.

Under the heading **Old value** click on **Range: ... through** and insert **1** and **2** in the boxes. Under the heading **New value** insert the value **2** and the label **agree**, then click the **ADD** button immediately beneath. In the **Added** box you'll see the text **1 – 2 → 2 : agree** appears. Repeat this process with the appropriate numbers to recode the values **4** and **5** to **4**, with the label **disagree**. If you do this successfully you should see the text **4 – 5 → 4 : disagree** in the **Added** box. Finally, in the **All other values** box click the option **Recode to *Sysmis***, enter a name for the new variable you have created in the box headed **Label** in the **New Variable** box at the bottom. The Recode dialog box should look like the one shown in Figure 3.8.

When you click on **OK** you should get a message telling you that the new variable has been added to the browse list in the left pane of the window; it will appear at the end of the list of variables for the dataset. We can now go back to our table (do so by clicking on the table icon **▦** in the toolbar). In the centre drop-down menu choose **Remove from table** to take our original gender role variable out, then choose the new variable you have created from the browse list of variables and click **Add to column**. Sort on one of the values of the variable to produce a list of countries ranked by the popularity of 'male breadwinner' gender role attitudes. Traditional gender role attitudes are common both in developing countries, and in Russia and eastern Europe (despite a half century of 'state socialism'). Austria is the

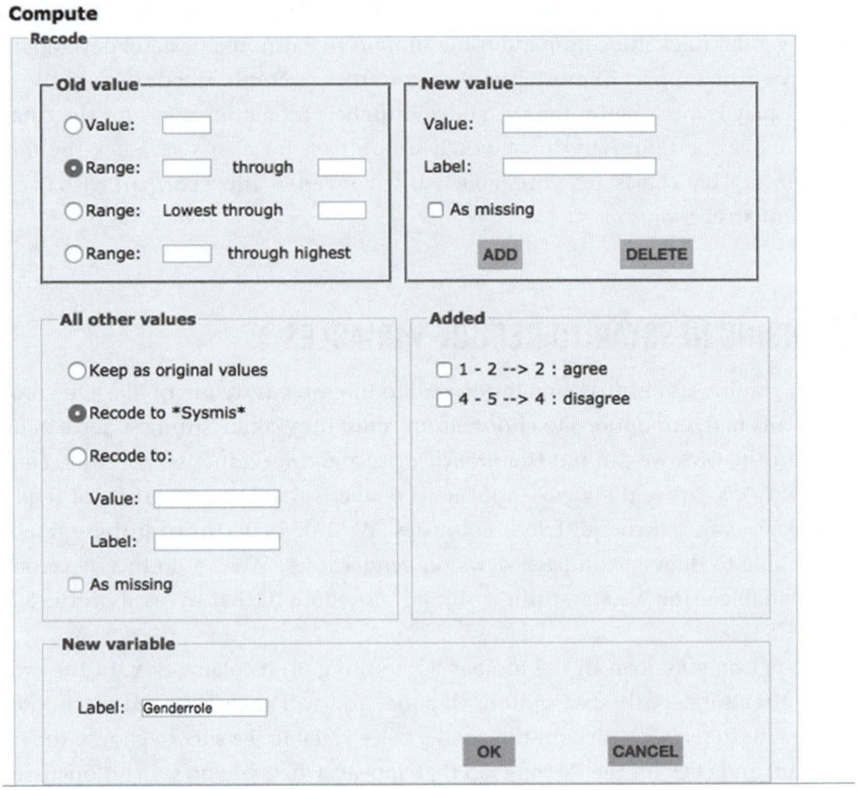

Compute

Recode

Figure 3.8 The Nesstar **Recode** dialog box

only country in western Europe where such views still have substantial support, while in Scandinavia only tiny proportions subscribe to them.

3 ⬤15 COMPARING DATA FROM 1988 AND 2012

Now you can produce a similar table for the survey fielded in 1988. That survey was fielded in a much smaller number of countries, but five took part in both the 1988 and 2012 rounds: Germany (in 1988 only what was then West Germany), Great Britain, USA, Austria and Ireland. You'll find that the corresponding variable in the 1988 survey was called **HOUSEHOLD IS WIFE'S JOB**, but the question used to produce it was similar to that used in 2012, except that instead of using the terms 'man' and 'woman' it used the terms 'husband' and 'wife'. We can see how much attitudes have changed over the last quarter century in these countries. Follow the same procedure as with the 2012 survey to produce results for 1988. Finally, compare the percentage agreeing with male breadwinner gender roles for each country in the two years. Your results should look like those shown in Table 3.3.

They certainly seem to suggest a substantial change in attitudes, especially in Europe. However, there are two qualifications we need to keep in mind. First, we have been working with unweighted data, and weighted data would have given us a more accurate picture. However, weighting the

Table 3.3 Adults' response to the statement 'A man's job is to earn money; a woman's job is to look after the home and family' in five countries, 1988 and 2012

	2012 % agree†	1988 % agree†	N 2012	N, 1988
Germany*	19	55	1,535	2,297
Great Britain	19	35	723	1,048
USA	27	35	1,054	1,091
Austria	44	68	881	773
Ireland	15	48	1,019	870

Source: ISSP Family and Gender Roles I and IV.

*Germany in 1988 refers to West Germany only.

†Responses 'don't know', 'can't choose' and 'neither agree nor disagree' were excluded from the totals. The percentage disagreeing is not shown but is obtained by subtracting the figures in the table from 100. The survey is a repeated cross-sectional design.

Source: ISSP Research Group (2014): International Social Survey Programme: Family and Changing Gender Roles IV – ISSP 2012. ZA5900 Data file Version 2.0.0, doi:10.4232/1.12022; Family and Changing Gender Roles I – ISSP 1988. ZA1700. GESIS Data Archive, Cologne.

data would be unlikely to shift the percentages by more than a point or two. Second, we have been working with sample data. There will be a margin of error in our estimates determined by the size and nature of the sample. For the figures here such error might be as much as 2–4%. This means that we can be confident that there has been substantial change in all these countries with the possible exception of the USA, where it is possible (although highly unlikely) that change was weaker and the apparent change is due to sampling fluctuation.

3 ● 16 GOOD TABLE MANNERS

As you explore data you'll find yourself producing many tables like the one above. If you want to make them available to others or put them in essays, reports or articles (rather than just keep them for your own analysis) then you should follow what Catherine Marsh (1988) called 'good table manners'. There are four key rules to follow.

A clear title

The title of a table should be as brief as possible, consistent with accurately describing the table contents. Table 3.3 could have been given an even shorter title, such as 'Gender role attitudes', but then the origin of the data for the table would have to be explained somewhere. Always number tables if there is more than one in any article, paper or report that you produce.

Less is more

When you've toiled for some hours to analyse your data and produce the results the natural temptation is to present them all. This is a temptation to be resisted at all costs. Nothing is more difficult to read than a table or graph that is packed with numbers. Rather your aim should be to tell a clear story in as few numbers as possible, so that readers can see the clear message.

Avoid spurious accuracy

Although we had results to one decimal place, in Table 3.3 these have been rounded to whole numbers. Including the decimal would have given a spurious impression of accuracy, since the margin of error for the numbers here is greater than a whole percentage point. We want to make a statement about the population, not our sample. Avoiding spurious accuracy also makes the table easier to read. There are few situations where you need more than three digits to convey the magnitude of any measurement.

Critical appraisal

The table should contain enough information about the origin of the data to allow a critical reader to verify it. This means *always* including the sample size (*N*) on which the data rests, the survey it comes from and where it can be accessed (using the citation format recommended by the survey originators) and definitions for all the components of the table. When presenting time series data you should report whether it comes from longitudinal or cross-sectional data.

3 ◖17 SUBSETTING IN NESSTAR

You can now try using Nesstar to explore how these gender role attitudes vary by such factors as age, gender or religion as we did for the USA. However, to do so you will find it useful to select particular countries or groups of countries to analyse. We wouldn't expect the patterns of views to be similar in, say, India and Brazil. To do this we can *subset* the data. Often when exploring or analysing data you want to look at a subset of the entire data: to select a group of cases defined by a common characteristic or group of characteristics. For example, you might want to look only at female respondents, or those from a particular area or of a certain age. This is called 'subsetting'. You define the subset you want to work with by the value or value range it takes on a variable or set of variables.

Click the subset icon on the **Nesstar** toolbar ▼ and when you then click on any variable on the variable list on the left of the window you will be given the option to **Add to subset**. Choose the country variable and click this option and you'll see a dialog box to the right like the one in Figure 3.9.

Let's select each of the countries in Latin America in the list for analysis. Click on 32 AR-Argentina and then click the **ADD** button. Then click **MORE**. Click on 152 CL-Chile, click **ADD** and click **MORE**. Repeat for 484 MX-Mexico and, finally, 862 VE-Venezuela; then click **OK**. Nesstar will now produce analyses for these four countries only. You can explore the impact of gender, age and religion in the same way as you did for the GSS. By clicking on the charts icon ▥ you can turn any table into a bar chart. Using the icons on the toolbar you can

Variable	Value	Categories	
Country/ Sample IS = ▲▼	ADD	32	AR-Argentina
		36	AU-Australia
		40	AT-Austria
		100	BG-Bulgaria
		124	CA-Canada
		152	CL-Chile
		156	CN-China
		158	TW-Taiwan
		191	HR-Croatia
MORE LESS CLEAR			OK

Figure 3.9   Subsetting in Nesstar

print ▤ the table or chart, **export** ☒ it as a PDF file or **link/embed** ⌖ it in a webpage. You can also export tables as Excel files ▤ for later reference.

what you have learned

Without leaving your web browser, in this chapter you've started using and developing some of the key skills you need in secondary data analysis. You've had practice in thinking in terms of variables, values and cases. You've learned to identify and manage data from four different datasets, one of them using aggregate data and three using microdata, and to use some of the metadata available online to guide your analysis. You've produced frequency tables, contingency tables, a three-way contingency table, summary statistics and charts from the data to explore it. You've manipulated data for further analysis by recoding variables and creating new ones, or subsetting the data in various ways to select specific groups of cases for analysis. You've downloaded the results of your work, and learned some rules for presentation of data.

Just as important are some of the 'softer' skills you will have started to use in following the examples in this chapter. The most important is to start to think always about the limitations of any data you work with: how valid is the survey question for the purposes of the analysis you are making? Also useful is to get into the habit of thinking about the difference between exploring data, informed by a (perhaps rather general or imprecise) set of questions and 'data dredging': wandering rather haphazardly through the data to see if anything turns up. In the course of the chapter you should have picked up some of the following skills:

- How to access summary statistics from sites such as Gapminder, the US General Social Survey, GSS Data Explorer, the World Values Survey, and the International Social Survey Programme
- How to interpret graphics plotted on a logarithmic scale
- *The Joy of Stats* is an excellent video introduction to statistics
- How to distinguish data exploration from theory testing
- How to use Nesstar and other online analysis applications to produce, edit and interpret frequency and contingency tables, including recoding variables and subsetting data
- How to produce and interpret a three-way contingency table
- How to use dialog boxes
- How to handle missing values
- Good table manners

━━━━━━━━━━━━━━ **exercises** ━━━━━━━━━━━━━━

If you've read and understood this chapter, and carried out the activities in it, try the following exercises to consolidate your skills. ♣ Answers are on the companion website.

Gapminder

Use the Gapminder site to answer the following questions:

1 Which country had the lowest rate of *child mortality* in 1900?
2 How much lower was it than that for India in the same year?
3 How did rates of child mortality for these two countries differ in the year 2000?
4 Which country had the lowest rate in 2000? and in 2015?
5 What was the range of life expectancy for women in 1965 across countries?
6 What was the range of life expectancy for women in 2015 across countries?
7 Which country in 2015 had with lowest female life expectancy outside sub-Saharan Africa?
8 Which countries had the highest and lowest fertility rates in 2015?
9 Compare the evolution of the fertility rate in Japan and France over the last 100 years. What are some of the similarities and differences?

The US General Social Survey

1 Do other gender role attitudes become more liberal over time?
2 Are non-whites more conservative or liberal in their gender role attitudes than whites?
3 Do people from the Southern states have more conservative gender role attitudes?
4 Does age or gender have more impact on gender role attitudes? Has this always been true in the period covered by the survey?

The World Values Survey

1 Do more adults in the United States or Russia think politics is important in their lives?
2 People are asked about the qualities it is important to encourage in children. In which country are people least likely to mention tolerance and respect, and in which country are they most likely to do so?
3 In which countries are people most likely to strongly disagree with the idea that men make better political leaders than women?
4 In which countries do more people say they trust people of other religions rather than not trust them?
5 In which countries do fewer people say they believe in God than say they do not believe?
6 Do proportionately more people in the USA, Japan or Iraq worry about terrorist attacks?

GETTING STARTED WITH SPSS

---
introduction

In this chapter we start working with IBM SPSS Statistics software using a simplified 'practice' dataset that you can download from the companion website. This introduction assumes no prior knowledge of SPSS, and only a basic knowledge of descriptive and inferential statistics. The focus of this chapter is on SPSS for secondary data analysis, rather than a comprehensive guide to all the features of SPSS. We'll see how to use SPPS analysis of microdata to generate the kind of tables that we produced using Nesstar, SDA or GSS Data Explorer in the previous chapter. You'll discover that SPSS gives you much more flexibility in how you organise, analyse and present your data. You will:

- Understand how the three main SPSS windows operate and what they represent
- Understand how microdata is organised and accessed
- Understand how weights are produced and used to keep data drawn from a sample representative of the population from which it has been drawn
- Use SPSS to produce frequency and contingency tables, descriptive statistics and charts from a dataset
- Use syntax as well as the GUI to issue commands and keep a record of your work
- Deal with missing values for variables
- Use SPSS to calculate and use confidence intervals and p-values
- Use SPSS to calculate measures of association
- Produce new variables using the **recode** procedure
- Use **Automatic Recode** to convert string to numeric variables
- Analyse subsets of cases
- Export output to other applications

---

4 ● 1 BEFORE YOU START

This chapter assumes that you know what variables, values and cases are, and can distinguish levels of measurement, know what a dataset comprises, and have some idea of what frequency distributions and contingency tables are. If you are unsure about any of these ideas, you'll find it useful to read Chapter 2 *before* reading this one. Conversely, if you already have some experience of SPSS you may skip this chapter and go straight to Chapter 5. There are many guides to SPSS online, and the book website has links to some of the better ones. You may find it helps to look at one or more of these as well as this chapter. SPSS also comes with a comprehensive tutorial, which you can access under the **Help** menu in the application itself.

4 ● 2 SPSS VERSIONS AND PLATFORMS

Like most software, SPSS is updated regularly, comes in versions for different computer operating systems such as PC and Mac and allows you to customise its appearance and procedures to suit your preferred way of working. This means that what you see on your computer screen may not be exactly the same as in the screenshots in this book or the animations on the book's website. However, changes across versions are fairly gradual so that what you see on your computer should not diverge too much from what you see here. In addition, whatever version or platform you are using, you can set the preferences to resemble those used here, so that what you see corresponds closely to the screenshots. However, there is no need to do so if you feel more comfortable with other settings you have chosen.

The system of menus and icons that you use in any computer application is known as a *graphical user interface* (GUI). To describe how to operate the GUI in the rest of this book I use the following rules to avoid lengthy descriptions. The phrase 'go to' means click on the relevant menu. An arrow → means go to the relevant sub-menu or click on the relevant final option within a hierarchy of menus. Thus 'go to **File**→**Open**→**Data**' means click on the **File** menu at the top of the window, select the option **Open** from that menu and then the option **Data** from the sub-menu that was displayed when you selected **Open**. Most SPSS menu commands open dialog boxes in which you either choose various options or enter information. Once you've entered the relevant information or chosen from the options offered, you issue the final command to SPSS by clicking on the **OK** button which is always situated to the bottom right of the dialog box. You'll notice that this button remains dimmed and will not operate until you've entered the information or choices needed to formulate the command.

4 ● 3 OPENING THE ESS6_PRACTICE.SAV DATASET

It is easier to get to grips with the basics of SPSS using a simple dataset, so that complexities in the data don't get in the way of understanding what the software does. ✎ A suitable practice dataset file, **ESS6_Practice.sav**, is on the book's website. Download the file (you may have to 'unzip' it, or your computer may do this automatically) and store it in a new folder with an appropriate name. Make a copy of the file within the folder, and open the original file. You now have a back-up copy of the original file should anything go wrong with the copy

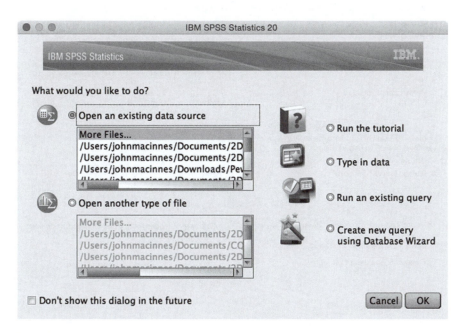

Figure 4.1 SPSS opening dialog box

you'll be working with. Your computer should select SPSS as the application to open it with automatically, or allow you to select SPSS as the application to open the file with. If you prefer you can open SPSS first, and then open the file from within SPSS. If you do the latter, SPSS first responds with a dialog box asking what you want to do (shown in Figure 4.1). This is not a feature of SPSS that you'll ever need to use, so check the box next to **Don't show this dialog in future** and click **OK**.

If you have started SPSS without opening the **ESS6_Practice.sav** file, SPSS presents you with an empty **Data Editor** window. To open the file go to **File→Open→Data** and in the dialog box that appears you can browse through the hierarchy of folders on your computer to locate **ESS6_Practice.sav**, or if you know the file path you can type that directly into the dialog box, and then click **OK**. SPSS then populates the **Data Editor** window with the file, and also posts a record of the commands you just issued using the GUI to the **Viewer**. (We'll review these windows in a moment.)

If you want the appearance of SPSS on your machine to resemble the screenshots here go to **Edit→Options** and select the **General** tab in the dialog box which will produce a window similar to that in Figure 4.2. Then choose the same options as shown.

As you can tell from this dialog box, there are many ways you can customise the performance of SPSS, but until you've had some experience of using it, it is best to leave most of the default settings as they are.

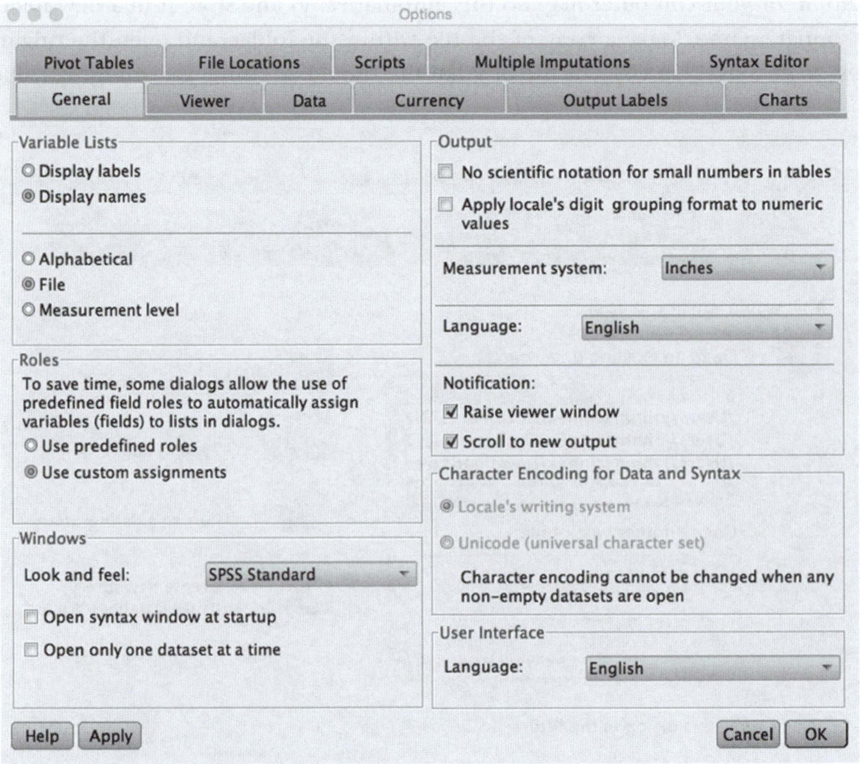

Figure 4.2 The SPSS **Options** dialog **box**

4 ● 4 SPSS: THE THREE MAIN WINDOWS

In most computer applications, such as word-processing packages, you work with only one window open at a time, although sometimes the package or your operating system might prompt you with a *dialog box*: a smaller window that displays options you choose from to complete some operation. For example, when you print a document it may ask you to confirm the page size, or ask if you want to print double-sided and so on. SPSS makes extensive use of such dialog boxes, and sometimes hierarchies of them (so that one box takes you to another). SPSS also has at least two, and sometimes more, main windows open and you must switch between them to do different tasks. Only one of the windows is active and ready to receive commands at any one time. This makes it convenient to use a machine with a large screen, or connect an external screen to it. However, as long as you manage your windows carefully, you can run SPSS perfectly well on a laptop.

The two main windows in SPSS are the **Data Editor** and output **Viewer** windows. The **Data Editor** window displays the dataset itself, in two different ways. In **Variable View** mode it lists all of the variables in the dataset, along with some information about them, such as the variable label (a brief description of the variable) and labels for the values the variable takes if it is nominal or ordinal. In **Data View** mode it displays the data matrix itself, with each record or case in the dataset displayed along a row and each variable displayed down a column. In each cell of the data matrix lies the value for the corresponding variable in that column and the case in that row, as shown in Figure 4.3.

At the top of the **Data Editor** window are *menus* and a *toolbar* of icons for issuing commands (just as in any other computer application). When working with SPSS you are always working with a dataset. However, unlike a word-processing package or a spreadsheet, the main output from your work rarely takes the form of changing that data itself, but rather of doing analyses that use it. Thus when you use SPSS you normally issue commands that tell SPSS to analyse or summarise your data in some way. For example, you might be working with census data and

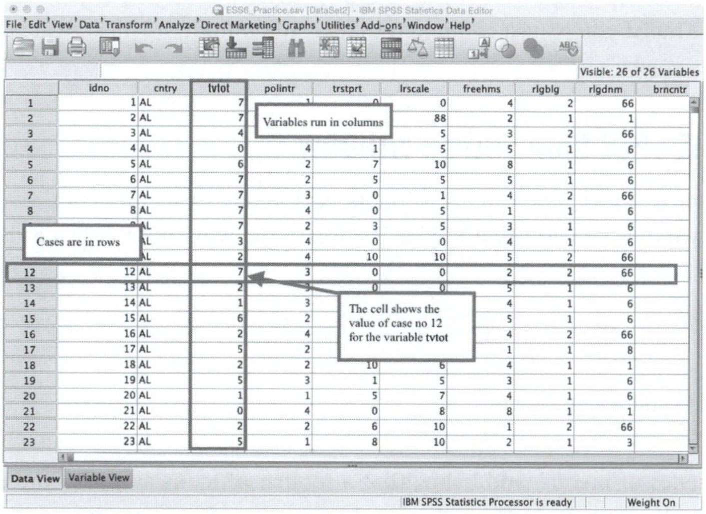

Figure 4.3 The SPSS **Data Editor** window, **Data View** mode

producing population totals for regions of a country. SPSS then posts the results of these analyses to a second window: the **Viewer**. Since the output from SPSS can sometimes be voluminous the **Viewer** has powerful search and editing functions allowing you to inspect output, file it away for later use, format it for printing or export it to another package or to the web. Using SPSS always involves these two windows, and each is generated by its corresponding file. Data files generating the **Data Editor** window have the suffix **.sav**. Output files generating the **Viewer** window have the suffix **.spo**. However, there is a third type of window that you will use: the **Syntax Editor**. Syntax files have the suffix **.sps** and are used to issue commands to SPSS.

4 5 USING SYNTAX TO RUN SPSS

GUIs are fine for situations where you need to issue simple, common commands (like using a word-processing package to change part of a text to italics or alter its font size) and do so irregularly because you're working with ever changing material. However, when you are working with data, this situation is reversed. You are often working with the same or similar data for substantial periods. And the commands you need to issue to work with that data are both heterogeneous (there are a lot of different things you can do) and complex (you must often specify precisely how you want to do it). Moreover, you may find yourself issuing very similar but complex commands many times. The upshot of all this is that using code to issue commands not only is quicker and easier than using the GUI, but also automatically creates a record of your work. It is the **Syntax Editor** window that you use to do this. This is not only vital for future reference, but also allows you, should you lose or damage a file, to recreate it quickly and easily. The downside, of course, is that you have to learn the syntax code, but as we shall see, you can quickly learn this by creating commands in the GUI, which SPSS itself then translates into syntax when you paste it to your **Syntax Editor** window.

There are many ways you can switch between windows in SPSS. Clicking on a window activates it. You can go to **Window** and select the window you want or click on the data icon in the toolbar to go to the **Data Editor** window. SPSS generally takes you to the window you need automatically. Thus if you issue a command that creates output, it will activate the **Viewer**.

4 6 THE SPSS DATA EDITOR WINDOW

Your **Data Editor** window should be in **Variable View** mode. If it isn't, click on the tab at the bottom of the window to select that mode. The top of the window is shown in Figure 4.4.

Figure 4.4   The **Data Editor** window toolbar

There is a series of menus, and below that a toolbar of icons as you'd find in almost any application, and then in the body of the window a series of columns beginning **Name**, **Type**, **Width**. In the rows of the body of the window are descriptions of each variable in the dataset, beginning with the variable **idno** and ending with **pweight**. You can customise this window to set which columns are displayed and the order they are presented in. It is worthwhile doing this as it helps to keep the appearance of the window tidy and avoid clutter by getting rid of information that you will not need to use. Go to **Edit→Options** and select the **Data** tab, then click on **Customize Variable View**. You'll see the window in Figure 4.5 which allows you to select which columns are displayed in the **Data Editor** window and the order in which they are displayed.

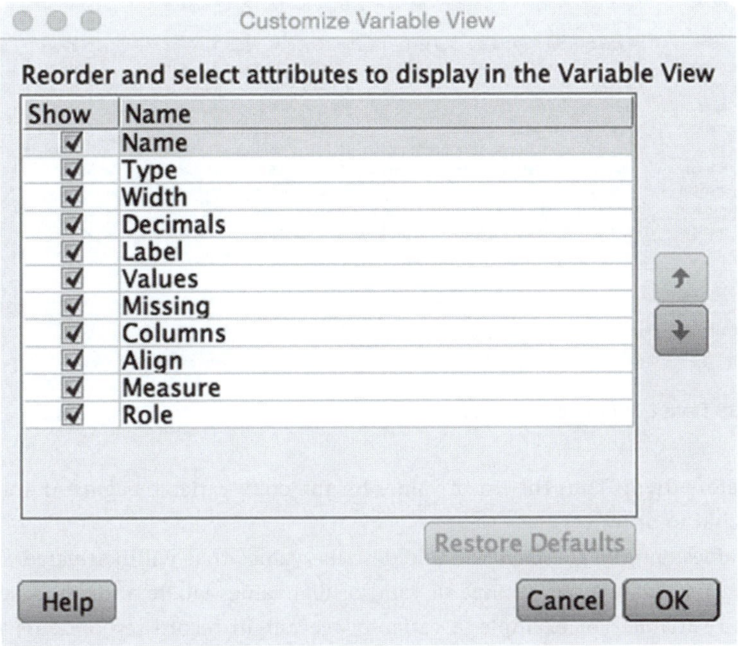

Figure 4.5 The **Customize Variable View** dialog box

Uncheck the columns **Role**, **Align**, **Columns**, **Decimals** and **Width** by clicking on the check boxes and reorder the remaining columns using the small arrows to the right of the list, so that you have them in the order **Name**, **Label**, **Values**, **Missing**, **Type**, **Measure**. Then click on **OK** which will return you to the original dialog box, where you click on **Apply** (at bottom left) and **OK** (at bottom right). Your **Data Editor** window will now look like the one in Figure 4.6.

Note that you can change the width of columns by dragging on the column dividers at the top of each column. It's usually convenient to make the variable **Label** column wider as variable labels are often quite long. We now have a window that lists the name of each variable stored in the dataset, the label for that variable (which gives a short description of the variable), the values that the variable takes, any labels for them, missing values defined for that variable, the type of variable and its level of measurement. SPSS can store several different types of variable, but the most common are **Numeric**, comprising only numbers, and **String**, storing text. You'll see that the variable **cntry** is a **String** variable, since it comprises two-letter codes for each country in the survey. Clicking in the **Values** column (where you will see a box with three small dots appear) for a variable tells us which values the variable can take, and the numerical codes

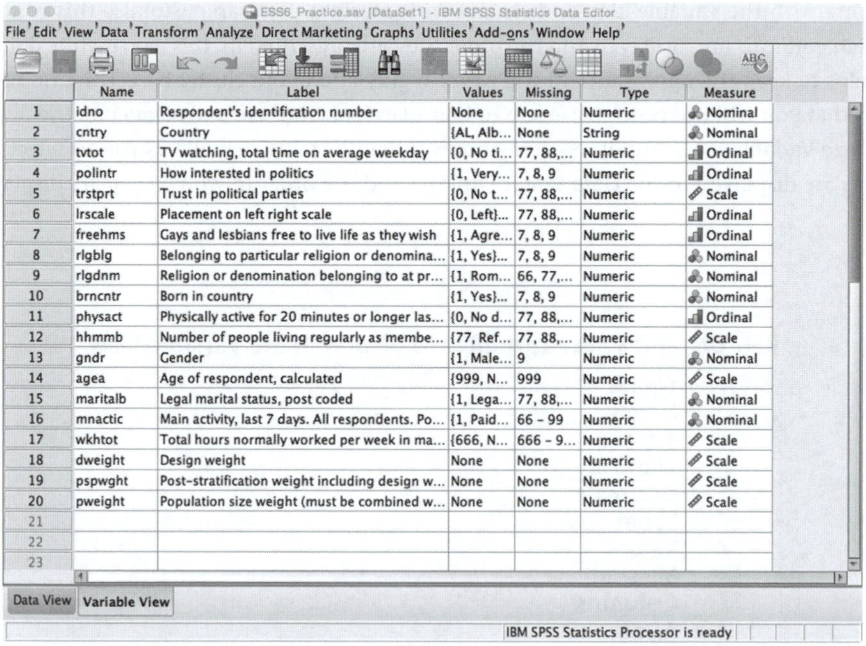

ESS6_Practice.sav [DataSet1] - IBM SPSS Statistics Data Editor

File Edit View Data Transform Analyze Direct Marketing Graphs Utilities Add-ons Window Help

	Name	Label	Values	Missing	Type	Measure
1	idno	Respondent's identification number	None	None	Numeric	Nominal
2	cntry	Country	{AL, Alb...	None	String	Nominal
3	tvtot	TV watching, total time on average weekday	{0, No ti...	77, 88,...	Numeric	Ordinal
4	polintr	How interested in politics	{1, Very...	7, 8, 9	Numeric	Ordinal
5	trstprt	Trust in political parties	{0, No t...	77, 88,...	Numeric	Scale
6	lrscale	Placement on left right scale	{0, Left}...	77, 88,...	Numeric	Ordinal
7	freehms	Gays and lesbians free to live life as they wish	{1, Agre...	7, 8, 9	Numeric	Ordinal
8	rlgblg	Belonging to particular religion or denomina...	{1, Yes}...	7, 8, 9	Numeric	Nominal
9	rlgdnm	Religion or denomination belonging to at pr...	{1, Rom...	66, 77,...	Numeric	Nominal
10	brncntr	Born in country	{1, Yes}...	7, 8, 9	Numeric	Nominal
11	physact	Physically active for 20 minutes or longer las...	{0, No d...	77, 88,...	Numeric	Ordinal
12	hhmmb	Number of people living regularly as membe...	{77, Ref...	77, 88,...	Numeric	Scale
13	gndr	Gender	{1, Male...	9	Numeric	Nominal
14	agea	Age of respondent, calculated	{999, N...	999	Numeric	Scale
15	maritalb	Legal marital status, post coded	{1, Lega...	77, 88,...	Numeric	Nominal
16	mnactic	Main activity, last 7 days. All respondents. Po...	{1, Paid...	66 – 99	Numeric	Nominal
17	wkhtot	Total hours normally worked per week in ma...	{666, N...	666 – 9...	Numeric	Scale
18	dweight	Design weight	None	None	Numeric	Scale
19	pspwght	Post-stratification weight including design w...	None	None	Numeric	Scale
20	pweight	Population size weight (must be combined w...	None	None	Numeric	Scale
21						
22						
23						

Data View Variable View

IBM SPSS Statistics Processor is ready

Figure 4.6 SPSS Data Editor window, customised

SPSS uses to store them. Thus the list of values for the **cntry** variable begins AL for Albania, BE for Belgium, and so on.

Missing values defined for each variable describe values that will be treated as missing in any analysis. Any variable has a range of valid or real values where a measurement has been recorded for a variable. For example, a variable 'age' might record respondents age in years. However, there may be some cases where a measurement was not made: perhaps the interviewer didn't record it, or the respondent couldn't remember or wasn't sure of their age. In such circumstances a missing value is assigned to the case. Such missing values usually also record why a valid value is missing for a case. Thus in the variable **freehms** in our dataset, values 7, 8 and 9 are defined as missing. Clicking on the **labels** box for the variable reveals that these correspond to the respondent refusing to answer the question (7), not knowing their answer to the question (8) or no answer being recorded (9).

The column **Measure** records the level of measurement of the variable (it uses the term *scale* for both interval and ratio variables), but you'll often encounter datasets where the data authors have not described this feature of the data so that what appears in this column is not always correct. In any case it is better to use your own judgement, if necessary, to decide on what level of measurement you have for any variable.

Clicking on the **Data View** Data View tab at the bottom of the **Data Editor** window takes you to the data matrix of the dataset itself with its cases along the rows and variables in columns, and the value recorded for each case for each variable in the cells. In the toolbar is a **Value Labels** icon that allows you to toggle between displaying the numerical value codes stored in the dataset and the value labels for these codes. You can use the sliders at the side and bottom of the window to scroll down through the cases or along the list of variables. In practice you will find that you rarely, if ever, have to use the **Data View** mode of the **Data Editor** window. It's reassuring to be able to 'see' all your data, but we need SPSS to organise and analyse it, since we can do little with it in its raw form. If you scroll down you'll see that we have 54,673 cases in the dataset (corresponding to each individual interviewed for the survey), each with 20 variables, so that we have just over 1 million pieces of data. To make any sense of it we need to summarise and analyse.

4 7 PRODUCING TABLES AND SUMMARY STATISTICS

Go to **Analyze→Descriptive statistics→Frequencies**. This produces the **Frequencies** dialog box in Figure 4.7.

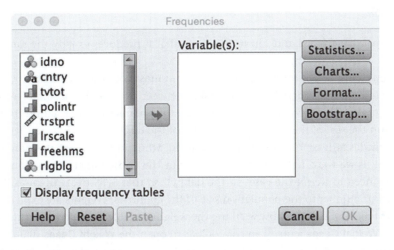

Figure 4.7 The **Frequencies** dialog box

On the left of the dialog box is a variable list. You can select variables from this list by dragging them across to the **Variable(s):** box on the right, or you can select them and then click on the small blue arrow, or just double-click on them. Any of these actions transfers one or more variables across to the box on the right. On the right-hand side of the window there are four buttons. These take you to further dialog boxes that enable you to produce summary statistics or charts for the variables you select. Select the variable **cntry** and put it in the **Variable(s):** box, then click on **OK** to run the command from the GUI, or better, choose **Paste** to open a syntax file and paste the command syntax into it. You'll see the following appear in the **Syntax Editor** window.

```
FREQUENCIES VARIABLES=cntry
  /ORDER=ANALYSIS.
```

Note that although SPSS uses a mixture of upper and lower case text for syntax, this is only to make it clearer to read: when writing your own syntax you can mix upper and lower case letters as you like. The main **FREQUENCIES** command tells SPSS to produce a table for the variable **cntry**, the **/ORDER** sub-command tells it to present the values for it in the order stored in the dataset. Finally the most important item in the syntax is the full stop after **ANALYSIS**, which signals the end of the command.

To run the syntax select it and click the run icon ▶, or from the keyboard hit **cmnd-R** if you are using a Macintosh, or **Ctrl-R** if you are using a PC. SPSS will then create a frequency table for this variable, post it to the **Statistics Viewer** and make this the active window. The frequency table shows the frequency with which all the cases in the dataset take each of the values for the variable **cntry**, that is, it shows the number of respondents to the survey in each country where Round 6 of the European Social Survey was fielded.

Don't be too intimidated by the syntax language. You'll quickly discover shortcuts and simpler ways of writing it. Go back to the Syntax Editor window and type

FREQ cntry.

Select what you have typed and run it. You'll see that it produces exactly the same output as before.

When you examine this output, you'll see that in most countries between 1,000 and 3,000 people were interviewed. There is no relationship between the population size of a country and the number of people interviewed. This is because the accuracy of information from a sample depends upon the size of the sample, not the size of the target population, so that even in the smallest countries at least 700 people were sampled, while in the largest no more than 3,000 were selected. If we want to make statements about the entire target population in these 29 countries we need to *weight* the cases in the dataset, so that SPSS treats them as if they were proportional in number to the population size of the countries. Weights are explained in more detail in the box opposite. For now we'll use the weight variable **pweight** to do this. To apply it click on the **Weight Cases** icon ▲ in the toolbar to open the **Weight Cases** dialog box. Select **Weight cases by** and then put the variable **pweight** into the box under **Frequency Variable:**, as shown in Figure 4.8, then click **OK** or **Paste**. You'll see that an alert appears at the bottom right of your **Data Editor** window stating **Weight On**.

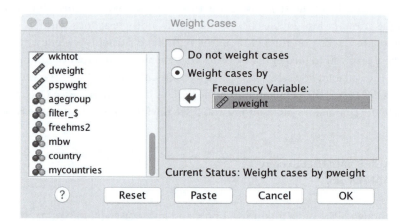

Figure 4.8   The **Weight Cases** dialog

━━━━━━━━━━ **weights** ━━━━━━━━━━

A simple random sample assumes that every member of the target population to be sampled has an equal probability of selection into the sample. This requires a list identifying all the population members from which such selection can take place, and the practical ability to contact and interview those selected. In the days when almost every household had a landline telephone a rough approximation to such a sample (at least of telephone subscribers) could be obtained by random digit dialling. However, unless a country maintains up-to-date population registers with names and addresses (people often move their address), such population sampling is difficult. Even if it could be achieved it would be prohibitively expensive if face-to-face interviewing were involved, as interviews would be randomly spaced out over the entire country. It makes more sense to cluster interviews geographically in some way (to reduce the costs of fieldwork) and use the resource to increase the size of the sample. For these and other reasons sampling usually means that different types of respondent have different probabilities of selection into the sample. As long as these probabilities can be accurately estimated this is just as good as a simple random sample. In addition, some characteristics of the target population may be available from a recent census. In such a situation weights can take account of this information so that the sample more closely resembles the target population from which it has been drawn. Weights are equal to the inverse of the probability of selection of the respondent into the sample, divided by the sample size. In a multinational survey such as the European Social Survey (ESS), the different country population sizes mean that the probabilities of selection vary widely: **pweight** takes account of this. *Within* each country **dweight** adjusts for different probabilities of selection of different kind of respondent. Finally **pspweight** uses census or other information to match the achieved sample to known information about the target population.

Now run the frequency table for **cntry** again. You can take a shortcut to go back to the **Frequencies** dialog box by using the **recall dialog** icon 🔳 which brings up a list of recently used dialog boxes to return to. Alternatively, just follow the procedure you used before, or run your syntax for frequencies again. When you produce the table this time you'll see that the number of cases in each country is now proportional to the population size of the country. SPSS still includes all the original cases in its calculations but assigns them a weight so that cases in more populous countries count for more in the calculations.

4 ⬤ 8 THE SPSS VIEWER WINDOW

Take a minute or two to explore the **Viewer**, which pretty much does what it says on the tin: it enables you to view, edit, store and export output from SPSS in a variety of formats. The **Viewer** window has two panes. In the left-hand pane are a series of nested icons that index all your output as you produce it. Clicking on an icon selects all the output associated with it. The right-hand pane displays the output itself. If you select any of this output in the right-hand pane, a small red arrow indicates its position in the index in the left-hand pane. Clicking on the small blue boxes 🔳 in the index pane collapses and displays the index items associated with it. Double-clicking on any output allows you to edit it, for example to give a table a title. There are further formatting options available under the relevant tabs in the **Edit→Options** dialog box. There is a wide range of formatting and editing options available for output in SPSS, but you may find that it is often more convenient to export the raw output as produced by SPSS into a word-processing, spreadsheet or web-authoring package to take advantage of the formatting facilities that they provide. The icons on the **Viewer** toolbar that you'll find most useful are those for returning to the **Data Editor** 🖳, for **recalling** recently used dialog boxes 🖳 and for exporting output 📄. Like any document or file you create, the **Viewer** needs to be saved regularly. The first time you save it, give it a name that associates it with the dataset you are using, and put it in the same folder.

Because you are working directly with microdata in SPSS, you can organise and analyse it much more easily than with Nesstar or the other online resources we examined in Chapter 3. First we'll produce some quick tables and statistics to get an idea of what can be done. Then we'll look in more detail at some of the issues that you need to keep in mind when working with data from samples in order to draw conclusions about the populations from which the sample has been drawn.

Debate on immigration has been a feature of European politics in recent years. But what proportion of people are immigrants? ESS asks respondents whether they were born in the country in which they live, recorded by the variable **brncntr**. Before looking at the data make your own guess of what the results might be. Approximately what proportion of the European population are migrants? Which countries do you think have the highest immigration? Now let's produce some evidence. Go to **Analyze→Descriptive statistics→Crosstabs** to call up the **Crosstabs** dialog box. We'll look at this dialog box in more detail later on. For the moment drag the variable **brncntr** from the variable list on the left to the **column(s)** box in the centre of the dialog box. Then drag the variable **cntry** to the **row(s)** box above. Click on the **cells** button to the right of the dialog box, and in the new **Cell Display** dialog which appears check **Row** under **Percentages** and click **Continue** at the bottom right. When back in the main dialog either choose **OK** or **Paste** as before, and if you have chosen to **Paste** the syntax, run the new syntax pasted in your syntax file window. You'll produce a table in your **Viewer** window listing the percentage of people in each country who are born there. You can make this table easier to read by sorting the rows in the table. Double click (Mac) or Right-click (PC) to activate it, and drag down the cells in the 'Yes' column in the body of the table, so that the numbers now appear highlighted as white against a black background. The go to **Edit→Sort Rows→Descending** and SPSS will sort the countries in order of their levels of immigration. What do you find?

Now consider how long it would have taken you to assemble this information from published sources. Although you might be lucky and find a ready-made table with exactly the data you wanted this is very unlikely. Moreover with microdata and the power of SPSS, you could go on to explore this question in greater detail, for example looking at the age, gender or ethnicity of migrants, where they are from, whether they are working or ways in which they resemble or differ from non-migrants.

4.9 PRODUCING GRAPHICS IN SPSS

Using the same procedure as you used for the variable **cntry**, run a frequency table for the variable **agea**, which describes respondents' age in years. However, before you click on **OK** in the dialog box, click on the **Charts** button on the right-hand side, choose **Histogram**, and click on

Continue. SPSS will now produce a histogram of this variable after the usual frequency table. The syntax for this is:

```
FREQ agea
/histogram.
```

Because it has so many values, being an interval-level variable, the frequency table for **agea** is not very useful, but note one feature. SPSS first lists the valid values for the variable, that is, the cases for which valid measurement were obtained, and then after this lists the missing values. You can see that there were 124 respondents for whom an age was not recorded, and who thus have a missing value for **agea**. Examining the histogram shows the kind of distribution of ages we might expect for a survey of this type: broadly similar proportions of respondents are aged up to around 70, after which the proportion declines as fewer people survive to older ages, or are more likely to be living in collective institutions such as care homes. The ESS surveys only adults living in private households so that the latter are excluded. As we'll see later on, you can edit graphics produced in the SPSS in many ways. If you like, you can explore this by clicking on your histogram, which will open it in a new **Chart Editor** window with a variety of editing options.

4 ● 10 USING SAMPLE DATA FOR POPULATION ESTIMATES: CONFIDENCE INTERVALS

The variable **freehms** describes respondents' attitudes towards homosexuality by asking how far they (dis)agree with the statement 'Gays and lesbians should be free to live life as they wish'. Run a frequency table for this variable to look at its distribution (Figure 4.9).

freehms Gays and lesbians free to live life as they wish					
		Frequency	Percent	Valid Percent	Cumulative Percent
Valid	1 Agree strongly	15905	29.1	30.8	30.8
	2 Agree	17379	31.8	33.7	64.5
	3 Neither agree nor disagree	7690	14.1	14.9	79.4
	4 Disagree	5067	9.3	9.8	89.2
	5 Disagree strongly	5557	10.2	10.8	100.0
	Total	51599	94.4	100.0	
Missing	7 Refusal	153	.3		
	8 Don't know	2858	5.2		
	9 No answer	63	.1		
	Total	3074	5.6		
Total		54673	100.0		

Figure 4.9 Frequency table for **freehms**

Note that respondents who didn't give a response or didn't know what their response to the statement was have been defined as missing, and that SPSS produces a table with the percentage distribution of *all* values, under **Percent**, and of valid values only, under **Valid Percent**. It is this **Valid Percent** column that we are usually interested in. Across the countries covered by the survey it looks as if tolerance of homosexuality is now widespread, but nevertheless just over one in five adults still disagrees with the attitude statement.

standard errors

No sample perfectly 'represents' the population from which it is drawn. Moreover, it is impossible to know how well or badly any single sample does so, since the only way to discover this would be to measure the whole population … yet it is the impossibility or impracticality of such a measurement that leads us to rely on samples in the first place! The escape from this 'catch-22' predicament was one of the most brilliant scientific advances of the nineteenth century. Provided any sample is *randomly* drawn, the probable divergence between the sample estimate and population parameter can be calculated. The standard error itself refers to the standard deviation of the distribution of results that would be obtained by drawing multiple samples. It varies according to the size of the sample, the nature of the parameter being measured and its variability in the population. Standard errors are used to calculate confidence intervals which describe how much uncertainty attaches to any estimate we make from a sample. It is good practice *always* to report this uncertainty and in ways a non-specialist audience can understand.

However, we have a further step to take in our analysis before it is complete. Our data is from a *sample*, not a population. We therefore have to estimate the amount of error our estimate is subject to because of this. We do this by calculating standard errors (see the explanation in the box), and then multiplying them by a factor corresponding to the level of confidence we wish to have in our result to produce a confidence interval. Unfortunately SPSS does not do this (a strange omission), so that we have to do it ourselves. The formula for the standard error of a proportion is

$$SE = \sqrt{\frac{p(1-p)}{n}}.$$

We multiply our sample proportion (p) by its complement ($1 - p$), divide it by the size of our sample (n) and take the square root of the result. The standard error of the proportion of people in our survey agreeing or strongly agreeing that gays and lesbians should be free to live life as they wish is therefore

$$\sqrt{\frac{0.645 \times 0.355}{51599}} = \sqrt{0.0000044} = 0.0021.$$

Notice that the standard error refers to the *proportion* (i.e. of 1) and not *percentage* (of 100). To obtain a confidence interval at the 95% level we need to multiply this standard error by 1.96 (= 0.0041) and then add it and subtract it from our estimate. Now we can say that we are '95% confident' that the true proportion of adults in the countries surveyed who explicitly agree that gays and lesbians should be free to live life as they wish (remember we've included the don't knows as a distinct category in our table) lies between 0.645 − 0.004 = 0.641 and 0.645 + 0.004 = 0.649, or between about 64% and 65%.

What does it mean to be 95% confident? Strictly, it means that were we to repeat our sampling procedure 100 times, the confidence interval produced by 95 of these samples would include the true but unknown population value we are estimating. Of course, we only ever draw *one* sample. We can never know if it is one of the 5 samples out of 100 that would produce a confidence interval that misses the true population value. Thus we describe our level of confidence as '95%'. More loosely it means that we can be pretty sure that the population value lies somewhere within our confidence interval. Often you will see confidence intervals referred to as a 'margin of error'.

✎ Since SPSS doesn't automatically calculate confidence intervals for proportions I've put a *confidence interval calculator* on the companion website using Excel. Enter the sample proportion (*p*) and the sample size (*n*), and out pops the relevant confidence interval. Notice that the sample (*n*) always refers to only that part of the target population on which the proportion (*p*) is based. In our example above the relevant sample was all 51,599 valid responses. Had we been looking at the responses of only one country or only men, the sample would have been the number of valid responses from that country or from men, not the entire sample.

Happily SPSS does calculate standard errors and confidence intervals for point estimates such as the mean value of an interval level variable. We'll see that later when we look at the **Means** and **Explore** commands.

4●11 OTHER SOURCES OF ERROR IN SAMPLE DATA

Does this mean we can be absolutely sure that 64–65% of the adult population of the countries surveyed think 'gays and lesbians should be free to live life as they wish'? Unfortunately not. Standard errors and confidence intervals take account of sampling fluctuation: the fact that each single random sample drawn from a population will differ slightly in its characteristics and that these differences will decline as sample size increases. They take no account of measurement error associated with validity and reliability. Maybe some or all of our respondents interpreted the question in unexpected ways, or have volatile views that shift from one month or year to the next, or privately deplore or champion homosexuality but see no reason to reveal their attitudes to an anonymous survey interviewer. Although the response rate for our survey is respectable, over one-third of adults declined to take part. Perhaps their views on homosexuality are more conservative or liberal than those of their genial fellow citizens who agreed to participate in the survey. However, even taking account of all these possibilities, our estimate is the best that can practically be achieved. We only need to remember the point made in Chapter 2 that measurement of social phenomena is not like taking the dimensions of an object with a ruler: rather it depends upon the operationalisation and capture of conceptual ideas and categories that are often hard to define precisely.

4●12 THE SIGNIFICANCE OF SIGNIFICANCE

Associated with confidence intervals are *significance* tests of various kinds that similarly take the form of asking: what is the probability that a result or pattern would appear in our sample data, because of sampling fluctuation, when no such pattern or result exists in the target population from which the sample has been drawn? If this probability (p-value) is low enough (conventionally below 5% or 0.05) the sample evidence is taken as 'significant' evidence of a population result. Whenever you discover an association or other results of interest in your data there are two possible explanations for it. One possibility is that the result does indeed represent a pattern or association in the target population that would have been revealed had it been possible to measure the entire target population, and which is captured by the sample. The other possibility is that no such pattern or association exists in the target population, and that the pattern or association observed only exists in the sample by virtue of the particular selection of cases that comprised the randomly drawn sample. The probability (p) value associated with a test such as the *chi-square* statistic represents the probability, given that the sample was randomly drawn, of obtaining the sample result were there *no* such pattern in the target population.

Calculating this probability requires formulating a hypothesis to test, usually a *null hypothesis* of no association or no pattern *in the population*. A value for the chi-square or other appropriate test statistic and a corresponding probability value are calculated by SPSS which gives us the probability that the null hypothesis is *true* for the target population, given what we observe in our sample data. If this probability is low enough (conventionally a value of 0.05 or 0.01 is usually taken as 'low enough'), then we reject the null hypothesis and provisionally accept the alternative hypothesis that there is indeed such an association. If our *null* hypothesis is *not* true, we accept our alternative hypothesis until more information comes along that may lead us to revise it.

Why this rather roundabout way of proceeding? It has its origins in the problem of induction and the nature of scientific knowledge. When we observe anything, there are two fundamental, and almost inevitable, errors we can make. One is that whatever system of concepts and categories we use to make sense of our experience is flawed or incomplete. Our knowledge might just be wrong. For example, until the process of oxidation or combustion was understood as the combination of oxygen with other elements, it was thought that fire was caused by a substance known as phlogiston, contained in combustible material and released by and manifested by fire. The experimental result that fire could not be sustained without supplies of air was interpreted as the limit of air's capacity to absorb phlogiston, and by the observably different properties of 'phlogisticated air' (in fact a mixture of carbon dioxide and nitrogen). The second error is that although our conceptual approach is basically correct, we don't collect sufficient information to test our ideas rigorously enough. This might be because there is information we have overlooked, or because the information has yet to be produced. Imagine a scientifically minded turkey (who really knows what occurs in a turkey's brain!). It might, using excellent empirical evidence, theorise an apparently perfect association between sunrise and the appearance of a farmer bearing food. Nothing could 'disprove' this association until the morning, perhaps shortly before Thanksgiving or Christmas, that instead of bearing food the farmer arrives with a sharp knife.

The theory of phlogiston might appear as risible to us now as the turkey's theory of the farmer's benevolence, but both these theories *were* consistent with the 'experimental' evidence. They were overthrown when they proved incompatible with other experimental evidence, including, for example, the finding that combustion increased rather than decreased the weight of a substance, or the fact of a decapitated turkey. How do we know that our current understanding of something is 'true' and the theory of phlogiston 'false'? The simple answer is that we do not and cannot, at least if 'truth' is defined as some form of perfect understanding. However, what we *can* do is make conjectures or hypotheses about the natural or social world, and try to *disprove* them. Until such time as they are disproven, we can accept them as *provisionally* correct.

Significance tests have attracted legitimate criticism because they can be misleading if applied in a mechanical and unthinking way. I don't enter this debate in this book, as a proper consideration of the issues takes us beyond what I have space to deal with here. However, three simple rules will keep you on the right track:

1   Any estimate or 'result' from sample data should be accompanied by an estimate of the sampling error it is subject to, and spurious accuracy in its presentation should be avoided. That is to say, it is better to report confidence intervals than point estimates alone, and when using the latter do not report more places after the decimal point than the data can actually sustain.
2   Effect sizes are usually more important than significance levels. 'Effect size' here means any measure of the strength of association between variables. With a large enough sample size, utterly trivial associations reach statistical but not *substantive* significance. Conversely, in populations which are hard to research and with very small sample sizes, even very strong patterns will not necessarily show up as 'significant' at conventional levels. Above all, avoid 'fishing' for significant associations without good analytical reasons to go looking for them.
3   The third is to keep a sense of proportion about significance levels, and keep in mind what significance means. It is not the case that a *p*-value of 0.051 means we have a 'result' while one of 0.049 means we do not. Both would be evidence that our risk of rejecting a null hypothesis that was in fact true is low (about one in 20). However, this must be balanced against the number of null hypotheses we set out to reject when we explore data. In any large dataset we might test dozens of hundreds of hypotheses. The simple rules of probability tell us that if we use a 5% significance level ($p < 0.05$) then one in 20 of our significant results will be a product of sampling variation, but that we will have no way of knowing *which* ones. The solution to this problem is not to devise some other form of test on the same data, but to search for similar results in *other* data: to use replication in the wider sense of repeating an investigation using new, different, data sources. The latter gives us much more robust information, especially if the data collection and measurement procedures used are different. If we find similar results we can be reasonably sure that sampling fluctuation, or the precise way in which our variables were operationalised, was not responsible for the results we obtained, but rather that these results are based in something going on in the real world.

the chi-square statistic

The chi-square statistic is widely used to test hypotheses and estimate the *p*-values associated with categorical data, including data organised as a contingency table. Note that 'chi' is the Greek letter χ, pronounced 'kye' rather than 'chai'.

4.13 EXPLORING DATA USING CONTINGENCY TABLES

You now have output building up in the **Statistics Viewer**, so that, just like any other file, it makes sense to save it so that you do not lose any work if your machine crashes. Go to **File→Save as** and give your output file a name and a location for it to be saved to. It makes sense to save it to the same folder that you put the dataset file in, and to give it a name that makes clear that it is output from that dataset. However, as we'll see in the next chapter, once you've finished a work session with SPSS, you may not wish to keep your output file.

What might affect respondents' attitudes towards homosexuality? It is not difficult to think of some potential factors. Perhaps women are more tolerant than men, or younger people more tolerant than older? What about those who describe themselves as religious, or those from different religions? Or perhaps those who describe themselves as left or right wing have different views. We can examine all this by looking at how the distribution of the **freehms** variable changes according to the values taken by these other variables. For categorical variables we can produce contingency tables using the **Crosstabs** procedure. Contingency tables show the conditional distribution of the values of one categorical variable for each of the values taken by (or conditional upon) another variable. You may find it helpful to think of a crosstab as a series of frequency tables for the variable of interest defined by each of the values of a second variable.

Go to **Analyze→Descriptive statistics→Crosstabs**. This brings up a dialog box similar to the frequencies dialog box we've just seen. It asks us which variable(s) we wish to put from the variable list in the rows and columns of our table. Put **freehms** in the **Row(s):** box and **gndr, rlgblg, rlgdnm** and **lrscale** in the **Column(s):** box. There is a list of buttons on the right-hand side of the dialog box. Click on the third one, **Cells**, which allows you to specify what will appear in each cell of the table. Our interest is in the distribution of **freehms** conditional upon the values of the other variables, so we want the percentages in the table to run down the columns of the table. Just as in a frequency table, we want to deal with percentages rather than raw numbers, since this will standardise for the different numbers of cases taking each value of the second variable. However, it is still useful to keep raw numbers in the table as well, to be able to check for cells with small numbers of cases. Choose **Observed** under **Counts** and **Column** under **Percentages**, then click on the **Continue** button at the bottom right to return to the main **Crosstabs** dialog box, and click **OK**. This will produce the four contingency tables you have specified and post them to the **Viewer**.

In the **Viewer** you'll first see a **Case Processing Summary** that reports how many cases were used to produce each contingency table. SPSS excludes cases for which one or both of the variables in the table has missing values from the analysis. You'll notice that the number of missing cases for **rlgdnm** is much higher than for the others. This variable is based on a question that asked only those who described themselves as belonging to a religion (at the question for the variable **rlgblg**) which religious denomination they saw themselves as belonging to. Those who did not describe themselves as religious at **rlgblg** are therefore treated as missing for the **rlgdnm** variable. The contingency tables for **freehms** by **gndr** and by **rlgblg** are shown in Figures 4.10 and 4.11.

We can examine the distribution of the variable **freehms** by comparing the column percentages along the rows of the table. Start with the table for **gndr** by **freehms**. It looks as if the sex of respondent has little impact on the distribution of views. Rather more women than men agree with the statement, and more men than women disagree, but the differences are small: a couple of percentage points. We could provisionally conclude that gender has only a small impact on views about homosexuality across all our countries taken together. Nevertheless, we can run a significance test on this contingency table and find that the difference is highly significant.

To run a significance test on a crosstab use the **Statistics** button on the right of the **Crosstabs** dialog box to call up the **Crosstabs: Statistics** dialog and select **Chi-Square**. You can

freehms Gays and lesbians free to live life as they wish * gndr Gender Crosstabulation

			gndr Gender		
			Male	Female	Total
freehms Gays and lesbians free to live life as they wish	Agree strongly	Count	6606	8907	15513
		% within gndr Gender	26.1%	31.8%	29.1%
	Agree	Count	8692	8966	17658
		% within gndr Gender	34.4%	32.0%	33.2%
	Neither agree nor disagree	Count	3775	4131	7906
		% within gndr Gender	14.9%	14.8%	14.8%
	Disagree	Count	2976	2773	5749
		% within gndr Gender	11.8%	9.9%	10.8%
	Disagree strongly	Count	3226	3213	6439
		% within gndr Gender	12.8%	11.5%	12.1%
Total		Count	25275	27990	53265
		% within gndr Gender	100.0%	100.0%	100.0%

Figure 4.10 Views on homosexuality by gender: adults, Europe, 2012

freehms Gays and lesbians free to live life as they wish * rlgblg Belonging to particular religion or denomination Crosstabulation

			rlgblg Belonging to particular religion or denomination		
			1 Yes	2 No	Total
freehms Gays and lesbians free to live life as they wish	1 Agree strongly	Count	7572	7875	15447
		% within rlgblg Belonging to particular religion or denomination	23.7%	37.9%	29.3%
	2 Agree	Count	11026	6532	17558
		% within rlgblg Belonging to particular religion or denomination	34.5%	31.5%	33.3%
	3 Neither agree nor disagree	Count	5186	2582	7768
		% within rlgblg Belonging to particular religion or denomination	16.2%	12.4%	14.7%
	4 Disagree	Count	3824	1816	5640
		% within rlgblg Belonging to particular religion or denomination	12.0%	8.7%	10.7%
	5 Disagree strongly	Count	4339	1956	6295
		% within rlgblg Belonging to particular religion or denomination	13.6%	9.4%	11.9%
Total		Count	31947	20761	52708
		% within rlgblg Belonging to particular religion or denomination	100.0%	100.0%	100.0%

Figure 4.11 Views on homosexuality by religious belonging: adults, Europe, 2012

use the same dialog to select various correlation coefficients such as *phi* or *Cramér's V* or *gamma* (for further information on correlation coefficients see the box on the next page). In syntax just add the sub-command **/statistics** as a separate line, with the statistics you want to request:

/statistics = chisq phi gamma

SPSS reports the value of the *chi-square* statistic and the associated *p*-value. The latter is the probability of obtaining the pattern of results in the table were there no pattern in the population from which the sample on which the table is based was drawn. A low value for *p* (conventionally below 0.05) is termed a significant result. Our result for differences in views by gender is *statistically* highly significant: a difference like this almost certainly really exists in the population and is not a product of sampling fluctuation. However, it is *substantively* of little or no interest. Our very low *p*-value is just a function of the very large sample we have when combining countries together, it is *not* a product of a strong pattern in our data. We can also see this if we examine the size of our correlation coefficients: both *Cramér's V* and *gamma* are very low, well under 0.1. You can also confirm this result by using the confidence interval calculator. Compare the confidence intervals for the 'strongly agree' response for men and for women and you'll see that they do not overlap, again suggesting that there is a real, but very small, difference between the views of men and women.

measures of association and correlation coefficients

Often we want to know if two variables are associated in some way if we have measured them both for the same set of cases. It is easiest to think of this in terms of two limiting cases. If two variables are independent of each other then there is no association between them. In such a situation knowing the distribution of values of one variable gives us no information about the distribution of values for the other variable. Think of the Gapminder data we looked at. Were we to measure the population size of countries and average the income per head, we'd find no association. There are large rich countries, like the USA or Japan, but there are also many small rich ones, like Andorra or Luxembourg. There are large, relatively poor countries, like Pakistan or Nigeria and also small ones such as Liberia or Haiti. Knowing how big a country was would tell us nothing about its wealth.

However were we to measure fertility and child mortality, we'd find a strong association. The higher the fertility rate in the country, the higher is its child mortality. In fact given the data about one of these variables for a country, we'd be able to make a fairly accurate guess about the value of the other. If this association were so strong that such guesses could be perfect, we'd have perfect association and our measure of association would take the value 1. If, on the other hand, knowing the value of one variable gave us no guide to the value of the other (as in the example of population size and income) our measure of association would be 0.

There are five further important points about measures of association to keep in mind.

1   A measure can be positive or negative. The correlation between fertility and child mortality is positive because higher values of one variable go together with higher values of the other. Had we examined the relationship between fertility and life expectancy we would have found a negative relationship, since higher levels of fertility go together with lower values for life expectancy.
2   Measures of association calculate the strength of the *linear* relationship. This terminology comes from the fact that the association can be represented as a line on a graph, or expressed as a mathematical formula that includes only multiplication or addition. Thus a very rough estimate of life expectancy in years could be obtained by multiplying a country's fertility rate by 7 and then subtracting the result from 90. However many relationships are not linear. This happens when the nature of the association between the two variables changes across the range of their values. There is a strong association between fertility and income across countries, as we saw in Chapter 3. At high levels of fertility even large differences in fertility rates are associated with relatively small differences in income per head. However at lower levels of fertility the differences in income become much larger. The result is that linear association is weak. To get a proper sense of the real strength of association we need to transform one of the variables, as we did by using a log scale for income.
3   The correct measure of association to use depends on the level of measurement of the variables involved. Pearson's r is suitable for interval level variables; Spearman's Rho and Gamma for ordinal variables and Phi and Cramers V for nominal variables.

4 Measures of association tell us about our *data*, not the population from which it has been drawn. To draw any conclusions about the latter, we need to look at confidence intervals, significance tests or other means of estimating how likely any sample result is likely to be true of the target population.

5 Finally, as we have already seen, evidence of correlation, revealed by a measure of association, is necessary but not sufficient evidence of causation.

What about religion? Look at the contingency table you have produced for **rlgblg**. Here there is a more substantial difference. You should find that 23.7 + 34.5 = 58.2% of those who describe themselves as religious either agree or strongly agree with the statement. However, 37.9 + 31.5 = 69.4% of those who are not religious do so. This is hardly a strong relationship, but it does suggest some difference. Perhaps views differ across different religions? Examine the table of **freehms** by **rlgdnm** (Figure 4.12). Because there are eight categories of religion described by the variable **rlgdnm** the table is a little unwieldy, with 40 cells in the body of the table. Nevertheless, by scanning along the table rows you can see that attitudes to homosexuality differ substantially according to religious denomination, with Eastern Orthodox and Islamic religions less sympathetic to homosexuality than Protestant or Eastern religions.

freehms * rlgdnm Crosstabulation

			1 Roman Catholic	2 Protestant	3 Eastern Orthodox	4 Other Christian denomination	5 Jewish	6 Islamic	7 Eastern religions	8 Other non-Christian religions	Total
freehms	1 Agree strongly	Count	4560	1514	638	169	232	255	116	53	7537
		% within rlgdnm	28.6%	29.6%	9.0%	29.0%	45.0%	12.3%	36.4%	36.6%	23.7%
	2 Agree	Count	6392	2441	1231	154	151	445	123	34	10971
		% within rlgdnm	40.0%	47.8%	17.4%	26.5%	29.3%	21.5%	38.6%	23.4%	34.5%
	3 Neither agree nor disagree	Count	2406	579	1518	105	47	428	44	24	5151
		% within rlgdnm	15.1%	11.3%	21.4%	18.0%	9.1%	20.7%	13.8%	16.6%	16.2%
	4 Disagree	Count	1393	349	1541	62	33	387	27	24	3816
		% within rlgdnm	8.7%	6.8%	21.7%	10.7%	6.4%	18.7%	8.5%	16.6%	12.0%
	5 Disagree strongly	Count	1210	225	2160	92	52	555	9	10	4313
		% within rlgdnm	7.6%	4.4%	30.5%	15.8%	10.1%	26.8%	2.8%	6.9%	13.6%
Total		Count	15961	5108	7088	582	515	2070	319	145	31788
		% within rlgdnm	100.0%	100.0%	100.0%	100.0%	100.0%	100.0%	100.0%	100.0%	100.0%

Figure 4.12 Contingency table of **freehms** by **rlgdnm**

Finally, look at the table for **lrscale**. It is even harder to make sense of, since **lrscale** can take a value from 0 to 10, but overall it seems to be the case that agreement that 'gays and lesbians should be free to live life as they wish' does decline slightly as we move to higher scores of **lrscale**, representing those who see themselves as more 'right wing'.

4 14 CREATING A BAR CHART IN SPSS

One of the reasons why **lrscale** is difficult to examine in a crosstab is that it has so many categories. Moreover, we could probably safely treat this as an *interval*-level variable. Keep in mind the assumption that we need to make in order to do so. This is that not only will people choose a higher number on the scale if they describe themselves as right rather than left wing, but also it makes sense to assume that respondents treated the scale as a linear one – that the difference between 1 and 3 is the same as that between 6 and 8, and so on. Is this a reasonable assumption? One way we could examine this is to look at the distribution of the variable itself. Run a frequency table for it, but this time, in the **Frequencies** dialog box, use the **Charts** button to select a **bar chart** with **percentages** as the **Chart Values**. This gives us a graphic display of the frequency distribution of the variable that is easier to deal with than a list of raw frequencies. It is clear that most respondents chose to describe themselves as middle of the road, with numbers falling away as we move away from the value '5' until the two extremes of the scale are met. Given this distribution, it seems that it would not be stretching things too far to treat this variable as an interval one and use relevant summary statistics such as the mean to describe its values for different groups.

4 15 USING THE MEANS PROCEDURE

We looked at the relationship between **freehms** and categorical variables using crosstabs. For interval-level variables we could look at the relationship in a slightly different way. We can examine the distribution of values for these variables, according to the values taken by **freehms**. This allows us to answer such questions as: are people sympathetic to the rights of gays and lesbians more likely to be older or younger than those less sympathetic? To do this we can use the **Compare Means** procedure in SPSS. Go to **Analyze→Compare Means→Means** to bring up the **Means** dialog box. Put the variables **lrscale** and **agea** in the **Dependent List** box, **freehms** in the **Independent List** box and click on **OK** or **Paste**. SPSS will compare the means and standard deviations (level and spread) of the variables **agea** and **lrscale** for each separate value of **freehms**, enabling you to compare the ages and position on the left–right spectrum of those with different views on homosexuality. You should obtain a table like the one in Figure 4.13.

Report			
freehms Gays and lesbians free to live life as they wish		agea Age of respondent, calculated	lrscale Placement on left right scale
1 Agree strongly	Mean	44.47	4.53
	N	15475	14099
	Std. Deviation	17.691	2.342
2 Agree	Mean	48.75	5.19
	N	17585	15487
	Std. Deviation	18.946	2.152
3 Neither agree nor disagree	Mean	47.12	5.39
	N	7886	6447
	Std. Deviation	19.050	2.073
4 Disagree	Mean	48.43	5.54
	N	5753	4607
	Std. Deviation	19.647	2.286
5 Disagree strongly	Mean	49.26	5.52
	N	6432	4718
	Std. Deviation	19.381	2.346
Total	Mean	47.29	5.08
	N	53131	45358
	Std. Deviation	18.833	2.270

Figure 4.13   Descriptive statistics for **freehms**

It looks as if there is no strong relationship to either age or whether respondents see themselves as left or right wing, except that the average age of those who agree strongly is a little lower than those with other views. Unlike proportions, SPSS happily calculates standard errors for means, and it's one of the statistics you can request using the **Options…** button or adding **SEMEAN** to the **/CELLS** sub-command in syntax, so that we could ask for Figure 4.13 but with standard errors shown as well by running the syntax

```
MEANS lrscale agea BY freehms
/CELLS=MEAN COUNT STDDEV SEMEAN.
```

✎ Remember that copies of all the syntax shown in the text are available on the companion website.

4 16 RECODING VARIABLES AND CREATING NEW VARIABLES

So far we have used all five categories of the **freehms** variable, but we could simplify it to make our exploration with this variable easier, by reducing it to two categories, all those who strongly agree or agree, and all those who strongly disagree or disagree. We could also treat those who neither agree nor disagree as missing. We can do this by *recoding* the variable to create a new variable, that is, put the existing values of a variable into one or more new groups. This is a technique you'll often use when analysing data. It makes sense to *disaggregate* categories as much as possible when *collecting* data, and, in contrast, to *aggregate* it as much as possible in its *presentation*. The former maximises the flexibility the analyst has to deal with the information in the dataset, while the latter ensures that the focus of any results reported is on the most important information or comparisons to be made. Recoding a variable allows you to aggregate data in the way that best facilitates the comparisons you want to make.

While it is possible to recode existing variables in a dataset, this is rarely a good idea, as we then lose the original, disaggregated, information that was collected. So we usually use recoding to create a new variable alongside the original variable. To do this we need to tell SPSS what the new values (categories) are to be, and how they are to be created out of the original variable values. We can create a new variable **freehms2** with one value corresponding to the codes 1 and 2 (strongly agree and agree) in **freehms**, and another value corresponding to the codes 4 and 5 (strongly disagree and disagree). We want to keep the existing values defined as missing (7, 8 and 9), but also add those cases taking the existing value 3 ('neither agree nor disagree') to this list. We already have the information on why different cases are missing in the original **freehms** variable, so we don't need to retain this information in our new variable. SPSS has a special value, represented by a dot, for values that it stores as *system missing*. We could use this option as our new value for cases taking values 3, 7, 8 and 9 in **freehms**. Thus our new variable is defined in terms of our original one as shown in Table 4.1.

Go to **Transform→Recode into Different Variables** which brings up the dialog box in Figure 4.14. This dialog box is a little tricky, but with practice soon becomes less annoying. It has the usual list of variables on the left-hand side and a box in the middle, **Input Variable→ Output Variable:**, into which you drag the variable(s) you wish to recode from the variable list. When you do this the **Name:** box on the right-hand side becomes available into which

Table 4.1 Value codes for **freehms** and **freehms2**

freehms value	freehms value label	freehms2 value	freehms2 value label
1	Strongly agree	1	Agree
2	Agree	1	Agree
3	Neither agree nor disagree		System missing
4	Disagree	2	Disagree
5	Strongly disagree	2	Disagree
7	Refusal		System missing
8	Don't know		System missing
9	No answer		System missing

you insert the name of the new variable you want to create. The name must be all one word, beginning with a letter, and using numbers, letters or underscores. Once you've entered the name for your new variable, the **Change** button underneath becomes active and you click on it to put the name in the **Input variable→Output variable** box.

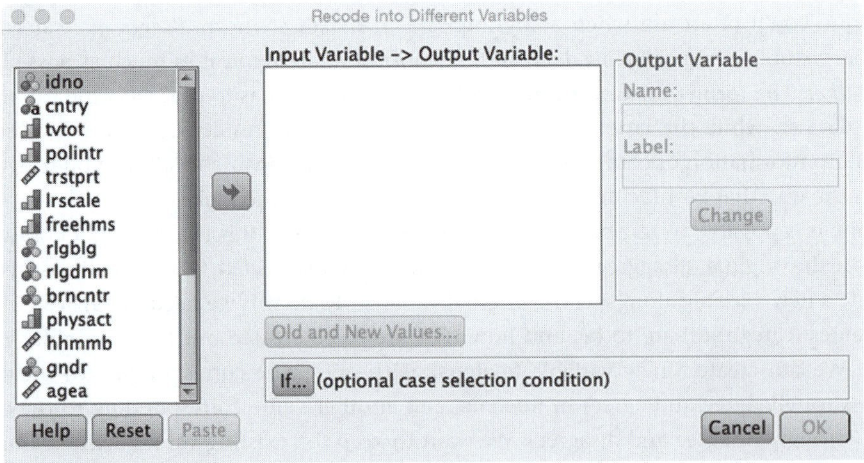

Figure 4.14 The **Recode into Different Variables** dialog box

You next need to click on the **Old and New Values** button beneath the **Input variable→Output variable** dialog box. This takes you to the next layer of the dialog box (shown in Figure 4.15) in which there are a variety of different options given for telling SPSS how to transform the value codes for the existing variable into those for the new variable.

You specify the individual value or value range you want to recode on the left-hand side under **Old Value**, and on the right-hand side the **New Value** code this value or range of values should take in the new variable. Once you have done this the **Add** button lights up to the left of the **Old→New** values list box, and when you click on this button, the instructions you have

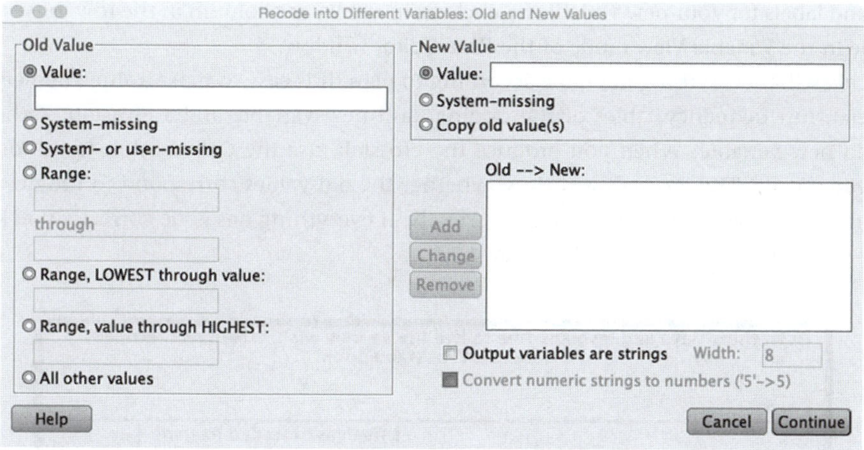

Figure 4.15 The **Recode into Different Variables: Old and New Values** dialog box

given SPSS are entered in this box. Note that one of the options under **Old Value** is **All other values**. Once you have told SPSS what to do with the 1s, 2s, 4s and 5s, you can thus tell SPSS to set all other values to system missing.

If you make an error in the instructions, you can go back by highlighting the instructions in the **Old→New** box and clicking on **Change** or **Remove**. At the end of the process the results should look like Figure 4.16 (note that I've also told SPSS what to do with any missing values).

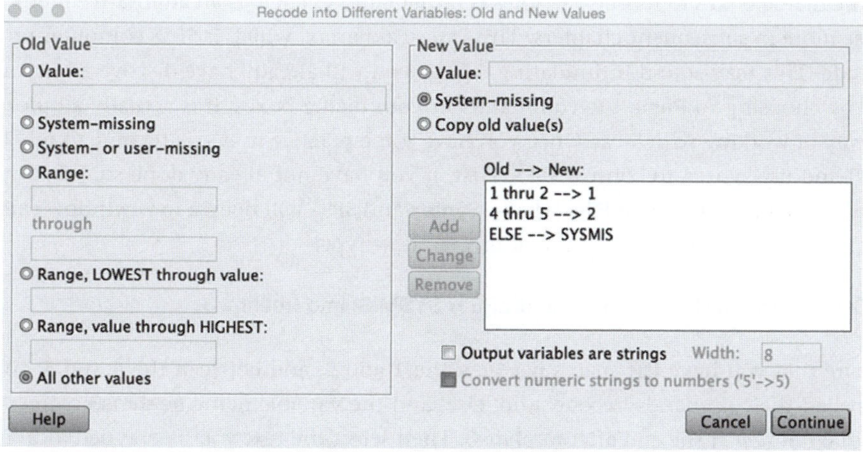

Figure 4.16 The completed **Recode into Different Variables: Old and New Values** dialog box

Now click on **Continue** which returns you to the main dialog box and click on **OK**. SPSS now creates your new variable and posts it to the end of the list of variables in the **Data Editor** window. Now you should give labels both to the new variable and to its values. It is tempting, especially when you are in a hurry, to overlook this step, and you can easily convince yourself that you will remember what the variable and value codes stood for. You won't! Enter value codes and labels for your new variable by clicking in the **Values** column in the row for your new variable in the **Variable View** mode of the **Data Editor** window.

To check that everything has gone according to plan (it is easy to make a slip when entering numbers), run frequency tables of the original and new variable and a crosstab of the original and new variable. When you produce the crosstab, use the **Cells** button to ask only for **Observed counts**. The crosstab will show whether the old values correspond to the new ones, and if missing values have been recoded correctly. If everything has gone correctly you should get the contingency table shown in Figure 4.17.

freehms Gays and lesbians free to live life as they wish * freehms2 recoded freehms Crosstabulation				
Count				
		freehms2 recoded freehms		
		1.00	2.00	Total
freehms Gays and lesbians free to live life as they wish	1 Agree strongly	15540	0	15540
	2 Agree	17676	0	17676
	4 Disagree	0	5760	5760
	5 Disagree strongly	0	6439	6439
Total		33216	12199	45415

Figure 4.17 Crosstab of **freehms** by **freehms2**

4●17 USING SYNTAX IN SPSS

Using the dialog boxes to recode variables is rather clunky. There is an alternative method that we'll use more in subsequent chapters. This is to use syntax, which is SPSS computer programming code. This may sound intimidating, but as you will already have discovered if you have tried it by choosing to **Paste** the commands in your dialog boxes, it is actually a quicker and better way of working with SPSS. Once you have some practice in it you'll come to rely less on the GUI and use syntax to control SPSS. First, if you have not already done so, you'll need to create a new syntax file. Go to **File→New→Syntax** and SPSS will open a new window called the **Syntax Editor**. In the right-hand pane of this window type:

RECODE freehms (1 2 = 1) (4 5 = 2) (ELSE = SYSMIS) into freehms3.

Make sure that you have left spaces between the 1 and 2, and between the 4 and 5; that you have spelled the commands 'recode' and 'else' and the variable name **freehms3** correctly, and have put a *full stop* at the end after **freehms3**. Then select the text you have typed (don't forget the full stop at the end) and click on the **Run Selection** icon ▶ in the toolbar. You will find that you've done exactly the same recode procedure as with the dialog boxes and commands, but with much less fuss. You need to learn some rules of syntax language to use it, but they are reasonably intuitive and you'll pick them up as you develop your skills.

We've now changed our dataset by adding new variables to it. We therefore have to save it, so as not to lose our new data. Go to **File→Save as** and, as you did with the output **Viewer** file, save the new version of your dataset to the folder alongside the back-up copy of the original, giving it a name that allows you to identify what it comprises.

4 ●18 SUBSETTING AND SELECTING CASES

When looking at the US GSS in Chapter 3 we saw how attitudes that supported a male bread-winner system had declined in the USA, and even more sharply in some European countries, over the last few decades. Let's look now at behaviour. We could look at how the activities of men and women in the home and in the labour market compare, and do this across different countries. It would make sense to compare men and women at the stage in life when they've completed their education and are working or forming and raising families but not yet so old that they might be contemplating retiring from the labour market. Thus we could look at, say, men and women aged 25–49.

You can select subgroups of cases, or respondents, to analyse by going to **Data→Select Cases** or clicking the **Select Cases** icon ▦ from the toolbar, to open the **Select Cases** dialog box, which controls how you select cases and what is to be done with them once selected. Under **Select** choose **If condition is satisfied**, and click the **If** button that then becomes available. You then have the usual variables list on the left-hand side of the box, together with a numeric key-pad in the middle. The top untitled box is where you put your formula for the cases you want to select (ignore the **Function Group** boxes to the right of the pane for just now). We want to select cases if the variable **agea** takes a value between 25 and 49 inclusive, so we can type

  agea ge 25 and agea le 49

directly into the box. You can drag the variable **agea** to the box instead of typing it, or use the arithmetic operators from the numeric keypad instead of **ge** (equal to or greater than) or **le** (less than or equal to). Your dialog box should look like the one in Figure 4.18.

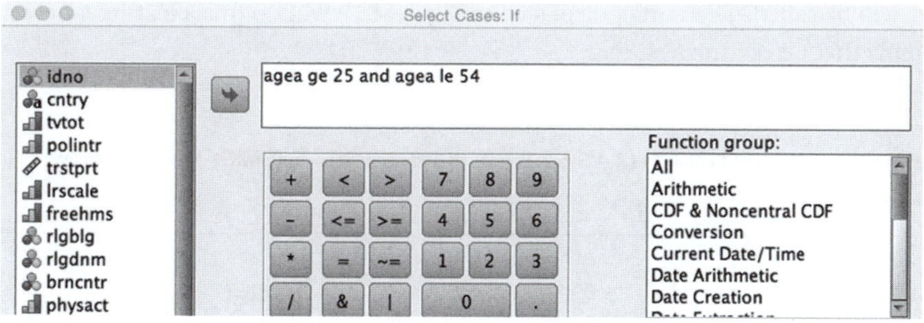

Figure 4.18 The **Select Cases: If** dialog box

Click on **Continue** to go back to the main dialog box (where you'll notice that your formula now appears next to **If**). You now have to tell SPSS what to do with the selected cases under **Output**. Choose **Filter out unselected cases** and click on **Paste**. You should have created the following syntax:

```
USE ALL.
COMPUTE filter_$=(agea ge 25 and agea le 54).
VARIABLE LABELS filter_$ 'agea ge 25 and agea le 54 (FILTER)'.
```

VALUE LABELS filter_$ 0 'Not Selected' 1 'Selected'.
FORMATS filter_$ (f1.0).
FILTER BY filter_$.
EXECUTE.

Notice that SPSS creates a filter variable to select the cases to analyse. If you wish to return to analysing all cases, you can select the relevant option in the **Select Case**s dialog, or in the **Syntax** window just type:

USE ALL.

If you examine your **Data Editor** window in **Data View** mode you'll see that SPSS has created a temporary variable called **filter_$** and that all the cases which have *not* been selected using the criteria you specified now have a diagonal bar striking through their case row number at the extreme left of the window. It is thus possible to visually check if your selection criteria have worked in the way you planned.

The variable **mnactic** records what the main activity of respondents was in the week before their interview. If you run a frequency table for this variable you'll see that it has nine categories, but that many of them account for a relatively small proportion of cases. Our focus of interest is in whether women are active in the labour market. We might therefore decide to put those in paid work and those looking for it (codes 1 and 3) together. We could also put together those in education (2), or not looking for a job (4) or sick and disabled (5), retired (6) doing community/military service (7) and others (9) together as a catch-all category. We can keep those keeping home or looking after children or others (8) as they are. Again, we can use the recode procedure to do this, and practice our syntax skills. The syntax needs to specify the variable to be recoded, how the old values will correspond to the new values, and what the new variable will be called. The syntax displayed in Figure 4.19 will do this, creating a new variable called **mbw** that takes three values.

RECODE   mnactic (1 3 = 1) (2 4 5 6 7 9 = 9) (8 = 8) (ELSE = SYSMIS)   into   mbw.

↑	↑	↑	↑	↑	↑
The SPSS command	The variable to be recoded	How each of the values of the original variable is to be recoded	What is to be done with any values not already specified	Create a new variable with the recodes	The name of the new variable

Figure 4.19 Syntax for recoding a variable to create a new variable

Note that I've used a mixture of upper- and lower-case letters. SPSS syntax does not distinguish between them. I've kept upper case for commands and keywords and put variables in lower case, but that's only to make them easier for me to distinguish: you do not have to follow a similar system. Enter this syntax on a new line in the **Syntax Editor** window and **Run** it in the same way as you did before, then label your new variable and its values in the **Data Editor** window. To do this click on the **Values** column next to your new variable in the **Data Editor** window in **Variable View** mode. This will display the **Value Labels** dialog box in Figure 4.20. To label the values enter the value you wish to label, the label for that value and click on the **Add** button that becomes available when you do so. When you have done this for all three values (1, 8 and 9) click on **OK** as usual.

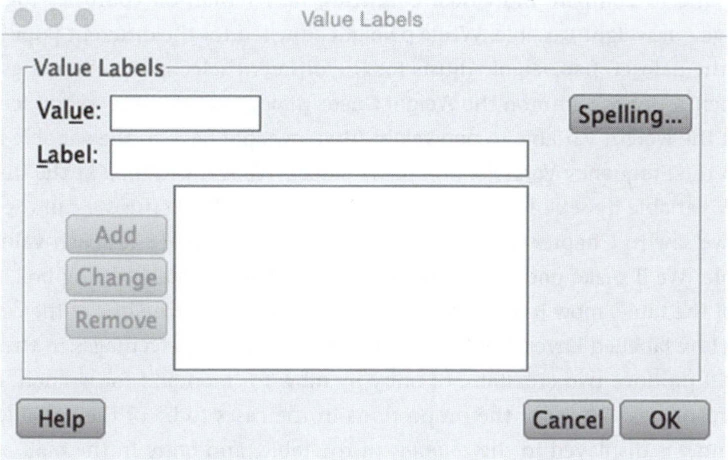

Figure 4.20   The **Value Labels** dialog box

Note that although we've created this variable while we have a subset of cases selected for analysis, SPSS nevertheless creates the new variable for *all* cases, selected or not. Run a crosstab, as before, to check that the recode has worked. It should look like Figure 4.21.

		mbw			
		1.00 (looking for)paid work	8.00 carer /homemaker	9.00 Other	Total
mnactic Main activity, last 7 days. All respondents. Post coded	1 Paid work	20180	0	0	20180
	2 Education	0	0	441	441
	3 Unemployed, looking for job	1817	0	0	1817
	4 Unemployed, not looking for job	0	0	695	695
	5 Permanently sick or disabled	0	0	530	530
	6 Retired	0	0	361	361
	7 Community or military service	0	0	4	4
	8 Housework, looking after children, others	0	2447	0	2447
	9 Other	0	0	212	212
Total		21997	2447	2243	26687

*mnactic Main activity, last 7 days. All respondents. Post coded * mbw Crosstabulation*

Count

Figure 4.21   Crosstab of **mnactic** by **mbw**

In countries where women still withdraw from the labour market either permanently or temporarily on the birth of children, we'd expect there to be a higher proportion of women reporting that they are homemakers/carers (the precise wording used by the survey was whether

'Doing housework, looking after children or others' had been the respondents 'main activity' in the previous week).

4 ● 19 PRODUCING A THREE-WAY CONTINGENCY TABLE

We're now going to compare individual countries, rather than all countries together, so we need to change our weight variable. While **pweight** adjusted for the different population size of countries in the dataset, **pspweight** adjusts for the different selection probabilities of respondents *within* each country. Summon the **Weight Cases** dialog box with the weight icon ⚖ on the toolbar to set the weight variable to **pspweight** (drag **pweight** back to the variable list and drag **pspweight** to the **Frequency Variable:** box in its place). We want to look at the distribution of our new **mbw** variable by sex of respondent and by country. To do this we can use a three-way crosstab. As we saw in Chapter 3, this produces a series of crosstabs for each value of a third, *control* variable. We'll make **gndr** this variable. Call up the **Crosstabs** dialog box, put **cntry** in the **Row(s):** of the table, **mbw** in the **Column(s):**, and drag **gndr** to the box at the centre bottom of the dialog box labelled **Layer 1 of 1**. Ask for counts and row percentages in the **Cells** of the table. This will produce two crosstabs, of **cntry** by **mbw** for men and for women. (Why do we want row percentages? We want the proportions in the cases to be of the variable of interest, **mbw**. Since **mbw** is displayed in the *columns* of the table, and **cntry** in the *rows*, we will need *row* percentages to see the proportions in the different values of **mbw**, within each country.) If you look first at the crosstab for men, it is clear that in almost all countries the overwhelming majority of men of this age, between 85% and 95%, are either in paid work or unemployed and looking for a job. Only a tiny percentage describe themselves as homemakers or carers. There is only one exception to this pattern: Kosovo. However, when we look at women we find a different pattern. There is much more variation across countries. In some countries, the proportion of women working is nearly as high as that for men, whereas in others it is somewhat lower. If we turn to look at the proportion of women who are carers or homemakers, it varies much more than that for men: from 3% in Sweden to almost ten times that level in Switzerland and Ireland and higher levels still in Kosovo and Albania.

4 ● 20 EXPORTING OUTPUT TO OTHER APPLICATIONS

If we wanted to examine this distribution of women's activity in different countries it would help to visualise it. While you can do this in SPSS, it is often more convenient to *export* your results to another package. We can export the results to Excel and create a bar chart. First select the table you have produced by clicking on it in the **Viewer** window. When you do this you'll see that a small red arrow appears to its left and the whole table is surrounded by a thin black border. Now go to **File→Export** to open the **Export Output** dialog box as shown in Figure 4.22.

Under **Objects to Export** choose **Selected**. The default option for file export is as an Excel file, so we can leave this setting unchanged. Under **File Name** you can supply a title for the file to be exported after the last slash and before the **.xls** suffix. You can also specify a destination for the file here, or use the **Browse** button to do this. If you are unfamiliar with how to describe file destinations using the directory hierarchy in your computer, it is often best to just accept the

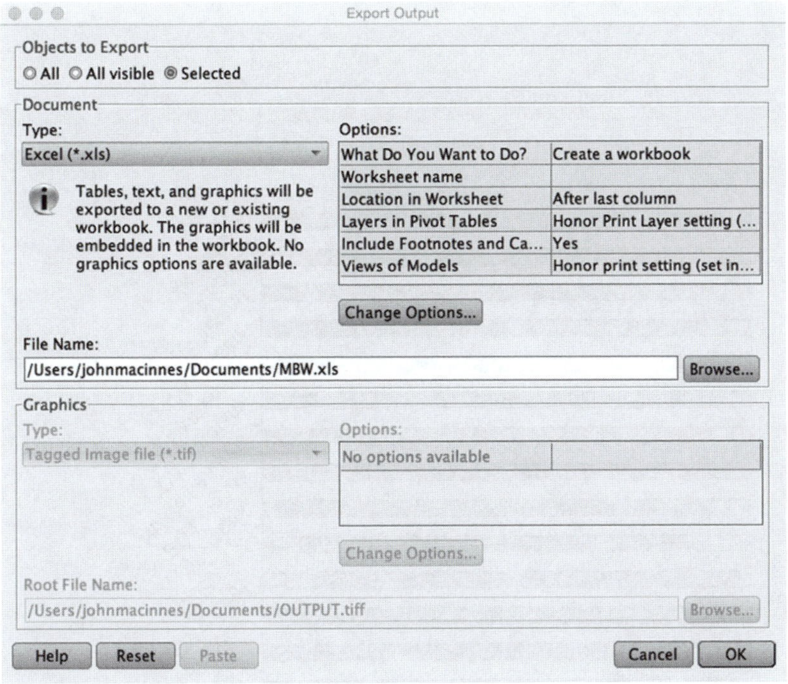

Figure 4.22 The **Export Output** dialog box

defaults that SPSS supplies. Click on **OK** or on **Paste** to place the syntax in your **Syntax Editor** window and run the syntax from there, and then open the Excel file that you have created. The top of the Excel workbook page should look something like Figure 4.23 depending on the version of Excel that you have and the computer platform you are using.

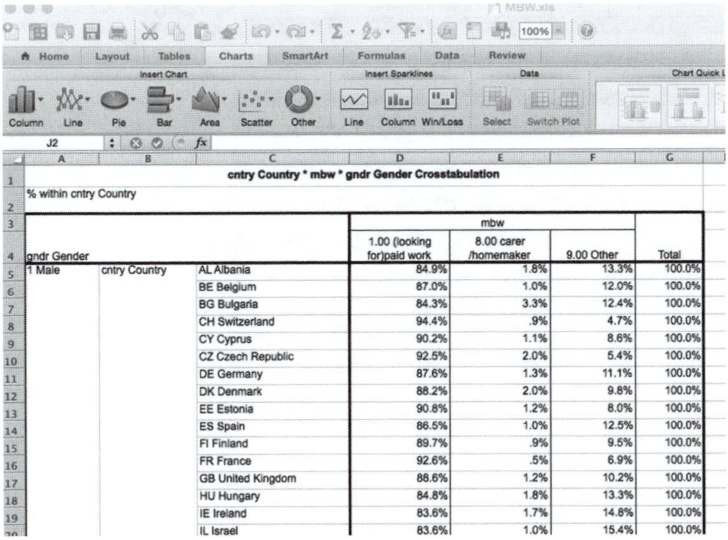

cntry Country * mbw * gndr Gender Crosstabulation

% within cntry Country

gndr Gender			mbw 1.00 (looking for)paid work	mbw 8.00 carer /homemaker	mbw 9.00 Other	Total
1 Male	cntry Country	AL Albania	84.9%	1.8%	13.3%	100.0%
		BE Belgium	87.0%	1.0%	12.0%	100.0%
		BG Bulgaria	84.3%	3.3%	12.4%	100.0%
		CH Switzerland	94.4%	.9%	4.7%	100.0%
		CY Cyprus	90.2%	1.1%	8.6%	100.0%
		CZ Czech Republic	92.5%	2.0%	5.4%	100.0%
		DE Germany	87.6%	1.3%	11.1%	100.0%
		DK Denmark	88.2%	2.0%	9.8%	100.0%
		EE Estonia	90.8%	1.2%	8.0%	100.0%
		ES Spain	86.5%	1.0%	12.5%	100.0%
		FI Finland	89.7%	.9%	9.5%	100.0%
		FR France	92.6%	.5%	6.9%	100.0%
		GB United Kingdom	88.6%	1.2%	10.2%	100.0%
		HU Hungary	84.8%	1.8%	13.3%	100.0%
		IE Ireland	83.6%	1.7%	14.8%	100.0%
		IL Israel	83.6%	1.0%	15.4%	100.0%

Figure 4.23 An SPSS contingency table in Excel

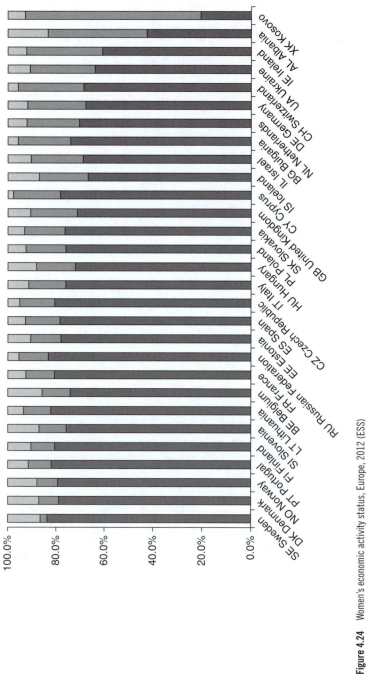

Figure 4.24 Women's economic activity status, Europe, 2012 (ESS)

Source: European Social Survey, Round 6 (2012), author's calculations

Now that you have your output in Excel you can use it to produce different kinds of graphical output from your table. Scroll down to the part of the table that deals with women. Select only the four columns with the country names, and the percentages of women in each of the three activity categories, from the first country (Albania) down to the last (Kosovo), go to **Data→Sort** and have Excel sort the data by the column with the percentages for carers/homemakers. Then, selecting the same columns and rows again, click on **Charts** and **Column** in the toolbar to have Excel produce a chart based on this part of the table. Excel creates a small chart in the same workbook. It is usually best to move the chart (go to **Chart→Move Chart**) to a new worksheet, to have a chart that is easy to read. The result should look similar to the chart in Figure 4.24.

It is now much easier to look at the pattern of women's activity across countries. At least in terms of women's activity in the labour market, it looks as if there is no longer much evidence of a male breadwinner system in the countries surveyed by the ESS. However, there are still some important differences between countries. In Scandinavia, France and Russia only around one in 10 women in the age group we are examining are homemakers/carers, while the proportion is around double that in the Netherlands, Germany, Switzerland and Ukraine.

4 ● 21 EXAMINING GENDER AND EMPLOYMENT USING ESS6-PRACTICE.SAV

The variable we have looked at only tells us if someone is in the labour market or not. However, the variable **wkhtot** captures how many hours a week those with employment normally work. How does this vary across countries and for men and women in this age group?

One way of looking at this would be to compare mean working hours for women and men across countries. Go to **Means→Compare Means** and in the **Means** dialog box put **wkhtot** in the **Dependent List:**, and **gndr** in the **Independent List:**. When you do this you'll see that the **Next** button above **Independent List:** becomes highlighted. Clicking on this button takes you to a new **Independent List:** box. Drag **cntry** to this box. We've now asked SPSS to calculate the mean of **wkhtot** for each value of **gndr** (men and women) *and* for each value of **cntry** (the countries in the survey). Click on **OK** or **Paste** the syntax to your **Syntax Editor** window and run it to have SPSS produce the output. Scanning the numbers in the table seems to suggest that average weekly working hours for men range from around 40 to 48, and for women from 30 to the low 40s.

However, the mean tells us nothing about the *spread* of working hours within a country. Perhaps most people have hours that are near the mean, or it might be that there is a wide spread of hours, with some working very long hours and others having only part-time work. We could look at the distribution of hours within countries. However, to do this for all the countries in our survey risks overwhelming ourselves with data, leaving us unable to tell the wood from the trees. Let's therefore select a smaller number of countries to examine. I'll choose France, Germany, the UK, the Netherlands, Portugal, the Russian Federation and Sweden.

It would be possible, but tedious and complex, to select this list of countries using the **Select Cases** feature that we used earlier. We have an additional challenge, too. The variable **cntry** is a string variable, less easy to manipulate and change than a numerical one. However, there is another, often easier and quicker, way to select groups of cases for analysis. We can create a new variable that defines the cases we want to select. We could use the **Recode into Different Variables** dialog to do this, but it is quicker to use syntax, and this will give us a little more practice with the **Syntax Editor**. Thus we'll first turn **cntry** into a numeric variable, and in turn use this variable to create another new numeric variable that describes the set of countries that we want to examine.

4 ● 22 CREATING NUMERIC VERSIONS OF STRING VARIABLES

The variable **cntry** stored in the ESS dataset is a **string** variable: it comprises text rather than numbers. SPSS lets you carry out various operations on such variables (so that you can use them in frequency or contingency tables) and sorts the values they take alphabetically rather than numerically. You can also recode string variables in a similar way to numeric ones. However, for some operations it is more convenient to have a numeric version of a string variable. The option **Automatic Recode** allows you to do this very quickly.

Go to **Transform→Automatic Recode** to open the **Automatic Recode** dialog box. Drag the string variable you wish to recode into the **Variable→New Name** box, and when you do this the **New Name:** box will become available. Type a name for the new variable you are going to create in the box (e.g. **country**), and the **Add New Name** button below it will become active; click on this button. You can leave all the other options at the default settings (your dialog box should now look like Figure 4.25) and click **OK,** or to create the syntax corresponding to these commands choose **Paste** and then run the syntax using the icon as we saw above. Your syntax should read:

```
AUTORECODE VARIABLES=cntry
/INTO country
/PRINT.
```

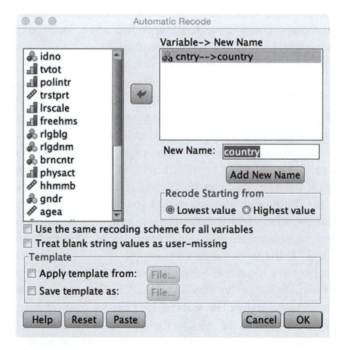

Figure 4.25 The **Automatic Recode** dialog box

SPSS then converts the text values of the original variable to a series of numbers in the new variable, but retains the value labels from the original variable. It posts a list of the old and new values and their labels to the **Viewer**, while you can also view the new variable that has been created in the **Data Editor** window: it will be in the final row of variables in **Variable View** mode.

In the numeric **country** variable that we have just created, the seven countries I want to select have the values 7, 12, 13, 20, 23, 24 and 25. The following syntax code will create a new variable, **mycountries**, that collects these countries together in one group and all the other countries in another group. I've also added a second line of syntax code to have SPSS run a **CROSS**tab of my new variable by the old variable, so that I can check that my new variable has been created correctly. Note that each command is on a separate line and that each ends with a full stop.

```
RECODE country (7 12 13 20 23 24 25 = 1) (ELSE=0) into mycountries.
CROSS country by mycountries.
```

We can now easily select our list of countries for further analysis by returning to the **Select Cases** dialog ▦ and we can edit the **If...** statement we currently have in operation there, by adding **and mycountries eq 1** so that the full expression becomes:

agea ge 25 and agea le 54 and mycountries eq 1

Once you have done this, go back to the main **Select Cases** dialog and click **OK** or **Paste**.

4 ● 23 CREATING A BOXPLOT IN SPSS

We can look at the distribution of working hours for men and women in these countries by looking at a boxplot. Boxplots display the range of values from the lower quartile (the value taken by a case ranked one-quarter of the way up all cases ranked in order from the lowest to the highest) to the upper quartile (the value taken by a case ranked one-quarter of the way down from the top of all cases ranked in order from the lowest to the highest) in a box, with a line across the box that corresponds to the median or middle-ranked case. 'Whiskers' extend from the box to more extreme values and markers indicate the position of 'outliers', unusually low or high values.

Go to **Graphs→Legacy Dialogs→Boxplot**, select **Clustered** and click **Define**. This will open the **Define Clustered Boxplots: Summaries for Groups of Cases** dialog box. Drag **wkhtot** to the **Variable:** box, drag **cntry** to the **Category Axis:** box and drag **gndr** to the **Define Clusters by:** box and click **OK** or **Paste**.

The chart that this produces in the **Viewer** looks rather messy, but we can clean it up to make it easier to read by editing it. To do this double-click on the chart and a **Chart Editor** window will open. Now double-click on any box within the chart and the **Properties** window will open. Here select the **Bar Options** tab and drag the **Bars** slider to the right to make the boxes in the boxplots wider. Click **Apply** and then **Close**. Now click on the Y icon **Y** in the **Chart Editor** toolbar, select the **Scale** tab and set the maximum to 80, click **Apply** and **Close**. After these alterations your chart should look like Figure 4.26.

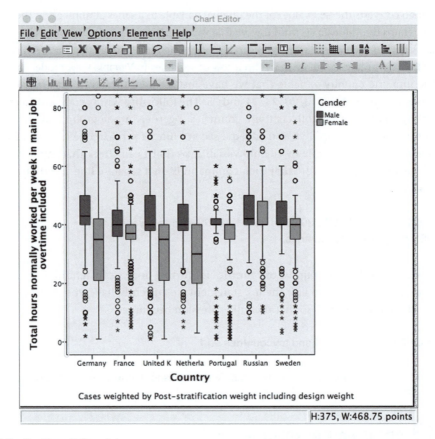

Figure 4.26 The **Chart Editor** window

It is usually more effective to examine a chart such as this one than long lists of numbers. Several features of the data stand out. Only in France is the spread of working hours for men greater than that for women, while in Germany, the UK, and Netherlands women's working hours are rather diverse, with about one-quarter of women working 20 hours or less per week. In most countries there are small numbers of men working very long hours, and very few men indeed working for less than about 35 hours a week. There seems to be little link between the hours that men and women work when we compare countries. The distribution of men's hours is broadly similar in the Netherlands, the Russian Federation and Sweden, but the pattern of women's hours quite different in these three countries. There are other stories that could be taken from this chart, and other possibilities to explore. For example, using the full ESS dataset, it would be possible to look at what happens to parents' working patterns when they have young children.

4 24 TIDYING UP

If you have followed the suggestions in this chapter, you'll now have five new documents in your computer:

1   The back-up of the original **ESS_Practice.sav** file
2   The new version of **ESS6_Practice.sav** which contains the original data plus the new variables you
    have created
3   The **Viewer** file which contains all the tables and charts you have created using the dataset
4   The **Syntax Editor** file in which you pasted or wrote commands for the data
5   The **Excel** file with the bar chart for women's activity.

When you finish working with SPSS it is important to clear up these files, otherwise you will soon
find that you have dozens of files and struggle to identify them or remember what they contain.
You will end up repeating work because you cannot find where you left the results of some earlier
analysis, or worse, you'll find that you have variables in your dataset but cannot remember how
they were defined, leaving them useless. It is good practice to keep all the files relating to one
dataset in the same folder or set of folders, to name the files systematically, to keep a record of the
file naming system you follow (like anything else, it may appear obvious at the time you create it
but will be easily forgotten), and to ruthlessly discard files that are not important. Always keep a
back-up copy of the original dataset file, and the latest version of that file that you've worked on.
Before closing SPSS, ensure that any new variables you've created are fully labelled, and if necessary described in a journal or log of your work. You can also discard variables that you do not wish
to keep. To do this, in **Variable View** mode in the **Data Editor** window, select the variable (so that
the row it occupies is highlighted) and then go to **Edit→Clear** to delete the variable.

Review the contents of your **Viewer** window and delete anything that you are not certain
you will wish to refer to again. Often you will find it better to export material for later use to
another program such as Word or Excel and delete the entire **Statistics Viewer** file. If you do
decide to retain output in this file, it is best to use the same output file for all your work on
the same dataset. When you next open SPSS, open both the dataset file and the corresponding
output file, and close the new output file that SPSS automatically opens along with the dataset,
without saving it. This avoids creating a plethora of output files in which it is almost impossible
to locate that table or chart you remember that you created one day!

The best way to keep a record of your work, once you have become more proficient at syntax, is in the **Syntax Editor** file. If you use the same syntax file for all your work on a dataset, it
builds up into a comprehensive journal of everything you've done. Until you find you are using
syntax for most work, you will need to keep a separate log or journal of your work, including
a list of the key things you have done and any details that you will need for future reference.

Good housekeeping is no more enthralling with SPSS than it is in real life. But just as living
with a grungy bathroom, a chaotic kitchen or overflowing waste bin is a pain, so too is wading
through a mess of files, vainly trying to work out what was in each one. A little time invested at
the end of each SPSS session really does save much more time and effort down the line.

what you have learned

That completes our introduction to SPSS. If you review this chapter you'll see that we've covered
a lot of ground. While some of the sequences of menu commands and dialog boxes may have
appeared confusing at first, you will be surprised at how quickly they will come to seem straightforward as you gain a little practice. The best way to master SPSS is through practice, and a good

(Continued)

(Continued)

way to practise is to try different things out as you explore different variables. Don't worry if the procedures you try don't work out in quite the way you expect at first, and remember that if you inadvertently destroy or damage your data, you can always go back to your back-up copy or download a new copy from the companion website. ✎ You will also find a video screen animation there to guide you through all the procedures we have covered in this chapter. You have learned:

- How to use the three **Data Editor**, **Viewer** and **Syntax Editor** windows in SPSS, and to travel between them
- How to download and open a dataset
- How to issue commands using the GUI and dialog boxes or using syntax
- How to customise the appearance of SPSS and its dialog boxes
- What missing values for a variable are and how to deal with them
- How to weight a dataset for analysis and understanding how to use them
- How to produce frequency and contingency tables (crosstabs)
- How to produce summary descriptive statistics
- How to understand standard errors, confidence intervals, significance tests and null hypothesis testing
- How to understand measures of association and correlation coefficients
- How to produce graphical output including bar charts, histograms and boxplots
- How to edit graphical output in SPSS or by exporting to another program
- How to create new variables by recoding existing variables, and label them appropriately
- How to transform string variables into numerical variables
- How to select groups of cases to examine by subsetting
- How to export output to other programs such as Excel
- How to keep a log of your work, and housekeep your data, so that you can identify and retrieve it later

---

▬▬▬▬▬▬ exercises using the ESS6 practice dataset ▬▬▬▬▬▬

1 Which countries have the (a) highest and (b) lowest proportion of their adult populations born in other countries?

2 Across all countries, what proportion of those not born in the country in which they are living are women? (Hint: use the correct weight variable!)

3 Across all countries, is the employment rate for those born in the country higher or lower than those not born there?

4 What is the average age of those not born in the country they live in, compared to those born there?

5 Are those born in the country or those not born in the country more likely to belong to a religious denomination?

6 In which countries do people report the highest and lowest level of trust in political parties?

7 What seems to have more impact on trust in political parties: age, gender or religion?

8 What proportion of men and women have married by the time they are 30 years old across all the countries in the survey?

9 In which country is the proportion of people who say they never watch television the highest?

10 Produce a chart of the mean size of households across the countries in the survey, ranking average household size from the smallest to the largest.

✎ Answers, and explanations of how to arrive at these results, are available on the companion website.

APPENDIX: A QUICK REFRESHER ON POWERS AND LOGARITHMS

If you are unsure about logs the best introduction to them is a short film *Powers of Ten*, available at https://www.youtube.com/watch?v=0fKBhvDjuy0.

In the film a camera records the view as it travels away from the earth, each time multiplying the distance away by a factor of 10. Thus it starts a metre away, then 10 metres, 100 metres, one kilometre, 10 kilometres, 100 kilometres ... and so on. By only the twenty fourth move the camera is billions of light years distant and the entire milky way is an invisible speck. If we use a simple arithmetic scale to measure this distance the numbers get unmanageably large very rapidly. However if we use a multiplicative scale, where each unit is a *multiplier of* the previous one, rather than an *addition to* it, the numbers can easily express the scale involved. We use **powers** to make the notation even more succinct. Thus, for example, instead of saying the camera is 1,000,000 metres away we express this number as the number of times 10 has to be successively multiplied to reach it: 10^6 (pronounced '10 to the power 6') is just 10*10*10*10*10*10. This is the same as the number of zero digits after the '1', or the number of steps the camera has taken.

Powers are a shorthand way of expressing how many times a **base** number is multiplied by itself, and are written either as a superscript to the number or after a caret (^) or two asterisks (**).

e.g. $2^3 = 2\text{^}3 = 2**3 = 2*2*2 = 8$

e.g. $10^5 = 10\text{^}5 = 10**5 = 10*10*10*10*10 = 100,000$

To avoid confusion, we call the number that is multiplied by itself the **base**, and the number of times it is multiplied by itself as the **power**, sometimes also called the **exponent** or **index**.

E.g. $2*2*2*2*2 = 2^5 = 2\text{^}5 = 2**5 = 32$

Here the **base** is 2 and the **power** is 5.

E.g. $10*10*10*10 = 10^4 = 10\text{^}4 = 10**4 = 10,000$

Here the **base** is 10 and the **power** is 5.

Arithmetic rules of powers

If two numbers expressed as powers *to the same base* are multiplied, this can be done by adding the respective powers.

E.g. $10^3*10^2 = 10^5$ [because (10*10*10)*(10*10) = 10*10*10*10*10]

E.g. $2^3*2^2 = 2^5$ [(2*2*2)*(2*2)= 8*4 = 32]

Thus we have the general rule: $a^m * a^n = a^{(m+n)}$

Similarly, if two numbers expressed as powers to the same base are divided, this can be done by *subtracting* the respective powers.

E.g. $10^3/10^2 = 10^1$ [because $(10*10*10)/(10*10) = 10$]

E.g. $2^3/2^2 = 2^1$ [$(2*2*2)/(2*2)= 8/4 = 2$]

Thus we have the general rule: $a^m / a^n = a^{(m-n)}$

From this it also must follow that:

Any base number to the power 0 is equal to 1: $10^0 = 1$

Any base number to the power 1 is just the base number itself: $10^1 = 10$

Powers can be negative

Here they express the **reciprocal** (that number by which the original number must be multiplied to obtain 1). The rules of addition/subtraction still apply (indeed we arrive at the meaning of negative powers from the rules of addition and subtraction outlined above).

E.g. $2^{-2} = 1/2^2 = \frac{1}{4}$

E.g. $2^3*2^{-2} = 2^1$ [$(2*2*2)*(1/4)= 8*1/4 = 2$]

Thus we have the general rules: $a^{-m} = 1/a^m$ and $1/a^{-m} = a^m$ and $1/a = a^{-1}$

Powers need not be whole numbers

From the symmetry of multiplication and division, and from the addition rule it must also follow that

$a^{n/m} = (a^{1/m})^n = (a^n)^{1/m}$

Therefore

This follows from the addition rule

$9^{1/2} *9^{1/2} = 9^1 = 9$

$9^{1/2} =$ the square root of $9 = 3$ (the number multiplied by itself that equals 9)

Therefore the **nth root** of a number x is a number a which, when raised to the power of n, equals x.

E.g. $16^{1/2} = 4$ the 2nd (square) root of 16 [because $4^2 = 4*4 =16$]

E.g. $16^{1/4} = 2$ the 4th root of 16 [because $2^4 = 2*2*2*2 =16$]

Logarithms

The logarithm of a number to a **base** is the **power** to which that base must be raised to express the original number. For example the log of 1,000 to base 10 is 3, since $10^3 = 10*10*10 = 1,000$. The log of 10,000,000 to base 10 is 7, because $10^7 = 10,000,000$. The log to base 10 of 10,000 is 4, because $10^4 = 10,000$. The base is usually written as a subscript so that we would write:

$$\log_{10}(1000) = 3$$

To re-express a log as the original number we take the *exponent* of the log. Since the log is the power to which the base has been raised to express the original number, the exponent of a log is given by raising the base to that power.

$$\exp_{10}(3) = 10^3 = 1,000$$

Logs are often useful because they represent relations of multiplication by addition. Thus adding the logs of two numbers gives the same result as multiplying the original numbers. For example:

$$\log_{10}(1,000) + \log_{10}(10,000) = 3 + 4 = 7$$

$$\exp_{10}(7) = 10^7 = 10,000,000 = 1,000 \times 10,000$$

This is why, as you may have noticed, the log to base 10 of the numbers we have used equals the number of zeros after the one, since our counting system also uses a base of ten. We often use logarithmic transformations when describing processes that are multiplicative rather than additive in nature, or where we have a distribution that is heavily skewed.

In practice, rather than use logs to base 10, we use *natural* logarithms which are to base e (= approximately 2.718). e is a number with various very desirable mathematical properties.

The feature that interests us here is that e is extremely useful for describing processes of growth or decay that are exponential in form. Imagine a process in which the value of something doubles in each time period:

Period	0	1	2	3	4	5	6	7	8
Value	1	2	4	8	16	32	64	128	256

We could express the value as a function of the time period by raising the number 2 to a power equal to the number of the period. For example $16 = 2^4$. However, a little reflection will show that the 2 we are using as a base here comprises *two* numbers: the original value (1) and the amount of growth (100% = 1). We could turn this into a general formula for the rise in any value subject to a constant process of growth over discrete periods of time:

$$\text{Growth} = (1 + \text{rate of growth})^{\text{period}}$$

However growth may not happen in this way. The key word in our definition was *discrete*, so that growth is imagined to occur in a finite series of distinct steps. An analogy would be a bank account in which interest was applied on the amount in the account at the end of each year. If you had such an account, deposited $100 and left it there, and the interest rate was 100% you would have $200 at the start of year 2, $400 at the start of year 3 and so on. However if the interest was applied more frequently (every month, or every day, or every second, or fraction of a second) growth would be larger, since interest would start to accrue earlier on both the principal and the interest gained so far. However there would be a limit to this process, which equates to the concept of growth being *continuous*. Using calculus we can calculate this limit and it turns out to equal the value of *e*.

The logit

The logit is the natural log of odds (i.e log to base *e* of odds). As we have seen, odds can take a value between 0 and infinity, with the value 1 representing a probability of 0.5, values less than one representing lower probabilities and values greater than one representing higher probabilities. The natural logarithm of odds will take a negative value when the odds are less than one (that is probabilities less than 0.5) and a positive value when the odds are over one (that is probabilities more than 0.5). The logit of odds of one (equally likely outcomes) will be zero.

DEALING WITH DATA
DOCUMENTATION

■ introduction ■

The documentation that accompanies datasets is often intimidating, if for no other reason than it often runs to hundreds or thousands of pages. However, if you know what are the key things to look for, it soon becomes easier to find your way around it. You will learn how to:

- Find the key information you need in data documentation
- Ask twelve questions about any dataset
- Understand the difference between cross sectional and longitudinal data
- Use the **count** command to combine data from several variables
- Standardise variables using the **descriptives** command
- Download a data extract from the US General Social Survey
- Produce a codebook you can refer to for your work

5 ● 1 WHAT IS DATA DOCUMENTATION?

There are two essential components of any secondary data. One is, of course, the data itself – the information collected by the survey. However, just as important is the second component, the data *documentation*, which contains such information as how the survey was organised, what the target population was, when fieldwork was undertaken, what the sampling frame was and what kind of sampling was done, whether the survey comprised different modules and whether they were used with only a subset of respondents, and whether the survey was one of a series of repeated inquiries.

The documentation will usually include the *survey instrument* – the questionnaire used to conduct the survey – along with how different responses were coded, the question routing, any *showcards* used, and how *missing values* have been defined and applied. Many surveys include a bewildering number of variables, so that the documentation may contain a *data dictionary* that allows you to quickly find the specific variables that you are interested in. We need all this information in order to make sense of the data in the dataset and use it properly.

Data documentation can be voluminous. For example, the codebook for the US General Social Survey is over 3,000 pages long, while the data documentation for the UK Labour Force Survey runs no less than 11 volumes. It would be tedious and unnecessary to read all of it, so it is essential to know what to look for, so that you can find the information you need to conduct the kind of analysis you intend to carry out.

5 ● 2 TWELVE QUESTIONS TO ASK ABOUT DATA

There are usually 12 pieces of key information that you'll be looking for when you browse data documentation. Finding them gives you the background information you will need to make good use of survey data.

1 *When was the survey fieldwork carried out?*

Clearly you need to know what time period your data relates to. It would be unwise to use data from a survey conducted many years ago to provide evidence about current social institutions or attitudes. However, there will also be occasions when the timing of the survey within a year is relevant to your analysis: some attitudes or behaviour may be seasonal (e.g. unemployment may be higher in winter months); or the timing of a particular event, such as a major change in the law, an election result or high-profile media story might influence how respondents answer questions.

2 *Is the survey one of a repeated series?*

Most major social surveys are repeated at regular intervals, such as every 2 years. This makes comparison of trends over time possible, but you must be careful to check for consistency in the target population and the way the data has been collected. As societies change and evolve over time, so too do surveys.

3 *Is there a panel element to the survey?*

Most surveys are *cross-sectional*: they sample a target population at a particular point in time. If the survey is repeated it draws on a new sample from the target population (and that population will also have changed as it loses some members who may die, migrate or drop out because they are no longer included in the definition, or acquires new members as they migrate into the survey area, are born or reach adulthood). The respondents to each round of the survey are different. However, some repeated surveys have a *panel* element. Successive rounds of the survey return to some or all of the original respondents so that they are interviewed in more than one round of the survey. This makes it possible to directly observe changes over time, which is especially useful when looking for evidence of causal processes. Some surveys are *longitudinal* rather than cross-sectional. In this case the survey returns to the same sample of respondents at regular intervals.

4 *What was the target population?*

The *target population* is the group of people, organisations or institutions that the survey sets out to collect information about. Most general social surveys aim to sample from the adult population of one or more countries. Sometimes special arrangements may be made to sample children or young people. However, 'adult population' is a rather vague concept, so it is important to understand what *sample frame* was used. Countries rarely have an up-to-date list of their population with names, ages, addresses and contact details. Even if they did, obvious ethical, privacy and confidentiality concerns would preclude releasing it to researchers. Often sampling frames are based on lists of addresses at which private households are located. However, there will often be more than one household at each address, or none at all, and households will contain different numbers of adults or comprise more than one family. Some people live at more than one address, having a holiday home or commuting to a work address during the week. Some adults will be in collective institutions rather than private households: elderly care or nursing homes, hospitals, prisons, hotels and so on. Students might live some of the year in halls of residence and at other times at their parental home. Social survey organisations in various countries have different ways of translating the information they are able to obtain about households into a reasonable sampling frame for adults, but the details of how they do this will vary, often with important implications for the coverage of students or of older adults who may be less likely to live in private households. If your study includes such groups, or it is comparing different countries, it is important to consider how adequate the target population is for your analysis.

5 *What was the sampling method and weighting strategy?*

Making inferences about a target population from a sample depends upon that sample being *random*: members of the population must have a known probability of selection into the sample. In a simple random sample each target population member has the same probability of selection. Most surveys use more complex sample designs. This can mean that more than one weight has been recorded for each respondent, depending on the target population that an analysis wants to make statements about.

6 *What was the response rate?*

The response rate is the proportion of people contacted by the survey researchers who participate in the survey. In an imaginary world, everyone approached might participate in a survey. In the real world this never happens. Sample frame information will have inaccuracies, so that some potential respondents are impossible to locate. Some respondents will be away, ill, too busy or simply disinclined to participate. In recent years some less than scrupulous marketing disguises itself as 'research', lowering public confidence in genuine research, as it may be difficult for people to distinguish a marketing ploy from a genuine inquiry. Response rates for most surveys have been declining, prompting researchers to find new ways to encourage participation to counteract this trend. Non-participation matters, because we cannot assume that the characteristics of non-responders are the same as those who do take part. Some surveys are able to estimate and account for some of the impact of non-response by oversampling types of respondent who are under-represented or least likely to respond. As a rough rule of thumb, a response rate below 60% may be a cause for concern. However, less important than the crude response rate is whether those who do respond are similar to those who do not. Some recent research has suggested that in some situations even very low response rates nevertheless produce samples that are sufficiently representative for robust research. It may be that the often costly effort required to increase the response rate by a couple of percentage points – for example, by repeated calls to hard-to-reach households – brings rapidly diminishing returns and low-quality responses with missing information or a surfeit of 'don't know' responses.

7 *Who answered the questions?*

To maintain response rates surveys sometimes permit 'proxy' responses. One member of a household may answer questions for another absent or unavailable member, for example. This often makes good sense, but sometimes judgement is needed about the value of this information. While it may be highly accurate for factual questions, it may be far less useful for questions about identity, attitudes or beliefs.

8 *Does the survey contain modules administered only to subsets of respondents?*

Any survey is a compromise between collecting all the data researchers would like, keeping the interview brief enough to maintain the goodwill and cooperation of the respondent and keeping the considerable costs of fieldwork down. Often a good way to manage these conflicting goals is to break the survey down into component modules with only a subset of respondents completing each module. This allows a single survey to cover a larger range of topics, but with smaller numbers of respondents asked about each one, to keep the overall length of the interview reasonable.

9 *What data did the survey collect?*

A survey may cover the subject you wish to investigate, but that is no guarantee that it collects the particular data you require, or that it does so on the type of respondent you need. To determine this you need to examine the variables in the dataset and the survey instrument that was used to construct them. However, keep in mind that most surveys have been developed with more resources and expertise than is usually available to an individual researcher. Their questionnaires will likely have been developed by teams of researchers with expertise in each topic; they will usually have been refined over time by cognitive interviewing or methodological experiments (the box opposite describes the development the sexual identity question for ONS surveys); they may be worded to facilitate comparisons with other surveys from different periods or countries; other researchers will have used the data, so that there will be research findings and literature that can be referred to. Especially in long-running surveys, you can usually assume that the quality of research instrument is high.

10 *What use have others made of the data?*

Most surveys require users to deposit copies of publications or other outputs, so that other researchers have ready access to them. This is a good way of discovering any methodological issues with the data: have other researchers encountered problems with it, or developed useful ways of working with it? It is also a good way of checking what analyses have been done with the data so far. You may find references that escaped your literature review; you may even find that others have already done what you propose to do!

11 *How can I access the data? Can I review it online without downloading?*

Most data can be downloaded over the internet, usually subject to registering and agreeing to any conditions for its use. You should make a careful note of these conditions and ensure that you abide by them. You have an ethical responsibility towards other researchers to do this. If data were to be misused or access conditions flouted, then data producers might well restrict access in the future, or public confidence in social research can be undermined, adversely affecting response rates.

Often you can review the data before downloading it using online tools such as Nesstar (see Chapter 3). While Nesstar is useful for a quick look at the data to ensure that it contains the kind of information you need, it is usually easier to manage and analyse data using a statistical software package such as IBM SPSS Statistics software: it has more flexibility and capacity, and most important of all, allows you to keep a detailed record of your work, and repeat similar analyses or procedures with much less effort.

12 *How do I cite the data I use?*

You should cite a dataset in the same way that you cite other bibliographic sources such as journal articles or monographs. Usually the data documentation gives you a preferred format for doing this. It also lets you know what obligations you agree to when you download the data. Usually this comprises a commitment not to use or publish any information that could disclose the identity of survey respondents (normally this should not be possible if the data have been properly anonymised) and to provide copies or references to any work that you publish using the data.

■ a question of sexual identity ■

One illuminating example of the difficulty of developing valid survey instruments comes from the recent work of the Office for National Statistics (ONS) to produce a question on sexual identity for use in government surveys. In order to produce evidence for use in equality legislation, where discrimination on grounds of sexual orientation can be unlawful, it was desirable to estimate how many people in the population identified as lesbian, gay or bisexual (LGB). However, ONS decided to ask questions about **sexual identity** rather that **sexual orientation**.

> This is because sexual orientation is an umbrella term that covers sexual behaviour, sexual attraction and sexual identity. During the development work, it became evident that in order to collect data on sexual orientation, we would need to develop a suite of questions. Such a suite would not only add to the cost of surveys but also increase the burden on survey participants. Sexual identity was identified as the one component of sexual orientation for which data would be robust enough to support the legislation. (Haseldon and Joloza, 2009: 3)

(Continued)

(Continued)

You can find background information on the development of the survey question here:

🔧 http://www.ons.gov.uk/about-statistics/measuring-equality/equality/sexual-identity-project/index.html

And on the question development here:

🔧 http://www.ons.gov.uk/about-statistics/measuring-equality/equality/sexual-identity-project/quest-dev/index.html

And question design and implementation here:

🔧 http://www.ons.gov.uk/about-statistics/measuring-equality/equality/sexual-identity-project/quest-test-and-implem/index.html

The team developing the question had to ensure that survey respondents understood the question, in the specific sense of having the *same* understanding of the categories involved as those undertaking analysis and reporting on any survey that used it. They also had to ensure that the question did not use language that respondents might not understand, pose questions which they would be unwilling to answer or feel uncomfortable doing so, and which interviewers could use without problems either in face-to-face interviews (using showcards) or telephone interviews where interviewers read out options for respondents to choose. This might be thought to be relatively straightforward, but it was not. For example, early cognitive testing (a process in which interviewers probe respondents to discover why they gave the answers they did to each question after administering a questionnaire) showed that a small but significant proportion of respondents confused the meaning of the terms *bisexual* and *heterosexual*, so that respondents who saw themselves as the latter nevertheless described themselves as the former! The final form of the question was as follows:

Box 3 Face to Face question (CAPI)

ASK ALL AGED 16 OR OVER

[NAME] SHOWCARD 1, [NAME] SHOWCARD 2, [NAME] SHOWCARD 3 etc

Which of the options on this card best describe how you think of yourself?

Please just read out the number next to the description.

27. Heterosexual/ Straight

21. Gay/ Lesbian

24. Bisexual

29. Other

(Spontaneous DK/ Refusal)

Results from the first couple of years of the use of the question found that around 2% of adults in the UK defined their identity as gay, lesbian or bisexual.

However, this has not been universally accepted as a definitive measurement, especially as it is significantly lower than the proportion of the population previously thought to identify as such. Spokespeople for LGB organisations have argued that in a 'straight' society respondents may not feel confident enough to answer the question truthfully. However, others have argued that the evidence and measurements used in the past to produce higher estimates were far less robust methodologically. The efforts of the ONS show how much care often has to be taken to produce even a relatively simple measurement.

5 3 THE EUROPEAN SOCIAL SURVEY

The European Social Survey (ESS), which started in 2001, is an excellent resource for developing your secondary data analysis skills. It was established by the late Sir Roger Jowell, a pioneer of social survey research in the UK, and is run by social scientists so that questions relate to issues that directly concern the social sciences, rather than being driven by other considerations, such as government departments' needs for data. The data documentation is clear, comprehensive and relatively easy to access and understand. The data is freely available for non-commercial use to anyone who registers by supplying their email contact address. So far there have been seven rounds of the survey and 36 countries have taken part, although not every country takes part every year. The survey is led by a coordinating team that develops a strict specification for the organisation of the survey, including sampling and fieldwork, interviewer training and question translation, to maximise comparability across countries. It has a high target response rate of 70%. Moreover, most of the documentation produced in the development of the survey (such as the translation history for different language versions of a question) is available on the website, so that an answer to even the most detailed methodology query can usually be found.

 http://www.europeansocialsurvey.org/

Start by going to the ESS website and look for the answers to our 12 questions. If you look at the bottom of the ESS homepage you will see a list of hyperlinks in grey text that take you to all the relevant documents. Try doing this yourself. If you find it difficult you can refer to the box below to see where you should have found the answers.

▬▬▬ twelve questions to ask about the ESS ▬▬▬

You can usually find each piece of relevant information in more than one place on the ESS website. In the following guide I've suggested some of the main alternatives.

When was the survey carried out?

Every second year from 2002 onwards.

(Continued)

(Continued)

Is the survey one of a repeated series? Is there a panel element to the survey?

Core questions are repeated in every survey; modules on specific topics are also included, with some modules repeated over longer periods of time. This means that it is a repeated cross-sectional design, not a longitudinal or panel study.

http://www.europeansocialsurvey.org/data/round-index.html

What was the target population?

Adults aged 15 and over in private households, regardless of nationality, citizenship or language.

What was the sampling method and weighting strategy?

A minimum sample size of 1,500 for each country with a population over 2 million, 800 for those with smaller populations. Weights are produced to adjust for the sample design, and also the population size of countries.

www.europeansocialsurvey.org/methodology/sampling.html

What was the response rate?

An answer to this question is not so easy to find. There are two places you could locate it. Each round of the survey produces a data documentation report available on the data and documentation download page. This report includes a figure for the response rate for each individual country.

www.europeansocialsurvey.org/docs/round6/survey/ESS6_data_documentation_report_e02_1.pdf

However, there is another source. Under the **Data and Documentation** menu is a **Fieldwork Summary and Deviations** option.

http://www.europeansocialsurvey.org/data/deviations_6.html

Alternatively, under **Data and Documentation by Round/Year** you will find a document called 'ESS6 Quality Report'.

www.europeansocialsurvey.org/docs/round6/methods/ESS6_quality_report.pdf

You can see from any of these documents that although the ESS has a target of a response rate of 70%, this is achieved only by a minority of countries. The average response rate across all countries in the survey has fluctuated between 60% and 65% since the survey was first fielded in 2002.

Who answered the questions?

In the ESS interviews are done face to face. Again this is a core feature of the survey that you have to dig around a little to discover. You can infer it from much of the documentation for the survey (for example, the questionnaire contains showcards: it would be difficult for these to be used in a phone interview) but the only actual confirmation of this is in the rather detailed technical document. This also makes clear that 'proxy' interviews are not permitted, nor can interviewers substitute an alternative respondent for one whom they are unable to contact or who declines to participate: they must count as a non-response.

Does the survey contain modules administered only to subsets of respondents?

No. All respondents get the same questionnaire, which comes in three parts: a core section common to every round of the survey; two modules on specific topics which change in each round but may be 'rotated', that is, they may be repeated in future rounds periodically; and a supplementary section which is used to make methodological checks on the survey.

What data did the survey collect?

You can find this information in many places. Under **Questionnaire** from the **Methodology** menu you can read about the development of the core questionnaire and rotating modules for each round of the survey.

    www.europeansocialsurvey.org/methodology/questionnaire/

What use have others made of the data?

References to many books and journal articles as well as key findings from some topics are at:

    http://www.europeansocialsurvey.org/essresources/findings.html

How can I access the data? Can I review it online without downloading?

You can download the data in various formats via the **Data and Documentation** menu. If you have not already registered, the system will prompt you to do so before you can login and access the data files.

    www.europeansocialsurvey.org/data/

You can also use Nesstar to do simple online analyses of the data. Click on **Online Analysis** under **Data and Documentation** on the homepage to go to

    http://nesstar.ess.nsd.uib.no/webview/

How do I cite the data I use?

    Full guidance is at http://www.europeansocialsurvey.org/data/conditions_of_use.html

---

5 ● 4   THE EUROPEAN SOCIAL SURVEY ROUND 6

In the previous chapter we used a simplified 'practice' dataset based on the ESS. However, we now have enough basic skills to work with the real thing. We'll analyse a set of variables from the *Personal and Social Wellbeing* module to see how learning how to find your way around data documentation is important for almost any secondary data analysis.

Go to the ESS website, register and download the SPSS data file for ESS Round 6. Remember to make a copy as a back up, and place it in a folder with an appropriate name. Open the file in **Variable View** mode in the **Data Editor** window. At first sight the data looks daunting, with just over 620 variables, while if you switch to **Data View** you'll see that there are 54,673 rows of data (with each row corresponding to one respondent), so that we have around 34 million pieces of data. You can use the extensive data documentation that comes with the ESS to guide you through the contents of the dataset.

The best place to start is the *source questionnaire* for that round, which gives you a comprehensive guide to what respondents were asked. You can also use it to check the details of variables that depend on question routing. For example, the variable **vote** records whether respondents voted in the last national election. If they answered that they did, they are then routed to a country-specific question which asks about how they voted and is recorded in the relevant variable from **prtvtal** to **prtvtxk**. If you widen the column for **Label** in **Variable View** mode in your **Data Editor** window you can scroll down through the variables to get a sense of what information has been collected.

In general, the order of the variables in the dataset follows the order in which they are generated by the interview questionnaire. After an 'icebreaker' question about TV watching comes a series of questions about politics; then some general questions about life satisfaction, social networks, religion, and discrimination, including where the respondent and their parents were born; then a series of questions about personal well-being and about democracy which come from two rotating modules; then questions about the composition of the household, the marital status, education and economic activity of the respondent and their partner if they have one, their parents' educational level and occupation if they were working when the respondent was aged 14; and finally, variables based on a supplementary questionnaire that measure the respondent's 'human values'. While some of the variables are straightforward, such as a respondents' gender or year of birth, so that we do not need to know much more about them, others are the result of extensive research and development to produce measures that are known to be valid and reliable. For variables in the rotating modules you can consult the module templates that describe the modules' contents and the research lying behind them in some detail.

5 ● 5 THE CES-D DEPRESSION SCALE

If you read the module template on personal and social wellbeing

⚲ http://www.europeansocialsurvey.org/docs/round6/questionnaire/ESS6_final_personal_and_social_well_being_module_template.pdf

you'll see that the variables from **fltdpr** to **cldgng** can be used to construct a depression inventory scale. From the wording of the questions it can be seen that higher scores on each item represent a greater likelihood of depression, with the exception of **wrhpp** and **enjlf**, where a *lower* score does so. You will often find in similar scales that the 'direction' of scoring is reversed in this way to minimise the impact of question wording on responses. In order to create the CES-D 8 depression inventory scale we need to bring these eight variables together. A simple way to do this is to add the scores for all eight variables, after first reversing the scoring used on **wrhpp** and **enjlf**.

However, before we do this we need to take account of missing values. Not every respondent will have given a definite answer to all eight questions. We can examine this by producing frequency tables for each of the variables. When checking through data before using it for analysis it is best to work with raw, unweighted data. Use syntax to run these frequencies, first giving your syntax file an appropriate name and saving it to a folder where you can keep your work on ESS6 together.

FREQ fltdpr to cldgng.

From these tables you'll see that the rate of refusal to answer is very low: between about 0.5% and 1.5% of respondents answer 'don't know' to each question. However, there is one exception to this. On the last variable in the series, **cldgng**, there are 1,201 system-missing responses: a curiously high number worth investigating further. It looks as if an entire group of respondents have returned this response for some reason. A quick way to check this is to examine the raw data. We can use the **Sort Cases** command to do this. From the GUI you can go to **Data→Sort Cases** and enter the variable **cldgng** in the **variable list** box, or use the syntax

SORT CASES BY cldgng(A).

The **(A)** after the variable name tells SPSS to sort the cases in ascending order of the values, which will place system-missing values in the first rows of the dataset. Go to the **Variable View** mode of the **Data Editor** window and locate the variable **cldgng** using the search function. Select the **Name** column by clicking on its title, click the search icon 🔍 and enter the variable name in the search box. Once you've located the variable, clicking on the row number to its left will take you to the corresponding column for that variable in the **Data View** mode of the **Data Editor** window, where you'll see that the cases taking a system-missing value now occupy the first 1,201 rows of the **Data Editor** window. Scroll to the left and you'll see that all these cases are from Albania. Now you can consult the *Data Documentation Report* for ESS6

🔗 http://www.europeansocialsurvey.org/docs/round6/survey/ESS6_data_documentation_report_e02_2.pdf

and on page 13 you'll find an entry that solves the mystery:

ALBANIA: D12 (CLDGNG): No data was collected for this variable due to a CAPI error.

(CAPI stands for 'computer-assisted personal interviewing': a system where an interviewer uses a handheld device rather than a paper questionnaire to ask questions and record answers to them). We now face a choice. If it was important to include Albania in our analysis we would need to think of a way of constructing our variable for depression taking account of the fact that respondents there could not answer this question. However, a simpler course of action for us would be to omit Albania from our analysis.

We created a numeric version of the **cntry** variable – **country** – for our ESS6_Practice dataset in the previous chapter. If you used syntax to create this variable you can copy and paste the syntax you wrote before to do exactly the same job here: one of the advantages of using syntax. Once you have a numeric version of **cntry** you can use it to select all cases that are not from Albania for analysis. You can do this using the select and filter commands from the GUI or using syntax, as we saw in Chapter 4. If using syntax, remember that we need to create a filter variable to do this. If you use the **select if** command in syntax without doing this, SPSS will permanently delete the cases you do not select from the dataset: something we do not want to do! We wish to select all cases where **country ne 1** (the value code of **country** for Albania), so our syntax will be:

```
USE ALL.
COMPUTE filter_$=(country ne 1).
VARIABLE LABELS filter_$ 'country ne 1 (FILTER)'.
VALUE LABELS filter_$ 0 'Not Selected' 1 'Selected'.
FILTER BY filter_$.
```

Now that we've dealt with the Albania issue, we can examine how other missing responses were distributed across respondents rather than across questions. Did most respondents only use this response once or twice, or were there respondents who used this response frequently? This matters as it affects how we treat this missing data. The simplest approach would be to drop any respondent who did not answer all eight questions. However, this could bias our results if it turned out, for example, that respondents who scored higher on the questions they *did* answer were more likely to use the 'don't know' response.

We have a quick and easy way of examining the pattern of don't knows, refusals and non-responses using the **count** command in SPSS. We'll also use this command in Chapters 7 and 8, so it's useful to get a little practice in now. The **count** procedure takes a group of two or more variables and counts the number of times a value or group of values occurs across these variables *within* each case. We can use this function to work out how many of our eight questions each respondent did not know or did not want to give an answer to. Our syntax will be:

```
COUNT missdep = fltdpr to cldgng(7,8,9).
FREQ missdep.
```

This tells SPSS to take our eight variables, count the number of times each of these takes a value between 7 and 9 (corresponding to *don't know*, *refusal* and *no answer*) for each individual case in the dataset and create a variable called **missdep** that stores the results. You should obtain the frequency distribution for **missdep** shown in Figure 5.1.

The vast majority of respondents (51,188) answered all eight questions, but almost 3 per cent did not answer one of the eight: if we can include these respondents in our analysis we need omit only the 794 respondents who failed to answer two or more questions.

To create our variable describing depression we first need to reverse the coding on **wrhpp** and **enjlf**. This is a procedure you'll often use, as questions with result scores running in opposite directions are common in surveys. The way to do this is to subtract the existing scores from a

missdep

		Frequency	Percent	Valid Percent	Cumulative Percent
Valid	.00	51188	95.7	95.7	95.7
	1.00	1490	2.8	2.8	98.5
	2.00	428	.8	.8	99.3
	3.00	150	.3	.3	99.6
	4.00	67	.1	.1	99.7
	5.00	35	.1	.1	99.8
	6.00	15	.0	.0	99.8
	7.00	18	.0	.0	99.8
	8.00	81	.2	.2	100.0
	Total	53472	100.0	100.0	

Figure 5.1 Number of missing values across eight depression variables

number one greater than the value of the highest score. Thus scores for all the variables except **wrhpp** and **enjlf** run from 1 (indicating absence of depression) to 4 (indicating its presence). For **wrhpp** and **enjlf**, in contrast, a score of 1 is associated with its presence and 4 with its absence. If we subtract the values of **wrhpp** or **enjlf** from 5 we will turn the current 4s into new 1s, 3s into 2s and so on. We can create new variables with these results, which we can call **wrhpp2** and **enjlf2**, or any other appropriate name. Our syntax will be as follows. Note that I've given the new variable a label and also labelled its values. This takes little time and creates a record of the changes for future work.

```
COMPUTE enjlf2 = 5-enjlf.
COMPUTE wrhpp2 = 5-wrhpp.
VAR LABELS enjlf2 "enljlf reverse coded".
VAR LABELS wrhpp2 "wrhpp reverse coded"
VAL LABELS enjlf2 wrhpp2 1 "All or almost all of the time" 2 "Most of the time" 3 "Some of the time" 4 "None or almost none of the time".
FREQ enjlf2 wrhpp2.
```

We can now construct our depression variable by adding together the values for our eight variables, using **wrhpp2** and **enjlf2** instead of the original **enjlf** and **wrhpp**. We can ask SPSS to carry this out *only* for those respondents who have answered at least seven of the questions, and set other cases to a missing value for the new variable. For those who have answered all eight questions our new variable will be equal to a score out of a total of $8 \times 4 = 32$ for these questions. For those who have answered only seven, we can make the 'missing' score equal to the mean of the scores on the other seven questions. The subcommand **SUM** can be followed by a full stop and a number which tells SPSS the minimum number of valid values for the variables to be added together that it must find before it carries out the calculation. If SPSS finds fewer real values than this (because the respondent gave *don't know, no answer* or *refusal* as a response) it will set the result of the operation to missing. We can then tell it to increase the value of this variable by 8/7 for those cases with only seven real values, so that their score is what it would have been had they answered their 'missing' question in the same way as the average of the others. We'll call our new variable **depress**, so that our syntax will be:

COMPUTE depress = sum.7(fltdpr, flteeff, slprl, fltlnl, fltsd, cldgng, enjlf2, wrhpp2).
IF (missdep = 1) depress = (8/7)*depress.
FREQ depress.

You'll see from the frequency table that because we took account of respondents who only answered seven questions our new variable takes a mixture of values that are not all whole numbers. We'll get a better sense of its distribution by looking at a histogram. To do this we can use the GUI, or add a subcommand to our syntax:

FREQ depress
/histogram.

Select the histogram produced in the **Viewer** to edit it, then select any of the bars on the histogram to bring up the **Properties** dialog box, and in the menu at the top select **Binning** and **Custom** under **X axis**. This allows you to select the number of 'bins' or intervals into which the values will be organised, or alternatively the width of these intervals in terms of the variable values, to produce the histogram. You can experiment with different numbers of bins or interval widths. I chose an interval width of 2 to produce the histogram in Figure 5.2.

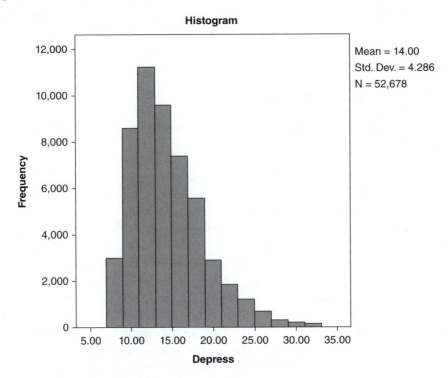

Figure 5.2   The distribution of the CES-D score, Europe (excluding Albania)

Source: European Social Survey, Round 6 (2012), author's calculations.

There is one final change we might make to our **depress** variable to make it more convenient to use. It currently takes a range of values from 8 to 32, with a mean of 14, so that it is
a little clumsy to work with. However, we could *standardise* it so that it takes a mean of 0, a
standard deviation of 1, and values for individual cases become *z-scores* denoting the number of
standard deviations above or below the mean at which the original score lies. The **descriptives**
command reports the mean and standard deviation for interval level variables and can also be
used to produce standardised versions of such variables by adding the subcommand **/save**. SPSS
automatically creates a new variable using the existing name and the prefix **z**. (You can also use
the GUI and check the **Save standardized values as variables** in the dialog for **descriptives**, but
syntax is easier and quicker.)

```
DESC depress
/save.
FREQ zdepress.
```

Now that we've created our new variable we can examine the correlates of depression across
the countries in the survey for various groups. First we must apply the relevant weights, as we
have been working with unweighted data so far. Let's look at the scores for our variable for
men and women across different countries. Since we are comparing individual countries rather
than all countries together, we can use **pspweight** as our weight variable and use the **means**
procedure, using the following syntax:

```
means zdepress by cntry by gndr
/cells = mean stddev count.
```

If you examine the results you can see that women score higher than men on our depression scale for all countries. This is a well-documented finding. However, it is also evident
that, except for Slovenia and Italy, scores are higher in eastern Europe. There are two possible
explanations for this: one is that the incidence of depression is indeed higher there; the other
is that for some reason our measuring instrument produces higher values there for the same
underlying incidence of depression. This could be because of the way the questions have
been translated, or because of cultural differences in the way questions are understood by
respondents.

Now we'll do a brief exercise that reveals the power of using syntax. The same questions were
fielded in Round 3 of the ESS in 2006. Twenty-two countries participated in both years:

Belgium	France	Poland	Sweden
Bulgaria	Germany	Portugal	Switzerland
Cyprus	Hungary	Russian Federation	Ukraine
Denmark	Ireland	Slovakia	United Kingdom
Estonia	Netherlands	Slovenia	
Finland	Norway	Spain	

For these countries we can compare the results for 2006 and 2012 to see if there has been any change, in what is a relatively short period of time. We can create a variable describing these countries to select them. However, we can now use all the syntax that we generated to examine ESS6 to carry out *exactly the same series of data management and analysis procedures* on ESS3 with a couple of mouse clicks! ⚡ The syntax to create the variables to select the set of countries from each dataset, as well as all the other syntax, is on the companion website. Try to compare levels of depression for men and women in these countries for the years 2006 and 2012. What do you conclude? The answer, as usual, can be found on the companion website. In Chapter 8 we'll see how to merge data files such as those for ESS3 and ESS6 to create a common dataset, so that you can analyse data from different rounds of the same survey more easily.

5 ● 6 THE US GENERAL SOCIAL SURVEY

As we saw in Chapter 3, the GSS has been running since 1972 and fielded every 2 years since 1994. It is a repeated cross-sectional survey, which uses a core of questions repeated in each round, together with one-off modules on particular topics which are also sometimes repeated. Over the years the precise design of the survey has changed, but there are cumulative datasets available that make taking account of these changes relatively straightforward. The GSS website has links to data documentation, datasets, publications using GSS data and online tools to explore and conduct simple analyses of the data. Because of the accumulation of data over the years and changes in the survey design, finding your way around the data and its documentation is not always easy, but the website has search tools and a list of FAQs to assist you.

⚡ www.gss.norc.org

Suppose we are interested in attitudes towards gender roles and gender equality, and want to see what the GSS has to offer. The website has no general introduction to and description of the survey and the methods it uses, but we can start to find our way around the wealth of information the website contains by looking at the FAQs which are available just under Quick Links on the main website page or at:

⚡ http://www.gss.norc.org/Pages/Faq.aspx

By skimming the FAQs we can find answers to many of our data documentation questions, as well as where to go in the website for any further information we might need. Since 1994 the GSS has sampled around 3,000 and since 2006 around 4,500 adults. Until 2006 it was a cross-sectional survey, but since 2006 it has shifted to a rolling panel design in which respondents are interviewed for three successive rounds of the survey. In each round about 2,000 new households are recruited and they stay in the panel for a further two rounds. Respondents are asked only a subset of questions or modules, in such a way that variables in different modules can still be correlated across a representative subset of respondents. Its sampling method is based on households, so that if we wish to generalise to adults rather than households we will need to use an appropriate weight. This also means that adults in collective institutions are excluded. Weights also correct for the procedures used to minimise non-response. Interviews for the survey are usually done face-to-face using CAPI and last about 90 minutes on average. The FAQs also direct you to the GSS codebook and questionnaire files for all the GSS surveys.

5.7 DOWNLOADING A DATA EXTRACT FROM THE GSS

It is possible to download the entire cumulative GSS dataset, with results from over 40 years of the study, but with almost 60,000 records and 5,600 variables this is daunting to anyone without significant experience of secondary data analysis. However, GSS also allows you to draw up bespoke download extracts of data covering a small selection of variables, years or respondent types. Go to the GSS home page given above, click on the orange **GSS Data Explorer** tab in the page header which will take you to the GSS Data Explorer that we saw in Chapter 3, and click on the **EXPLORE GSS DATA** tab under **Access and Analyze GSS Data**. This takes you to a **Search Data** page with a **Keyword** search function as shown in Figure 5.3.

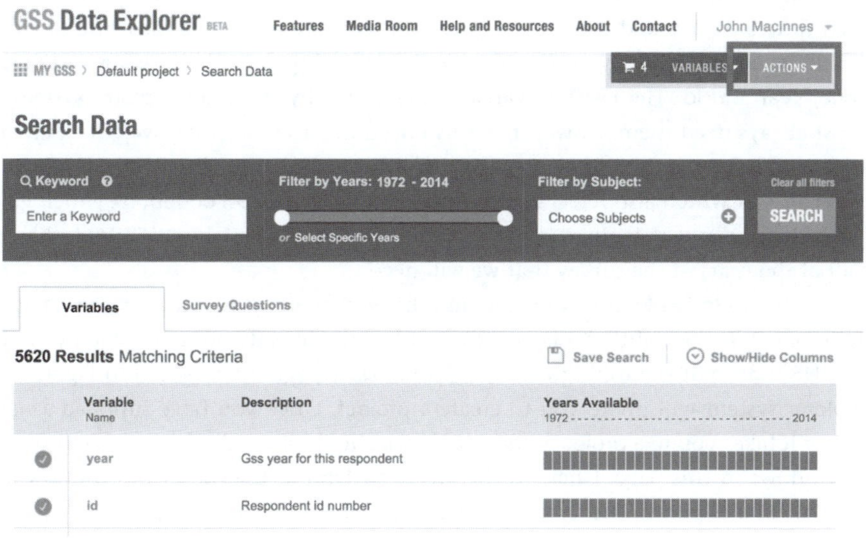

Figure 5.3   The GSS Explorer Search Data page

Enter the word **gender** and click on **SEARCH**. This throws up around 20 variables that might be what we are looking for. Most of these are variables describing the gender of the members of households interviewed in the survey; however, some cover attitudes to gender. Clicking on any variable name (coloured in green at the left-hand side of the window) brings up further information about that variable. For example, **mrmom** is a variable based on a question about gender role reversal in households, fielded in 1994. This is not really what we are looking for, but you'll see that the page with details for this variable also suggests some related variables to explore. Sometimes this feature can be useful, other times less so. On this occasion it doesn't suggest anything very useful. You will often find that using search functions is a hit-and-miss affair, since the tagging of dataset information depends upon the cataloguer and researcher having the same sense of meaning of the terms used – something that is rarely the case. The solution is a little lateral thinking in guessing effective search terms. In this case it turns out that a better search term to use is 'women'. You should find that this returns around 120 variables to explore. Note that the page also records which years the question(s) on which a variable is based were fielded, and frequency distributions for the variable. This is very useful in deciding whether a variable is likely to be relevant to any analysis we have in mind, and also provides a quick check, when we download data to work on it, that we've done so correctly. Explore the variable **wrkbaby** which asks respondents opinions about mothers of preschoolers working outside the home. It looks as if this is an example of where gender attitudes have shifted. In 1988 roughly half of those who expressed an opinion said that the mothers of preschool-age children should stay at home rather than work. By 2012 this proportion had dropped to one-third.

To create a data extract you must first add variables to a 'cart' by clicking on the icon at the top right of the page, as if you were buying something in a shop. If we want to carry out an analysis we'll almost certainly be interested in the age, race, education level and sex of any respondent answering the questions. Locate these variables by using the word *respondent* in the search function, and add them to your cart in the same way. The most useful education variable will be **educ**. By now you should have the following variables in your 'cart': **age**, **sex**, **race**, **educ**, **year** and **id**. The last two variables are added by the **Data Explorer** system as you will almost always need them. However, we also need to check out what weights if any will be required. If you return to the GSS homepage and click the link on the right to **GSS FAQs** you'll find a brief answer which also refers you to Appendix A of the **GSS codebook** which gives further details. It turns out that there is a comprehensive weight variable **WTSSALL** that we can use for all of the years of the survey that we will need.

Return to the **Data Explorer** system and add this variable to your 'cart' (if you have trouble locating it, search for 'weight' as a keyword). If it has not already done so, when you click on the **ACTIONS** button at the top right of the **Search Data** page (highlighted in Figure 5.3), the **Data Explorer** system will invite you to create a **project**. Once you have supplied a name for your project it takes you to a **project page** where you should find all your variables listed. There are five windows in this page. Click on the green ⊕ icon at the top of the window labelled **Extracts** which takes you to the **Create Extract** page where you are asked to give your extract a name (see Figure 5.4). Choose a short one as this name will be the root of the name for the file you will download. Next go to the **Choose variables** pane and click **ADD ALL** at the top of your **VARIABLE CART** highlighted in Figure 5.4 the left side of the pane to place your variables in the **ADD VARIABLES** box to the left, and click **NEXT**. The next screen asks if you want to add a variable describing the case selection. This would allow you to use one or more variables to select subsets of cases for analysis, such as women, or young people and so on. We don't want to do this, so click **NEXT** again which takes you to the **Choose output options** pane. We don't want all years of the data, since our main variable of interest was fielded only in 1988, 1994, 2002 and 2012. Click on **Select certain years** (in green) and check the boxes to the left of the relevant years. Finally, select the SPSS control file option and click **CREATE EXTRACT**. Now is a good time to make a coffee: extracts often take 10–15 minutes to generate. Don't assume there is an error or that the system is hanging: just be patient. The icon to the right of your extract name changes to a download symbol ⬇ when your extract is ready.

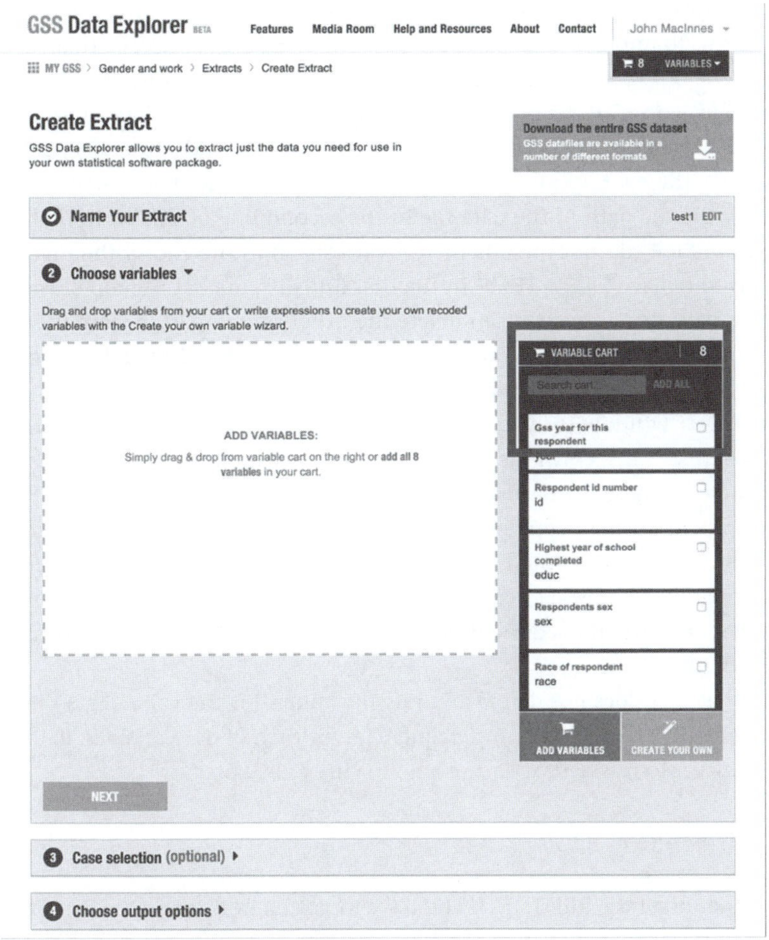

Figure 5.4   The GSS Data Explorer **Create Extract** page

Your extract download comes in a zipped folder. When you unzip it there will be an SPSS syntax file with the suffix **.sps** and a file with the data extract with the suffix **.dat**. Launch SPSS and go to **File→Open→Syntax...** which will open an **Open Syntax** dialog box so that you can select the folder you've just downloaded and open the **.sps** file. This is an SPSS syntax file that describes the data in the **.dat** file to SPSS. The first line of the syntax file will read

DATA LIST FILE=TEMP FIXED RECORDS=1 TABLE /

You need to replace the term **TEMP** with the file path in your computer to the **.dat** file. If you are familiar with computer file path syntax you may be able to do this yourself. I find it usually takes me a few attempts to get it right. However, you can trick SPSS into telling you the file path. Go to **File→Read Text Data...**. This will open the **Open Data** dialog box. At the bottom of the dialog is a menu labelled **Files of type** where you should select **Text (*.txt, *.dat,**

*.csv, *.tab). Navigate to, select and open your **.dat** file. This will open the **Text Import Wizard**. We could use this to import the data, but it is easier to use the syntax file that GSS has created to do this, so the only piece of information we want from the Wizard is the correct file path to our data. Thus ignore all the options in the wizard and click **Continue** at each stage till you reach **Step 6 of 6**. Here click on the **Yes** radio button under **Would you like to paste the syntax?** SPSS then pastes the syntax into the bottom of the syntax file that you already have open. This will show the file path to the data file in the second line of this section of syntax. Copy everything from **FILE** (do not include the forward slash) to the end of the inverted commas, and paste this to replace **FILE = TEMP** in the first line of syntax at the top of the same syntax file. Once you have done this you can delete the other syntax pasted from the **Get Data** procedure. Then run all the syntax from **DATA LIST** down to the **EXECUTE** command (include the full stop which ends the list of commands). The syntax will create an SPSS data file and open a **Data Editor** window for you to view it. **Save** this file, giving it an appropriate name. It is easy to overlook this, continue to edit and change the file, and then when SPSS or your operating system crashes, as they do from time to time, you've lost your work! Save regularly! Your next step is to create a copy of this file. This is insurance against anything happening to the file your work is on. Should it be damaged (it is surprisingly easy to delete some vital piece of information by mistake) you can re-create your file from this back-up. ✎ If you find the above series of instructions difficult to follow, remember that you can consult the relevant video on the book website.

You'll see that GSS does not define any missing values for the variables, so this is our next task. We can identify them by running frequencies for each of our variables. Rather than using the GUI, its quicker to use syntax. Create a new syntax file, enter

```
FREQ age to wrkbaby.
```

and run it (don't forget the full stop). If you have forgotten how to use the **Syntax Editor**, revise the relevant part of Chapter 4. From the frequency tables we can define the following values as missing: **age**, 99; **educ**, 98, 99; **wrkbaby**, 0, 9. You can use the missing-values cells in the **Variable View** of the **Data Editor** window to define these values as missing, but again syntax is quicker and, more importantly, keeps a record of your work. This is the syntax to define these values as missing for these variables:

```
MISSING VALUES age ( 99) educ (98 99) wrkbaby (0 9).
```

Note that we need only write the variable name and then the missing values in round brackets separated by a space or comma. You can also specify value ranges by using the term **thru** as in **(0, 97 thru 99)**.

Next we need to apply the weight variable to our data. Again let's use syntax:

```
WEIGHT by wtssall.
```

Now we can run a three-way crosstab to look at the relationship between **sex** and **wrkbaby** by **year**. Again, instead of the GUI, we can use syntax to do this:

```
CROSSTABS wrkbaby BY sex BY year
/CELLS=COUNT COLUMN
/COUNT ROUND CELL.
```

Note that the main command tells SPSS the variables to put in the rows, columns and layers of the table in that order. The **/CELLS** sub-command tells SPSS what to put in each cell (the observed count of cases and this count standardised as a column percentage), and the **/COUNT** sub-command tells SPSS to round these counts to whole numbers (since weights may produce counts which are not integers). Remember that you can always produce SPSS syntax by building commands in the GUI, then pasting the syntax and running it from the **Syntax Editor**. It is good practice to get into the habit of doing this. Syntax files build up into a useful journal of your work without your having to record anything!

You should find that the main shift in attitudes seems to have come in the second half of the 1990s, and has continued since then, accompanied by a large increase in the number of respondents who say they 'cannot choose' the answer to the question. Throughout women are less likely than men to argue that preschooler mothers should stay at home. If you examine the influence of race you should find that across all periods blacks are more likely to favour women working, but the numbers of black and other races in the sample are small, so we have to treat these results with some caution. What about the impact of age? We can examine this by looking at the mean age of respondents who choose different answers. Try this syntax:

```
MEANS TABLES=age BY year BY sex BY wrkbaby
/CELLS=MEAN STDDEV.
```

You should find that in all years, and for both men and women, respondents who think that mothers of preschoolers should not work are older. You can also explore the impact of education this way.

You can use the data documentation supplied online with the GSS to check the original questions wording from the relevant survey years, as well as the way in which variables such as sex, education and race were defined.

5 ● 8 MAKING A CODEBOOK FOR YOUR WORK

As you will have realised by now, the full data documentation that accompanies most surveys is extensive. As such you can spend a lot of time locating the precise piece of information you need. If you are going to do more than occasional work with a survey, it can be useful to create a codebook for the variables you use, cutting and pasting the most important relevant information from the data documentation. For each variable you are going to use it is helpful to have a note of the values it takes and their labels, including missing values and an unweighted frequency table of the distribution of the variable across all cases for categorical variables, or summary descriptive statistics for interval-level ones. You will find that the convenience of having such a resource to quickly refer to more than makes up for the time invested in preparing it. You can also use it to make notes about questions in the survey instrument, or other useful details about the dataset that you need to refer to in your work.

what you have learned

- What information you need to glean from data documentation and how to find it
- How to extract specific variables from an online dataset and use them to produce an SPSS data file
- How to create a codebook for your work
- How to download and edit a complete dataset
- How to use data documentation to check the coding of variables and search relevant literature for an analysis
- How to use the **compute, count, descriptives, filter, if, means, sum** and **weight** procedures in SPSS
- How to create and edit a histogram
- How to create a standardised variable

exercises

1 Make a codebook for ESS3 and ESS6 containing the following variables: **essround, cntry, ppltrst, pplfair, pplhlp, stflife, happy, sclmeet, sclact, health, rlgblg, rlgdgr, fltdpr, flteeff, slprl, wrhpp, fltlnl, enjlf, fltsd, cldgng gndr, agea, yrbrn, domicil, eisced, mnactic, dweight, pspwght, pweight**.

2 Use the **means** procedure to produce data that you can use to produce a chart of the incidence of depression by age.

3 Use the variables **ppltrst, pplfair** and **pplhlp** to create a variable that describes how much the respondent thinks other people can be trusted. Is there an association between this variable and the depression score for respondents? Do you find any association in both 2006 and 2012?

4 Is there an association between the economic activity (use **mnactic**) of adults and their risk of depression? What might the causal direction(s) in any such association be?

5 'Money can't buy you love'. Were people happier in 2006 or 2012? Ensure that you select only countries surveyed in both years to give your answer. List at least two reasons why your answer could be criticised.

6 How does race affect US adults' attitudes towards mothers of preschool children working?

7 How do the attitudes of women who themselves worked as mothers of preschool children compare to others?

8 What (if anything) limits our ability to answer question 7 from our data extract?

9 How does the number of years of school completed affect gender role attitudes?

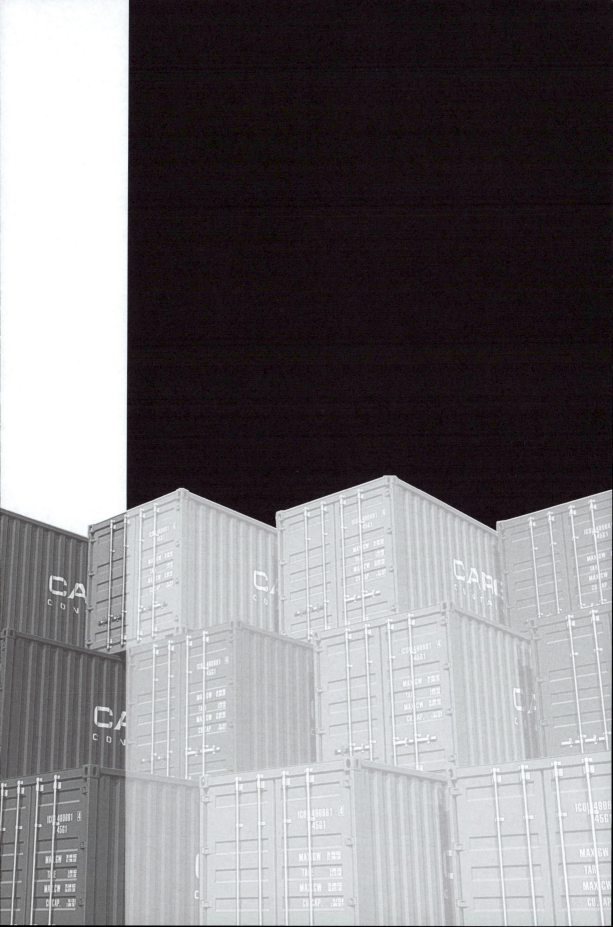

REPLICATING PUBLISHED ANALYSES

introduction

We set out to replicate the data analyses made in two recent articles. Replicating the analyses reported in journal articles and elsewhere using the same original data is not only an excellent way to develop your data analysis skills, but also gives you a much better understanding of the published work than even the closest reading. As well as replication studies with the same data, doing so with a different dataset is even more valuable, since such replication may be a much stronger evidence of any result than statistical significance.

- It is not unusual to find it difficult to replicate work exactly: datasets may be revised as errors are discovered, and unfortunately journals rarely insist that authors supply enough information on their data analysis procedures to make perfect replication possible
- Working out how authors have defined their variables, how they have dealt with missing values, which weights they have used and which cases they have selected my require some detective work
- Replicating others' work is an excellent way to practice new skills
- Replication often uncovers small errors, but sometimes it brings more serious ones to light. It ought to be a far more widespread practice

6 1 REPLICATION

Replication is fundamental to scientific work. Because our thinking can be influenced by all kinds of conscious and unconscious biases, findings only become well established when more than one scientist or team of scientists has independently produced the same results. The greater the consistency of these results across the use of different methods, the more robust the findings. In secondary data analysis, the most elementary stage of such replication is to take the same dataset that others have used, carry out exactly the same analysis, in so far as this can be determined from the information they publish, and check that the same results are obtained.

Replicating published work in this way is not only a good way to develop your data analysis skills, but also gives you a much deeper insight into a research paper than you gain from simply reading it, since it takes you through the many analytic choices faced by the researchers that are seldom discussed fully when results are published. Undertaking such replication work often makes it clear that many other interpretations might have been made of the data and different conclusions drawn. You may well find, after doing such replication work, that you come to regard many of the findings reported in published work as being rather less conclusive than they appear to be. Occasionally, too, you will unearth errors. Researchers are human beings and make mistakes. Often these are inconsequential, but occasionally you may find errors that undermine the substantive conclusions drawn.

In principle it should always be possible to replicate the results in a published paper exactly, but this is not always the case in practice. Partly because of constraints on space, authors do not always give sufficiently precise and comprehensive information to enable an exact replication. This is unfortunate since such replication is the most basic critical check on the conclusions reached in any scientific work. Fortunately, electronic versions of journals now frequently include supplementary material that facilitates this. The other barrier to exact replication is that datasets typically evolve over time, either as those curating them add or refine information in them or correct errors that have been discovered by researchers. Thus it often happens that we replicate an analysis using a dataset that has some differences from the one the original authors worked with.

6.2 BRITISHNESS, ETHNICITY AND RELIGION

Karlsen and Nazroo (2015: 773) use the 2008/9 UK Home Office Citizenship Survey (HOCS) to explore 'whether there are variations in levels of "Britishness" and perceptions of the compatibility between Britishness and other cultural/religious identities among different minoritized groups in England and Wales'. The survey has a large sample size with a minority ethnic boost of around 4,000 respondents that facilitates the analysis of distinct ethnic and religious groups that would otherwise produce too small a number of respondents to be analysed separately. This means, however, that we have to pay attention to the weights used when analysing the results, to take account of the differential probabilities of selection of different kinds of respondent.

Table 1 of the article (Karlsen and Nazroo, 2015: 767–8) presents descriptive statistics for the main variables that they use. Take a little time to study the table. You should see that although it might look like a contingency table at first glance, it is not. It contains information on the distribution of several different variables according to the minority ethnic categories they have created. They divide minority ethnic respondents into nine groups based on their reported ethnicity and religion. They then explore three dimensions of Britishness: (1) whether the respondent agrees that they 'personally feel part of Britain'; (2) how strongly they feel they belong to Britain; and (3) whether they agree that it is possible to 'fully belong to Britain and maintain a separate cultural and religious identity'. They record whether respondents believe 'they would be the victim of institutional racism' based on their answers to 15 questions in the survey about the expectation of being treated differently according to race or ethnicity by a variety of institutions and service providers. Finally, they report some demographic variables for their nine groups: mean age, sex composition, economic activity, and whether they were born in the UK. Using their description of their methods in the text, we ought to be able to replicate this table. The data from HOCS is available for download from the UK Data Service (SN 6388) and can also be analysed online using Nesstar. Download the dataset and its accompanying documentation. You can either use this documentation to identify the relevant variables for analysis, or you can use the Nesstar interface at the UK Data Service to do so. We'll take the latter approach here, to illustrate how we can use online analysis to help us find our way around the IBM SPSS Statistics software file.

6.3 DOWNLOADING AND PREPARING THE HOCS DATA

Register and login to the UK Data Service website.

🔗 https://www.ukdataservice.ac.uk/

Either use the *Discover* catalogue or the search functions on the site to go to the page for the Home Office Citizenship Survey 2008–2009 and click on the **Access online** link (Figure 6.1).

Table 1 Differences in the attitudes towards being 'British' and cultural integration among those with different ethnic and religious affiliation (in %)

Ethnic group / Faith group	Caribbean Christian	African Christian	Asian Christian	Indian Hindu	Indian Sikh	Indian Muslim	Pakistani Muslim	Bangladeshi Muslim	African Muslim
To what extent do you agree or disagree that you personally feel a part of Britain?									
Strongly agree	45	41	45	47	51	51	50	56	37
Tend to agree	48	49	43	45	47	42	45	38	50
Tend to disagree	5	7	9	6	2	5	4	5	8
Strongly disagree	2	3	3	2	0	2	1	1	4
Unweighted bases	*871*	*803*	*211*	*779*	*337*	*251*	*955*	*339*	*195*
How strongly do you belong to Britain?									
Very strongly	42	40	38	41	48	45	48	49	32
Fairly strongly	44	40	41	47	44	45	43	39	53
Not very strongly	11	16	18	10	7	7	8	9	10
Not at all strongly	4	3	3	2	1	3	1	2	5
Unweighted bases	*874*	*809*	*211*	*788*	*337*	*252*	*961*	*345*	*200*
To what extent do you agree or disagree that it is possible to fully belong to Britain and maintain a separate cultural or religious identity?									
Strongly agree	25	32	31	39	36	54	45	36	38
Tend to agree	43	49	51	47	56	38	42	40	48
Tend to disagree	21	12	14	11	6	5	9	12	12
Strongly disagree	11	7	3	3	2	3	3	12	2
Unweighted bases	*843*	*780*	*203*	*752*	*322*	*238*	*934*	*327*	*190*
Mean age	43.5	35.5	40.9	39.3	39.5	37.5	35.1	34.2	34.3
Unweighted bases	*888*	*816*	*212*	*793*	*339*	*254*	*968*	*345*	*204*

Ethnic group Faith group	Caribbean Christian	African Christian	Asian Christian	Indian Hindu	Indian Sikh	Indian Muslim	Pakistani Muslim	Bangladeshi Muslim	African Muslim
Gender:									
Male	43	54	44	61	51	58	57	61	41
Female	57	46	56	39	49	42	43	39	59
Unweighted bases	*889*	*816*	*212*	*793*	*339*	*254*	*968*	*345*	*204*
Economic activity									
Employed	64	81	72	76	72	65	61	60	58
Unemployed	10	9	9	6	8	9	9	12	13
Sick	3	1	1	3	6	3	5	5	3
Retired	17	2	9	9	8	4	6	5	1
Looking after home	6	7	9	6	7	17	19	18	25
Unweighted bases	*883*	*812*	*212*	*793*	*338*	*254*	*964*	*344*	*204*
Not born in UK	47	81	84	76	56	74	60	75	91
Unweighted bases	*885*	*812*	*212*	*794*	*339*	*254*	*967*	*345*	*202*
Believes they would be the victim of institutional racism	49	40	29	24	27	33	33	35	32
Unweighted bases	*888*	*816*	*212*	*794*	*339*	*254*	*968*	*345*	*204*

Source: (Karlsen and Nazroo, 2015: 767–8)

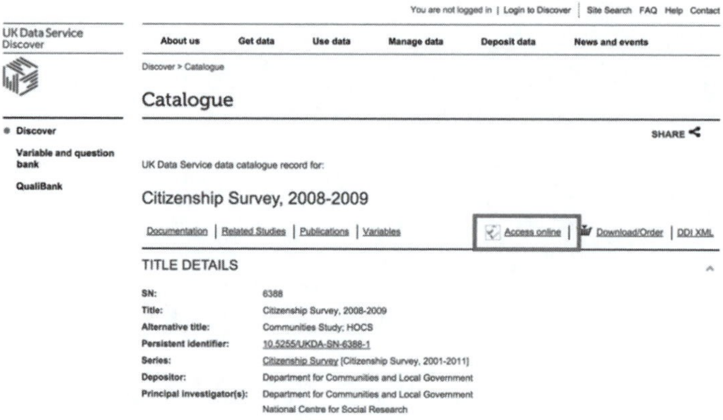

Figure 6.1 Accessing Nesstar pages from a UK Data Service catalogue entry

This will take you to the Nesstar interface, where you'll see the survey listed in the left-hand column. Click on the icon to its left and then on **Variable Description** to reveal a list of variable categories (Figure 6.2).

Selecting **Demographics** and then **Ethnicity/Country of Birth** takes you to the list of variables used to capture ethnicity, and selecting 'which of these best describes your ethnic group' gives you a frequency table whose categories correspond to those used in the article. The categories are those used in all UK Office for National Statistics surveys and censuses to measure ethnicity. You can also see from the table heading that the variable in the dataset corresponding to this question is **ethnic**. You can now run a frequency table of this variable from the dataset you have downloaded and check that your results correspond exactly to the Nesstar table. If they do, you know that you have successfully downloaded the correct dataset (Figure 6.3).

If you do *not* find that that you have exactly the same data in the Nesstar and SPSS frequency tables, then something has gone awry. Check that you are using the correct year of the survey (2008–9), that you are *not* applying weights or selecting a subset of cases, and that you have identified and used the correct variable.

Our next task is to identify the variable used to capture respondents' religion. In the **Variable Description** list on the Nesstar page, go to **Religion** and then **General** to find the variable **relig**: 'What is your religion even if you are not currently practising?' Our next task is to produce a crosstab of this variable with **ethnic**, since the article authors use ethnicity and religion to create the groups of respondents that they analyse. However, before producing this crosstab, set both variables to take no missing values (otherwise cases with missing values on either variable will be omitted from the crosstab and we need to check that our treatment of any such case is consistent with that of the article authors). You should get the results shown in Figure 6.4.

Your next task is to re-create the ethnic and religious groups studied by Karlsen and Nazroo:

Caribbean Christian (888)	Indian Muslim (254)
African Christian (816)	Pakistani Muslim (968)
Asian Christian (212)	Bangladeshi Muslim (345)
Indian Hindu (794)	African Muslim (204)
Indian Sikh (339)	

Figure 6.2 Citizenship survey variables in Nesstar

It is possible to do this because the authors provide the unweighted *N*s for each group (shown above) from which we can infer how they were created. You may find it useful to download and printout the Nesstar version of this table (use the ▣ icon on the toolbar to download an Excel file of the table). We can see that to create their categories the authors have included both respondents describing themselves as having an Asian, black African or black

Ethnic Which of these best describes your ethnic group? (QInter.QResp.Ethnic)

		Frequency	Percent	Valid Percent	Cumulative Percent
Valid	1 White British	8001	53.6	53.7	53.7
	2 White Irish	139	.9	.9	54.6
	3 Any other White background	350	2.3	2.3	56.9
	4 Mixed White and Black Caribbean	229	1.5	1.5	58.5
	5 Mixed White and Black African	129	.9	.9	59.4
	6 Mixed White and Asian	98	.7	.7	60.0
	7 Any other mixed background	114	.8	.8	60.8
	8 Asian or Asian British – Indian	1553	10.4	10.4	71.2
	9 Asian or Asian British – Pakistani	990	6.6	6.6	77.8
	10 Asian or Asian British – Bangladeshi	354	2.4	2.4	80.2
	11 Any other Asian/Asian British background	252	1.7	1.7	81.9
	12 Black or Black British – Caribbean	874	5.9	5.9	87.8
	13 Black or Black British – African	969	6.5	6.5	94.3
	14 Any other Black or Black British background	44	.3	.3	94.6
	15 Chinese	185	1.2	1.2	95.8
	95 Any other ethnic group	627	4.2	4.2	100.0
	Total	14908	99.9	100.0	
Missing	–9 Refusal	9	.1		
Total		14917	100.0		

...nd economic data resources

DESCRIPTION   TABULATION   ANALYSIS

Dataset: Citizenship Survey, 2008-2009

Variable Ethnic: Which of these best describes your e (QInter.QResp.Ethnic)

LITERAL QUESTION
Please could you look at this card and tell me which of these best describes your ethn...

Values	Categories	N	
1	White British	8001	53.7%
2	White Irish	139	0.9%
3	Any other White background	350	2.3%
4	Mixed White and Black Caribbean	229	1.5%
5	Mixed White and Black African	129	0.9%
6	Mixed White and Asian	98	0.7%
7	Any other mixed background	114	0.8%
8	Asian or Asian British - Indian	1553	10.4%
9	Asian or Asian British - Pakistani	990	6.6%
10	Asian or Asian British - Bangladeshi	354	2.4%
11	Any other Asian/Asian British background	252	1.7%
12	Black or Black British - Caribbean	874	5.9%
13	Black or Black British - African	969	6.5%
14	Any other Black or Black British background	44	0.3%
15	Chinese	185	1.2%
95	Any other ethnic group	627	4.2%
-9	Refusal	9	
-8	Don't Know	0	
-2	Schedule not applicable	0	
-1	Item not applicable	0	

SUMMARY STATISTICS
Valid cases   14908
Missing cases   9
This variable is numeric

INTERVIEWER INSTRUCTIONS
SHOWCARD 2. CODE ONE ONLY.

UNIVERSE

Figure 6.3   A comparison of Nesstar and SPSS frequency tables

Ethnic Which of these best describes your ethnic group? (QInter.QResp.Ethnic) * Relig What is your religion even if you are not currently practising? (QInter.QRace.Relig) Crosstabulation

Count

			Relig What is your religion even if you are not currently practising? (QInter.QRace.Relig)										Total
		-9 Refusal	-8 Don't Know	-1 Item not applicable	1 Christian	2 Buddhist	3 Hindu	4 Jewish	5 Muslim	6 Sikh	7 Any other religion	8 Or no religion at all	
Ethnic Which of these best describes your ethnic group? (QInter.QResp.Ethnic)	-9 Refusal	0	0	0	2	1	0	0	2	0	0	4	9
	1 White British	8	5	3	6354	23	3	33	9	0	194	1369	8001
	2 White Irish	0	0	0	117	0	0	2	2	0	5	13	139
	3 Any other White background	2	1	0	247	1	1	5	24	1	20	48	350
	4 Mixed White and Black Caribbean	2	1	0	164	0	0	0	2	0	8	52	229
	5 Mixed White and Black African	0	0	0	89	1	0	0	16	0	4	19	129
	6 Mixed White and Asian	0	0	0	38	2	2	0	18	2	2	34	98
	7 Any other mixed background	0	0	0	65	3	2	2	16	0	2	24	114
	8 Asian or Asian British – Indian	2	0	2	87	11	794	1	254	339	42	21	1553
	9 Asian or Asian British – Pakistani	1	1	0	6	1	3	0	968	2	5	3	990
	10 Asian or Asian British – Bangladeshi	0	1	0	0	0	3	1	345	0	3	1	354
	11 Any other Asian/Asian British background	0	0	1	81	29	43	0	70	2	11	15	252
	12 Black or Black British – Caribbean	0	1	1	724	1	1	0	10	0	44	92	874
	13 Black or Black British – African	2	0	2	727	2	5	1	188	1	11	30	969
	14 Any other Black or Black British background	0	0	0	32	0	0	1	7	0	1	3	44
	15 Chinese	0	0	0	56	39	1	0	2	3	7	77	185
	95 Any other ethnic group	0	0	0	238	39	44	4	202	5	29	66	627
Total		17	10	9	9027	153	902	50	2135	355	388	1871	14917

Figure 6.4   Crosstab of **relig** by **ethnic**

Caribbean ethnicity with those who reported having a 'mixed' ethnicity of white and one of these backgrounds. We can also see that they have used the variable describing respondents' religious affiliation whether or not they describe themselves as actually practising that religion (which is captured by another variable, **relact**). These may both be sensible decisions, but are not explicitly reported in the article. Excluding those with mixed identities or those who did not currently practise their religion may have produced different conclusions.

The easiest way to create a variable describing the authors' ethnic and religious groups is to use the **compute** command together with a series of **if** statements. **Compute** is the command that SPSS uses to create a new variable. We want to use the information currently stored in the variables **ethnic** and **relig** to make a new variable that combines information from both these variables. For example, we want to create a category that brings together those from the black British, black Caribbean and mixed black and white Caribbean ethnic groups who describe their religion as Christian. That means taking cases with values 4 or 12 on **ethnic** and value 1 on **relig** into one category of our new variable. Similarly, we want those taking values 5 or 13 on **ethnic** and 1 on **relig** to form a category describing black or mixed ethnicity African Christians, those taking values 8 on **ethnic** and 3 on **relig** to describe Indian Hindus, and so on. Let's call the new variable **ethrelig**. We begin the syntax by creating the new variable and setting its value for all cases to one that we'll later define as missing. We then use the command **if**, followed by a series of logical statements that describe the conditions under which our new variable will take each of the values we define. Note how logical statements are contained within parentheses. This ensures that SPSS tackles the various calculations in the right order. Note, too, that each statement ends in a full stop.

```
COMPUTE ethrelig = 99.
IF (ethnic = 4) and (relig = 1 ) ethrelig = 1.
IF (ethnic = 12) and (relig = 1 ) ethrelig = 1.
IF (ethnic = 5) and (relig = 1 ) ethrelig = 2.
IF (ethnic = 13) and (relig = 1 ) ethrelig = 2.
IF (ethnic = 6) and (relig = 1 ) ethrelig = 3.
IF (ethnic = 8) and (relig = 1 ) ethrelig = 3.
IF (ethnic = 9) and (relig = 1 ) ethrelig = 3.
IF (ethnic = 10) and (relig = 1 ) ethrelig = 3.
IF (ethnic = 11) and (relig = 1 ) ethrelig = 3.
IF (ethnic = 8) and (relig = 3 ) ethrelig = 4.
IF (ethnic = 8) and (relig = 6 ) ethrelig = 5.
IF (ethnic = 8) and (relig = 5 ) ethrelig = 6.
IF (ethnic = 9) and (relig = 5 ) ethrelig = 7.
IF (ethnic = 10) and (relig = 5 ) ethrelig = 8.
IF (ethnic = 13) and (relig = 5 ) ethrelig = 9.
IF (ethnic = 5) and (relig = 5 ) ethrelig = 9.
IF (ethnic lt 4) and (relig = 1) ethrelig = 10.
IF (ethnic lt 4) and (relig = 8) ethrelig = 10.
```

Next we need to give our new variable value labels. Although you can do this in the GUI in the **Variable View** mode of the **Data Editor** window, it is better to use syntax to do this as this keeps a record of your work. The **Value Labels** command is followed by the name of the variable you wish to label, followed by each value and its associated label placed within double inverted commas:

VALUE LABELS ethrelig 1 "Caribbean Ch" 2 "Africa Ch" 3 "Asian Ch" 4 "Indian Hindu" 5 "Indian Sikh" 6 "Indian Muslim" 7 "Pak Muslim" 8 "Bang Muslim" 9 "Africa Muslim" 10 "white Ch or no relig" 99 "Other".

Next we define missing values for our new variable using the **Missing Values** command. It makes sense to define all white ethnic groups as missing, since our analysis is about other groups. However, if we later want to make comparisons with this group we can always change value 10 for **ethrelig** to a valid value by issuing the **Missing Values** command again but omitting the value 10. The format of the command is to list the variable(s) it applies to, and place up to three values, separated by spaces or commas, within parentheses, followed, as ever, by a full stop. Finally, we run a frequency table of our new variable to check that it has turned out the way we wanted:

MISSING VALUES ethrelig (10, 99).
freq ethrelig.

You should obtain the frequency table shown in Figure 6.5. If you check the numbers in the frequency column you will see that they correspond to the those in Figure 6.4. For example, there were 164 mixed ethnicity black Caribbean Christians + 724 black Caribbean Christians = 888 Caribbean Christians.

ethrelig

		Frequency	Percent	Valid Percent	Cumulative Percent
Valid	1.00 Caribbean Ch	888	6.0	18.4	18.4
	2.00 Africa Ch	816	5.5	16.9	35.4
	3.00 Asian Ch	212	1.4	4.4	39.8
	4.00 Indian Hindu	794	5.3	16.5	56.2
	5.00 Indian Sikh	339	2.3	7.0	63.3
	6.00 Indian Muslim	254	1.7	5.3	68.5
	7.00 Paki Muslim	968	6.5	20.1	88.6
	8.00 Bang Muslim	345	2.3	7.2	95.8
	9.00 Africa Muslim	204	1.4	4.2	100.0
	Total	4820	32.3	100.0	
Missing	10.00 white Ch or no relig	8148	54.6		
	99.00 Other	1949	13.1		
	Total	10097	67.7		
Total		14917	100.0		

Figure 6.5 Frequency table of **ethrelig**

Next we can identify the other variables used in Table 1 from Karlsen and Nazroo (2015). In the Nesstar variable list, go to **Identity and Social Networks** where you'll find the variable **febrit** ('To what extent do you agree or disagree that you personally feel a part of Britain?'). Then go to the heading **Your Community – Feelings about Neighbourhood and Local Area** where you can locate the variable **sbegb** ('How strongly do you belong to Britain?'). Finally, under **Values**, find the variable **dualid** ('Is it possible to fully belong to Britain and maintain a separate cultural or religious identity?'). You should also be able to find the variables **rsex**, **rage** and **hcoba** (for sex, age and country of birth). While you can use the first two variables as they are, the variable **hcoba** needs to be recoded to collapse the different non-UK categories into a single value.

We can recode the values of **hcoba** using the **recode** command and the following syntax. Note that first I ask for a frequency table of the existing variables. This enables me to check for anything I need to be aware of such as missing values, or possibly cases that do not take an expected value because of a data entry error or for some other reason. The **recode** command requires the name of the variable that is to be recoded, and then a series of parentheses in which we list the value(s) to be recoded to the left of the equals sign and the new value they are to take to the right. There must always be *only one* value to the right of the sign (SPSS must have a single value to reset the others to!). When listing a series of values you can use the keyword **thru**, so that **2 thru 5** would mean **2 3 4 5**. You can also use the keywords **lo** and **hi** to stand for the lowest occurring and highest occurring values in the variable being recoded. You also have the option of using the keyword **ELSE** in the final parenthesis in the series to refer to every value in the existing variable that has not been specified in the **recode** command so far. Finally, and crucially, follow the parentheses by the subcommand **into** and the name of the new variable you wish to create. If you omit this final step SPSS recodes the original variable and leaves you only with the new, recoded, version. Thus the following syntax tells SPSS to:

- produce a new variable called **birth** that takes the value 1 where the existing **hcoba** variable took values 1 to 5, takes the value –9 when **hcoba** equalled –9, and takes the value 0 for all other values of **hcoba**;
- make –9 in the new variable a missing value;
- label the new variable so that 0 = non-UK and 1 = UK;
- produce a frequency table of the new variable.

```
FREQ hcoba.
RECODE hcoba (1 thru 5 = 1) (-9 = -9) (ELSE = 0) into birth.
MISSING VALUES birth (-9).
VALUE LABELS birth 0 "non UK" 1 "UK".
FREQ birth.
```

The variables for economic activity and beliefs about institutional racism require a little more work. The variable **dvilo3a** divides respondents into those who are employed, unemployed and inactive. The authors have kept the first of these two categories, but divided the third into those who are sick, retired and homemakers using the variable **yinact**. Try to work out the syntax to create this new variable yourself, following the example of how we created **ethrelig**, and then check it against mine, shown below. I've called the new variable **ecact**.

```
MISSING VALUES yinact dvilo3a ().
CROSS yinact by dvilo3a.
COMPUTE ecact = 9.
IF (dvilo3a ne 3) ecact = dvilo3a.
IF (dvilo3a eq 3) and (yinact = 1) ecact = 3.
IF (dvilo3a eq 3) and (yinact = 2) ecact = 4.
IF (dvilo3a eq 3) and (yinact = 3) ecact = 5.
IF (dvilo3a eq 3) and (yinact = 4) ecact = 6.
IF (dvilo3a eq 3) and (yinact = 5) ecact = 7.
IF (dvilo3a eq 3) and (yinact = 6) ecact = 8.
```

```
VALUE LABELS ecact 1 "empl" 2 "unempl" 3 "student" 4 "LAFH" 5 "temp sick"
6 "long sick" 7 "retd" 8 "other".
MISSING VALUES ecact (9).
FREQ ecact.
```

For the variable describing beliefs about racism the authors have collected information from 15 variables **rdis01** to **rdis16** (the authors mistakenly report this as 16, an error caused by the way variables in the dataset are named). These variables ask respondents whether they would expect to experience unfavourable treatment compared to others because of their race in a variety of different organisational settings, from council housing departments to the prison service. Each variable is coded as 0 'not mentioned' or 1 'mentioned'. We will also need to check if there are cases with missing values on these variables. We could create a new variable that counts the number of times a respondent did mention (i.e. takes the value 1) an organisation across these 15 variables. To do so we use the **count** command in SPSS. Let's call the new variable **discrim**.

6 ● 4 USING THE COUNT FUNCTION TO SUMMARISE INFORMATION FROM SEVERAL VARIABLES

The **Count** procedure counts the occurrence of a value or set of values across multiple variables in the dataset. We can construct our commands in the GUI and paste the syntax to learn the format it takes, and then edit that syntax if need be. Go to **Transform→Count Values within Cases** to open the **Count Occurrences of Values within Cases** dialog box. Enter the name for our new variable in the **Target Variable** box at the top left of the dialog box, and give it an appropriate label (e.g. 'N discriminatory orgs'). From the variable list select all the variables from **rdis01** to **rdis16** (remember that to select a list of consecutive variables you can select the first one and then shift-click on the last one) and then drag them across to the **Numeric Variables:** box on the right of the dialog box. Then click the **Define Values** button, which opens the **Count Values within Cases: Values to Count** window. We want to count how many times the value 1 appears across all these variables within each case in the dataset, so we enter this value in the **Value:** box and click on **Add** and then **Continue** (as shown in Figure 6.6). Now **Paste** the syntax we have created, which should look like this:

```
COUNT discrim= rdis01 rdis02 rdis03 rdis04 rdis05 rdis06 rdis07 rdis08 rdis09 rdis10 rdis12a
rdis13a rdis14 rdis15 rdis16(1).
VARIABLE LABELS discrim 'N discriminatory orgs'.
EXECUTE.
```

If you're already comfortable with syntax you'll notice that you can shorten the version SPSS produces if you write the syntax from scratch. The same command could read:

```
count discrim = rdis01 to rdis16(1).
var labels discrim 'N discriminatory orgs'.
```

You may notice, if you run frequency tables on these 15 variables, that there are many system-missing responses and don't knows, which are worthy of further investigation. If you

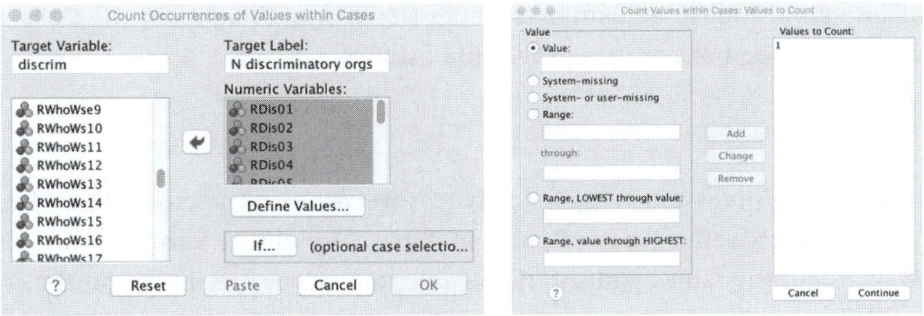

Figure 6.6 The **Count** dialog boxes

consult the data documentation you'll discover that in the fourth quarter in which the survey was administered some questions were dropped in order to create space to pilot some new questions, giving rise to the missing values on four of our variables. However, the survey sampling was done in such a way that each quarter produced a random sample, so that we can safely ignore the fact that these four questions were fielded in only three quarters. The high level of don't knows, ranging from around two-thirds to three times the total of all those reporting they expected to be treated either better or worse, ought to lead us to treat the answers to these questions with some caution. As a general rule answers to hypothetical questions such as these are unreliable, in so far as respondents may find them difficult to interpret and may have little concrete experience upon which to base their answers.

You should now have all the variables you need to replicate Karlsen and Nazroo's Table 1: the original variables **rsex**, **rage**, **febrit**, **sbegb** and **dualid**, the recode of **hcoba** and the newly created variables **ethrelig**, **discrim** and **ecact**. The frequency distributions of these variables are shown on the companion website, so that you can check that your syntax has worked correctly.

To replicate the data in Table 1 of the article we can run crosstabs of **ethrelig** by **febrit**, **sbegb**, **dualid**, **rsex**, **ecact** and **discrim**, and then calculate mean values for **rage** by the categories of **ethrelig**. First we must weight the data by the appropriate weight, which is **WtFlnds**. We looked briefly at how to apply weights in Chapter 4: consult this again if you've forgotten how to do it. If you run a frequency table of **ethrelig** for unweighted data and then repeat this using the weight you will find that the number of respondents we are analysing falls from 4820 to 950. This is what we might expect given that there was a minority ethnic boost in the sample, and weights restore equal probabilities of selection for the whole sample. However, if we use the weights as they stand when analysing our results, the much smaller number of weighted cases can cause two problems. When the absolute numbers of weighted cases in crosstab cells are small and they are rounded to the nearest whole number (the default option in SPSS) this introduces errors. If we use the weighted cases to produce any inferential statistics these may also be wrong, if calculation of standard errors and other values is based on the weighted rather than the raw number of cases. We can get round both these problems by adjusting the weight so that the absolute number of weighted cases we are working with is the same as the total of raw unweighted cases (i.e. setting the average weight to 1). We can do this by multiplying **WtFlnds** by 4820/950 = 5.0737. In addition, we can ask SPSS to report the weighted numbers in crosstab cells rather than rounding them to the nearest integer (its default practice). You can do this in the GUI by deselecting **Round** cell counts and choosing **No adjustments** under **Noninteger Weights** in the **Cells** sub-dialog of the **Crosstabs** dialog box, or using the syntax sub-command

/COUNT ASIS.

as the last line of your crosstab syntax. Apply this weight, run the crosstabs and you should find that you perfectly replicate the figures in Table 1 for all the variables *except* Economic Activity. ❦ As usual, the tables you should be able to produce are shown on the companion website.

6●5 RECONSTRUCTING THE ECONOMIC ACTIVITY VARIABLE

Here, something appears to have gone wrong with our replication. The article authors' variable on economic activity has five categories: employed, unemployed, sick, retired, and looking after home. It must have been constructed out of the two variables **dvilo3a** and **yinact**. However, the second of these two variables also contains the category *student*. We can infer that these cases are included in the data presented in Table 6.1 because of the unweighted *N*s: these total 4804, so that only 16 cases have been dropped. Set **dvilo3** and **yinact** to take no missing values, turn weights off, and run a crosstab of these two variables. You should get the results in Table 6.1.

It looks as if the 16 cases coded as economically inactive at **dvilo3a** yet given a 'not applicable' coding at **yinact** may be the cases dropped by the authors. But this raises the question of what has happened to the students, to the 3 cases coded as not applicable at **dvilo3a** and to the 138 cases who gave 'other' reasons for not being economically active. To pursue this further we will need to apply weights again in order to use the information on the distribution of weighted cases in the body of Table 1 from the published article.

If we use the **Split File** procedure we can reproduce the information in Table 1, but keeping sight of those cases treated as missing. Splitting a file by a variable carries out any procedure as if the data were in separate files defined by the values of that variable. You can use the **Split File** icon ▦ on the toolbar to issue the command. This brings up the **Split File** dialog box where you choose **Organize output by groups** and enter the variable you wish to use to define the split in the **Groups Based on:** list box (Figure 6.7).

However, it is quicker and better to use syntax. First you must **sort** the file by the variable on which it is to be split, then tell SPSS which variable to split the file by. To analyse the entire file again, turn off the **SPLIT FILE** command:

```
SORT CASES BY ethrelig.
SPLIT FILE SEPARATE BY ethrelig.
FREQ dvilo3a yinact ecact.
SPLIT FILE off.
```

SPSS will now produce a set of frequency tables for our three variables taking each single value of **ethrelig** in turn. Thus it will produce frequency distributions for **dvilo3a**, **yinact** and **ecact** for only those cases where **ethrelig** = 1 (Caribbean Christians), then for **ethrelig** = 2 (African Christians) and so on. We can use this information to produce Table 6.2.

Table 6.1 Economic inactivity (**yinact**) by employment status (**dvilo3a**)

DVILO3a	8 Don't know	−1 Item not applicable	1 Student	2 Looking after the family/ home	3 Temporarily sick or injured	4 Long-term sick or disabled	5 Retired from paid work	6 Other reasons	Total
−1 Item not applicable	0	3	0	0	0	0	0	0	3
1 InEmp	0	2671	0	0	0	0	0	0	2671
2 Unemp	0	230	0	0	0	0	0	0	230
3 EcInAct	3	16	291	692	26	245	505	138	1916
Total	3	2920	291	692	26	245	505	138	4820

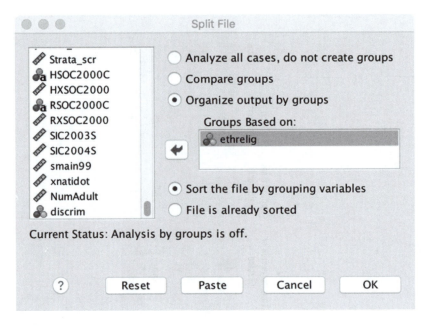

Figure 6.7   The **Split File** dialog box

Comparing these results to those presented in Table 1 of the published article, it looks as if 'others' and the 'temporarily sick' have been included with the unemployed and 'students' have been included with the employed to produce the results in the table. It is unclear whether this was the intention of the authors and an explanation of how the categories were created was somehow omitted from the final version of the article, or whether this was the result of an error in the creation of the variable used to produce Table 1. We can re-create the variable for economic activity used by the authors by **recoding** our **ecact** variable, merging the categories for the 'temporarily sick' and 'others' into 'unemployed' and 'students' into 'employed'.

There is one other feature of the results in Table 1 that ought to catch our attention. You will see that the proportion of the sample who are male varies from 41% to 61%. However, a quick check of the census data for England and Wales shows the adult gender distribution in each of these ethnic categories to be much more equal than this. One could surmise that non-response is behind the pattern we find in our table.

Finally we can re-create the authors' statistics for the mean age of the different ethnic religious categories they explore by using the **means** procedure with the variable **ethrelig**. You should be able to reproduce their results exactly. You can go to **Analyze→Compare Means→Means...**. In the dialog enter **DVAge** in the **Dependent List:** and **ethrelig** in the **Independent List:** boxes. However, let's use syntax, which takes the form of the **MEANS** command followed by the variable for which you wish to calculate mean values, and any variable you wish to subset the original variable by. The **/CELLS=** sub-command lists which statistics you'd like SPSS to calculate. As well as means you can ask for medians, minima, maxima, standard deviations and other statistics.

```
MEANS DVAge BY ethrelig
/CELLS=MEAN COUNT STDDEV.
```

Table 6.2 Economic activity by ethnicity and religion

(col. %)	1 Carib-bean Chr	2 African Chr	3 Asian Chr	4 Indian Hindu	5 Indian Sikh	6 Indian Muslim	7 Pakis Muslim	8 Bangla Muslim	9 African Muslim	Total
employed	59.6	69.5	65.8	67.2	62.6	59.6	50.6	50.9	42.5	60.2
unemployed	6.9	5.3	5.3	3.8	4.0	4.8	5.6	7.0	6.9	5.4
student	4.6	11.0	6.3	8.7	10.1	7.0	10.7	9.1	15.4	9.1
LAFH	5.8	7.4	10.1	6.4	6.5	17.4	19.7	18.7	25.1	11.6
temp sick	0.7	0.2	0.2	0.3	0.2	0.8	0.5	0.8	0.2	0.4
long sick	3.4	1.4	1.5	2.9	5.7	3.1	5.1	4.6	3.0	3.5
retired	16.8	1.6	9.2	8.8	7.7	3.8	5.5	5.0	1.3	7.1
other	2.3	3.5	1.6	1.9	3.1	3.5	2.2	3.8	5.7	2.7

6●6 SOME PRELIMINARY CONCLUSIONS

We will look at the logistic regression analysis reported by the authors in Chapter 12. However, already our replication efforts should have prompted the following reflections. The first is that it usually takes some detective work using the data documentation and, if it is available, the Nesstar interface, to accurately identify the variables and weights used and how variable values or missing cases have been defined in a published analysis. In the days of hard-copy journals with tight space restrictions journal editors were often reluctant to devote space to such technical methodological considerations at the expense of discussion of substantive results and the rationale of the analysis. In my view such priorities were unfortunate, since any development of cumulative knowledge in science ultimately depends upon precise methodology. In the era of online journals, it is straightforward for authors and editors to post supplementary technical material about methods online, including the software syntax they used. This would not only facilitate more rapid and accurate replication, but also make the implicit analytical decisions made by authors more visible, encourage more debate about them and bring any errors to light far more quickly.

A second conclusion you may have drawn is that in replication, the analysis takes much less time than the data management and preparation preceding it. Here, as elsewhere in secondary data analysis, patience is a virtue. Rushing the data preparation makes errors more likely and turns out to be a false economy of time, since it is wasted later on hunting through syntax for the origin of some slip.

The third conclusion that I hope you will draw is that although it takes longer to replicate the analysis in a piece of published work rather than simply read it, replication gives you a much deeper and more critical insight into what the authors have done, and how robust their conclusions are, because in the course of replicating their analysis you are almost certain to become alert to a range of different approaches that the authors could have adopted but didn't. Usually exploring some of these other options not only gives you a much better insight into the object of the original analysis, but also may suggest other conclusions beyond those signalled by the original authors, or even call the arguments of these authors into question.

To hone your replication skills further, we'll take another example, this time using European Social Survey data.

6●7 RESPONSIBLE CITIZENSHIP

Purdham and Tranmer (2014) use data from Round 3 of the ESS (2006) to examine 'responsible citizenship' by looking at how far people expect help in return for offering help of their own in different circumstances. We'll replicate their analyses, using their description of their methods, and attempt to obtain the same results that they publish in their article.

The first question we face is to locate the data the authors used. They specify that they used data from the 23 countries in ESS3. However, when you go the ESS website you should find that this wave of the survey was fielded in *25* countries. A look at Table 6 in the article (Purdham and Tranmer, 2014: 72) reveals that the discrepancy is accounted for by Latvia and Romania, and if you consult the data documentation you will find that design weights are still not available for

Table 3 The expectation of help in return for helping by age.

If I help someone I expect some help in return

Age (years)	Agree strongly (%)	Agree (%)	Neither agree nor disagree (%)	Disagree (%)	Disagree strongly (%)
15–24	7	32	26	28	8
25–30	5	28	24	32	11
31–40	5	23	25	35	12
41–50	5	21	24	35	15
51–65	5	21	21	37	15
66–80	4	23	20	35	18
Total	5	24	23	34	14

ESS 2006. $N = 39, 683$; chi-square: 666 ($p < 0.000$).

these two countries, so that they have not been included in the integrated data file. Since the analysis in the article uses weights, it is clear why these countries have not been included. You'll also see that the latest edition of the data file that you can download is edition 3.5 released in November 2014. This will be a later version than that used by the authors, who submitted their article in 2013. However, if you consult the version notes for the various editions in the data documentation, it looks as if there have been no major corrections or changes since the release of the edition that would have been available to the journal authors.

Our next task is to identify the variables used by the authors. We can use the data documentation such as the main questionnaire or the Nesstar data page on the ESS website to identify variables as we did for our first replication. Table 6.3 shows how each variable is described by the authors, and the corresponding variable in the ESS dataset. Remember that to locate these variables you can use the search function within SPSS using the 🔍 icon on the toolbar: select the **Name** column in the **Variable View** of the **Data Editor** window, click on the icon and enter the name of the variable you are looking for as your search term.

In compiling this list we can note a couple of features that we might otherwise have overlooked. The variables **pplhlp** and **pplahlp** come from different sections of the questionnaire. We might want to be alert to how the preceding questions may have led respondents to interpret these questions in particular ways. The categories used to construct 'value helper' and 'helper in practice – local activities' are fairly broad, including both quite infrequent help and 'attendance' at local activities rather than specifically help with them. The authors have also chosen not to use the variable describing whether respondents are involved with volunteer or charitable work. Finally, although the authors report that they have used weights in their analysis, they do not indicate whether they used only the design weight in the dataset or also the post-stratification weights.

The authors first report some descriptive statistics for the variables they are to use. The first is a frequency table of **hlprtrn** for all respondents in all countries taken together. The authors note that 'all analyses were weighted to take account of the population size of the different countries and the country specific sampling strategies' (2014: 68), so we can assume that the

Table 6.3 Purdham and Tranmer main variables

Article description	ESS question	ESS3 variable and author changes
Expectation of help in return for helping (reciprocity)	Using this card, please say to what extent you agree or disagree with each of the following statements: If I help someone I expect some help in return	**hlprtrn** Those responding 'Don't know' and 'Neither agree nor disagree' excluded
Help and care for others' well-being as a value (value help)	Now I will briefly describe some people. Please listen to each description and tell me how much each person is or is not like you. Use this card for your answer. It's very important to her/him to help the people around her/him. She/he wants to care for their well-being. Very much like me … Not like me at all.	**iphlppl** *Very much like me* and *Like me* coded as 'value helper', other responses coded as 'not important'
Help in practice – (local activities)	And in the past 12 months, how often did you help with or attend activities organised in your local area?	**atnoact** Those who help or attend activities 'At least once every six months' or more often are coded as a 'Helper in practice – local activities'
Informal helping others (excluding family, work, or voluntary orgs)	Not counting anything you do for your family, in your work, or within voluntary organisations, how often, in the past 12 months, did you actively provide help for other people?	**hlpoth** Help at least once every six months coded as 'Informal helper'
Help – perceived local context	Using this card, please tell me to what extent … you feel that people in your local area help one another? 0 Not at all … 6 A great deal	**pplahlp** Recoded: 0–2 No or low level of help; 3–6 area of helping/high helping
Help – perceived social context	Would you say that most of the time people try to be helpful or that they are mostly looking out for themselves? Scale 0–10	**pplhlp**

authors applied the weight variable **pweight** (to account for the different population sizes of participating countries), but we do not know whether they applied either **dweight** or **pspweight** as the country-specific weighting variable. We can therefore try to replicate Table 2 in their article by running a frequency table of **hlprtrn** for each of four weight statuses: no weights; **pweight** only; **pweight*dweight** and **pweight*pspweight**. The latter two weights can be created using the **compute** command. I've called them **dpweight** and **popweight**:

```
compute dpweight = (pweight*dweight).
compute popweight = (pweight*pspweight).
```

You should find that none of the three weights return the exact distribution of responses as shown in Table 2 of the article, so unfortunately we cannot yet be sure which weighting variable the authors employed. Table 2 (2014: 72) gives an N of 42,855 but doesn't state if it is weighted or not. This N is quite close to the N of 42,576 valid responses you obtain for the 23 countries without weights, but since this uses data from more than one country it would be wrong not to use at least **pweight** to take account of the differences in the sampling fraction across countries. Unless this is done we'd be treating countries as if their adult populations were proportional to the numbers sampled in each country, making tiny Cyprus half the size of France! Yet if we weight the data with **pweight** (which accounts only for population differences and not the sample design) our N rises to 48,579.

Next the authors report that 29% of men and 24% of women across all countries respond *strongly agree* or *agree* to the variable **hlprtrn**. Again try to replicate this using the variable for respondent's sex (**gndr**) and trying different weights. While it is not possible to replicate the percentages quoted in the paper exactly, it is not difficult to get within a percentage point of them, as shown in Table 6.4. The small number of missing cases is not enough to change these percentages if they are included.

Table 6.4 Percentage of respondents agreeing or agreeing strongly that they expect some help in return if they help someone, by sex: all countries

	Men	Women	*N* (inc. missing cases)
Article text	29	24	
No weights	29	23	42,903
pweight only	31	27	50,504
dweight*pweight	31	28	49,207
pspweight*pweight	31	27	50,484

We can also check whether the authors included some missing cases in the denominator when calculating these percentages. After all, it could be argued that respondents who said they 'didn't know' the answer to this question might be classified along with those who 'neither agreed nor disagreed', but if you do this, you'll find that it makes little difference to the final percentage distributions.

The authors also cite the results by sex for some individual countries. Let's see how closely we can replicate this. Table 6.5 shows the results for the percentage of respondents taking the values *strongly agree* or *agree* for **hlprtrn** by gender and country, with *N*s for the number of respondents returning a valid response on the variable. You can produce the results for this table by running a three-way crosstab, with column percentages. SPSS will produce contingency tables with as many dimensions as you supply variables, but in practice tables with more than four dimensions are extremely difficult to read or interpret. In the GUI **Crosstabs** dialog you can produce *n*-way crosstabs by entering third and subsequent variables in the **Layer 1 of 1** box, clicking **Next** to create extra layers. However, as usual, syntax is quicker and simpler.

```
CROSSTABS gndr BY hlprtrn BY cntry
/FORMAT=AVALUE TABLES
/CELLS=COUNT ROW
/COUNT ASIS.
```

Remember that since we are now comparing individual countries we do not need to use **pweight**, only the alternative design weights for the study. It looks from Table 6.5 as if **dweight** does the best job. Again, we cannot match the percentages in the article text perfectly, but we are within one or two percentage points.

We can now try to replicate their Table 3 (2014: 70), which reports the distribution of **hlprtrn** by age for all countries together. Note that in the age group variable the authors have created they exclude respondents over 80 years old. Again you should find that nothing

Table 6.5 Agreement with expectation of help in return for helping by gender and selected country

	Denmark		Norway		United Kingdom		Russian Federation		Slovenia	
	Men	Women	Men	Women	Men	Women	Men	Women	Men	Women
Article	43	28	30	17	17	13	50	47	45	42
no weight	44	*28*	31	*17*	*17*	11	48	46	44	*42*
N		1,474		1,746		2,391		2,363		1,473
dweight	44	*28*	31	*17*	*17*	13	*50*	46	44	*42*
Weighted N		1,474		1,746		2,392		2,365		1,473
pspweight	46	30	32	18	18	*13*	49	45	46	*42*
Weighted N		1,489		1,741		2,976		2,357		1,473

replicates the percentages perfectly, but almost all the differences are minor: within one percentage point (see Table 6.6). The most worrying discrepancy is that between the *N* of cases which is reported as 39,683 by the authors, but as 40,809 (unweighted) or 48,187 (weighted) in our replication. It is unclear where these extra 1,100 cases come from.

Next the authors present results from their recoding of the **iphlppl** variable by **hlprtrn**. They collapse the five valid categories of **hlprtrn** into three: merging the values *agree* and *strongly agree* together and *disagree* and *strongly disagree* together. They collapse the values for **iphlppl** into two groups: 'Value helper' for values 1 and 2 and 'Do not see helping others as important' for values 3–6.

Recode the variables accordingly and use the weight **popweight**, and you should find that you can replicate the results in the body of their Table 4 (2014: 71) perfectly. You can try producing this table both for all respondents and for those aged up to 80 years: the differences are not large enough to affect the rounded percentages. Ask for a chi-square significance test so that we can compare the result with that in the article by including the subcommand

/STATISTICS=CHISQ

Table 6.6 Age (grouped) by **hlprtrn** (replication of article Table 3)

(Row %) Age	Agree strongly	Agree	Neither agree nor disagree	Disagree	Disagree strongly
15–24	6.9	32.1	25.6	27.4	8.1
25–30	4.8	27.0	23.7	33.6	11.1
31–40	5.3	22.7	24.8	35.4	11.9
41–50	5.0	21.1	24.1	35.0	14.7
51–65	5.2	21.1	21.8	36.9	15.0
66–80	4.4	21.5	19.6	35.6	18.9
Total	5.3	23.8	23.2	34.2	13.4
N (unweighted)	1,811	8,773	9,145	15,431	5,649

in the syntax for the crosstab. The authors don't explicitly report if they have excluded those aged over 80 or not and whether their denominator includes those who gave no response to the question on which the **iphlppl** variable was based. The results to one decimal place for all those aged up to 80 are shown in Table 6.7. ✎ You can check the syntax to do all this on the companion website.

Table 6.7   Expectation of return help by importance of helping others; all countries, respondents aged 15–80 years

(Row %)	Agree/strongly expect help in return	Neither agree nor disagree	Disagree/strongly don't expect help in return	All
'Value helper'	27.3	20.6	52.1	100
'Not important'	31.8	27.2	41.0	100
All	29.0	23.1	47.8	100
Unweighted *N*	10,186	8,823	20,522	39,531
Pearson chi-square	574.2			

Our *N* for weighted cases is 47,300 and for unweighted cases is 39,531, neither of which corresponds to the 42,856 which they report. Our value for chi-square, 574, is also rather higher than the 516 they report, but since this value is so high it makes no substantive difference to the interpretation of the results.

6●8   EXPECTATION OF HELP BY HELPING ACTIVITIES

Their next table (Table 5, p. 71) reports the distribution of the recoded **hlprtrn** variable by each of the recoded **atnoact** and **hlpoth** variables, in order to demonstrate an association (albeit a rather weak one) between expectation of reciprocal help and people's reports of their own helping activities. Use the information in Table 6.3 above to produce these two crosstabs, again using **popweight** as the weight variable. Again you should find that your results do not match those in the paper exactly, but are within a percentage point, as shown in Table 6.8.

Table 6.8   Expectation of help by helping activities

	If I help someone I expect some help in return		
	Yes agree/agree strongly (%)	Neither agree nor disagree (%)	No disagree/disagree strongly (%)
Helper in practice – local activities	24.6	22.3	53.1
Not a helper in practice – local activities	30.6	23.4	46.0
Total	29.0	23.1	47.9
N weighted 47,185, unweighted 40,251, chi-square 213 (252)			
Informal helper of people	26.5	21.2	52.2
Not informal helper of people	31.1	25.0	43.9
Total	28.9	23.1	48.0

N weighted 46,554, unweighted 39,931, chi-square 322 (338)

The article presents a bar chart of the distribution of the recoded **hlprtrn** variable by country in ascending order of agreement. To reproduce this variable, first produce a crosstab of the variable with **cntry**. Although it is possible to produce the bar chart directly in SPSS, it is usually easier to do so in Excel, which also gives you more formatting options. Produce a crosstab putting **cntry** in the rows and **hlprtrn3** in the columns, and asking for row percentages in the table cells. Copy this table and paste it into an Excel worksheet, or export it direct to Excel using the techniques you learned in Chapter 4. Once in Excel, drag to select both the body of the table and the variable value labels (but not the variable names or labels) and select the **Sort** command under the **Data** menu to order the results by the 'agree' column. Then select a **100% stacked column chart** using the toolbar icon or menus. Once Excel has produced the chart, go to the **Chart** menu and select **Move Chart** to put the chart in a new worksheet so that you can work with a larger copy that is easier to edit and format. ✎ If you are unsure of these techniques you can review Chapter 4 and also follow the commentary and screen animations on the companion website.

━━━━━ what you have learned ━━━━━

Replication takes time, most of which is spent managing and preparing the data, identifying and recoding variables or creating new ones, and checking which weights, if any, have been used. Thus it uses all the skills you have practised so far. Once this data management and preparation has been done, the actual analysis itself is rapid. Going through this whole process is an excellent way to learn how to go about secondary data analysis. You've probably realised that most of your effort went into data preparation and management, thus our next chapters focus on this.

Replication gives you a much better sense of the data and its possibilities than even the most meticulous reading of the research reported in a finished article. It enables you to think about other possibilities of analysis that could have been explored. Perhaps the authors also envisaged these but preferred the analyses they report as more insightful or informative. But it may also be that there are analyses they did not consider that you can pursue and shed new light on the subject.

Keeping a syntax record of what you have done enables you to return to your work later and carry on where you left off. It also protects you against any problems that you might encounter with your data. In a few clicks you can go back to the original data and rerun all the transformations or revisions of it that you have carried out. It is also invaluable for tracing errors. It is easy to slip up when recoding or creating variables. With a syntax record you can quickly identify where something may have gone wrong. You have learnt how to:

- Locate and download a dataset from the UK Data Service, using the data documentation or Nesstar online to identify relevant variables
- Use **Compute** and **If** statements to produce a new variable
- Use syntax to produce **Value Labels**
- Use the **Missing Value** and **Recode ... Into** commands in syntax
- Use the **Count** command
- Use the **Sort** and **Split File** procedures
- Use the **Search** function to locate variables in large datasets
- Use the **Means** procedure to produce summary descriptive statistics

- Create super-tables from their composite frequency or contingency tables
- Create weights by multiplying original weights
- **Export** crosstabs to Excel and produce graphics
- Appreciate the time and effort that go into data preparation and management

exercises

1 In their analysis, Karlsen and Nazroo (2015) combined minority ethnic categories with 'mixed' ethnicity categories, and included those who did not actively practise their religion to produce their ethnic religious groups. Locate the variable in the HOCS dataset that records whether respondents practise their religion and use this to produce new categories based on unmixed minority ethnic groups and those practising their religion. Produce contingency tables of this new variable with **febrit**, **sbegb**, **dualid**, **rsex**, **ecact** and **discrim**. Do you find any important differences between these results and the ones we obtained earlier using the variable **ethrelig**?

2 Purdham and Tranmer (2014) use the frequency 'at least once every six months' or more often in the variables **atnoact** and **hlpoth** to define 'helpers in practice' and 'informal helpers'. Reproduce the contingency tables for these variables with **hlprtn** but instead using the frequency 'at least once a month' or more often to define these categories. Do you find any important differences in the results obtained?

3 Formulate and test a null hypothesis for the association between sex and expectation of help in return when helping others for respondents in the following individual countries: Switzerland, Germany, United Kingdom, Poland, Ukraine. Then do the same for all countries included in the survey together. What do you find?

PREPARING YOUR DATA

━━━━━━━━━━ **introduction** ━━━━━━━━━━

Most of the work in secondary data analysis is in the management and preparation of the data so that it is in the right format for analysis. This is essential preparatory work that has to be done with some care to avoid errors. However, with a few key skills you will soon be able to reorganise datasets to get them in the shape you need. In this chapter you will learn how to:

- Organise your files and folders clearly
- Keep a record of your work using a journal or editing syntax files to include comments and notes
- Remove unwanted variables or cases from datasets and save new versions using the **Keep** and **Drop** commands
- Assemble data from different sources into one data file
- Import data from Excel to IBM SPSS Statistics software
- Take information from several existing variables to produce new ones using the **Count**, **Compute**, **If**, and **Do Repeat - End Repeat** commands
- Deal with 'hierarchical' data by attaching household level data to individual respondents
- Clean errors in data revealed by inconsistencies in variable values

7 ● 1 INTRODUCTION

By now you'll have realised that one of the secrets of good secondary data analysis is good data preparation and management: reviewing the data documentation to check the definition of variables and selection of respondents, selecting groups of cases, recoding variables or creating new ones out of combinations of existing ones, dealing with weights, keeping track of missing values and so on.

Up till now we've been using datasets that include all the variables you need in one location. However, there will be times when the data comes in less convenient forms and you have to do more work with it. This chapter looks at some of the skills you will need to assemble data from different sources, or restructure data within a file if it comes in a format that is not easy to analyse. Often datasets based on respondents also carry information about other members of the household in which the respondent lives. We'll see how to extract such 'hierarchical' data so that we can describe not only the respondents themselves but also their households. In the next chapter we'll look at restructuring and merging data files.

As you go further with analysis of secondary data you will need to develop your data management skills. There is thus a temptation to rush the data management to get on to the more interesting and exciting part of the work. Resist this temptation! It is best to think of data management as the equivalent of fieldwork or of setting up an experiment: the vital work that produces the data that makes the results or the analysis possible in the first place. Those without experience of secondary data analysis tend to imagine that it's a quick matter of downloading the data, pouring it into a statistics package and reading off the results. On the contrary, careful study of the relevant data documentation, good data management and preparation and a thorough record of what has been done are an essential foundation for robust analyses and take time. Get into the habit of working methodically, avoiding shortcuts and checking your procedures for errors. It is easy to make an error. However, it is also easy to check for them as you go, so that it is you who spot it, and not the reader of your final analysis.

7 2 CATALOGUING YOUR DATA

First you will need a set of routines for cataloguing your data so that you don't lose it, and recording your work so that you know what you have done. This might appear obvious, but once you find yourself working with a large number of datasets, or successive editions of the same dataset, you'll soon discover how difficult it is to locate the data you worked with some weeks or months ago, and recall exactly what you did with it, what modifications you made to the original dataset and so on. Data rarely comes in exactly the format you need to carry out the analysis you want. You may need to assemble components of your dataset from different sources. You will almost certainly have to recode or merge variables, create new variables or manage the definition of missing data. All this work has to be fully recorded, so that you know how to describe your data accurately when you report it in projects or publications, and so that you can return to data you have previously used in future analyses.

In order to store and retrieve your data you need a consistent naming system for files and folders. Put all the files relating to a survey in a single folder, with subfolders for different waves of the survey or work projects using it. Always keep a copy of the original data you downloaded and the latest version of the dataset you are working on. Ensure that you back up files regularly. Delete unnecessary files. Only keep files that you are certain you will use again. Delete previous editions of your dataset (except of course the original) and ensure that the latest edition is backed up. Unless you do this you will soon have many slightly different and incompatible versions of a data file, which are easy to confuse.

It is rarely a good idea to save output files unless you are sure that you will need to use their contents for future work. Often it is easier to reproduce output when you need it by running the relevant section of your syntax file. If you do save an output file, edit it first to remove content you will not need. Scrolling through endless output files searching for a table or statistic can waste a lot of time. Alternatively, you can keep a master output file for a dataset in which you store output you wish to use later on. Each time you work on the corresponding dataset open this output window and delete the default new **Viewer** window SPSS creates at the start of each work session. Keep this output file in the same folder, or within the same folder hierarchy as the relevant data files, and label it clearly. You can also input text directly to an output file. Click anywhere in the **Viewer** window where you want to add notes about your work, go to **Insert→New Text** or click the **New Text** icon in the **Viewer** toolbar to have SPSS create a box in which you can enter text.

7 3 RECORDING YOUR WORK: KEEPING A JOURNAL

Recording your work, whether or not you use syntax files, takes a little time. It is tempting to overlook it because it's boring (exploring data is far more interesting than recording what you did), because it is easy to convince yourself that you'll remember what you did when you return to a piece of work later on, or because you have to break off working at short notice. Resist these temptations!

The easiest way to keep a work journal is to spend a little time on your syntax file at the end of each work session. Edit the syntax file to ensure that all amendments you made to the original data are recorded, and are annotated with any information you used to do this that you may need to refer to in the future. You can insert comments in your syntax file in two ways. Start a new line with an asterisk and then finish your comment with a full stop. It can extend over as many lines as you wish and can use any characters or symbols. You can also insert comments after the end of a command on the same line if you precede it with a slash and an asterisk and finish it within the same line. However you cannot put comments in the middle of a command: that would cause an error. Below is an example of comments inserted in a series of commands using both techniques:

```
compute dpweight = (pweight*dweight). /* dweight is sample design only.
compute popweight = (pweight*pspweight).
weight by dpweight.
CROSSTABS gndr BY hlprtrn2 BY cntry
/FORMAT=AVALUE TABLES
/CELLS=COUNT ROW
/COUNT ASIS.
weight off.
weight by popweight.
*xtab run with both weights to attempt to replicate article N.
CROSSTABS gndr BY hlprtrn2 BY cntry
/FORMAT=AVALUE TABLES
/CELLS=COUNT ROW
/COUNT ASIS.
```

You will see that SPSS greys out comments, so that you can easily distinguish them from a sequence of commands. You will also find it helpful to leave blank lines between successive chunks of syntax: it is much easier on the eye than long blocks of computer code.

If you have used the GUI and not syntax, you will have to ensure that you keep a separate journal of your work. It must record all the changes you have made to your data including:

- any changes made to existing values from data 'cleaning'
- how any new variables were defined and created
- which original variables if any were deleted
- the criteria used for deleting any cases
- the sources of any new data (variable or cases) added to the dataset

The best place for such a journal is alongside any codebook you produce for your data, as I suggested you should do in Chapter 5. You will usually find that it is much less effort to use syntax as it saves a great deal of irksome journal writing. Nevertheless, keeping such a record will save you endless frustrating effort later on as you try to reconstruct your work from inadequate notes or scribbles. Inevitably you'll find yourself repeating work you have already done, in order to check how in fact you did it first time around.

7.4 EDITING DATASETS: REMOVING VARIABLES OR CASES

Often the data you want to use comes as an SPSS file that's fine as it is. But often it has to be assembled or edited in some way, or the original data is not in SPSS format. Even when it is usable as it is, it can be convenient to edit it to create a dataset that is easier and quicker to use – for example, because it contains only the subset of cases or variables that you will be working with. Thus we'll look first at removing redundant data. Then we'll look at assembling a dataset from different component sources.

7.4.1 Removing variables

Getting rid of cases or variables you don't need is straightforward. But first, check that you are sure that you are not going to need them as your work develops. If you later decide you need them after all, you will have to go back to the original data and then repeat all the modifications you may have made to it meanwhile, or merge your modified data with sections of the original data, a more complex task than the original editing.

To delete a few variables from a dataset you can use the command **delete variables** in the **Syntax Editor**. List the variables you wish to delete after the command and end with a full stop as always. You can use the **to** keyword to define a variable list. It is also possible to select a variable in the **Data Editor** window and go to **Edit→Clear**, but this is not recommended as it does not leave you with a record of what you have done.

To delete a large number of variables it is easier to save a new edition of your data file, instructing SPSS to **drop** variables when it does so. You can also use the GUI to do this. Within the **Data Editor** window, go to **File→Save As** which will open the **Save Data As** dialog box. This asks you for a file name and directory location for your file (as a default it offers the file name and location of the dataset you are working with) and also the format in which you wish to save it (the default is as an SPSS **.sav** file, but you can also save it in other formats including **.csv**, **.dat**, Excel, SAS and Stata). Clicking on the **Variables** button takes you to the **Save Data As: Variables** dialog box shown in Figure 7.1 that enables you to specify the variables to be written to the new file (or overwritten to the existing file if you have kept the same file name) in a number of different ways. There is a box in which you can check and uncheck variable names in order to keep or drop them. The **Keep All** and **Drop All** buttons allow you respectively to check and uncheck all the variables – especially useful if you only wish to retain a few variables, as it saves you checking every variable you wish to delete. Clicking **Continue** takes you back to the main dialog box where you can **Paste** to your syntax file to establish a record of what you have done.

Alternatively, you can write the syntax directly. It takes the form

```
save outfile='directory path ending in filename'
/drop var1 var2 var3
/compressed.
```

Here you can instead use the **/keep** sub-command to specify which variables are to be retained. The order in which the variables are listed will be the order they take in the new file, and any variables not specified after the command will be dropped. Note that if you supply a new file name SPSS will save the file to the location you have specified, but the original dataset will continue to be the active one in your **Data Editor** window. You will need to open the new file you have created in SPSS to work with it. If you specified the existing file name to overwrite it, your changes take immediate effect. Specifying directory paths correctly for the **Save Outfile**

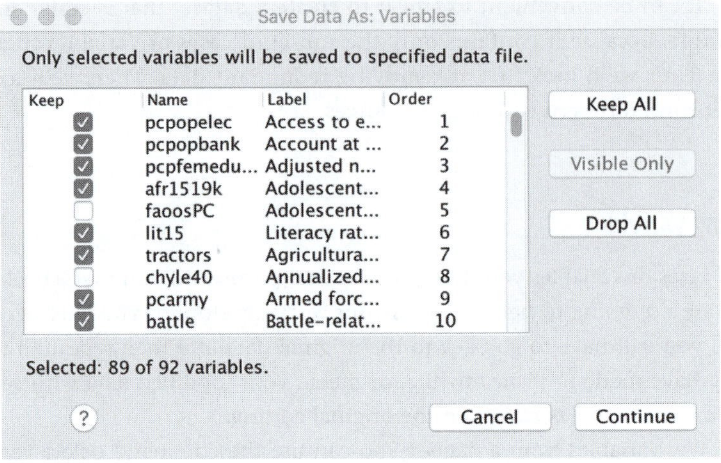

Figure 7.1   The **Save Data As: Variables** dialog box

command is best achieved by calling the **Save Data As** dialog box from the GUI and choosing **Paste**. You can then edit the result in the **Syntax Editor**.

7.4.2 Removing cases

When you want to drop cases you must first work out how best to identify the cases to be dropped. It might be that you have identified one or a few cases in the dataset which you wish to remove because they contain a large number of errors or for some other reason. Here you can use any unique identifier (such as a case number or identifier number) to drop them using the **Select Cases** routine. However, you must select the cases *you do not wish to drop* and then delete those cases not selected. For example, if you wished to drop the case where an identifier variable **ident** took the value 12345 your syntax would take the form

> use all.
> select if (ident ne 12345).

More often you will want to drop cases that share some common characteristic: all the cases from a county or group of countries, respondents in an age range or of a given educational level, and so on. It only makes sense to drop cases if you are absolutely sure that you will not want to include them in later analyses. Remember that you can select groups of cases for analysis by filtering out other cases temporarily using the **Filter** command that we saw in Chapter 4, or using the **Select Cases** dialog and choosing the option **Filter out unselected cases**.

7 ● 5   CREATING A WORLD DEVELOPMENT INDICATORS DATASET FROM THE WORLD BANK SITE

The World Bank oversees a very extensive data collection, cataloguing and analysis operation focused on global development. In recent years it has made a substantial and welcome effort to make the data it collects available in a readily accessible format and in no fewer than five languages. However, finding the right data and downloading it in a usable configuration can be a challenge simply because of the sheer volume of data available and the different formats it is available in. Fortunately, the data webpages also host a range of excellent guides to the data that are easy to follow. At the time of writing the Bank was trialling a new data interface and the instructions I give here refer to that. As the Bank's data provision develops, expect details to change; however, the main principles will almost certainly stay the same.

In what follows I assume that you've watched the short video which gives an excellent rapid overview of the DataBank at:

🔗 http://databank.worldbank.org/data/FAQ/Video/databank-tutorial-overview.html

The FAQs option takes you to a print version of the information in the video at:

🔗 http://databank.worldbank.org/data/faq/html/databank-faq.html

We will create a dataset in SPSS of a number of development indicators for the 214 countries of the world drawn from the *World Development Indicators* database. This holds over 1,400 variables, with some measured annually for up to 50 years, giving a vast amount of data. It is possible to download the complete dataset, but this is not advisable: there is too much data to deal with effectively. It is better to select the data you need and create a customised dataset. We'll use this dataset for some linear regression exercises in Chapter 9. You'll find that the skills you use in doing this will be relevant to downloading data from any database system, including those managed by Eurostat, the Organisation for Economic Co-operation and Development (OECD) and other organisations.

7 ● 6   LOCATING AND ASSEMBLING THE DATA

From the World Bank homepage select the **Data** tab that is displayed at both the head and foot of its homepage which takes you to the **Open Data** homepage. In the header of the page click on the link to **World DataBank**. Here click on **World Development Indicators** under the **EXPLORE DATABASES** heading and the page in Figure 7.2, or one very like it, will appear.

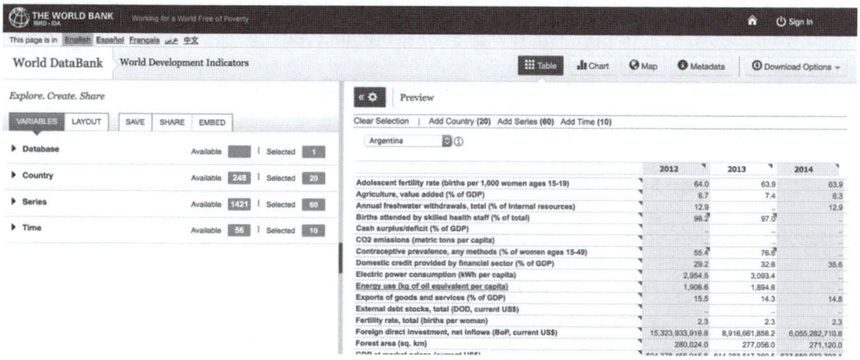

Figure 7.2   World DataBank World Development Indicators

On the left-hand side of the page click on ▸ **Country** and a list of countries and groups of countries will appear as well as three buttons to the right of the panel. [All | Countries | Aggregates] Click on the middle **Countries** button and then on the check icon [✓] to the left of the panel. You should see a small blue check box display against the name of each country, while at the top right of the panel opposite ▸ **Country** the boxes next to **Available** and to **Selected** should now contain the number of countries in the world that you have selected. Meanwhile you will see that in the right-hand **Preview** panel of the page a dialog box has appeared inviting you to [APPLY CHANGES]. Click on this button and the **Preview** panel will refresh its contents in line with your instructions.

Now return to the left-hand panel and select ▸ **Series**. This opens a list of the several hundred data series in the database. Use the keyword search function or alphabetical buttons to locate the following series and check the box adjacent to them to select them. If you click on the wrong check box, simply click it again to uncheck it. (In the list below I've also suggested variable names for these series in SPSS, which we'll use later.)

Access to electricity (% of population) [**elecpc**]

Literacy rate, adult female (% of females ages 15 and above) [**litf15pc**]

Births attended by skilled health staff (% of total) [**birthspc**]

CO2 emissions (metric tons per capita) [**co2mtpc**]

Contraceptive prevalence, any methods (% of women ages 15–49) [**cprev1449**]

Government expenditure on education, total (% of government expenditure) [**educpcge**]

Fertility rate, total (births per woman) [**tfr**]

Fixed broadband subscriptions (per 100 people) [**broadbpc**]

GDP per capita, PPP (constant 2011 international $) [**gdppc$2011ppp**]

GINI index (World Bank estimate) [**gini**]

Hospital beds (per 1,000 people) [**bedspk**]

Immunization, DPT (% of children ages 12–23 months) [**dptpc1223**]

Immunization, measles (% of children ages 12–23 months) [**measlespc1223**]

Improved water source (% of population with access) [**imph2opc**]

Incidence of tuberculosis (per 100,000 people) [**tubercp100k**]

Internet users (per 100 people) [**netpc**]

Life expectancy at birth, female (years) [**e0f**]

Life expectancy at birth, male (years) [**e0m**]

Lifetime risk of maternal death (%) [**mmrpc**]

Low-birthweight babies (% of births) [**lobirthpc**]

Military expenditure (% of GDP) [**milipcgdp**]

Mobile cellular subscriptions (per 100 people) [**mobiilepc**]

Mortality rate, infant (per 1,000 live births) [**infmort**]

Mortality rate, under-5 (per 1,000 live births) [**under5 mort**]

Population growth (annual %) [**popgrow**]

Poverty headcount ratio at $1.90 a day (2011 PPP) (% of population) [**povhr$190**]

Prevalence of HIV, total (% of population ages 15–49) [**HIV1549**]

Primary completion rate, female (% of relevant age group) [**comp1fpc**]

Research and development expenditure (% of GDP) [**rdpcgdp**]

Rural population (% of total population) [**rurlapc**]

Survey mean consumption or income per capita, bottom 40% of population (2011 PPP $ per day) [**conpc40$ppp**]

Women who believe a husband is justified in beating his wife (any of five reasons) (%) [**beatpc**]

Women who were first married by age 18 (% of women ages 20–24) [**married18pc**]

Feel free to add other series, but ensure that you choose at least the ones above, as we will use several of them later on. When you have selected all the series you want, click APPLY CHANGES once more. Now select ▶ Time, but rather than selecting specific years click on the **Create Time Function** button at the bottom right of the panel so that the dialog box in Figure 7.3 is displayed.

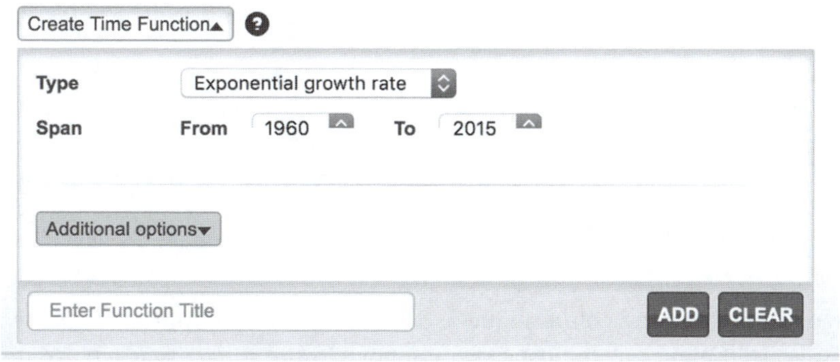

Figure 7.3 The **Create Time Function** dialog box

Against **Type** scroll down the list of functions to select **Most Recent Value** and against **Span** select the years 2009 to 2015. In the box called **Enter Function Title** give the time function you have just created a name, such as MRV0915, and click **ADD**. You should then see a pop-up dialog telling you that you have 'successfully added a **New Custom Period**'. Deselect any years that are currently checked so that the number of time points selected should read '1' in the grey box to the right of **Time**. Once again click APPLY CHANGES.

7 ● 7 DOWNLOADING AND FORMATTING THE DATA YOU HAVE SELECTED

You are now ready to download the data. Select **Excel** under the **Download Options** tab to the top right of the panel and an Excel file will download to your machine. It will have two worksheets. One will have the data, while a second will contain useful metadata on definitions and sources for each one of the series that you've selected. In the worksheet with the data, select all five columns and create a pivot table (how you do this will depend on the version and platform of Excel that you are using, but usually the command is under the **Data** menu). In the **PivotTable Builder** put **Country Name** in the **Rows**, **Series Name** in the **Columns** and **MRV0915** in **Values**. Click on **Count of MRV0915** and change this to **Max of MRV0915** in the **PivotTable Field** dialog box which will open when you click on **Count of MRV0915**. The worksheet should now look like Figure 7.4.

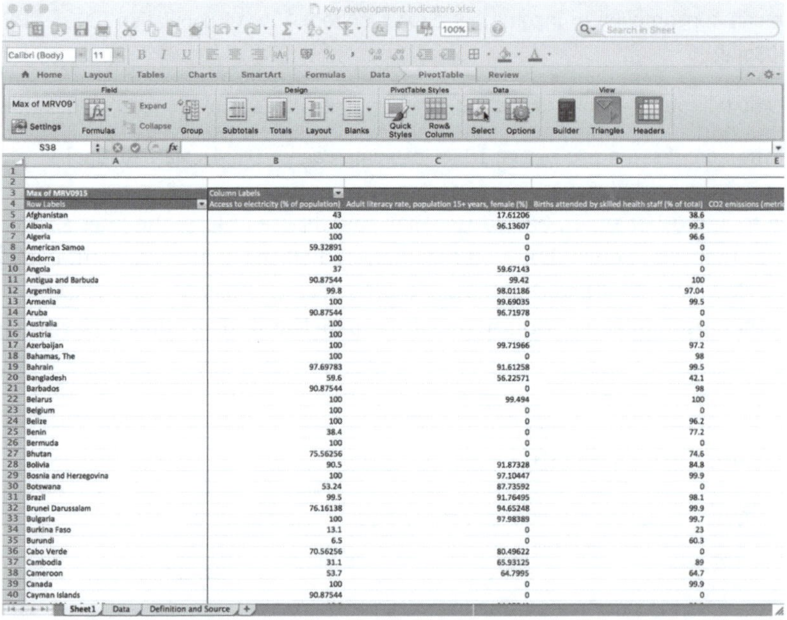

Figure 7.4 Excel worksheet of downloaded data

Next, replace the existing column labels so that they take appropriate variable names for SPSS. I've suggested names in the list of series above in the square brackets. To do this, first copy the contents of the worksheet to a new workbook and use **Paste Special** to copy only values to the new sheet, omitting the rows for **Grand Total** and the rows up to and including **Max of MRV0915** and **Column Labels** but including the row with the column descriptors themselves. You should find that this means omitting the first three rows. This strips out the pivot table formatting so that the data can be imported to SPSS without problems. Now you can substitute the suggested variable names for the existing column headings, including replacing **Row Labels** with **country**. Scroll down the data and you may find one or more rows that instead of a country name contain the text 'Data from database: World Development Indicators' or 'Last updated...'. Delete these rows. You should now have a worksheet with

215 rows, one with the list of variable names, and 214 with the data for each country in alphabetical order. It should look like Figure 7.5. Remember to save your work as you go and give this new workbook an appropriate name.

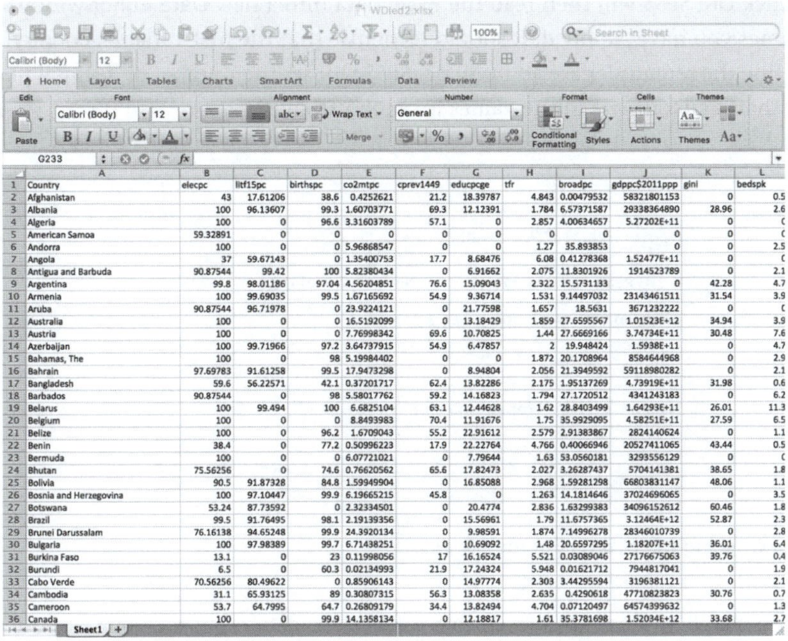

Country	elecpc	litf15pc	birthspc	co2mtpc	cprev1449	educpcge	tfr	broadpc	gdppc$2011ppp	gini	bedspk
Afghanistan	43	17.61206	38.6	0.4252621	21.2	18.39787	4.843	0.00479532	58321801153	0	0.5
Albania	100	96.13607	99.3	1.60703771	69.3	12.12391	1.784	6.57371587	29338364890	28.96	2.6
Algeria	100		96.6	3.31603789	57.1	0	2.857	4.00634657	5.27202E+11	0	0
American Samoa	59.32891	0	0	0	0	0	0	0	0	0	0
Andorra	100	0	0	5.96868547	0	0	1.27	35.893853	0	0	2.5
Angola	37	59.67143	0	1.35400753	17.7	8.68476	6.08	0.41278368	1.52477E+11	0	0
Antigua and Barbuda	90.87544	99.42	100	5.82380434	0	6.91662	2.075	11.8301926	1914523789	0	2.1
Argentina	99.8	98.01186	97.04	4.56204851	76.6	15.09043	2.322	15.5731133	0	42.28	4.7
Armenia	100	99.69035	99.5	1.67165692	54.9	9.36714	1.531	9.14497032	23143461511	31.54	3.9
Aruba	90.87544	96.71978	0	23.9224121	0	21.77598	1.657	18.5631	3671232222	0	6.2
Australia	100	0	0	16.5192099	0	13.18429	1.859	27.6595567	1.01523E+12	34.94	3.9
Austria	100	0	0	7.76998342	69.6	10.70825	1.44	27.6669166	3.74734E+11	30.48	7.6
Azerbaijan	100	99.71966	97.2	3.64737915	54.9	6.47857	2	19.948424	1.5938E+11	0	4.7
Bahamas, The	100	0	98	5.19984402	0	0	1.872	20.1708964	8584644968	0	2.9
Bahrain	97.69783	91.61258	99.5	17.9473298	0	8.94804	2.056	21.3949592	59118980282	0	2.1
Bangladesh	59.6	56.22571	42.1	0.37201717	62.4	13.82286	2.175	1.95137269	4.73919E+11	31.98	0.6
Barbados	90.87544	0	98	5.58017762	59.2	14.16823	1.794	27.1720512	4341243183	0	6.2
Belarus	100	99.494	100	6.6825104	63.1	12.44628	1.62	28.8403499	1.64293E+11	26.01	11.3
Belgium	100	0	0	8.8493983	70.4	11.91676	1.75	35.9929095	4.58251E+11	27.59	6.5
Belize	100	0	96.2	1.6709043	55.2	22.91612	2.579	2.91383867	2824140624	0	1.1
Benin	38.4	0	77.2	0.50996223	17.9	22.22764	4.766	0.40066946	20527411065	43.44	0.5
Bermuda	100	0	0	6.07721021	0	7.79644	1.63	53.0560181	3293556129	0	0
Bhutan	75.56256	0	74.6	0.76620562	65.6	17.82473	2.027	3.26287437	5704141381	38.65	1.8
Bolivia	90.5	91.87328	84.8	1.59949904	0	16.85088	2.968	1.59281298	66803831147	48.06	1.1
Bosnia and Herzegovina	100	97.10447	99.9	6.19665215	45.8	0	1.263	14.1814646	37024696065	0	3.5
Botswana	53.24	87.73592	0	2.32334501	0	20.4774	2.836	1.63299383	34096152612	60.46	1.8
Brazil	99.5	91.76495	98.1	2.19139356	0	15.56961	1.79	11.6757365	3.12464E+12	52.87	2.3
Brunei Darussalam	76.16138	94.65248	99.9	24.3920134	0	9.98591	1.874	7.14996278	28346010739	0	2.8
Bulgaria	100	97.98389	99.7	6.71438251	0	16.69092	1.48	20.6597295	1.18207E+11	36.01	6.4
Burkina Faso	13.1	0	23	0.11998056	17	16.16524	5.521	0.03089046	27176675063	39.76	0.4
Burundi	6.5	0	60.3	0.02134993	21.9	17.24324	5.948	0.01621712	7944817041	0	1.9
Cabo Verde	70.56256	80.49622	0	0.85906143	0	14.97774	2.303	3.44295594	3196381121	0	2.1
Cambodia	31.1	65.93125	89	0.30807315	56.3	13.08358	2.635	0.4290618	47710823823	30.76	0.7
Cameroon	53.7	64.7995	64.7	0.26809179	34.4	13.82494	4.704	0.07120497	64574399632	0	1.3
Canada	100	0	99.9	14.1358134	0	12.18817	1.61	35.3781698	1.52034E+12	33.68	2.7

Figure 7.5 The final version of the Excel file

7.8 IMPORTING THE DATA TO SPSS

You can now close this excel file. Go to SPSS and select **File→Read Text Data…** which will open the **Open Data** dialog box shown in Figure 7.6.

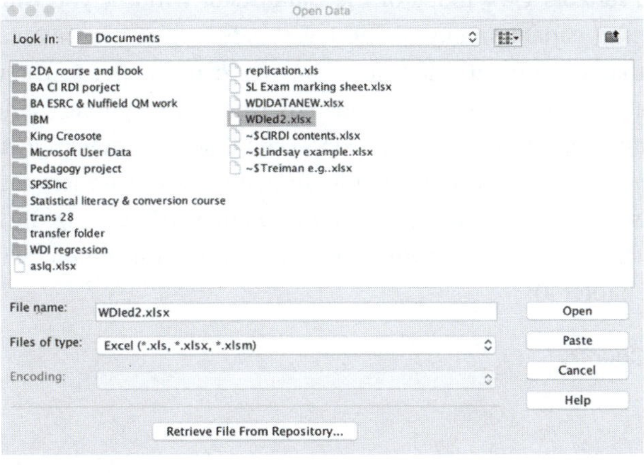

Figure 7.6 The **Open Data** dialog box

In the **Files of type:** option box choose Excel and then use the **Look in:** directory display to locate and select the Excel file you have just prepared. Its name will populate the **File Name:** box. Click **Open** and a further dialog box will open (Figure 7.7) which should have the option **Read variable names from the first row of data** already checked; if it is not then check this manually and click **OK**. SPSS will then read the Excel data into a new **Data Editor** window, with the variable names you have supplied. It should recognise that the first variable, **country**, is a string variable, while the remainder are all numeric. SPSS will set the number of decimal places to the maximum that it encounters in the values for each variable.

Figure 7.7 The **Opening Excel Data Source** dialog box

We have a couple of final tasks to do to complete our dataset. In the course of the data management, missing values will have been set to zeros. This could present a problem if we expected any 'real' zeros in our data, although this is unlikely. We can therefore set all zeros in the data to be missing values. SPSS requires this to be done separately for numeric and string variables, so we need to specify a variable list in the syntax beginning with the first numerical variable and ending with the last. Your syntax will be as follows, depending on the names you have given your variables:

MISSING VALUES elecpc to married18pc (0).

If you go to the **Variable View** mode of the **Data Editor** window you will see that SPSS will either have posted the variable name to the **Label** column, or left this blank. Return to the original Excel file that you downloaded from the World Bank site. In the worksheet labelled **Definitions and Source** you will find a list of **Indicator Names** that provide suitable variable labels and can be copied and pasted direct into the SPSS **Data Editor** window in **Variable View** mode.

Our variable for country is a string variable. In general these are less easy to manage than numeric variables, so it is a good idea to create a numeric version using the **Automatic Recode** command (**Transform→Automatic Recode...**) in the GUI or with the following syntax (we saw how to do this in Chapter 4):

AUTORECODE Country
/INTO cntrynum
/PRINT.

Finally, ensure that you save your new SPSS file and give it an appropriate name.

Now take a few minutes to explore the dataset. You'll see that most of the variables are at the interval level of measurement, in contrast to the categorical variables we have tended to deal with so far. You'll find it useful to use the **Frequencies** procedure to produce histograms and/or summary statistics for these variables. If you use the GUI check the **suppress tables** option in the dialog, or if using syntax use the subcommand

/format = notable.

otherwise you'll produce useless frequency tables with a row for each case! Put this subcommand on a new line after the **Frequencies** command. Remember that the full stop comes after any subcommands that you use with a command, not after the command itself.

You may also like to explore some of the associations between variables by producing scatterplots. Go to **Graphs→Legacy Dialogs→Scatter/Dot→Simple Scatter**. The dialog box (shown in Figure 7.8) has the familiar variable list on the left and boxes into which to select the variables to be displayed on the X (horizontal) and Y (vertical) axes. It is a good idea to place the variable for country in the **Label Cases by:** box, as this will allow you to inspect individual coordinates in the scatterplot to identify the relevant country. The syntax takes the form

GRAPH
/SCATTERPLOT(BIVAR)=*name of X variable* **WITH** *name of Y variable* **BY** *name of labelling variable*
(IDENTIFY).

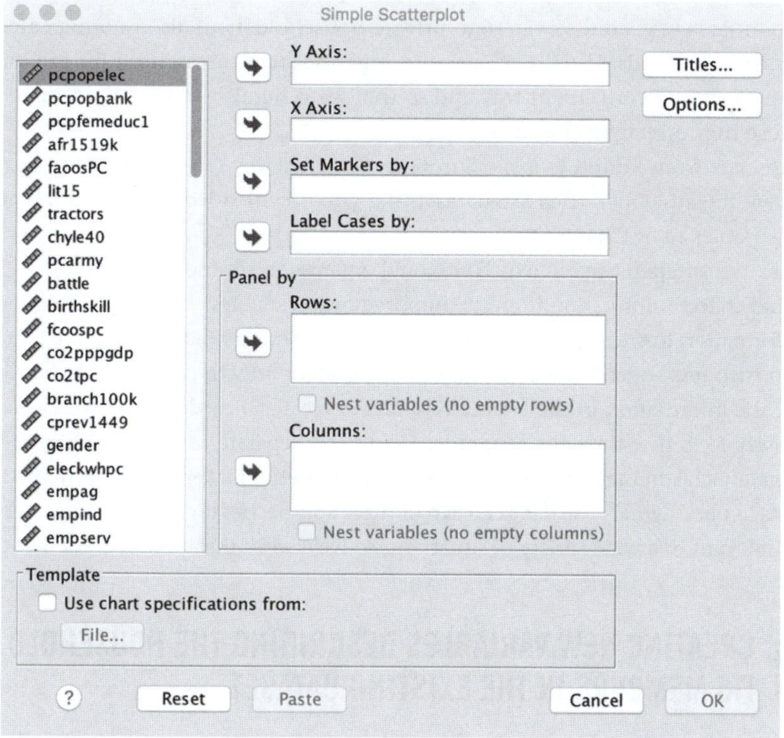

Figure 7.8   The **Simple Scatterplot** dialog box

Finally, store both your new SPSS dataset and the Excel file with the variable definitions and sources in the same folder, so that you have access to the key information about your dataset without having to go to the World Bank website.

You'll find that both the OECD and Eurostat offer similar systems for downloading data series that you can assemble in Excel and import in to SPSS.

7●9 HIERARCHICAL DATA: DEALING WITH HOUSEHOLDS

Datasets are flat two-dimensional affairs. Every variable has a column. Every case has a row. But social life does not resemble such a flat matrix. It is inherently hierarchical. Individuals live in a family, which in turn may or may not be coterminous with a household, which in turn may share an address with others. School pupils are taught in classes, in schools, in educational authority areas …

Many social surveys ask respondents questions both about themselves and about their households, often including a set of questions such as the age, sex and relationship to the respondent of other members of the household, details of the respondent's partner if they have one, such as their economic activity, and perhaps other features of the household. Because of this the information in our dataset may be 'hierarchical' rather than 'flat' since households come in different shapes and sizes. Thus instead of having exactly the same range of information for all respondents (and therefore perfectly well represented by a flat data matrix) the presence of some of the information will depend on the characteristics of the households within which the respondents are found. We can use the household information in the dataset to generalise not only to individual respondents (e.g. adults over 16 in private households) but also to other categories such as families or households. Usually we need to organise such hierarchical information both so that we can use it in a convenient way and so that we generalise to the appropriate unit and if necessary use the correct weights to do so.

We'll use data from Round 6 of the European Social Survey to see how data can be reorganised in different ways. Open the ESS6 dataset that you downloaded and added the **depress** and **zdepress** variables to in Chapter 5.

There are two different ways in which we could organise the household information in the dataset. We could collect information from the hundred or so variables about household members and use this information to create new variables describing the household that become part of the data we have on each respondent, since there is one respondent only in each household. Alternatively, we can use the information in these same variables to create a *new* dataset in which each member of the household, rather than the respondent only, is a separate case in the dataset. Later, if we wish, we can attach summary information about the household taken from this new dataset to the respondents in our original ESS6 dataset. Each of these approaches uses data management skills that you'll find relevant to a wide variety of situations, so we'll work through them each in turn.

7●10 CREATING NEW VARIABLES DESCRIBING THE HOUSEHOLD AND ITS MEMBERS IN THE EXISTING DATASET

We can begin by consulting the *source questionnaire* to check exactly how this data was collected from respondents. Here we find that they were first asked 'Including yourself, how many people – including children – live here regularly as members of this household?' This information was used to produce the variable **hhmmb**. In the ESS6 dataset household information begins with the variable **hhmmb** at line 277. From the **Variable View** mode of the **Data Editor** window you'll see that information was collected on the gender (**gndr2** to **gndr24**), year of birth (**yrbrn2** to **yrbrn24**), and relationship to the respondent (**rshipa2** to **rshipa24**) of up to 24 people living in the same household. Where there is no information to collect (e.g. on the third person in a household with only two people in it) these variables are coded 6, 66 or 6666 'not applicable' or take a system-missing value represented by a dot in the **Data View** mode of the **Data Editor** window. If the respondent had a partner, they were also asked about the latter's educational qualifications and economic activity, including occupation and hours of work if applicable. They were also asked about each parent's educational qualifications and occupation (if any) at the time of the respondent's 14th birthday.

This information is in a disaggregated form that is of little use as it stands. We'd rarely want to know the sex of the fourth household member, for example, since not all households will have a fourth member. However, because it is in this form, we can assemble it in whatever way captures features of the household or family that interest us. For example, we might want to know the number of young children in households, regardless of their position in the household grid. However, as we proceed we will need to take care with missing information. It is unlikely that all respondents were sure of the details of all household members, such as their year of birth.

Care must also be taken to correctly specify the populations to which we can generalise from the survey data. While the sampling procedures adopted in the ESS mean that respondents ought to represent the population of adults in a country, our collection of households in which these respondents are located will *not* represent the population of households. The inclusion of households in our sample will be proportional to the number of adults in them (since if each adult has a similar probability of selection, households with many adults will be more likely to be included). Were we to examine the data on parents' occupations it would *not* give us a good picture of the occupational structure a generation ago. First, respondents will have had their 14th birthday at any point from a year to 80 or more years ago. Second, the probability of selection of a parent will depend directly upon the number of children they have had who were adults at the time of the ESS survey round and therefore have a chance of being selected for its sample. Adults from earlier generations who did not have children would have no such chance of selection. Data on partners presents fewer problems. Since the ESS attempts to achieve a random sample of adults, either member of a partnership should have an equal chance of selection (as long as both are adults) and we can generalise to the populations of 'couples' or 'members of partnerships' in a straightforward way.

Before we start constructing new variables it makes sense to turn weights off in the dataset. Although they will not affect the construction of variables, non-integer weights can affect how some results are displayed, so that turning them off avoids this complication. Then we can start by reviewing the variable **hhmmb** containing responses to the question about the number of people in the household. Its frequency distribution is shown in Table 7.1. You'll see that 33 respondents did not know or did not give an answer to this question. We can safely ignore these responses since they are such a tiny fraction of our sample.

The distribution looks quite sound. There are no households with no members, most have only a few people and there is a reassuringly small proportion of households with many members.

Table 7.1 Number of people in household **(hhmmb)**

N	Frequency
1	10,528
2	17,619
3	10,483
4	9,493
5	4,003
6	1,539
7	543
8	203
9	85
10	44
11	46
12	29
13	8
14	4
15	4
16	3
17	1
18	2
22	1
23	1
24	1
Refusal	11
Don't know	6
No answer	16
Total	54673

7 ● 11 USING THE COUNT FUNCTION TO DESCRIBE HOUSEHOLD MEMBERS

Let's think about the gender composition of households. To produce information on this we need to bring together the values recorded across the original 24 variables from **gndr** to **gndr24**. For each respondent or case in the dataset we want to count up how many times these variables take the values 1 (male) and 2 (female). We will also need to check if there are variables with missing information (e.g. when a respondent didn't know or refused to disclose the gender of a household member). To do all this we can use the **count** procedure that we saw in Chapter 5.

We will begin by counting males. We want to count how many times the value 1 appears across all 24 **gndr** variables within each case in the dataset. Our syntax will be:

COUNT malehhn=gndr gndr2 gndr3 gndr4 gndr5 gndr6 gndr7 gndr8 gndr9 gndr10 gndr11 gndr12 gndr13 gndr14 gndr15 gndr16 gndr17 gndr18 gndr19 gndr20 gndr21 gndr22 gndr23 gndr24(1).
VARIABLE LABELS malehhn "N males in household".
FREQ malehhn.

Here the command **count** is followed by the name of the target variable (i.e. the new variable we are going to create), an equals sign, then the list of variables where the value or set of values is to be searched for and counted, and finally, in parentheses, the value or set of values to count. Remember that SPSS allows us to describe lists of consecutive variables in the dataset by using the word **to**, so that the long list of variable names here could also have been defined by specifying **gndr to gndr24**. You can also use the GUI to produce this syntax, as shown in Figure 7.9.

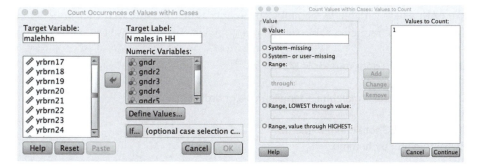

Figure 7.9   The **count** procedure dialogs

The syntax tells SPSS to count the number of times the value 1 appears across all these variables within a case and then set the value of our new **malehhn** variable for that case to be equal to that count. We'll want to check our results, so we can use the instruction **freq malehhn.** (don't forget the full stop). We can repeat this exercise for females very quickly by copying and pasting the syntax we used for males and editing it to alter the name of the target variable, changing the value to be counted to 2 and the variable label to **'N females in household'**. You will find that this is much quicker than using the GUI. However, it is important to double-check that you have edited the syntax consistently. It is easy to forget to edit all the elements that you need to change. Check your results against Table 7.2. I've also recoded the higher values to reduce the number of categories in the table.

These results seem quite reasonable. However, we can also check them against the distribution of **hhmmb**. To do this we'll need to take account of any household members for

Table 7.2 Numbers of men and women in surveyed households (ESS6)

	Men	Women
None	8,180	5,075
1	27,698	30,090
2	12,402	13,016
3	4,841	4,883
4	1,171	1,191
5	242	292
6+	139	126

whom respondents did not give gender information. Create a variable using the **count** command again (I've suggested the name **gndrdkr**). When you do so you will find about 400 such cases. Given that there were over 50,000 survey respondents and that some were faced with answering questions about large numbers of household members, it is not surprising that in a very small proportion of cases (0.7%) interviewers were unable to collect comprehensive information about everyone. Then compute a new variable formed by adding this variable to our variables for the numbers of men and women in each household, and finally produce a crosstab of this new variable by **hhmmb**. The syntax is below. Note that each time I create a new variable I run a frequency table so that I can quickly check if it has been correctly created.

```
COUNT gndrdkr = gndr to gndr24 (7, 9).
FREQ gndrdkr.
COMPUTE totalhhn = malehhn + femalehhn + gndrdkr.
FREQ totalhhn.
MISSING VALUES totalhhn hhmmb ().
CROSS totalhhn by hhmmb.
```

When you produce the crosstab you'll find that **hhmmb** and the new variable for the total number of household members give very similar but not identical results. With over 50,000 households it would not be surprising if a few respondents miscalculated the number of people in the household, but we'll examine some of these small discrepancies later on. We can safely ignore them for now.

Next we can identify children in the households. Unfortunately, we cannot do this exactly. We have the year but not the month of birth of household members and the year and month in which the interview was undertaken. Subtracting the birth from interview years will give us the correct age in years for people whose birthday took place *before* the date of the interview, but it will give us an answer one year too high for those whose birthday is still to take place, given that we usually reckon age in terms of completed years of life. However, this small inaccuracy should not matter too much for most purposes. The variable **inwyys** records the year of the start of the interview, which was either 2012 or 2013, while the relevant variable in the series **yrbrn** will record the year of each household member's birth.

7 ● 12 THE DO REPEAT – END REPEAT COMMAND

It would very tedious to write out the syntax for each of 24 variables to calculate an age in years for every household member. Fortunately, SPSS has a syntax command **do repeat – end repeat** which allows us to tell SPSS to do something with one or more variables and then repeat it with a similar list of variables that we give it. This saves a great deal of effort. We need to define a *placeholder* that stands in for the list of variables we want SPSS to carry out the same actions on, and also for any list of new variables that we want those repeated actions to replace. We want SPSS to subtract the year of birth of each household member from the year in which the interview occurred in order to produce their ages. We can do this with the following syntax (as usual, note that each of the commands ends with a full stop):

```
DO REPEAT Y=yrbrn to yrbrn24 / A=A1 to A24.
COMPUTE A = (inwyys - Y).
END REPEAT print.
```

The first line tells SPSS to carry out anything it is told to do, on each of the variables **yrbrn** to **yrbrn24**. It creates a set of new variables as a result, named **A1** to **A24**. The second line tells SPSS to make the set of variables defined in the first line (**A1** to **A24**) equal to the value for the year of interview (**inwyys**) minus the value for each **yrbrn** variable (**yrbrn** to **yrbrn24**). The third line tells SPSS to finish repeating commands and to print out a list of the commands that it carried out. SPSS then reports what it has done in the **Viewer** as shown in Figure 7.10.

```
Do repeat Y = yrbrn to yrbrn24 / A = A1 to A24.
compute A = (inwyys - Y).
end repeat print.

104  0 +compute        A1 = (inwyys - yrbrn)
105  0 +compute        A2 = (inwyys - yrbrn2)
106  0 +compute        A3 = (inwyys - yrbrn3)
107  0 +compute        A4 = (inwyys - yrbrn4)
108  0 +compute        A5 = (inwyys - yrbrn5)
109  0 +compute        A6 = (inwyys - yrbrn6)
110  0 +compute        A7 = (inwyys - yrbrn7)
111  0 +compute        A8 = (inwyys - yrbrn8)
112  0 +compute        A9 = (inwyys - yrbrn9)
113  0 +compute        A10 = (inwyys - yrbrn10)
114  0 +compute        A11 = (inwyys - yrbrn11)
115  0 +compute        A12 = (inwyys - yrbrn12)
116  0 +compute        A13 = (inwyys - yrbrn13)
117  0 +compute        A14 = (inwyys - yrbrn14)
118  0 +compute        A15 = (inwyys - yrbrn15)
119  0 +compute        A16 = (inwyys - yrbrn16)
120  0 +compute        A17 = (inwyys - yrbrn17)
121  0 +compute        A18 = (inwyys - yrbrn18)
122  0 +compute        A19 = (inwyys - yrbrn19)
123  0 +compute        A20 = (inwyys - yrbrn20)
124  0 +compute        A21 = (inwyys - yrbrn21)
125  0 +compute        A22 = (inwyys - yrbrn22)
126  0 +compute        A23 = (inwyys - yrbrn23)
127  0 +compute        A24 = (inwyys - yrbrn24)
```

Figure 7.10 The output from the **do repeat – end repeat** syntax

With just three short lines of syntax we've created 24 new variables (**A1** to **A24**). You may wish to check the **Data Editor** window where you'll see the new variables at the end of the dataset. We can now use these variables to count the number of people in different age groups in each household using the **count** procedure on our new variables for age.

Depending on our interests we might want to distinguish between infants, older children, working-age adults and older people. How much detail we require here depends upon what we are interested in. For example, were we wanting to look at households with preschool-age children, we might want to define this differently according to the age at which children in different countries normally start school. Were we interested in older people, we might want to take account of the state pension ages in different countries, or whether they are the same for men and women, and so on. Let's define infants as those aged under 5, children as those aged 5–14 years, adults of working age as all those aged 15–64, and older people as those aged 65 or over. We can use similar syntax to that which we used before to create variables describing the total number of household members in each category. As with gender, there will be cases where respondents were unable to give the year of birth of some household members, so that we will also need to take account of this. Try to work out the necessary syntax and then compare it with that suggested in the box. Remember to calculate how many households have members for whom we do not have information. You should find that this is the case for about 1,000 households, or 2% of the sample: an acceptable level of missing information. You should also be able to tell from the frequencies for these variables that around three in ten households have an older person in them, around one in ten have infants and two in ten have school-age children in them, but keep in mind that these proportions are based on unweighted data.

Syntax for producing age groups for household members:

```
COUNT infanthhn = a1 to a24 (0 thru 4).
COUNT childhhn = a1 to a24 (5 thru 14).
COUNT wagehhn = a1 to a24 (15 thru 64).
COUNT oldhhn = a1 to a24 (65 thru hi).
COUNT noage = yrbrn to yrbrn24 (7777,8888, 9999).
VARIABLE LABELS infanthhn "N children 0-4 in HH" childhhn "N children 5-14 in HH"
    wagehhn "N adults 15-64 in HH" oldhhn "N adults 65+ in HH" noage "N no age data in HH".
FREQ infanthhn to noage.
```

---

7 ● 13 USING THE COMPUTE COMMAND TO CREATE NEW VARIABLES

We may often think of households as comprising one or more adults and their children, but a little reflection suggests that the composition of households steadily changes over time. Children grow up and eventually leave the household, establishing their own, elderly relatives may move into it, or couples may separate or live apart. Household structure therefore has many possible dimensions and no single workable typology can capture all of these at once.

Moreover, in operationalising them we need to keep in mind that the respondent from the household randomly picked for the survey might be (among other things):

A (step)parent living alone or with their partner and/or with children

An older (15+) child living with parents and/or grandparents

A grandparent of another household member

An adult who has no family relation with other household members (e.g. a lodger, friend or au pair)

Because ESS collects information on household members in terms of their relationship to the respondent, we will have no information on the interrelationships of other household members when someone in the last of our categories was the respondent. We can identify such households as follows. Each of the **rshipa** variables will take the value 6 (other non-relative) and their total number should be equal to the total number of household members minus 1 (since the respondent is a member of the household included in this total). We can use the **count** procedure to identify such cases as follows. First we'll create a variable that tells us the number of people in the household not related to the respondent:

```
COUNT norelative = rshipa2 to rshipa24 (6).
FREQ norelative.
```

Then for households comprising more than one person, and in which there were one or more people who were not related to the respondent, we can identify cases where the non-relatives comprised all the other members of the household as follows:

```
COMPUTE onlynonrel = 0.
IF (hhmmb gt 1) and (norelative gt 0) and ((hhmmb - norelative) = 1 ) onlynonrel eq 1.
FREQ onlynonrel.
```

Often the best way to produce a new variable is first to set all cases to one value, using the **Compute** command, and then use a series of **if** statements to reset this value dependent upon the characteristics of the categories you want the new variable to have. In the syntax I've created a new variable **onlynonrel** and set its value to zero for all cases. I've then set out a series of logical statements that tell SPSS the conditions under which the value of **onlynonrel** should be set to 1: when there is more than one person in the household *and* there is a non-relative in the household *and* the number of non-relatives is equal to one less than the total number of household members (i.e. comprises everyone except the respondent). I've used brackets to separate each statement or logical operation. Note that SPSS syntax is at home with mathematical and logical operators, so that for example '=' has the same effect as **eq**. Other common symbols and their alphabetic equivalents are:

>	**gt**	Greater than
≥	**ge**	Greater than or equal to
<	**lt**	Less than
≤	**le**	Less than or equal to

When you produce this variable you should find that 468 respondents reported that they were not related to any other member of the household.

Now we can look at the distributions for other kinds of relationships of household members to the respondent. We can count children of the respondent, partners, parents and siblings. Instead of using the **count** command multiple times, SPSS allows you to issue the same command several times by using a slash to separate out the details of each new variable you want to create. The following syntax asks SPSS to create a new variable for each of these categories:

```
COUNT partners = rshipa2 to rshipa24 (1) /
offspring = rshipa2 to rshipa24 (2) /
parents = rshipa2 to rshipa24 (3) /
sibs = rshipa2 to rshipa24 (4).
VARIABLE LABELS partners "N partner of R" offspring "N (step)children of R in HH"
/ parents "N parents(in-law) of R in HH"
/ sibs "N (step)siblings of R in HH".
FREQ parents to sibs.
```

If you look at the frequency table for the new **partners** variable you will see a very small number of households where the data records more than one partner. It is possible that these are accurate accounts. A respondent might be living with a new partner and a spouse whom they have not yet separated from. They may come from a country where polygamy is still lawful. However, both these situations would be rather rare; so these cases might be data entry errors. Later we'll select them and examine them further to see if other evidence helps us identify if an error has been made.

It is of course also possible that some of the single partners reported are errors. We'd usually expect partners to be of a similar age to the respondent, so let's first create a variable describing the partner's age. To do this we need to use the correct variable for the year of birth of the partner, defined by the number in the household grid allocated to the partner. To save effort we can first identify the range of these numbers. Since the value corresponding to partner in the variables **rshipa2** to **rshipa24** is 1, the minimum value, we can run frequencies for all these variables, suppress the output of the tables, and ask SPSS to report the minimum value for each variable. Where this value is 1, this will tell us the range of **rshipa** variables where a partner is reported. Including the subcommand **/FORMAT=NOTABLE** tells SPSS not to produce frequency tables in the output, while **/STATISTICS=MIN** tells it to report the minimum value each variable takes.

```
FREQ rshipa2 to rshipa24
/FORMAT=NOTABLE
/STATISTICS=MIN.
```

7 ●14 USING IF STATEMENTS TO CREATE VARIABLES

You'll find that no partners were reported as tenth or subsequent household members, so we need only deal with variables **rshipa2** to **rshipa9**. We can now calculate partners' ages as follows:

```
COMPUTE partdob eq 9999.
IF (rshipa2 = 1) partdob = yrbrn2.
IF (rshipa3 = 1) partdob = yrbrn3.
IF (rshipa4 = 1) partdob = yrbrn4.
IF (rshipa5 = 1) partdob = yrbrn5.
IF (rshipa6 = 1) partdob = yrbrn6.
IF (rshipa7 = 1) partdob = yrbrn7.
IF (rshipa8 = 1) partdob = yrbrn8.
IF (rshipa9 = 1) partdob = yrbrn9.
RECODE partdob (sysmis = 9999).
MISSING VALUES partdob (9999).
FREQ partdob.
```

Note that before the **if** statements, I first set the value of the new variable **partdob** to a value that will become the missing value for the variable. If SPSS finds no value 1 (a partner) in any of the variables **rshipa2** to **rshipa9** it will do nothing, and so leave this as the value 9999 already stored for **partdob**. Note too that I've recoded system-missing values to 9999. SPSS will produce a system-missing value if it finds a missing value at **yrbrn** for a case. Recoding these to 9999 just keeps things tidy. You will be able to see from the frequency table that there are some suspiciously young partners with dates of birth after 1997.

We can use very similar syntax to identify the gender of respondent's partners when they live in the same household. The quickest way to do this is to edit the syntax we've just used to identify their age. Try to produce this syntax yourself and then compare it with the syntax shown in the box.

Syntax for identifying the gender of respondents' partners

```
COMPUTE pgndr eq 9999.
IF (rshipa2 = 1) pgndr = gndr2.
IF (rshipa3 = 1) pgndr = gndr3.
IF (rshipa4 = 1) pgndr = gndr4.
IF (rshipa5 = 1) pgndr = gndr5.
IF (rshipa6 = 1) pgndr = gndr6.
IF (rshipa7 = 1) pgndr = gndr7.
IF (rshipa8 = 1) pgndr = gndr8.
IF (rshipa9 = 1) pgndr = gndr9.
RECODE pgndr (sysmis = 9999).
MISSING VALUES pgndr (9999).
FREQ pgndr.
```

We might want to identify the age of the youngest member of each household. The amount of care children need is generally higher the younger they are, which influences such factors as the economic activity of parents in the household. Again we can use the **compute** procedure to collate information from the variables **A1** to **A24** that we made earlier and use it to identify the age of the youngest person in the household by setting the value of our new variable equal to the minimum value encountered in the age variables:

```
COMPUTE youngest = min(A1 to A24).
VAR LABELS youngest "age of youngest hh member".
FREQ youngest.
```

When you do this you'll see that SPSS sets the values of 107 cases to system missing. It does this when it cannot calculate the value of the new variable because the relevant information is missing in the original variables.

7 ●15 DATA CLEANING

We can also create a variable that is equal to the age difference between respondents and partners and look at its distribution:

```
COMPUTE agediff = (yrbrn–partdob).
FREQ agediff.
```

You should find that most partners are only a few years younger or older than each other. However, there are some very large values that bear investigating, since although they are not impossible, they are rather unlikely and may be errors in the data. Identifying errors in the data that can be corrected from using other information is referred to as *data cleaning*. Data cleaning is a matter of judgement. The amount of effort invested in it depends upon the quality of the data, the scale of errors and the prospect of being able to correct them using other data available within the dataset, and the importance of accuracy in the data values. The quality of data can only be inferred from the number of errors visible in the data, which can be assessed by looking for inconsistent combinations of data values for a case across different variables. For example, men cannot give birth, school-age children in affluent countries are unlikely to have long hours of paid employment, and so on.

The European Social Survey produces exceptionally clean data, so that we need not devote much time and effort to cleaning it. Unfortunately, this is not always true of datasets you will encounter. How should we proceed if we found a problematic error rate and wanted to inspect our data further? First we would need to identify cases with problematic information, and then inspect those cases to see if we can infer what may have gone wrong at the data collection stage and correct errors in our data. Let's do this here, even though the scale of error in the data is remarkably low so that we could normally skip such work as being unlikely to be worth the effort invested.

Let's examine cases where a respondent has reported more than one partner. Use the following syntax:

```
USE ALL.
COMPUTE filter_$=(partners gt 1).
```

FILTER BY filter_$.

LIST VARS = cntry idno yrbrn gndr hhmmb partdob agediff yrbrn2 to yrbrn6 rshipa2 to rshipa6 gndr2 to gndr6.

First we select the cases with more than one partner, and then the **list vars** subcommand asks SPSS to produce a report listing the values of every case for each of the variables that we list. A selection of the output is shown in Figure 7.11.

cntry	idno	yrbrn	gndr	hhmmb	partdob	agediff	yrbrn2	yrbrn3	yrbrn4	yrbrn5	yrbrn6	rshipa2	rshipa3	rshipa4	rshipa5	rshipa6	gndr2	gndr3	gndr4	gndr5	gndr6
CY	194	1976	1	4	2010	−34	1989	2005	2010	6666	6666	1	2	1	66	66	2	2	1	6	6
CY	1032	1972	1	5	1993	−21	1974	1993	1997	2006	6666	1	1	2	2	66	2	1	1	2	6
ES	1283	1953	2	4	1983	−30	1952	1980	1983	6666	6666	1	2	1	66	66	1	1	2	6	6
ES	1696	1970	1	4	9999	.	1973	2002	9999	6666	6666	1	2	1	66	66	2	2	1	6	6
ES	2252	1965	2	4	2001	−36	1962	1999	2001	6666	6666	1	2	1	66	66	1	1	1	6	6
FI	12266	1980	2	5	1980	0	1974	1980	2005	2011	6666	1	1	2	2	66	1	1	2	1	6
IE	38898	1962	1	3	1960	2	1960	1960	6666	6666	6666	1	1	66	66	66	2	2	6	6	6
IE	41772	1974	1	3	2010	−36	1973	2010	6666	6666	6666	1	1	66	66	66	2	1	6	6	6
IL	2264	1965	2	3	1998	−33	1966	1998	6666	6666	6666	1	1	66	66	66	1	2	6	6	6
IT	2965	1977	2	3	2009	−32	1972	2009	6666	6666	6666	1	1	66	66	66	1	1	6	6	6
IT	3126	1974	9	4	2011	−37	1979	2005	2011	6666	6666	1	2	1	66	66	2	2	2	6	6
NL	602015	1965	2	3	1996	−31	1966	1996	6666	6666	6666	1	1	66	66	66	1	1	6	6	6
NL	602714	1970	2	5	1973	−3	1957	1973	2000	2002	6666	1	1	2	2	66	1	2	1	1	6
NO	12954	1987	2	3	1987	0	1987	1987	6666	6666	6666	1	1	66	66	66	2	1	6	6	6
SE	2282	1972	2	6	1997	−25	1960	1997	2002	2004	2010	1	1	2	2	2	1	1	1	1	1
SE	2417	1974	2	4	2004	−30	1974	1994	2004	6666	6666	1	2	1	66	66	1	2	1	6	6
SE	2850	1982	1	3	2010	−28	1985	2010	6666	6666	6666	1	1	66	66	66	2	1	6	6	6
SK	201409	1975	1	5	2008	−33	1974	1999	2001	2008	6666	1	2	2	1	66	2	2	1	1	6
SK	212104	1943	1	3	9999	.	9999	9999	6666	6666	6666	1	1	66	66	66	1	1	6	6	6
SK	220301	1933	2	5	1956	−23	1954	1956	1973	1976	6666	1	1	2	2	66	1	2	1	1	6
SK	220602	1965	2	6	1988	−23	1931	1932	1959	1986	1988	3	3	1	2	1	1	2	1	2	1
SK	221207	1950	2	4	1993	−43	1992	1993	2006	6666	6666	1	1	2	66	66	1	2	2	6	6
XK	96	1993	2	5	1964	29	1954	1964	1988	1990	6666	1	1	3	3	66	1	2	2	1	6
XK	288	1944	1	4	1969	−25	1945	1969	1972	6666	6666	1	1	5	66	66	2	1	2	6	6
XK	734	1938	1	8	1963	−25	1943	1963	1986	1989	1992	1	1	2	2	2	2	2	2	2	1
XK	845	1981	1	7	2012	−31	1958	1982	2001	2003	2005	3	1	2	2	2	2	2	2	1	2
XK	1401	1974	2	4	2012	−38	1974	1975	2012	6666	6666	1	5	1	66	66	1	2	1	6	6
XK	1542	1964	1	7	2008	−44	1969	1997	2000	2001	2004	1	2	2	2	2	1	2	1	1	1
XK	1716	1947	2	3	1985	−38	1945	1985	6666	6666	6666	1	1	66	66	66	1	1	6	6	6
CZ	4224	1972	1	8	1973	−1	1973	1995	1997	9999	9999	1	2	2	99	99	2	1	1	9	9
IT	1957	1985	2	4	9999	.	9999	9999	9999	6666	6666	1	1	1	66	66	1	2	2	6	6
IT	2464	1969	1	4	2009	−40	1979	2007	2009	6666	6666	1	1	1	66	66	2	2	2	6	6

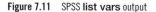

Number of cases read: 32   Number of cases listed: 32

Figure 7.11 SPSS **list vars** output

The first case, from Cyprus, **idno** 194, is a man born in 1976. There are three other household members. The second member of the household is his *partner* born in 1989. The third is a *daughter* born in 2005. The fourth, born in 2010, is a boy, coded as a *partner*. We could confidently conclude that this is a coding error and set the value for **rshipa4** for this case to 2 for son/daughter. The next case, also from Cyprus, is a man born in 1972 with a partner born in 1974. The third member of this household is another boy *partner* born in 1993, followed by children born in 1997 and 2006. Again we could conclude that this is another case of a son being miscoded as a partner and can recode **rshipa3** to 2. Many other cases are similar examples of miscodes, which I've summarised in Table 7.3.

We can correct these errors by using syntax to give SPSS the correct values. Given the volume of data collected on over 50,000 respondents, the error rate is extremely low. Moreover, in these few cases we're proceeding on the balance of probabilities, given contradictory information captured in the survey. For example, it could be that in our second case the man might have recently separated from his partner born in 1974, but while she remains a member of the

Table 7.3 Probable miscodes in ESS6

country	idno	Variable	correct value
5	194	rshipa4	2
5	1032	rshipa3	2
10	1283	rshipa4	2
10	2252	rshipa4	2
15	41772	rshipa3	2
16	2264	rshipa3	2
18	2965	rshipa3	2
18	3126	rshipa4	2
20	602015	rshipa3	2
25	2282	rshipa3	2
25	2417	rshipa4	2
25	2850	rshipa3	2
27	201409	rshipa5	2
29	288	rshipa3	2
18	2464	rshipa3	2
18	2464	rshipa4	2
29	1401	rshipa4	88
11	111851	yrbrn2	1979
14	10212	yrbrn2	8888
29	1210	yrbrn2	1979
29	1542	rshipa7	2
6	4224	rshipa7	99
6	4224	rshipa8	99

household, his mistress born in 1993 has already moved in. It's a highly improbable scenario, but it might nevertheless crop up once in a sample of over 50,000 households, which is what we are working with.

The following **if** statements can be used to correct what appear to be errors in the data. ✎ If you prefer you can copy and paste this syntax from the companion website.

IF (country =5) and (idno = 194) rshipa4 = 2.
IF (country =5) and (idno = 1032) rshipa3 = 2.
IF (country =10) and (idno = 1283) rshipa4 = 2.

```
IF (country =10) and (idno = 2252) rshipa4 = 2.
IF (country =15) and (idno = 41772) rshipa3 = 2.
IF (country =16) and (idno = 2264) rshipa3 = 2.
IF (country =18) and (idno = 2965) rshipa3 = 2.
IF (country =18) and (idno = 3126) rshipa4 = 2.
IF (country =20) and (idno = 602015) rshipa3 = 2.
IF (country =25) and (idno = 2282) rshipa3 = 2.
IF (country =25) and (idno = 2417) rshipa4 = 2.
IF (country =25) and (idno = 2850) rshipa3 = 2.
IF (country =27) and (idno = 201409) rshipa5 = 2.
IF (country =29) and (idno = 288) rshipa3 = 2.
IF (country =18) and (idno = 2464) rshipa3 = 2.
IF (country =18) and (idno = 2464) rshipa4 = 2.
IF (country =29) and (idno = 1401) rshipa4 = 88.
IF (country =11) and (idno = 111851) yrbrn2 = 1979.
IF (country =14) and (idno = 10212) yrbrn2 = 8888.
IF (country =29) and (idno = 1210) yrbrn2 = 1979.
IF (country =29) and (idno = 1542) rshipa7 = 2.
IF (country =6) and (idno = 4224) rshipa7 = 99.
IF (country =6) and (idno = 4224) rshipa8 = 99.
```

7 ● 16 WORKING PARENTS

Respondents with a partner were asked about the latter's education and economic activity as well as their age and sex. Let's examine the economic activity of parents of young children. First we need to note that the information on couples in the ESS, as in any survey, is shaped by its sampling strategy. Remember that the respondent from a household might be one of the members of a couple, but they might also be an adult child of a couple who has not yet left the family home, or an older relative of others in the household who might also have a partner. Only in the first of these cases will we have information on the respondent's partner of a couple with young children, even though such partnerships may exist within the household.

We can identify households with a couple with a child (0–14 years) where one of the members of the couple is a respondent. We can do this by selecting households where **offspring**, **partners** and either **infanthhn** or **childhhn** each take the value 1 or greater. We can create a new variable to flag such cases. Try to produce the syntax for creating this variable and then compare it with my suggestion below.

```
COMPUTE flag eq 0.
IF ((childhhn ge 1) and (partners ge 1) and (offspring ge 1)) flag = 1.
IF ((infanthhn ge 1) and (partners ge 1) and (offspring ge 1)) flag = 1.
VALUE LABELS flag 0 "other" 1 "child 0-14yrs & partner of R in HH".
FREQ flag.
```

You should find that 19.6% of households in the survey (unweighted) satisfy this condition. Let's see how many of these couples are dual-earner couples where both are working.

We can use the variables **pdwrk** and **pdwrkp** to identify cases where the respondent and partner are working, and the variables **gndr** and **pgndr** to identify the gender of the partners. Try to produce the syntax necessary to identify the working status of heterosexual couples with young children and compare it to my suggestion below. You'll see that I've set out a series of **if** statements for the six possible combinations of **gndr** (gender of respondent) **pdwrk** (whether respondent works) and **pdwrkp** (whether partner of respondent works).

```
COMPUTE dualearn = 9.
IF ((flag = 1) and (pdwrk = 1) and (pdwrkp = 1)) dualearn = 1.
IF ((flag = 1) and (gndr = 1) and (pdwrk = 1) and (pdwrkp = 0)) dualearn = 2.
IF ((flag = 1) and (gndr = 2) and (pdwrk = 0) and (pdwrkp = 1)) dualearn = 2.
IF ((flag = 1) and (gndr = 2) and (pdwrk = 1) and (pdwrkp = 0)) dualearn = 3.
IF ((flag = 1) and (gndr = 1) and (pdwrk = 0) and (pdwrkp = 1)) dualearn = 3.
IF ((flag = 1) and (pdwrk = 0) and (pdwrkp = 0)) dualearn = 4.
VALUE LABELS dualearn 1 "both work" 2 "man works" 3 "woman works" 4 "neither works"
9 "NA".
MISSING VALUES dualearn (9).
FREQ dualearn.
```

Let's compare this across countries. To do this we will need to weight the cases by **pspwght**. Produce a contingency table of **cntry** by **dualearn** and you should find that in most countries the most common arrangement is for both partners to be in paid work. You may also want to produce a graphic of these results in Excel, as I've done in Figure 7.12. Only in Albania, Kosovo and, surprisingly, Italy is this not the case. However, we have to be cautious in interpreting the results. Although ESS6 records data from over 50,000 households, the number of respondents from households in each country with a partnership and school-age children is modest: between about 100 and 400 in each country. This means that the confidence intervals we need to place around the proportions in our contingency table will be correspondingly broad. I've shown those for the proportion of dual earner couples in each country. You can use the confidence interval calculator on the companion website to do this. Table 7.4 shows a selection of the results: check them against the results you get. As usual, the syntax is available on the companion website if you run into trouble. Note several things that the table reveals.

Notice that I've used no decimal places in the table, because that would have been 'spurious accuracy'. Given the modest sample numbers in each country, our estimates for the percentages of dual-earner households in each county have a margin of sampling error of 4–5 percentage points above and below our sample estimate. It looks as if dual-earner families are the most common working arrangement everywhere except Italy and Ukraine. However, in both these countries the confidence intervals are wide enough for us to be unsure whether this is in fact the most common working arrangement. This illustrates a common challenge in using survey data. Although our number of respondents across all the countries in ESS6 is very large, once we drill down to specific categories of respondent within individual countries our sample size rapidly becomes too small to make precise estimates.

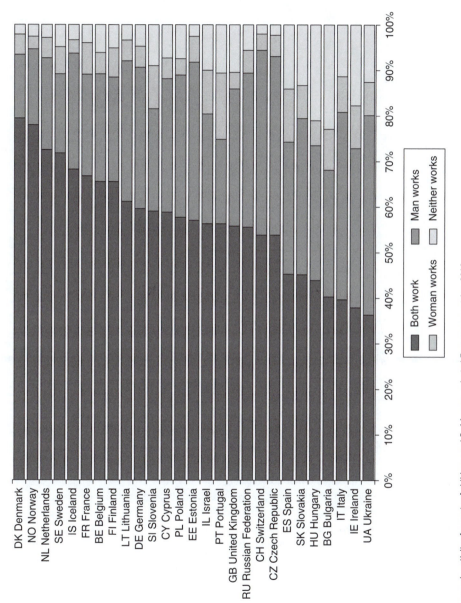

Figure 7.12 Economic activity of parents of children aged 5–14 years, selected European countries, 2012

Source: ESS6 post-stratification weights applied; author's calculations.

Table 7.4 Economic activity of parents of children aged 5–14 years, selected European countries, 2012

	Both work		95% CI	Man works	Woman works	Neither works	N
Denmark	79	75	84	13	6	2	336
Netherlands	72	68	77	20	4	3	413
France	69	65	74	21	6	4	408
Germany	60	56	64	31	5	4	526
Poland	58	53	62	32	3	7	458
United Kingdom	55	51	60	30	4	11	447
Russian Federation	55	50	60	34	5	6	386
Switzerland	53	47	59	42	3	2	289
Spain	46	41	51	29	12	13	397
Bulgaria	41	36	45	28	9	22	456
Italy	40	32	48	42	7	11	139
Ireland	38	34	42	34	10	18	568
Ukraine	36	32	41	44	7	13	457

Source: ESS6, post-stratification weights applied. Author's calculations.

what you have learned

This chapter should have given you some insight into different aspects of managing data, from downloading and importing data that is not originally in an SPSS format, through to identifying and cleaning errors in the data and then coping with data that is hierarchical. Hopefully it has also shown you how flexible and powerful the **count, compute** and **if** commands are in SPSS, especially when combined with the **do repeat – end repeat** procedure. You have seen how to:

- Take time with data management and preparation
- Make record keeping and file management systematic, saving a great deal of time
- Remove redundant cases and variables from a dataset
- Use the **Keep** and **Drop** sub-commands
- Assemble a custom dataset from components available on websites
- Import Excel data to create an SPSS **.sav** file
- Use the **Count, If** and **Compute** commands to create new variables from many different original ones
- Use the **Do Repeat – End Repeat** procedure
- Clean data to correct errors you find
- Save new versions of your data file

exercises

1 The ESS6 dataset you have been working with contains many country-specific variables that you are unlikely to use. These include the political party that respondents report having voted for or feeling close to, the precise religion that respondents report belonging to or having belonged to, and their own, their partner's and their parents' highest level of education using national qualifications. **Drop** these variables and save a new version of the dataset.

2 Review all the SPSS and other files you have created so far in working through this book. Delete redundant files (but ensure your latest version of each file is backed up). Arrange the remaining files methodically in folders, renaming them if need be. Examine and edit your syntax (**.sps**) files and add any commentary necessary to enable you to return to earlier work and understand what has been done.

3 Use ESS6 to calculate the mean weekly working hours of the members of the dual-earner couples you identified by the variable **dualearn**. Use the confidence interval calculator on the companion website to calculate 95% confidence intervals for your results.

MANAGING AND MANIPULATING DATA

introduction

Sometimes it is useful to go further than restructuring data within a dataset and instead use it to create an entirely new dataset. There are also situations where you will wish to merge two or more datasets in order to add new variables or new cases, or to take information from several cases to produce brake and aggregate variables. We learn how to:

- Merge two datasets together and to use the **Restructure Data Wizard**
- Work with more than one dataset at once
- Check and reorganise missing values codes to ensure your data restructuring is successful
- Create new cases from existing variables
- Create consistent identifiers for the new cases
- Use the **Summarize, Merge** and **Aggregate** commands
- Merge files to add variables
- Merge files to add cases
- Use syntax created for one dataset to run procedures on another one

8 ● 1 USING VARIABLES TO CREATE NEW CASES

The procedures we looked at in Chapter 7 rearrange the information in the dataset in order to extract information from several variables at once and summarise it, for example, information about the household within which the respondent was located. However, it may be that the focus of your interest is the household composition itself, so that using these procedures to produce all the data you might want could become time-consuming and tedious. An alternative, which needs rather more investment in the preparation of the data but is then faster once such data has been created, is to use the information in household roster variables to create a new dataset where there is one record for each household member, whether or not they were the respondent, so that each household member becomes a case in the dataset. This is illustrated in Figure 8.1 for data on six households with a total of 16 members.

In order to do this we have to take the existing *variables* describing other household members in the respondent's data and use them to create new *cases*. The number of new cases created will *not* be the same for each respondent: it will depend upon the number of other household members for whom we have information. We'll create a new case for each of the second to 24th household members defined by **gndr2** to **gndr24**, **yrbrn2** to **yrbrn24** and **rshipa2** to **rshipa24**. Then we'll delete all the cases that comprise only missing values (because the corresponding household members do not exist) and end up with a dataset that has as many cases as there were people in the respondents' households.

The syntax for restructuring operations can be complex, so this is an occasion where using the GUI as well as syntax is helpful. Even experienced IBM SPSS Statistics software users can make mistakes when restructuring data, and so it is essential to ensure that you have backed up the latest version of your dataset before embarking on any restructuring. Having done this, we'll next create a much smaller dataset with only a few variables from which we'll construct a dataset that will comprise a record for each household member recorded in the survey.

Current dataset

01	HH 1	R1 data	M12 sex	M12 age	M12 rel R	M13 sex	M13 age	M13 rel R	M14 sex	M14 age	M14 rel R
02	HH 2	R2 data	M22 sex	M22 age	M22 rel R						
03	HH 3	R3 data	M32 sex	M32 age	M32 rel R	M33 sex	M33 age	M33 rel R	M34 sex	M34 age	M34 rel R
04	HH 4	R4 data									
05	HH 5	R5 data	M52 sex	M52 age	M52 rel R	M53 sex	M53 age	M53 rel R			
06	HH 6	R6 data	M62 sex	M62 age	M62 rel R						

New dataset

01	HH1	R1 data		
02	HH1	M12 sex	M12 age	M12 rel R
03	HH1	M13 sex	M13 age	M13 rel R
04	HH1	M14 sex	M14 age	M14 rel R
05	HH2	R2 data		
06	HH2	M22 sex	M22 age	M22 rel R
07	HH3	R3 data		
08	HH3	M32 sex	M32 age	M32 rel R
09	HH3	M33 sex	M33 age	M33 rel R
10	HH3	M34 sex	M34 age	M34 rel R
11	HH4	R4 data		
12	HH5	R5 data		
13	HH5	M52 sex	M52 age	M52 rel R
14	HH5	M53 sex	M53 age	M53 rel R
15	HH6	R6 data		
16	HH6	M62 sex	M62 age	M62 rel R

Figure 8.1   Restructuring data to create new cases out of existing variables

Our first task is to create a new version of our ESS6 dataset with only the following variables (some of which you created in Chapter 7):

name

idno

cntry

hhmmb

gndr to rshipa24

icpart1

rshpsts

eisced

eiscedp

pdwrkp to wkhtotp

eiscedf

eiscedm

country

dweight

pspwght

pweight

popweight

infanthhn to noage

parents

partners

offspring

sibs

pgndr

malehhn

femhhn

gndrdkr

totalhhn

To do this go to **File→Save As...** which will open the **Save Data As** dialog box. Click on the Variables button to the right of the box and the **Save Data As: Variables** dialog will appear (Figure 8.2). You'll see that it lists all the variables in the dataset by their name, label and order in the dataset, and with a small blue check box adjacent to each variable. To the right are three buttons, the last of which is **Drop All**. If you click this button all the variables become unchecked. We can now check those variables we want to retain in the new dataset by clicking on the corresponding check boxes. You should have checked 121 variables when you finish. As usual, click **Continue** to return to the main dialog. Here you need to give the new dataset a **File name**. Remember to use file and folder names that are logical and that will enable you to quickly locate the right dataset in the future. You can use the folder and file directory at the top of the main dialog to determine where your new file will go. Finally, click **Paste** to copy the syntax, run the syntax to create the new dataset, and open it.

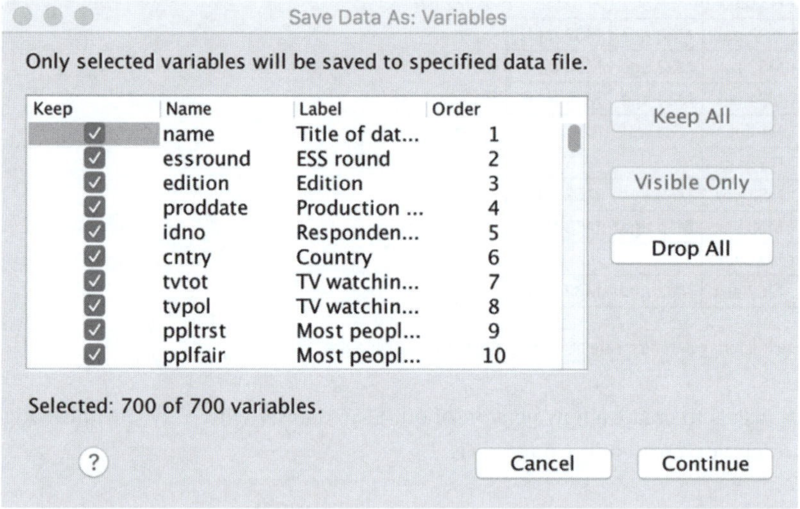

Keep	Name	Label	Order
✓	name	Title of dat...	1
✓	essround	ESS round	2
✓	edition	Edition	3
✓	proddate	Production ...	4
✓	idno	Responden...	5
✓	cntry	Country	6
✓	tvtot	TV watchin...	7
✓	tvpol	TV watchin...	8
✓	ppltrst	Most peopl...	9
✓	pplfair	Most peopl...	10

Only selected variables will be saved to specified data file.

Keep All

Visible Only

Drop All

Selected: 700 of 700 variables.

Cancel   Continue

Figure 8.2   The **Save Data As: Variables** dialog box

Note that SPSS does *not* close the original dataset you were working with. It allows you to toggle between datasets. This can be a useful feature, but it must be handled with care. You have to ensure that you are working on the correct dataset when more than one is open at once. It can be all too easy to issue commands meant for one dataset and carry them out on the wrong one, with sometimes disastrous consequences. The *active* dataset will be whichever one has the **Data Editor** window active, as indicated by the title of the dataset above the menu bar appearing in black. The inactive dataset has its title greyed out. If you are using the GUI the active **Data Editor** window will be the one you are using to issue commands. If you are using syntax, the number of the dataset will appear in the toolbar opposite **active:**. You can use the dialog box there to toggle between datasets. SPSS refers to different datasets by a number which it allocates to them and this appears in square brackets after the file name.

8 ● 2 CHECKING THE EXISTING HOUSEHOLD VARIABLES

Before we restructure our data so that each household member for whom we have information is a case, we need to double-check how information on household members has been
collected and recorded in our existing data. In the **gndr2** to **gndr24**, **yrbrn2** to **yrbrn24** and
rshipa2 to **rshipa24** variables values of 6, 66 or 6666 indicate that there was no corresponding
household member. However, if you look at the dataset in **Data View** mode, you'll see that
the variables for the 13th household member onwards are defined as system missing if there
was no corresponding household member. We can first use this information to count how
many people there were in each household and see if it corresponds well with the variable
hhmmb. If you check the document *European Social Survey Round 6 (2012) Project Instructions
(CAPI)* you'll discover that this variable is based on the question asked of respondents before
the interviewer proceeds to fill up the household grid that records the information captured
in the variables **gndr2** to **rshipa24**.

      ☞ https://www.europeansocialsurvey.org/docs/round6/fieldwork/source/ESS6_source_project_
instructions.pdf

Thus discrepancies between our two totals could be due either to data recording or entry mistakes, or to confusion on the part of interviewees who may, for example, have forgotten to
include themselves or another member of the household in their answer to the question. With
over 50,000 cases it would be surprising not to have some discrepancies.

First we can count the number of all household members for each respondent by counting the
number of not applicable and system-missing values in the **gndr2** to **gndr24**, **yrbrn2** to **yrbrn24**
and **rshipa2** to **rshipa24** variables, checking that they are the same total for each case, and then
subtracting the result from 24. This should give us a result equal to the value for **hhmmb** for each
case. Again, try to produce the syntax yourself and then compare your result with that in the box.

Counting household members by summing not applicable and system-missing cases

```
COUNT yearn = yrbrn2 to yrbrn24 (6666, SYSMIS).
COUNT gndrn = gndr2 to gndr24 (6, SYSMIS).
COUNT rshipan = rshipa2 to rshipa24 (66, SYSMIS).
FREQ yearn to rshipan.
CORR yearn to rshipan.
COMPUTE hhmmb1 = (24-yearn).
FREQ hhmmb1.
MISSING VALUES hhmmb ().
CROSS hhmmb by hhmmb1.
```

All three sets of variables tell us the same story about the number of additional household
members, and you can check this quickly by asking for a correlation coefficient for them, using

the command **corr**, which if the variables are identical will be equal to 1. We can compare these results with those recorded in the variable **hhmmb**. Set missing cases to *valid* on **hhmmb** and produce a crosstab of **hmmb1** by **hhmmb** to identify any discrepancies. You'll see that if we look at the cases for which we have a non-missing value for **hhmmb**, there are only 12 minor discrepancies, a very low number. In these cases respondents may have given one answer about the number of people in the household and then proceeded to give details about a different number of household members. Interviewers may have miscoded answers to household grid questions recording 'no answer', 'refusal' or 'don't know' as answers to questions about one or more other household members when they should have recorded 'not applicable' because no such member existed, and so on. Our new **hhmmb1** variable also gives a value for the number of household members in some cases where **hhmmb** is defined as missing because of a refusal, don't know or no answer being recorded. We'll need to check these cases to see if there is enough information in the variables **gndr2** to **rshipa24** to allow us to attribute a value to **hhmmb** rather than leave it as missing.

8●3 DATA CLEANING: THE SUMMARIZE COMMAND

If you study the contingency table you produced of **hhmmb** and **hhmmb1**, you'll see that something rather strange is going on when **hhmmb1** takes the value 12. About half the cases (29) are unproblematic, where **hhmmb1** has the same value as **hhmmb**. But we also find most of the cases where **hhmmb** is missing here, which seems odd. Earlier we used the **list cases** procedure to check the values of individual cases for a range of variables. There is another similar procedure in SPSS that can be used, the **summarize** command. We'll use it here to see how it works.

First we'll create a filter variable to identify our cases, then run the **summarize** command:

```
USE ALL.
COMPUTE filter_$=((hhmmb1 eq 12) and (hhmmb ne 12)).
FILTER BY filter_$.
SUMMARIZE
/TABLES=idno cntry hhmmb hhmmb1 gndr to gndr24,
yrbrn to rshipa24
/FORMAT=LIST CASENUM TOTAL LIMIT=40
/CELLS=NONE.
```

The **summarize** command and its sub-commands ask SPSS to produce a table with a column for each of the variables listed after **/TABLES=** and which **LIST**s the cases in the rows of the table up to a **TOTAL LIMIT** of 40. Putting in a limit like this avoids the risk of producing a massive table because of some error in the syntax. **/CELLS=NONE** suppresses the calculation of summary statistics for each variable. You can also use the GUI to construct this command. Go to **Analyze→Reports→Case Summaries**. As usual, the dialog box requests a list of variables to insert in the report and offers various options activated by the buttons on the dialog. Figure 8.3 shows part of this table, with some of the columns removed. If you find it hard to produce it yourself you can view the rest of it on the companion website.

	Case Number	idno	cntry	hhmmb	hhmmb1	gndr	gndr2	gndr3	gnc
1	2	4	AL Albania	99 No answer	12	1 Male	9 No answer	9 No answer	9 No a
2	70	217	AL Albania	99 No answer	12	1 Male	9 No answer	9 No answer	9 No a
3	95	308	AL Albania	77 Refusal	12	2 Female	7 Refusal	7 Refusal	7 Refu
4	165	529	AL Albania	99 No answer	12	1 Male	9 No answer	9 No answer	9 No a
5	195	616	AL Albania	99 No answer	12	1 Male	9 No answer	9 No answer	9 No a
6	207	645	AL Albania	99 No answer	12	2 Female	9 No answer	9 No answer	9 No a
7	232	686	AL Albania	99 No answer	12	2 Female	9 No answer	9 No answer	9 No a
8	4169	11024262	DE Germany	77 Refusal	12	1 Male	7 Refusal	7 Refusal	7 Refu
9	4611	11060544	DE Germany	88 Don't know	12	2 Female	1 Male	2 Female	2 Fem
10	4830	11078213	DE Germany	77 Refusal	12	2 Female	7 Refusal	7 Refusal	7 Refu
11	4839	11079213	DE Germany	77 Refusal	12	1 Male	9 No answer	9 No answer	9 No a
12	12750	1476	IL Israel	77 Refusal	12	2 Female	9 No answer	9 No answer	9 No a
13	12871	1922	IL Israel	77 Refusal	12	1 Male	9 No answer	9 No answer	9 No a
14	12903	2020	IL Israel	77 Refusal	12	1 Male	9 No answer	9 No answer	9 No a
15	13992	3529	IT Italy		1	12	9 No answer	9 No answer	9 No answer	9 No a
16	16445	1296	PL Poland	99 No answer	12	1 Male	9 No answer	9 No answer	9 No a

Figure 8.3 Results of the **summarize** command

If you scroll through this report it becomes possible to see what seems to have happened. Interviewers have entered missing values such as no answer or refusal against variables **gndr2** onwards for members of the household whose existence is unknown. At the 13th person, however, presumably as part of the data entry process, system-missing values are recorded, giving us a value for **hhmmb1** that is at odds with **hhmmb**. The existing, missing, value for **hhmmb** makes more sense. We can leave the existing values for **gndr2** to **rshipa24**, but set all refusals, no answers, don't know's and not applicables to system-missing values. If we do this, then, when we come to restructure the data, cases in which there are no details for household members, either because they do not exist or because there is no information on them, will be dropped.

```
USE ALL.
RECODE gndr2 to gndr24 (6 thru 9 = SYSMIS).
RECODE yrbrn2 to yrbrn24 (6666 thru 9999 = SYSMIS).
RECODE rshipa2 to rshipa24 (66 thru 99 = SYSMIS).
```

8 ● 4 CREATING A UNIQUE IDENTIFIER VARIABLE

We are now almost ready to create our new dataset, but we have two final tasks first. Up till now we have used a combination of the variables **cntry** and **idno** to identify individual cases in the dataset. It would be better if we had a variable that uniquely identified each case. Here we discover something that isn't easy to tell from the documentation. Although **idno** takes values from 1 to 11119221, these numbers are *not* unique to each case: some are repeated by country. This can be quickly checked by going to **Data→Identify Duplicate Cases** and entering the variable **idno** as shown in Figure 8.4.

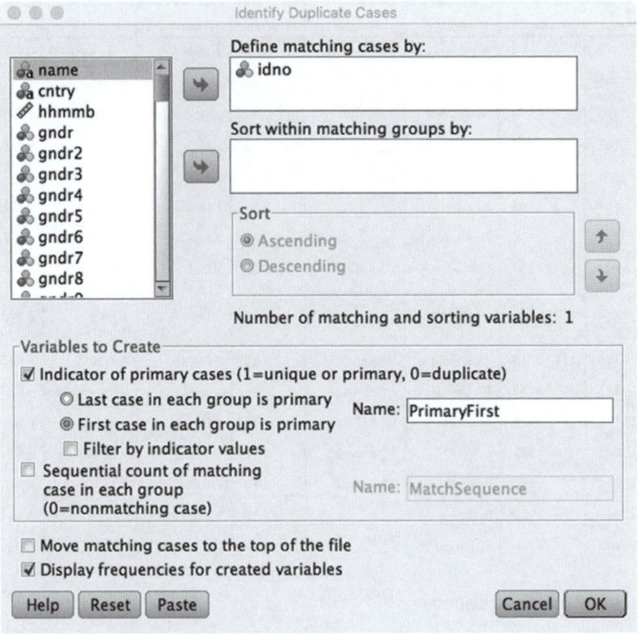

Figure 8.4 The **Identify Duplicate Cases** dialog box

We can use **country**, our numeric automatic recode of **cntry**, to produce unique identifiers. We could either multiply **idno** by 10^2 and add **country**, or multiply **country** by 10^8 and add **idno**. In either operation we create a series of zeros (equal in number to the power to which 10 is raised) after the first variable, to which the value of the second variable is added. The second of our two procedures is preferable, because if we then **Sort** on the new identifier variable, cases from each country will be grouped together:

COMPUTE newid = (100000000*country) + idno.

We now have a variable that identifies each case uniquely.

Finally, create a new variable **rshipa1** and have it take the value 0 for all cases. The reason for this will become clear shortly.

COMPUTE rshipa1 = 0.

8 ● 5 RESTRUCTURING THE DATA

We are now ready to produce a restructured data file. This is a procedure where it is best to construct commands in the GUI and then paste syntax. Go to **Data→Restructure**, which will open the **Restructure Data Wizard**. Before it does so, SPSS asks if you wish to save the existing dataset. Always accept this invitation! That way, if you make a fatal error in the restructuring, you can revert to the version of the dataset you have just saved and no work is lost. Once in the **Restructure Data Wizard**, choose the first option, **Restructure Selected**

Variables into Cases. Click **Continue** and in the next dialog choose **More than one** for the number of variable groups, enter '3' in the **How Many** box and click **Continue**. In step 3, **Variables to Cases: Select Variables** (shown in Figure 8.5), under **Variables to be Transposed** replace the name **trans1** with **gender** in the **Target Variable:** box and then select the variables from **gndr** to **gndr24** and put them in the variable list box beneath **Target Variable:**. Now replace the name **trans2** with **dob** and put in the variables **yrbrn** to **yrbrn24**. Next replace **trans3** with **rshipa** and first put the variable **rshipa1** and then the variables **rshipa2** to **rship24** into the list box. We need to have the same number of variables (24) in each of the three groups to be transposed. Creating a variable that describes the relationship of the respondent to themselves allows us to do this.

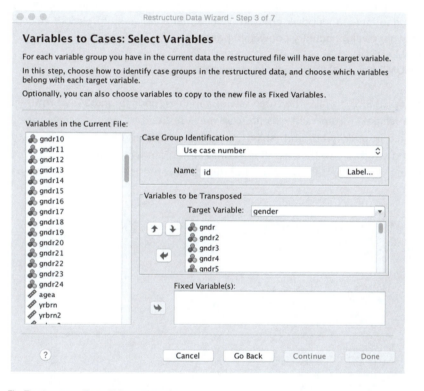

Figure 8.5 The **Restructure Data Wizard** (step 3)

Now select the remaining variables, excluding **gndr2** to **rshipa24**, and transfer them to the **Fixed Variable(s):** list box and again click **Continue**. In step 4, the next dialog, choose to create **one index variable** and click **Continue**; in step 5 make this index variable **sequential**; in step 6 choose to **Drop** variables not selected from the file and to **Discard the Data** if there are **System Missing or Blank Values in all Transposed Variables**, and choose to create a **Case Count Variable**. Give it an appropriate name such as **hhmmb2**, since this will count the number of new cases generated by each case in the current file. Finally, choose to **Paste** the syntax which should look like the syntax below ( it is also available on the companion website).

```
VARSTOCASES
  /MAKE gender FROM gndr gndr2 gndr3 gndr4 gndr5 gndr6 gndr7 gndr8 gndr9 gndr10
  gndr11 gndr12 gndr13 gndr14 gndr15 gndr16 gndr17 gndr18 gndr19 gndr20 gndr21
  gndr22 gndr23 gndr24
  /MAKE dob FROM yrbrn yrbrn2 yrbrn3 yrbrn4 yrbrn5 yrbrn6 yrbrn7 yrbrn8 yrbrn9 yrbrn10
  yrbrn11 yrbrn12 yrbrn13 yrbrn14 yrbrn15 yrbrn16 yrbrn17 yrbrn18 yrbrn19 yrbrn20 yrbrn21
  yrbrn22 yrbrn23 yrbrn24
  /MAKE rshipa FROM rshipa1 rshipa2 rshipa3 rshipa4 rshipa5 rshipa6 rshipa7 rshipa8
  rshipa9 rshipa10 rshipa11 rshipa12 rshipa13 rshipa14 rshipa15 rshipa16 rshipa17 rshipa18
  rshipa19 rshipa20 rshipa21 rshipa22 rshipa23 rshipa24
  /INDEX=Index1(24)
  /KEEP=newid name idno cntry hhmmb icpart1 rshpsts eisced eiscedp pdwrkp edctnp
  uemplap uemplip dsbldp rtrdp cmsrvp hswrkp dngothp dngdkp dngnapp dngrefp dngnap
  icomdnp mnactp icppdwk crpdwkp isco08p emprelp wkhtotp eiscedf eiscedm dweight
  pspwght pweight country popweight pgndr
  /NULL=DROP
  /COUNT=hhmmb2 "N household members".
```

We've asked SPSS to take the three sets of variables, **gndr** to **gndr24**, **yrbrn** to **yrbrn24** and **rshipa1** to **rshipa24**, from each existing case and use them to create 24 new cases, using the values stored in **gndr**, **yrbrn** and **rshipa1**, in **gndr2**, **yrbrn2** and **rshipa2**, in **gndr3**, **yrbrn3** and **rshipa3**, and so on. We've then asked it to **Drop** all cases in which these three new variables all take missing values (because the corresponding household member does not exist), to create

	newid	id	name	idno	cntry	hhmmb	icpart1	rshpsts	eisced
1	100000001	1	ESS6e02_2	1	AL	2	1	1	2
2	100000001	1	ESS6e02_2	1	AL	2	1	1	2
3	100000002	2	ESS6e02_2	2	AL	7	2	66	4
4	100000002	2	ESS6e02_2	2	AL	7	2	66	4
5	100000002	2	ESS6e02_2	2	AL	7	2	66	4
6	100000002	2	ESS6e02_2	2	AL	7	2	66	4
7	100000002	2	ESS6e02_2	2	AL	7	2	66	4
8	100000002	2	ESS6e02_2	2	AL	7	2	66	4
9	100000002	2	ESS6e02_2	2	AL	7	2	66	4
10	100000003	3	ESS6e02_2	3	AL	3	1	1	4
11	100000003	3	ESS6e02_2	3	AL	3	1	1	4
12	100000003	3	ESS6e02_2	3	AL	3	1	1	4
13	100000004	4	ESS6e02_2	4	AL	99	9	77	88
14	100000005	5	ESS6e02_2	5	AL	7	1	1	1
15	100000005	5	ESS6e02_2	5	AL	7	1	1	1
16	100000005	5	ESS6e02_2	5	AL	7	1	1	1
17	100000005	5	ESS6e02_2	5	AL	7	1	1	1
18	100000005	5	ESS6e02_2	5	AL	7	1	1	1
19	100000005	5	ESS6e02_2	5	AL	7	1	1	1

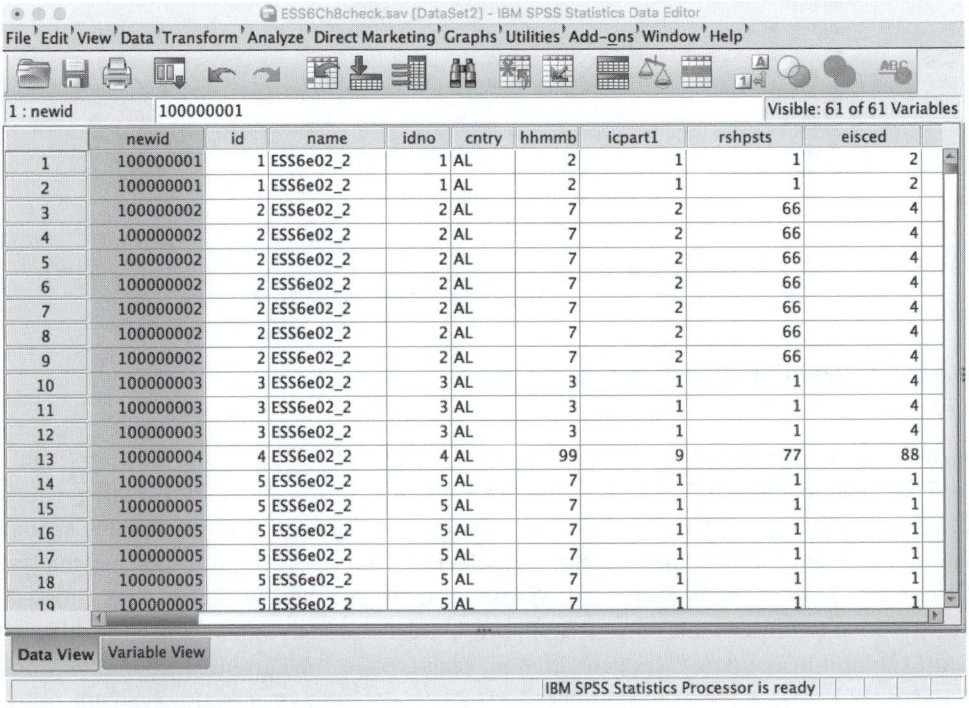

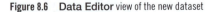

Figure 8.6 **Data Editor** view of the new dataset

an index variable that will assign a sequential number to each new case created out of the same original case (so that each household member will have a unique identifier) and to create a variable **hhmmb2** that counts the number of cases corresponding to each original case (which will correspond to the number of household members). We've also asked it to attach the *fixed* variables that we've specified using the **/KEEP** sub-command to each new case. Figure 8.6 shows part of the **Data Editor** window in **Data View** mode for our new dataset. If everything has gone according to plan, save and name the new dataset you have created.

If you look at the first few rows of data, you can see how SPSS has restructured the file. In our original dataset the second respondent was from a household in Albania with seven members. This case has now become seven cases: one for each member of this household. The values for **hhmmb** and **hhmmb2** are the same, as they should be, and our index variable gives each household member a number from 1 to 7. The fourth household is a male respondent from Albania who gave no information about himself or other members of his household. Next is a household comprising seven people, and so on. If we run frequencies on some of our new variables we can describe some of the characteristics of the household members of respondents. You'll find for example, that they comprise around 32,000 partners of respondents, 36,000 offspring, 15,000 parents and about 8,000 siblings, that the oldest household member recorded in the survey was born in 1900 and that almost 1% of household members were babies born in the year the survey was carried out (2012/13).

8 ● 6 WORKING WITH THE NEW HOUSEHOLD MEMBERS DATASET

We can now create a new variable describing children in households. Let's first create a variable for age and then define household members who are the son or daughter of the respondent (since respondents themselves are all adults aged 15 or older) and aged 14 or below as children. Note that this will not identify all the children in the survey. If the respondent in a household is a grandparent, then children of this grandparent's son or daughter in the household would appear in the household grid as 'other relation' rather than as a son or daughter. We can define age by subtracting year of birth from 2013 (the latest year of birth appearing in the data), but, as we noted before, precise age would depend upon the unknown month of birth of the household member. Again compose the syntax for this and compare it to my suggestion below:

```
COMPUTE age = 2013-dob.
RECODE age (lo thru -1=999).
FREQ age.
COMPUTE child eq 0.
IF (age le 14) and (rshipa eq 2) child = 1.
FREQ child.
```

You should find that there are 18,654 children in the survey households.

8 ● 7 THE AGGREGATE COMMAND

We have just created a dataset that transforms information about a household attached to one respondent into separate cases for each person in that household. However, there will also be occasions when you want to do the reverse. You may encounter a dataset in which each case represents an individual person, but these people can be grouped into households or other aggregate units, and you wish to create a dataset that is about these units rather than the people within them. To see how this is done we'll take the dataset that we've just created and use it to take data describing all household members and make a single case for each household from it. We'll then see how we can merge this new data to our original **ESS6** dataset.

Our dataset currently comprises just over 152,000 records – one for each household member – and we want to transform this into one where each household has one record, that is, constitutes a single case that nevertheless contains information about the household and its members. To do this we use the **Aggregate** command. Go to **Data→Aggregate** to open the **Aggregate Data** dialog. This dialog allows you to do three things.

First, you can define one or more *break* variables. A break variable is one that takes the same value for each of the cases that you wish to aggregate together. A suitable variable for us would be **newid**, since it takes the same value for all members of the same household, but different values for each distinct household, because it was based on the original ESS survey respondent's identifier.

Second, you can produce *aggregated variables* that summarise the values of variables describing individual cases in the existing dataset. Thus each case in our dataset has a value for year of birth. We could select this variable and ask for a summary statistic of it: the mean or median, largest or smallest value and so on. This would produce a new variable describing the average age (calculated via the year of birth) of members of the household, or the age of the youngest or oldest member and so on. To produce an aggregated variable in this way transfer the variable to the **Summaries of Variable(s):** list box. SPSS will automatically suggest a name for the new variable to be created, but you can override this by clicking the **Name & Label...** button beneath the list box. Clicking on **Function...** allows you to specify a range of ways of summarising the data in a variable, in terms of either the values themselves or their order within the cases within the break group (the household). An example of the former would be the lowest value of a variable within the group (e.g. the earliest year of birth of any household member), while an example of the latter would be the value for year of birth of the first case encountered in the break group (the household). SPSS will also create a variable describing the **Number of cases** in the break group. The default name for this variable is **N_BREAK**, which can be overridden.

Finally, you can append the variables you have just created to the existing dataset (where the variables will take the same value for every member of the same break group) or create a new dataset with only the aggregated variables and one case for each break group. You can create this new dataset in a new **Data Editor** window directly, or you can create a new **.sav** file.

Let's create aggregate variables that describe:

the age of the oldest household member;

the age of the youngest household member;

the number of children aged 14 or below of the respondent in the household;

the number of people in the household.

The first variable will be the *maximum* value that our new variable **age** takes within each break group. Similarly, the second variable will be equal to its *minimum* value. Since a child is coded as 1 and others as 0, the *sum* of the values of our **child** variable will give us the number of children in the household. Finally, the number of people in the household will equal the number of cases in the break group. We can change the SPSS default name for this variable to **hhmmb4**. We'll use the aggregate data to create a new dataset called **ESS6hhdata**. The **Aggregate Data** dialog box should now look like Figure 8.7. The syntax it creates when you **Paste** it is as follows:

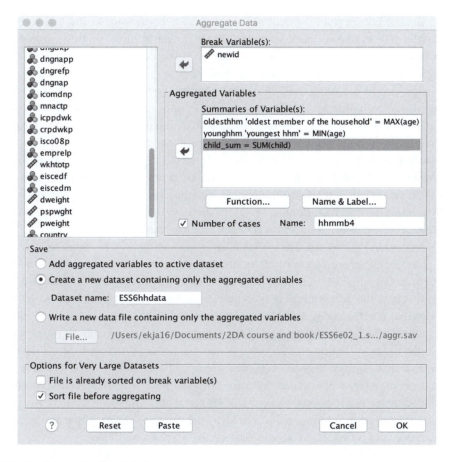

Figure 8.7 The **Aggregate Data** dialog box

```
DATASET DECLARE ESS6hhdata.
SORT CASES BY newid.
AGGREGATE
/OUTFILE='ESS6hhdata'
/PRESORTED
/BREAK=newid
/oldesthhm 'oldest member of the household'=MAX(age)
/younghhm 'youngest hhm'=MIN(age)
/child_sum=SUM(child)
/hhmmb4=N.
```

This creates a dataset with five variables. **Save** it to an appropriate location. If you run frequencies on **hhmmb4** you should see a familiar distribution of results! Similarly, a frequency table of **child_sum** will give you a description of the numbers of children in the survey households.

8●8 MERGING FILES WITH COMMON CASES AND NEW VARIABLES (ADD VARIABLES)

Our new dataset **ESS6hhdata** contains variables that we might want to add into our original **ESS6** dataset. To do this we need to **merge** our two dataset files. For this purpose we can use our **newid** variable to ensure that the data from the correct household is attached to each respondent. Although this variable exists in the two new datasets we've created there is no version of it in our original **ESS6** dataset. This is a good example of where syntax is so convenient. We need only locate the relevant syntax in our syntax file, activate our original dataset by clicking on it or using the **dataset activate** command in syntax, and run the syntax again. Still in the original dataset, go to **Data→Merge Files→Add Variables…** to open the **Add Variables** dialog. From now on SPSS will refer to the dataset you issued the merge command from (our original **ESS6** dataset) as the *active* dataset. It now asks which dataset or **.sav** file you wish to merge with it: select **ESS6hhdata**, or whatever name you gave to the file you recently created, and click on **Continue** to go to the next dialog which has three variable list boxes: **Excluded Variables:**, **New Active Dataset:** and **Key Variables:**.

You'll see that in the first two lists the variable names are followed by either an asterisk (*) or a plus sign (+). The former refers to variables SPSS has identified as from the active dataset, while the latter refers to variables from the dataset that is being merged with it. SPSS will identify variables that it thinks are common to both datasets and exclude such duplicate variables from the dataset that is being merged with the active one. Hence since we have the variable **newid** in both datasets, the version in the file **ESS6hhdata.sav** will be removed from the new dataset.

SPSS allows you to rename any excluded variable in order to include it in the new dataset (since two variables cannot have the same name in any one dataset). It also allows you to drop variables from the new merged dataset by transferring them from the **New Active Dataset:** list to the **Excluded** list. SPSS also provides a key variables and table facility which allows you to merge files that do not share a common, sequential identifier variable. This facility requires some care in its operation and is best left to advanced users, so I do not cover it here.

Before we **merge** the datasets, we must ensure that each case is in exactly the same order in both datasets. We can do so by sorting the data on **newid** in *both* datasets, either using the GUI (**Data→Sort Cases**), or using syntax (the **A** instructs SPSS to sort the cases in ascending order of their values):

SORT CASES by newid (A).

Let's also rename the excluded **newid** variable from our **ESS6hhdata** dataset and include it with the new dataset (by clicking **Rename**, supplying a name, and transferring it to the **New Active Dataset:** list). We can use it to double-check that our merge has worked as we wanted it to by correlating the id variables from each dataset. The dialog box should look like Figure 8.8. Note how the variables from **ESS6hhdata** come at the end of the **New Active Dataset:** variable list and include our renamed **newid** variable which I've called **newidcheck**. The pasted syntax is as follows:

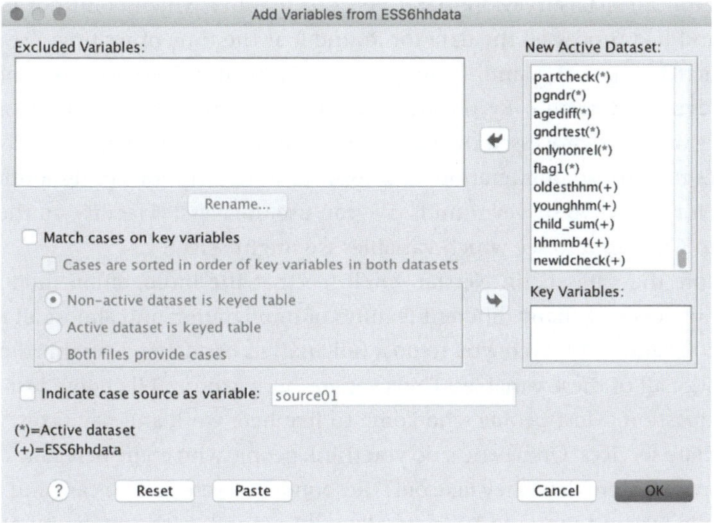

Figure 8.8 The **Add Variables** dialog box

```
MATCH FILES /FILE=*
/FILE='ESS6hhdata'
/RENAME newid=newidcheck.
```

Use the dataset you have just created to find the average age of the oldest child in the household, in each country. As usual the answer can be found on the companion website.

8 ⬤ 9 MERGING FILES WITH COMMON VARIABLES AND DIFFERENT CASES (ADD CASES)

Sometimes the data you want to use comes in the form of multiple datasets so that you have to merge files together to construct the dataset you want. A common situation is where you have two or more datasets for the same survey, and with the same or similar variables for different years. In such a situation you are adding *new cases* to your existing dataset (since the sample of respondents in each year will be different). Adding new cases is something you may need to do if, for example, you want to merge cases from different waves of a *cross-sectional* survey. Thus many surveys, including the ESS, collect information on many of the same, or very similar, variables in successive waves, allowing comparisons over time. It is often convenient to bring these variables together in a dataset that covers more than one wave of data. (If you are dealing with longitudinal or panel data it is always new variables that you are concerned with, since, at least in principle, the units of observation remain the same.) Alternatively, you may have a dataset that is split into sections, with the information about the same set of cases spread across datasets comprising the variables for each section.

Just as with adding variables, SPSS allows you to **Merge** two files at a time, working from the *active* dataset in your **Data Editor** window and a second file that you add cases from. Let's look at the example of immigration. There was a module on this topic in the very first round of ESS fielded in 2002, and in the latest round, ESS7, fielded in 2014. From the webpage at http://www.europeansocialsurvey.org/data/ you can identify which countries participated in both rounds and had processed the data for Round 7 at the time of writing: Austria, Belgium, Czech Republic, Denmark, Finland, France, Germany, Ireland, Netherlands, Norway, Poland, Slovenia, Sweden, Switzerland. By the time you read this the list will be incomplete, since more countries will have processed the data from Round 7. We can create a dataset with some of the variables relevant to immigration, and some basic descriptions of respondents for these countries and for these two survey rounds. We can use the Nesstar facility on the ESS site that we looked at in Chapter 3 to see which variables we might select.

If you explore the datasets on Nesstar you'll see that the immigration module comprised several questions covering many different features of immigration and almost all of which were used in both 2002 and 2014. Were you to do a full analysis of change over this time you'd want to look at most or all of these variables. However, for our purposes I'll choose just one, **imbleco**, based on the question 'Most people who come to live here work and pay taxes. They also use health and welfare services. On balance, do you think people who come here take out more than they put in or put in more than they take out?' Respondents were given a card and asked to score from 0 (generally take out more) to 10 (generally put in more), with a midpoint at 5.

We'll also need to extract some other variables: some 'face-sheet' variables about the respondent (**cntry, ctzcntr, brncntr, agea, gndr, eisced, chldhm**), a variable to differentiate the survey rounds (**essround**), and the weight variables **pweight** and **dweight**. You can also use Nesstar to confirm that these variables have the same name and definition in both datasets. Download the SPSS version of the integrated data files for Rounds 1 and 7 from the ESS website and open the **.sav** file for Round 1. Using the same commands as in Chapter 7, we'll save a new version of this dataset that contains only the variables we are interested in. Here we can use a useful shortcut to 'trick' SPSS into writing some of our syntax for us. Were we to use the **Save As…** dialog to construct our syntax, we would first need to drop all our variables from the dataset and then check the variables we want to keep. SPSS would then convert this into a **/DROP** subcommand listing all the 500 or so variables to be dropped. Instead, use the **Frequencies** dialog in the GUI to ask for frequencies of our 11 variables, and **Paste** the resulting syntax. Then use the **Save As…** dialog to save a new version of the file with only one variable (say **essround**) and an appropriate name, and again **Paste** the syntax. Now, in the **Syntax Editor** window, delete the **/DROP** sub-command and its contents and replace it with the **/KEEP** sub-command together with the list of variable names produced by the **Frequencies** command. When you've done this your syntax should read as follows (keep in mind that the first part of the directory path will depend upon the directory layout on your computer):

```
SAVE OUTFILE='…/ESS1e06_4.spss/ESS1imm.sav'
/KEEP =essround cntry idno ctzcntr brncntr imbleco gndr agea eisced chldhm dweight
pweight
/COMPRESSED.
```

If you open this file you should see that it contains the 11 variables we asked for.

Now open the **.sav** file for ESS Round 7. We can edit our syntax to produce the new Round 7 dataset. All you need do is specify a different name for the output file to distinguish it from the file we've just created. For example, you could delete **ESS1imm.sav** and replace it with **ESS7imm.sav** in the first line of the syntax. It is best to copy and paste the original syntax and edit the pasted copy, so that you are left with a record of all your operations. Run the edited syntax, and once you have both files open select either one and go to **Data→Merge Files→Add Cases**. As in the **Add**

Variables option, SPSS first produces a dialog which asks you which dataset you wish to add cases from; select the other file that you have just produced and SPSS responds with a dialog which lists all the variables to be included in the **Variables in the New Active Dataset:** box. To the left of this dialog there is also an **Unpaired Variables:** list which should be empty, since all 11 variables are common to both datasets, and there are no other variables specific to either one. You can merge datasets that do not have every variable 'paired'; unpaired variables in the new dataset will take a system-missing value for cases from the other dataset. You can also pair variables that have the same definition but different names, and SPSS can create a new variable that describes which one of the original datasets each case in the new merged dataset came from. We will not need this last feature, as the variable **essround** already does this job for us. As usual, **Paste** the syntax and run it and you will create a new dataset that contains the cases from both rounds of the ESS survey for these 11 variables.

Our next task is to produce a numeric version of **cntry**. Copy, paste, edit and run the **Autorecode** syntax you produced earlier to do this. We now need to select the countries for which we have data in both rounds (you can confirm which countries these are by running a contingency table of **essround** by **cntry**). Create a temporary variable that takes the value 1 for countries present in both rounds, and use the **SELECT IF** command to delete the other countries. Finally, produce a weight that combines **pweight** and **dweight**. You now have a new dataset that can be used to explore any differences between 2002 and 2014. When you do so you should find that on average respondents have a rather more positive attitude towards immigrants in 2014, that there is little difference by gender, but education has some impact, as does whether respondents were themselves born in the country or have citizenship. However, there are some differences between countries. Austria stands out as the only country where attitudes became substantially less positive over this period.

what you have learned

That completes our review of data management procedures in SPSS. If you look back over this chapter you'll see that you've developed a versatile set of skills that allow you to edit and arrange the contents of an existing dataset not only by creating new variables, but also by creating new datasets out of existing ones and merging different datasets together, adding either new variables to existing cases, or new cases to existing variables. Together with the skills you covered in Chapter 7 you are now equipped to deal with almost any situation the data can throw at you. As data sources multiply and the formats that data comes in become more diverse you'll find that these skills become ever more useful. However these are not skills to memorise. Unlike recoding variables or producing tables, statistics or graphical output, these are not skills you will use every day. However you do need to have a sense of what is possible, so that when you can see that restructuring your data in some way is the best way to proceed, you can turn to these two chapters to guide you through the work.

exercise

1   Go back to the World Bank website, select a variable available for recent years for most countries, download the data for all countries and import it from Excel into a new SPSS data file. Using the variable for country as your identifier for cases, merge the new data with your existing World Development Indicators SPSS dataset.

INTRODUCING LINEAR REGRESSION

━━━━━━━━━━━ **introduction** ━━━━━━━━━━━

In this chapter we learn how to do ordinary least squares linear regression analyses in IBM SPSS Statistics software. Regression is fundamental to social science work as it allows us to examine the relationship between a pair of variables, *controlling* for the impact of other variables. Since we usually depend upon observational rather than experimental data, this is a very useful and versatile procedure. We use linear regression when our dependent variable is at the interval level of measurement. Categorical variables require a different technique, logistic regression, which we cover in Chapters 10–12. In this chapter we learn about:

- What is 'regression to the mean' and why is it important?
- Defining any straight line by two numbers
- Producing and interpreting raw and standardised regression coefficients
- Fitting a regression line to the coordinates for two variables
- Use logged variables or scales to examine relative rather than absolute change
- Checking for the impact of missing values
- Drawing causal path diagrams
- Checking for multicollinearity
- Interpreting linear regression diagnostics
- Creating dummy variables
- Reporting the results of a model

9 ● 1 WHAT IS REGRESSION?

Regression is a curious term. It carries a negative connotation: to regress to something usually implies a return to a lower or less developed state. It also carries with it an aura of complexity and confusion. Kahneman (2012: 182) points out that the statistician David Freedman used to remark that in court cases, whichever side had to explain regression to the jury lost. People who can easily make sense of contingency tables or other descriptive statistics can be stumped when confronted with regression coefficients. This is perhaps why regression is seen as not only more difficult, but also more suspicious: as statistical obfuscation rather than enlightenment, or as a way of 'torturing the data until it talks'.

This is unfortunate, since regression and inference from samples to populations are two of the greatest scientific achievements of the nineteenth century. Regression is the basic building block of almost all statistical modelling in the social sciences and the gateway to all kinds of multivariate analysis because it offers something no other approach can offer: the ability to estimate the impact of one variable on another variable, *while controlling for the effects of other variables*. This is as close as most social research can come to the experimental method, and is therefore tremendously valuable. The most basic form of regression is ordinary least squares linear regression. Understanding this well provides a secure foundation on which to build a much wider range of analyses.

The best way of understanding regression is to retrace its origins in the work of its inventor, the polymath Francis Galton. An excellent account of this is given by Ellenberg (2015: Chapter 15). Galton was impressed by the work of Darwin, and interested in exploring its relevance to the study of human beings by analysing heredity. He wanted to investigate the heritability of intelligence or 'genius' but faced the obstacle that defining and measuring intelligence or genius itself was difficult. Instead he focused on something more tangible: height. He showed that, on average, tall parents had tall children. There was a positive correlation between the height of parents and the height of their children. However, it was *also* clear that on average, while these children were tall, they were *less tall* than their parents. This phenomenon gave rise to the expression 'regression to the mean' since the heights of the children of tall parents were closer to the mean for all children than those of their parents to the mean for all parents. *Why* were children of tall parents on average less tall than these parents?

A simple but counter-intuitive thought experiment tells us that this *must* be so. Imagine a population where both average height and the distribution of heights (as measured, for example, by their standard deviation) remain constant over generations. Imagine also that instead of two sexes there is only one and that reproduction occurs via parthenogenesis: a single parent produces a single child. This simplification avoids the problem of having to measure the heights of two parents and take account of sex differences in heights: it does not affect the logic of the argument we are dealing with.

In such a population there are two mutually exclusive but comprehensive possibilities for the association between parents' and children's heights. Either the correlation coefficient between parents' and children's height in this population is 1 or it is less than 1: either the association is perfect or it is not perfect. If the association were perfect, the height of each child would need to be exactly the same as that of their parent, and we would also have to conclude that it was the unique explanation of their height: no other variables could enter into its determination. Were we to look at our population over time we would find each lineage (i.e. succession of descendants from the same parent) occupying exactly the same place in the hierarchy of heights: there would be fixed 'castes' of 'talls' and 'shorts'.[1] If we want our imaginary population to resemble a real-world one we cannot have such perfect association. In the real world, some children turn out taller than their parents, some shorter. This leaves the other, more realistic possibility, that the correlation coefficient between height of parent and height of child is *less than* 1, and that therefore *other* factors play some part in the determination of children's heights.

If the correlation is less than 1, then we *must* have 'regression to the mean'. Tall parents will produce children who are on average less tall, short parents will have children who are on average less short. At first sight this would lead us to expect that over time the spread of heights in the population would decrease until eventually the height of all children converged to the mean and the standard deviation of heights was zero. Why does this not happen? Here we only need to remember that we have been dealing with averages (the measure of central tendency) and not distributions (the measure of spread). On *average* taller parents will have less tall children, but the *distribution* of these children's heights will include some very tall and some rather short children. Conversely, short parents will have some very short and some quite tall children.

The less visible obverse of 'regression to the mean' is what might be called 'expulsion from the mean'. Where does it come from? The answer can only be those *other* factors that play a part in determining children's height if the association between parents' and children's height

---

[1] Eagle-eyed readers will have spotted that it would also be possible for the association to be perfect but for all children's heights to be a multiple of their parents, so that, for example, every child was 10% taller or every child was 10% shorter than their parent. This makes no difference to the argument advanced here.

is less than perfect. Let's call all these other, unobserved, factors 'environment'. I use this as a convenient term, but note that some of these factors might be biological, while some of the factors captured by heredity may be social (e.g. taller parents on average may also be better off, provide an above average environment for their children and so on). Environment factors will have a distribution just as parents' heights do. Some will push children to be taller, others to be shorter. It is these factors that push children's heights away from those of their parents (in either direction) and stop the spread of heights diminishing.

We can now do two things. We can divide the association between parents' and children's heights into these two components, parent's height and environment, and measure their relative importance. However, we can now explain why not only the average height *but also the distribution of heights* remains steady in our population over the generations. By contrast, the people occupying the different locations in the distribution of heights *will* change. There will be no fixed strata of tall and short families: successive generations of each single family will move up and down the hierarchy of heights. Indeed, this is the *only* way such a structure could reproduce itself.

There is one final step in our argument, which we can make by thinking of the limiting case which is the converse of perfect association between the heights of parents and children: perfect independence. In such a situation both 'regression to the mean' and 'expulsion from the mean' would be total. The average height of children of the very tallest parents would be the same as the average height of all children. The same would be the case for the children of the very shortest parents. Indeed, since parental height now has no association with children's height we could take any selection of parents we wanted and would find that, on average, the heights of their children were the same. Just as important, we would also find this with the *distribution* of their heights, which would include the same range from very short to exceptionally tall children. In such a situation lineages would simply jump randomly up and down the height hierarchy.

What regression therefore does, which is invaluable to the social and natural sciences, is show how a structure can be reproduced over time or across space *while its constituent components change*. A way I find useful to think of regression coefficients is that they measure the relative contribution of different variables to that reproduction. In some circumstances, but by no means all, we can interpret such reproduction as causal, depending on how we think of the meaning of 'cause'. When we can be confident that we have measured all the relevant prior variables (see Chapter 2) and when we are prepared to interpret 'cause' as meaning 'increasing the probability of', we can use regression to make causal inferences: this makes it a very powerful tool. It also enables us to make estimates of not only the strength of the correlation between different variables, but also *how much* of a change or difference in the value of one variable is associated with a change or difference in the value of the other.

9.2 WHY *LINEAR* REGRESSION?

Regression is also a powerful tool because it reduces the association between two variables to its simplest form by expressing one variable as a *function* of another, that is as an equation, and by having no power terms in this equation so that it can be represented as a straight line. As we will see, this just constrains our summary of the relationship between the variables to be unchanged across their value range: that it works the same way for low values as for high values. However the best way to understand regression is to do some.

Go to the *World Development Indicators* dataset that you produced in Chapter 7. Produce a scatterplot of the variable **tfr** (on the vertical or *Y*-axis) against **infmort** (on the horizontal or *X*-axis). Label the cases by either **code** or **country**. (If you don't remember how to produce a scatterplot, see Chapter 7.) Your results should look like Figure 9.1.

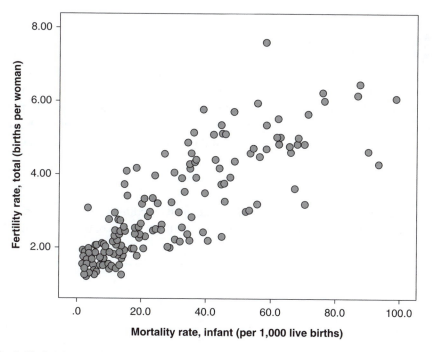

Figure 9.1   Fertility by infant mortality, countries, 2014 or latest available year

Source: World Bank World Development Indicators downloaded from http://databank.worldbank.org/data/reports.aspx?source=world-development-indicators; author's analysis.

The total fertility rate (TFR) is a measure of the average number of children produced by each woman across the span of their fertile years, while infant mortality records the number of children who die before the end of their first year of life (expressed as a rate per thousand live births). Just by looking at the scatterplot we can see that the variables are associated (*r* is about 0.85). Fertility rates range from around 1 to 8, while infant mortality rates range from under 2 to almost 100. Only one country with infant mortality below 1% (10 per thousand live births) has fertility much above 2 children per woman (Israel). Conversely, very few countries with high infant mortality have fertility rates below 4 (Pakistan is the main exception). Overall the coordinates take the approximate form of an ellipse; a cloud of points like a circle stretched in one direction. Note too that this association tells us nothing about the direction of cause and effect, if any. It might be that high fertility leads to higher infant mortality, or that low infant mortality encourages parents to have fewer children, or it could also be that both are products of other variables: affluence, education, public health, use of contraception, social attitudes and so on.

The correlation coefficient tells us how much two variables vary together. However, we can also specify this association in another way. We can model it as the straight line on our scatterplot that best summarises the position of *all* the coordinates. This would give us *two* measures:

1 a description of the line itself in terms of an equation that described the relationship between *Y* (**tfr**) and *X* (**infmort**).
2 a description of how good a summary that line was of all the coordinates.

9.3 THE REGRESSION EQUATION

Summarising all the individual coordinates by depicting them as a straight line is analogous to summarising all the individual values a variable takes by calculating a mean. Double-click on the scatterplot of **tfr** by **infmort** you produced to open the **Chart Editor** window. In the toolbar above the chart click on the **Add Fit Line at Total** icon. SPSS then adds a line to the chart that summarises the data points (we'll look at how it does this shortly), along with a label,

$$y = 1.53 + 0.05x,$$

as shown in Figure 9.2. The label is a *regression equation*. It describes the regression line, which in turn expresses the values of *y* as a function of *x*, or fertility in terms of infant mortality.

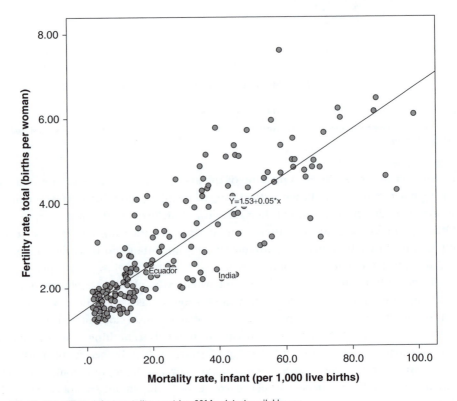

Figure 9.2 Fertility (TFR) by infant mortality, countries, 2014 or latest available year

If we know the infant mortality rate for a country we could estimate its fertility by multiplying its infant mortality rate by 0.05 and adding 1.53. For example, Ecuador has an infant mortality rate of 19 per thousand. We could estimate its TFR as

$$\text{TFR} = 1.53 + (0.05 \times 19) = 1.53 + 0.95 = 2.48.$$

This is quite a good estimate as the actual TFR for Ecuador is 2.54. We can use our equation to tell us the change in the value of our Y or dependent variable associated with a unit change in the X or independent variable. For each increase of 1 in the infant mortality rate (measured as infant deaths per thousand live births), TFR increases by 0.05, so that an increase of 20 in this rate would be associated with an increase of 1 in the TFR. We can also see that this value of 0.05 describes the *slope* of our regression line. Every move of one unit to the right on the X-axis is associated with a move up of 0.05 units on the Y-axis. Because it is positive it indicates that the line slopes upwards from the bottom left to the top right of the plot. Had it been negative the slope would have been in the other direction – downwards towards the right (and we'll see an example of this shortly). The value 0.05 is called the *regression coefficient*. Finally, we can see that the value 1.53 is the point at which our regression line crosses or intercepts the vertical axis (if the latter is placed where $X = 0$) and gives us an estimate for the value of TFR when infant mortality is zero. This is called the *intercept* or *constant*. (Later we'll consider whether such a scenario makes substantive sense: we might well have countries with extremely small rates of infant mortality, but a rate of zero would surely be impossible to achieve.)

The simplest form a regression equation can take is

$$y = a + bx,$$

where y is the dependent variable, a is the constant or intercept, b is the regression coefficient and x is the independent variable. The two values, a and b, can describe *any* straight line that could possibly be drawn in two-dimensional space. The regression coefficient describes the slope of the line: if it is positive the line slopes upwards from left to right, if it is negative it slopes downwards. The higher the absolute value of b, the steeper the slope. There is a special case, a third alternative where the line is horizontal. Here the value of the regression coefficient a is zero and the intercept b will be equal to the mean of y.

9.4 SUMS OF SQUARES AND ANALYSIS OF VARIANCE

We can also see that, because our coordinates are scattered around the line, the estimates of TFR that we would get from the infant mortality rate are not equally good for all countries. In **Chart Editor** mode, click on the **Data Label Mode** icon ⊞ and you can identify individual countries by clicking on their individual coordinates. If you examine your scatterplot you can see that Ecuador lies close to the regression line. For other countries the estimate is not as close: India has an infant mortality rate of 39.3, so that we'd estimate its TFR as $1.53 + (0.05 \times 39.3) = 3.4$, when in fact its fertility rate is 2.43 – slightly lower than that of Ecuador.

Thus, as well as our regression line and its equation, we need a second measure that describes *how well or badly* our regression line summarises the coordinates. To understand how this measure is constructed it is best to think of two limiting cases. Imagine infant mortality was perfectly associated with fertility, so that knowing the value of one told us the value of the other, and that this relationship was also linear. Our scatterplot would comprise coordinates that were all located on the regression line, as shown in Figure 9.3, so that our regression line and the individual data coordinates would be indistinguishable. Conversely, imagine a situation in which our two variables were independent, so that there was no association between them. The scatterplot would look something like Figure 9.4. Rather than taking the form of an ellipse, the coordinates are now scattered all over our graph with no discernible pattern. If we had to draw a line to summarise these coordinates our best guess would be a horizontal line that would lie along the mean value of **tfr**. Knowing the value of **infmort** for a country would be no useful help in estimating the value of **tfr**.

Where we have any sort of linear relationship, then, the pattern of coordinates will take the form of an ellipse, similar to the one in the scatterplot in Figure 9.1. How do we draw the regression line that can summarise these coordinates? There are several possibilities, but the most fruitful one, following the principle of how the standard deviation is calculated, is to produce the line that minimises the *sum of the squared vertical distances between the line and the coordinates*. This vertical distance between the regression line and a coordinate is called the *residual*. If the regression line is below the coordinate the residual for that coordinate is positive; if the line falls above the coordinate the residual is negative. Minimising the sum of squared residuals to obtain the best-fitting line is how we get linear regression's full name, *ordinary least squares* (OLS) regression.

The relationship between the regression line and the coordinates it summarises is given by examining and comparing two sets of *residuals*. We have just met the first set: the residuals

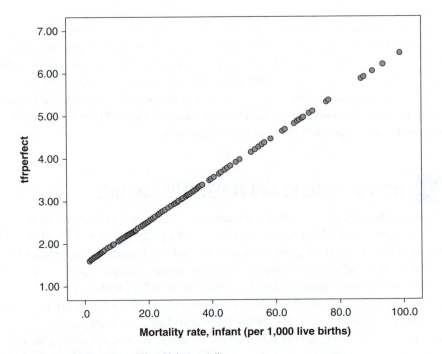

Figure 9.3 A perfect association between TFR and infant mortality

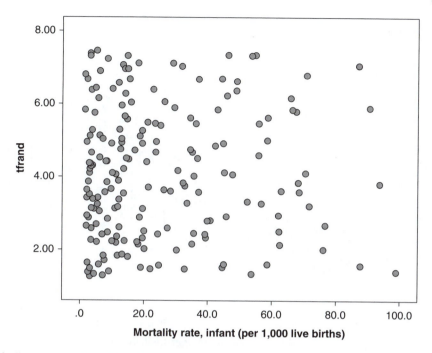

Figure 9.4 No association between TFR and infant mortality

from the regression line to the coordinates. However, we can also consider a second set: the residuals from the coordinates to a line describing the mean of Y. We have already met this second set of residuals as well, when we considered how to calculate the variance and standard deviation of a variable (see Chapter 2). We calculated the variance by summing the squared deviations of each value from the mean value, then dividing by the number of cases. These deviations are the residuals formed by the vertical distance of each coordinate from the horizontal line representing the mean of Y. The sum of these squared residuals (before we divide by N to obtain the variance) is known as the *sum of squares*. In statistical notation it is

$$\Sigma(y - \bar{y})^2.$$

It is shown in Figure 9.5, where the lines trace the vertical distance from the line representing the mean of Y to each of the coordinates. The length of each line is equal to $y - \bar{y}$. We can think of this sum of squares as representing the total amount of variation in our Y (dependent) variable.

Now think of what our *regression line* represents. Remember that it was our attempt to summarise all the coordinates in our scatterplot. A good summary is one where the line goes as close vertically to all the coordinates as possible, while still being a straight line. We need the line to be straight for two reasons: straight lines are mathematically simple and tractable, but, still more important, the slope of a straight line will tell us not only whether the association between X and Y is positive or negative, but also by how much, on average, a change in the value of X yields a change in the value of Y. It thus *also* gives us an estimate for the mean of

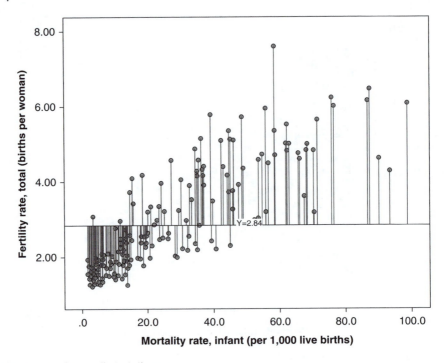

Figure 9.5   Residuals from coordinates to the mean

Y, but now *conditional upon* the value of *X*. Each of these estimated values for the mean of *Y* conditional upon the value of *X* will also be our best estimate for the value of *Y* if we only had information on the value of *X*. These estimates are represented by placing a circumflex or 'hat' above the *y*, pronounced '*y*-hat' ($\hat{y}$).

The sum of squares from the regression line, the *residual sum of squares*, tells us how much variation in *Y* is left *after* we have taken account of the variation it shares with *X*. The residual sum of squares,

$$\Sigma(y - \hat{y})^2$$

tells us how good a fit our line is (Figure 9.6). If all the coordinates cluster close to our line, the residual sum of squares will be small. Conversely, coordinates far from the regression line will make it larger.

9 • 5   THE GENIUS OF THE REGRESSION LINE

Drawing a regression line thus gives us yet another useful result. It divides the total variation in *Y* (given by the sum of squares) into two parts. We've just seen how the *residual* sum of squares describes the variation in *Y* left *after* we have taken account of its association with *X*. The *difference* between this amount (the residual sum of squares) and the total sum of squares must therefore be *the variation in Y that it shares with X*. This is known as the *regression sum of squares*.

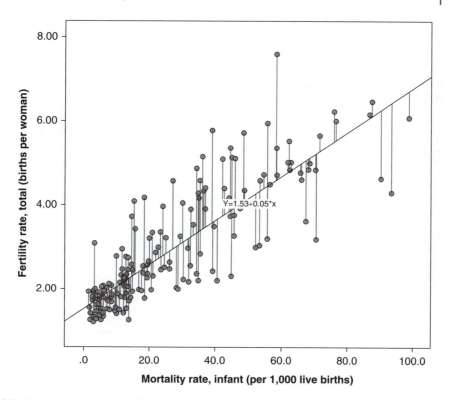

Figure 9.6 Residuals from coordinates to the regression line

It also follows mathematically that if we divide this by the total sum of squares and take the square root we arrive at r: the Pearson correlation coefficient between the two variables.

Thus from our regression line and the equation describing it we have:

- a formula for estimating the value of Y from the value of X, and how much of a change in Y we might expect from a change in X;
- a measure of how well we can predict Y from X (from the size of the *residual* sum of squares);
- a measure of the association between X and Y (from Pearson's r).

Not bad for one straight line!

9 ● 6 LINEAR REGRESSION IN SPSS

We can obtain these statistics that come from calculating a regression line by using the linear **regression** procedure in SPSS. Go to **Analyze→Regression→Linear...**, which brings up the **Linear Regression** dialog box shown in Figure 9.7.

When we run a linear regression it is customary to talk of regressing the dependent variable on the independent variable. To produce the calculations we have just discussed, put **tfr** in the **Dependent:** list and **infmort** in the **Independent(s):** list. You can leave all the other settings at their default values for now. Either click on **OK** or choose **Paste** to first obtain the syntax, which we'll examine later. You'll obtain the output in Figure 9.8.

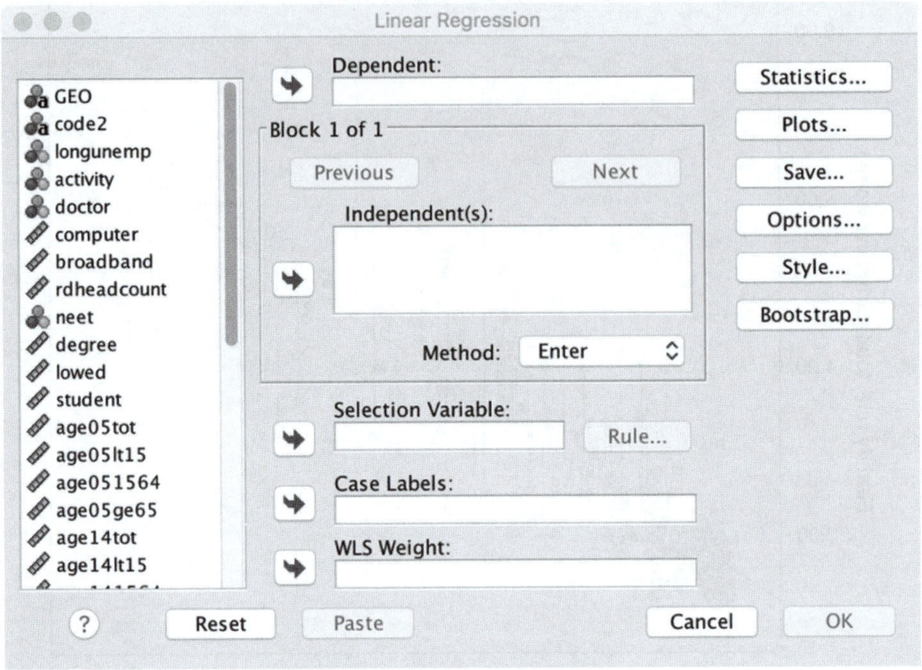

Figure 9.7 SPSS **Linear Regression** dialog box

The first block of output records the model being run. When you come to run more complex models with several independent variables, this keeps a record of which variables are being used; it also records (for some curious reason in a footnote!) the dependent variable, in this case, **tfr**.

Model Summary reports the value for *R*, and its square, *R*-square (R^2), known as the *coefficient of determination*. Because our regression uses only a single independent variable, *R* is the same as *r*, the Pearson correlation coefficient between our two variables, which is also the value of the standardised (beta) regression coefficient for our independent variable. R^2, the *coefficient of determination, gives us the proportion of the variance of our dependent variable that is accounted for by our independent variable*. It tells us how much of the variation in *Y* is accounted for by variation in *X*. Looking at a scatterplot, if our coordinates cluster tightly around the regression line, R^2 will be high, the values of *y* and $\hat{y}$ close together and our residuals small. Conversely, if there is only weak association between our variables, then R^2 will be low, the values of *y* and $\hat{y}$ distant and our residuals large.

ANOVA (*analysis of variance*) reports the regression, residual and total sums of squares that we discussed above. You can check for yourself that 267.544/370.140 = 0.723. The significance or *p*-value reported at the right of the ANOVA table is the based on an *F* statistic. It is calculated by dividing each sum of squares by its corresponding degrees of freedom. Since we have only one independent variable and a constant in the regression we have one degree of freedom for the regression sum of squares, and because we have 187 coordinates we have

Regression

Variables Entered/Removed[a]

Model	Variables Entered	Variables Removed	Method
1	infmort[b]	.	Enter

a. Dependent Variable: tfr
b. All requested variables entered.

Model Summary

Model	R	R Square	Adjusted R Square	Std. Error of the Estimate
1	.850[a]	.723	.721	.74470

a. Predictors: (Constant), infmort

ANOVA[a]

Model		Sum of Squares	df	Mean Square	F	Sig.
1	Regression	267.544	1	267.544	482.433	.000[b]
	Residual	102.596	185	.555		
	Total	370.140	186			

a. Dependent Variable: tfr
b. Predictors: (Constant), infmort

Coefficients[a]

Model		Unstandardized Coefficients		Standardized Coefficients	t	Sig.
		B	Std. Error	Beta		
1	(Constant)	1.527	.081		18.888	.000
	infmort	.053	.002	.850	21.964	.000

a. Dependent Variable: tfr

Figure 9.8 SPSS linear regression output

185 degrees of freedom for the residual sum of squares. Dividing the sum of squares by the degrees of freedom gives the mean squares, and the ratio of the regression mean square to the residual mean square produces the F statistic. From its distribution a significance value can be calculated that tests the null hypothesis that all the regression coefficients in the equation are equal to zero. You will rarely need these raw statistics, except for the last one, the significance level, but the ratio of the regression to the total sum of squares provides us with our vital estimate for R^2.

Coefficients gives us two sets of coefficients: standardised and unstandardised as well as the associated t statistic and level of significance. We use these to produce our regression equation. The intercept is referred to as the **(Constant)** by SPSS. Unstandardised coefficients, in the original units of the variables, are in the column headed **B** along with their standard errors (which we discuss below), and standardised coefficients under the **Beta** column. Standardised coefficients express the relationship between the variables in units of standard deviation rather than the original variable unit. Thus just as an increase of one infant death per thousand live births will raise the estimate of the fertility rate by 0.053 children, an increase in one standard deviation of infant mortality will increase the fertility rate by 0.85 standard deviations. Standardising using standard deviations allows us to compare variables measured in different scales directly. If you recall how the Pearson correlation coefficient was calculated (which includes standardising by dividing by the product of the standard deviations of each variable) it will be no surprise to see that the standardised beta coefficient for **infmort** is the same as the Pearson correlation coefficient: they are the same thing!

We can use these coefficients to produce our regression equation,

$$\mathbf{tfr} = 1.527 + 0.053 \times \mathbf{infmort}.$$

This is the same equation that we saw above that SPSS produced with our scatterplot, but now to one extra decimal place. It gives us a summary of the relationship between x and y such that we can predict values of $\hat{y}$ from the values of x.

9●7 STRAIGHTENING OUT CURVES: TRANSFORMING VARIABLES

Although OLS regression requires a linear relationship – one that can be summarised by a straight line – this is much less of a constraint than it might appear to be. We can see this by examining the relationship between per capita GDP and fertility. We'd expect it to be negative – that is, higher levels of GDP to be associated with lower rates of fertility – but we might also expect it to be nonlinear. In many poor countries a difference in GDP of $1,000 per person would be a very substantial contrast, and we might expect it to be associated with others, including the level of fertility. However, in an affluent country we'd expect the impact of such a difference in GDP to be much smaller, since it would represent a much smaller proportion of the absolute level of GDP. This is indeed what we find if we plot **tfr** against **gdppc$2011** You should obtain a scatterplot like Figure 9.9.

Fertility falls dramatically for any increase in GDP at low values of GDP, but once a value of GDP per person of around $10,000 is reached the fall in fertility becomes much less so that the cluster of points looks more like an 'L' than an ellipse, and the linear regression line becomes a very poor summary of the data. However, we need only take the logarithm of GDP (if you are unsure about logarithms, see the appendix to Chapter 4) to transform it into a variable whose values are multiplicative rather than additive, so that a unit change now represents the same *relative* change anywhere along the scale, and not the same *absolute* change. Create the variable **lnpcgdp** by taking the natural logarithm of our existing per capita GDP measure, using the syntax below, and you should be able to produce

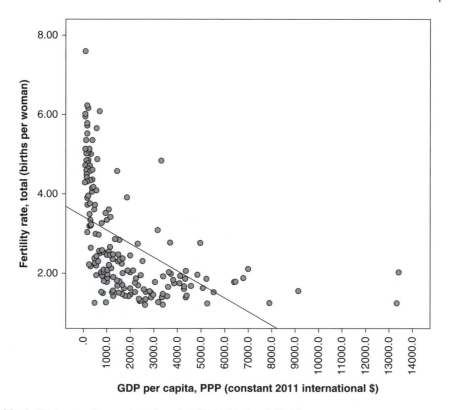

Figure 9.9   Fertility by per capita gross domestic product, 2014 or latest available data

the scatterplot shown in Figure 9.10 (SPSS interprets **ln** after the equals sign as 'take the natural log of'):

    COMPUTE lnpcgdp = ln(gdppc$2011).

We now have a much better distribution of coordinates round the line, and this makes substantive sense too: fertility is more strongly associated with relative rather than absolute differences in GDP. There are a variety of such transformations that can be applied to variables so that their relationship to the dependent variable becomes at least approximately linear. However, like most benefits, it comes with a price. Our interpretation of results will be initially in terms of the transformed rather than original variables, and this can sometimes be complex to report, especially to a non-expert audience. If I report that fertility is linked to levels of GDP, so that a difference in per capita GDP of $5,000 is associated with a fall in the fertility rate of one child per woman, most people would understand what I mean. Not so if I use terms such as the log of per capita GDP. It is therefore usually useful to report the final results also in terms of untransformed variables, and use typical values to illustrate their effect.

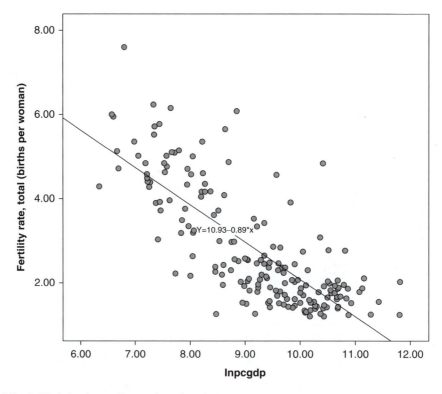

Figure 9.10 Fertility by log of per capita gross domestic product

9●8 THE (REALLY) COOL BIT

All this might seem like an exceptionally cumbersome way of making a small improvement on what the correlation coefficients could have told us: that there is a strong positive linear association between infant mortality and fertility, or that there is a substantial negative linear association between fertility and the log of per capita GDP. We can now put a number on not only the strength of the association (as measured by r) but also its size in terms of the original units of the variables. Given this general relationship, we could also compare different countries to see if their fertility rates fitted these pictures or deviated from them, and if so, in which directions. We also now have standard errors for our estimates, which may be useful in some circumstances. So why all the fuss?

Although we can only visualise two variables in two-dimensional space, exactly the same calculations that we have performed so far can be done *for any number of independent variables.* Each predictor or independent variable will have its own regression coefficient b, which will tell us the amount of change in our independent variable Y for a one-unit change in *that* dependent X variable, *holding all the other dependent X variables constant.* Given that most social sciences depend upon observational data, where it is often vital to control for prior variables when looking at the relation between a pair of variables of interest, it is an invaluable procedure. Small wonder that it is the workhorse of social science investigation.

It is worth pausing to reflect on this for a moment, as it is such an important point. Most social relationships or institutions whose behaviour we wish to model involve several variables. If we wished to model educational achievement we might be interested in spatial social deprivation, household income, type of school, social class, gender, ethnicity, a variety of social attitudes and so on. We'd probably prefer as simple a model as possible, and thus to weed out variables which have little independent impact. But how to do this? We often think in terms of the impact of factor X, 'other things equal', that is, taking account of everything else. While this is not difficult to do in the imagination, it is more difficult to achieve in empirical reality. The nearest we can get is in an experimental set-up where 'other things', whatever they may be, and whether or not we have even envisaged them, are 'made equal' by the process of random allocation of subjects to experimental and control groups, so that any differences in the outcome of the experiment can be attributed solely to the manipulation of the experimental variable. However, few social processes can be reduced to or mimicked by an experiment in ways that are ethical or practical, and unlike individuals, institutions, processes and structures cannot be 'randomised' in the same way. The next best alternative that we have is observation and *statistical* control, and the easiest way to achieve the latter is through multiple regression. Multiple regression gives us estimates for the direct effect of each independent variable, controlling for the effects of all the other variables in the model.

9 9 MULTIPLE LINEAR REGRESSION

The general form of the linear regression equation is

$$\hat{Y} = a + b_1 X_1 + b_2 X_2 + b_3 X_3 + \ldots + b_n X_n.$$

Each regression coefficient gives us an estimate for the effect of the corresponding independent variable on our dependent, controlling for the effects of all the other dependents. Let's continue looking at fertility and now use the capacity of regression to 'hold other things equal' to explore what might be some of the major variables associated with fertility rates in different countries around the world. Before we do so, note that there are various ways in which we could pose this question, each of which might lead to different answers.

First we might want to look only at countries above a certain size. One of the background assumptions of almost all statistics is the independence of observations; for example, it is built into the idea of random sampling. Can we treat very small countries as independent? No country within our global system is totally independent, but some countries are more independent than others, and some small countries may be so totally bound up with the larger units that surround them that it may not really be sensible to measure them at all: places like Luxembourg, Andorra, Monaco or the Virgin Islands. Tuvalu has a population of less than 10,000 so that it is about 140,000 times smaller than China. However, since there is no clear way of establishing what might be an appropriate cut-off size, let's analyse all countries, regardless of size.

Next we might consider looking only at relatively poor or relatively affluent countries. We can see from our scatterplot by per capita GDP that there appear to be two worlds of fertility: poor countries where fertility is still relatively high and richer countries where it is almost uniformly low. It would be surprising if exactly the same factors were associated with fertility levels in both these regimes. However, once again, especially if we look at our scatterplot for logged GDP, there is no obvious cut-off point that we might make, so let's once again analyse all countries.

Finally, there is a less obvious factor that will influence the kind of regression analysis we might make: missing data. When using only a couple of variables, missing data often doesn't matter very much. However, if we are using several variables, each with missing values for different cases in our data, we can very soon end up analysing a small and potentially highly selective and unrepresentative group of cases. It is easy to overlook this in linear regression as SPSS does not report on the number of cases excluded from the analysis (although you can infer it from the degrees of freedom for the residual in the ANOVA table in the output). We can only work with whatever data we have. One solution is to use imputation methods to estimate what the values for missing cases might have been, but such techniques take us beyond the scope of this book. The alternative is to look for data that is as comprehensive as possible. Thus in our World Development Indicators dataset we can often substitute a similar variable with fewer missing cases for one that suffers from this drawback.

One way of checking the impact of missing values is to first produce summary descriptive statistics for all the variables that you are considering for inclusion in a regression model, and to produce an *n*-way crosstab of all the independents (but be sure to check the option **Suppress tables** in the dialog box or add the sub-command **/FORMAT=NOTABLES** to your syntax, or you'll produce an enormous, and useless, contingency table). This allows you to see how many cases you will have in your model, as well as letting you identify variables with large amounts of missing data. Alternatively, as we will see below, you can have SPSS produce descriptive statistics as part of its regression output. It will include only those cases for which values are available for all the variables used in the regression.

The second thing that you must *always* do is produce scatterplots for each of your candidate independent variables by the dependent variable in order to check that their relationship is at least approximately linear, and that if it is not linear, it can be rendered so by some appropriate transformation.

Let's now produce a multiple linear regression model of **tfr** using both the independents we've looked at so far together. Missing data is not too much of a problem since we have 204 observations for **tfr**, 192 each for **infmort** and **lnpcgdp** and 180 for all three variables together. Either use the **Analyze→Regression→Linear...** dialog box or copy the syntax below. If using the dialog box, first put **lncpgdp** in the **Independent(s):** box, click **Next** under **Block 1 of 2** and enter **infmort**. This asks SPSS to first regress **tfr** on **lnpcgdp** alone, and then to regress on both our independent variables, so that we can compare the results. Instead of accepting all the defaults, click the **Statistics...** button then select both **Descriptives** and **Collinearity diagnostics**, as shown in Figure 9.11, click **Continue** and, back in the main dialog, ensure that **Enter** is selected as the **Method:**.

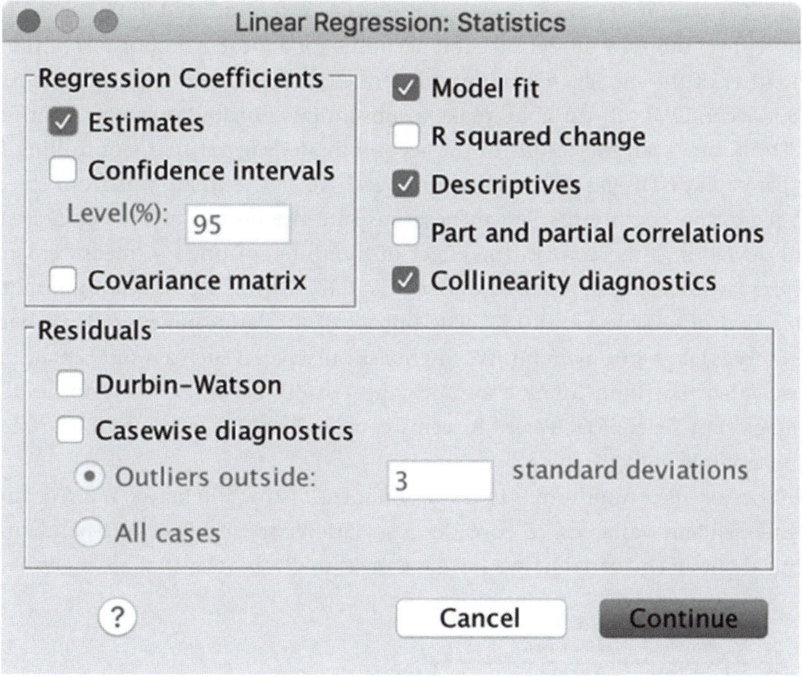

Figure 9.11   SPSS **Linear Regression: Statistics** dialog box

Alternatively, use the syntax below:

```
REGRESSION
/DESCRIPTIVES MEAN STDDEV CORR SIG N
/MISSING LISTWISE
/STATISTICS COEFF OUTS R ANOVA COLLIN TOL
/DEPENDENT tfr
/METHOD=ENTER lnpcgdp
/METHOD=ENTER infmort.
```

/MISSING LISTWISE instructs SPSS to exclude any case from the analysis that does not have values for all variables. **/STATISTICS** tells SPSS which output to produce. **COLLIN** and **TOL** are diagnostic outputs we are asking for. **/DEPENDENT** specifies the dependent variable, and **/METHOD=ENTER** instructs SPSS to force each independent into the model whether or not its estimate of their regression coefficient is zero. As alternatives to forced entry there are various forms of statistical selection of independent variables for the model, such as **STEPWISE**. Such approaches may be justified when there is no available theory or previous evidence to guide model construction, but they carry the real danger that we end up analysing the noise in our data rather than the signal, or simply getting the wrong variables in our model. However, if we are interested *only* in making predictions this *can* be a useful procedure. I discuss this further below.

Now study the output: the most important sections are reproduced in Figure 9.12. The first thing we note from our new model is that it accounts for a greater proportion of the variation in **tfr** than either of the models with one independent variable, but the gain is modest, from 0.85 to 0.87. Secondly, both variables make a substantial contribution to accounting for that variation. Third, however, the results of the second model suggest that, controlling for infant mortality, per capita GDP has only a modest effect. We can estimate this from the standardised (beta) regression coefficients. Since these measure the impact of the coefficient in units of standard deviation, this removes the effect of the different units of measurement used in producing the raw coefficients reported under **B**. At 0.62 the impact of infant mortality is more than double that of GDP level, at 0.29. The impact of the latter has more than halved once infant mortality is taken into account. We might ask ourselves if such a result is plausible. We've already speculated that both infant mortality and fertility are more likely to be determined (albeit indirectly) by level of GDP, and it seems counter-intuitive that infant mortality should play such a large role.

The solution to this conundrum is to think about the distinction between direct and indirect effects of independent variables, to consider associations between our independent variables and to think about all the variables we have *not* measured: variables that are *unobserved*.

Variables Entered/Removed[a]

Model	Variables Entered	Variables Removed	Method
1	lnpcgdp[b]	.	Enter
2	infmort[b]	.	Enter

a. Dependent Variable: tfr
b. All requested variables entered.

Model Summary

Model	R	R Square	Adjusted R Square	Std. Error of the Estimate
1	.774[a]	.599	.597	.88887
2	.866[b]	.750	.747	.70337

a. Predictors: (Constant), lnpcgdp
b. Predictors: (Constant), lnpcgdp, infmort

ANOVA[a]

Model		Sum of Squares	df	Mean Square	F	Sig.
1	Regression	209.985	1	209.985	265.776	.000[b]
	Residual	140.635	178	.790		
	Total	350.620	179			
2	Regression	263.053	2	131.526	265.853	.000[c]
	Residual	87.568	177	.495		
	Total	350.620	179			

a. Dependent Variable: tfr
b. Predictors: (Constant), lnpcgdp
c. Predictors: (Constant), lnpcgdp, infmort

Coefficients[a]

Model		Unstandardized Coefficients B	Std. Error	Standardized Coefficients Beta	t	Sig.	Collinearity Statistics Tolerance	VIF
1	(Constant)	11.026	.506		21.786	.000		
	lnpcgdp	-.896	.055	-.774	-16.303	.000	1.000	1.000
2	(Constant)	4.929	.712		6.922	.000		
	lnpcgdp	-.333	.070	-.288	-4.793	.000	.391	2.560
	infmort	.039	.004	.622	10.357	.000	.391	2.560

a. Dependent Variable: tfr

Figure 9.12 SPSS linear regression output

9 ●10 CAUSAL PATH DIAGRAMS

The best way to do this, and which is good practice before any multiple regression, is to draw up a causal path diagram (regardless of whether or not we intend to draw causal inferences from our data). In such a diagram we can represent variables as circles and potential casual paths as arrows. This helps you to think through both what might be important independents, and also what might be direct and indirect paths of impact of an independent on the dependent. It also guards against what might be called 'kitchen sink regression' where large numbers of independents are poured into a model in the search for variables with large coefficients or that are 'statistically significant'. Such an approach is an open invitation for the noise in your data to drive the model construction. Figure 9.13 shows a causal path diagram for our two independents.

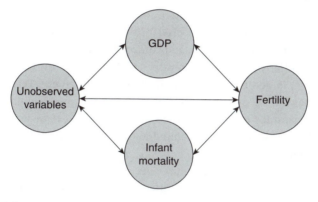

Figure 9.13 Causal path diagram I

We could speculate that both GDP and infant mortality might have both direct and indirect effects on fertility. Greater affluence, as measured by GDP, increases the resources that potential parents will have for rearing children, provides them with an increased range of choices about how to spend their time and money, and creates different opportunities for the children they may decide to have. Existing research suggests that the last two effects are the most important, and that there is a strong negative impact of GDP, at least in less affluent countries. Social demography describes the shift to lower fertility rates as the 'demographic transition'. It is clearly associated with economic development and social modernisation, and with falls in mortality, but the timing of change (which can be exceptionally rapid) is more difficult to explain and the direction of cause and effect is not completely clear. Early versions of the theory saw fertility change as a response to industrialisation and urbanisation, but later versions (arguably under the political impact of the cold war) came to see fertility change as a driver of modernisation, and a way of preventing population growth overwhelming economic 'take-off' in developing countries. Birth control became a mantra for development aid, and governments eager to receive it sometimes paid little attention to women's or potential parents' rights. What does seem to be crucial is for parents to come to have realistic aspirations of social mobility for their children, which in turn encourages them to use birth control and limit the number of children they have in order to concentrate their limited resources upon them (e.g. paying for schooling or medical care).

Thus we'd expect some *direct* impact of GDP on fertility, but also a range of indirect effects as GDP growth, for example, changes the health or education system in a country or parents' opportunities to do things *other* than have children, as well as influencing potential parents' fertility preferences. We'd also expect there to be some impact of fertility on GDP. Smaller families leave parents more time and energy to devote to production rather than reproduction. Thus we can draw arrows in both directions between GDP and fertility and between GDP and unobserved variables.

How might infant mortality affect fertility? Its *direct* effect may be low. In many traditional societies there is a preference for having at least one son. High infant mortality rates may encourage families to have more sons as insurance against their premature death and may drive them to have large families in order to achieve two or three sons. However, infant mortality is also associated with a range of unobserved variables that change with economic development, such as public health, sanitation, clean water supplies, diet, medical care (including vaccination against the main diseases of childhood) and education. Because we have not observed such variables directly, and controlled for them, we will therefore capture a whole range of *other* differences between countries with high and low rates of infant mortality through this variable, in addition to the infant mortality difference. Fertility will also affect infant mortality. We could expect high rates of fertility, and corresponding demand for neonatal health services and for resources devoted to child rearing, to be associated with higher infant mortality. Thus, as with GDP, we could draw arrows in both directions to both fertility and unobserved variables.

We can now think about our coefficient results again. Our coefficient for GDP gives us its *direct* effect on fertility, controlling for the effect of infant mortality. This direct effect will also contain the *indirect* effects of our unobserved variables that are *not* captured by infant mortality. This is one of the causes of the fall in the size of the GDP coefficient. Meanwhile our infant mortality coefficient will capture both any direct effect of infant mortality and all the direct and indirect effects of our unobserved variables with which infant mortality is associated.

9●11 PREDICTION AND EXPLANATION

When we draw up causal path diagrams we are concerned with explanation. However, sometimes our goal in regression is simpler: to produce a model that predicts a dependent variable from the values of one or more independent predictor variables. In the latter case we do not need to worry about the distinction between correlation and causation. For example, a model designed to forecast the sales of a product might rely on predictors that had correlated well with this in the past, whether or not they have any obvious causal link to sales performance. Recall from Chapter 2 that there is a robust correlation between ice-cream sales and the level of robbery. This is not because robbers like ice-cream, but because there are both more opportunities for committing robberies and reasons to eat ice-cream when the weather is good. If we were interested in predicting the incidence of robbery either predictor variable would suit our purpose, even though only one had a causal relationship to robbery.

9 12 MULTICOLLINEARITY

However, we have one final factor to consider, found in the collinearity statistics that we asked for. Multicollinearity arises when independent variables are highly correlated with each other, as is the case here. The r for **infmort** and **lnpcgdp** is 0.78. When independents share so much variance it is *not* possible for regression to distinguish the variation in the dependent accounted for by each variable individually. What tends to happen is that small differences in the strength of their relationship with the independent variable get magnified, so that the stronger of the two variables takes the lion's share of the variation in the regression model. This does not affect the overall performance of the model. The estimates for R will still be correct; rather it is the estimates of individual regression *coefficients* and their standard errors (which are artificially inflated) that are affected.

This might appear to be paradoxical. We use linear regression to distinguish the impact of independent variables controlling for each of the others – which implies that these independents are correlated – and now we're discovering that their correlation is a problem for the analysis! The resolution of this paradox lies in the fact that multicollinearity only arises when such correlation is high: a decent rule of thumb would be an r of 0.6 or more between independent variables. The solution to the issue lies in routinely asking for collinearity diagnostic statistics when running a regression. The *tolerance* statistic is produced by regressing each independent on all the other independents and subtracting the resulting R^2 from 1. Where an independent is highly correlated with the others this tolerance statistic will fall to low values: anything below about 0.4 is a problem. Its reciprocal, the *variance inflation factor*, gives an estimate of how much the standard errors for regression coefficient have been inflated by the multicollinearity. We can see that in our model our two independents are highly correlated and the collinearity diagnostics alert us to this. (You can confirm how they are calculated by squaring the correlation coefficient r for our two independents, $0.78^2 = 0.61$, and subtracting, $1 - 0.61 = 0.39$, which is the value reported under **Tolerance** in our output in Figure 9.12.)

What can be done about collinearity? The most important point to keep in mind is that collinearity is often a function of the real world, not necessarily a problem in our data. One solution can be to produce a single variable out of two highly correlated ones. In a situation like ours, where alternative variables are available, careful selection can sometimes get round problems of collinearity.

9 13 A BETTER MODEL

Let's now try to improve on our existing model, using both theory and data availability to guide its construction. We might hypothesise that GDP, education, public health and prevalence of the use of contraception affect a country's fertility rate. Our causal path diagram would look like Figure 9.14. Note that I've included **mortality**, a variable that isn't observed in the model, to illustrate how some of the effects of the variables we are observing could be indirect as well as direct.

To operationalise our model we can use the variables **comp1edfpc** (percentage of girls completing primary school), **imph20** (percentage of population with improved water supplies),

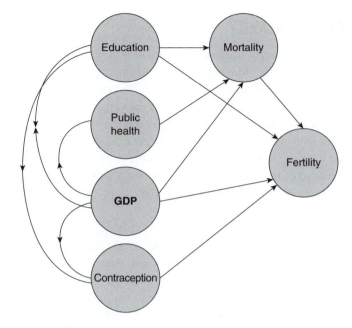

Figure 9.14 Causal path diagram II

cprev1449 (percentage of women aged 14–49 using any form of contraception) and **lnpcgdp**. Our first task is to run scatterplots for each of these independents with **tfr**. There are four reasons for doing this:

1   It may alert us to *unusual* values taken by either variable. We can check that these are not the result of a mistake in the data capture and recording process. If they are valid values it may make us rethink how we understand this variable. How might unusual values be possible? Are they of special interest because of that? Unusual values are referred to as *outliers* or *extreme values*.
2   It tells us at a glance what kind of association may exist between our two variables, and whether that association is *linear*. If the coordinates are best summarised by a curved line, that would mean that the amount of change in the values of the *Y* variable would also depend upon the range of values taken by the *X* variable. (As we shall see, it would mean that the *slope* of the line is not constant.)
3   If the association *does* seem to be linear it can tell us whether it is *positive* (high values on variable 1 tend to go with high values on variable 2) or *negative* (high values on variable 1 go with low values on variable 2 and vice versa).
4   To the extent that coordinates cluster close to a regression line, it tells us how *strong* the association is likely to be.

If using the dialog box, enter the dependents and independents, click the **Statistics...** button and choose the **Descriptives** and **Collinearity** diagnostics options as before, but this time, in the bottom half of the dialog box under **Residuals**, select **Durbin–Watson** and **Casewise diagnostics**, and change the setting under the latter to **2** standard deviations rather than **3**. Back in the main **Linear Regression** dialog box, click **Plots...** and select the option **Normal probability plot**; then place the variable ***ZPRED** in the **X** axis and ***ZRESID** in the **Y** axis under **Scatter 1 of 1**. Again return to the main dialog box and now select **Save...**, which brings up the **Linear Regression:Save** dialog box of statistics calculated for each case that can be saved.

Choose **Unstandardized Predicted Values, Cook's Distance, Leverage Values, Standardized Residuals** and **DfBeta(s) Influence statistics.** To use syntax, follow the syntax below, 🖉 which is also available on the companion website.

```
REGRESSION
/DESCRIPTIVES MEAN STDDEV CORR SIG N
/MISSING LISTWISE
/STATISTICS COEFF OUTS R ANOVA COLLIN TOL
/DEPENDENT tfr
/METHOD=ENTER lnpcgdp comp1edfpc imph20 cprev1449
/SCATTERPLOT=(*ZRESID ,*ZPRED)
/RESIDUALS DURBIN NORMPROB(ZRESID)
/CASEWISE PLOT(ZRESID) OUTLIERS(2)
/SAVE PRED COOK LEVER ZRESID DFBETA.
```

The options we have chosen give us a variety of diagnostic statistics to help us assess the fit of our regression model, which we will discuss as we go through the output that is reproduced in Figure 9.15.

Descriptive Statistics

	Mean	Std. Deviation	N
tfr	3.3925	1.44269	109
lnpcgdp	8.5675	1.07430	109
imph20	82.9844	15.66615	109
cprev1449	45.0899	22.37676	109
comp1edfpc	85.8490	22.13291	109

Correlations

		tfr	lnpcgdp	imph20	cprev1449	comp1edfpc
Pearson Correlation	tfr	1.000	-.726	-.717	-.763	-.728
	lnpcgdp	-.726	1.000	.587	.585	.560
	imph20	-.717	.587	1.000	.584	.634
	cprev1449	-.763	.585	.584	1.000	.709
	comp1edfpc	-.728	.560	.634	.709	1.000
Sig. (1-tailed)	tfr	.	.000	.000	.000	.000
	lnpcgdp	.000	.	.000	.000	.000
	imph20	.000	.000	.	.000	.000
	cprev1449	.000	.000	.000	.	.000
	comp1edfpc	.000	.000	.000	.000	.
N	tfr	109	109	109	109	109
	lnpcgdp	109	109	109	109	109
	imph20	109	109	109	109	109
	cprev1449	109	109	109	109	109
	comp1edfpc	109	109	109	109	109

Figure 9.15   SPSS linear regression output I

If you review the correlations between the independent variables you will see that multicollinearity threatens to be a problem since the smallest correlation between any independent and another is 0.58, uncomfortably close to the 0.6 borderline. There is little that we can do about this. Industrialisation, modernisation and development take a broadly similar path in many countries, so that we often find high levels of association between its different aspects when comparing across countries at different stages of development. You will also see that our selection of five variables has whittled down what were originally 214 countries to just over half that number. This would usually be a cause for concern. The next step would usually be to identify which observations were missing and to attempt to fill them, either by selecting an alternative variable, using other sources of data to get relevant estimates, or accepting observations from earlier time periods if they were available. However, since much of our missing data comes from either small or affluent countries that did not provide the full range of statistics to the World Bank, we'll proceed with the countries for which we have data.

Next review the main output for our new model shown in Figure 9.16. The new model accounts for a little over three-quarters of the variance in the dependent, and all the independents are significant. The collinearity statistics confirm what we saw in the descriptive statistics: that multicollinearity is an issue, but none of our tolerance statistics are below 0.4. However, we might want to be cautious in our interpretation of the individual beta coefficients.

Model Summary[b]

Model	R	R Square	Adjusted R Square	Std. Error of the Estimate	Durbin–Watson
1	.874[a]	.764	.755	.71413	2.055

a. Predictors: (Constant), comp1edfpc, lnpcgdp, imph20, cprev1449
b. Dependent Variable: tfr

ANOVA[a]

Model		Sum of Squares	df	Mean Square	F	Sig.
1	Regression	171.748	4	42.937	84.192	.000[b]
	Residual	53.039	104	.510		
	Total	224.786	108			

a. Dependent Variable: tfr
b. Predictors: (Constant), comp1edfpc, lnpcgdp, imph20, cprev1449

Coefficients[a]

Model		Unstandardized Coefficients		Standardized Coefficients	t	Sig.	Collinearity Statistics	
		B	Std. Error	Beta			Tolerance	VIF
1	(Constant)	10.583	.616		17.189	.000		
	lnpcgdp	-.396	.086	-.295	-4.622	.000	.557	1.796
	imph20	-.022	.006	-.240	-3.599	.000	.508	1.968
	cprev1449	-.021	.005	-.319	-4.420	.000	.436	2.296
	comp1edfpc	-.012	.005	-.184	-2.498	.014	.417	2.398

a. Dependent Variable: tfr

Figure 9.16 SPSS linear regression output II

We can now produce a regression equation describing the relationship between our dependent and four independent variables from the information in the **Coefficients** table:

$$\text{est. } \textbf{tfr} = 10.58 - (0.40 \times \textbf{lngdp}) - (0.02 \times \textbf{imph20}) - (0.02 \times \textbf{cprev1449}) - (0.01 \times \textbf{comp1edfpc}).$$

We can use this equation to estimate what the model would predict for given values of our independents, or to compare the impact of the independent variables. For example if we had a country where per capita GDP was $10,000, all the population had access to improved water supplies, contraceptive prevalence was 85%, and 100% of girls completed primary education, we'd have the following result (remember we need to take the natural log of 10,000 for the GDP figure, which is 9.21) :

$$\text{est. } \textbf{tfr} = 10.58 - (0.4 \times 9.21) - (0.02 \times 100) - (0.02 \times 85) - (0.01 \times 100)$$
$$= 10.58 - 3.68 - 2 - 1.7 - 1$$
$$= 2.2.$$

What would be the estimated impact of doubling per capita GDP to $20,000? The natural log of 20,000 is 9.90 so we'd expect **tfr** to be $(9.9 - 9.21) \times 0.4 = 0.28$ lower.

9 14 LINEAR REGRESSION DIAGNOSTICS

Now examine the new diagnostic output that we've requested (Figure 9.17). Under **Casewise Diagnostics** SPSS reports on any residuals whose value is more than two standard deviations from the mean. If our residuals are approximately normally distributed (i.e. our prediction

Casewise Diagnostics[a]

Case Number	Std. Residual	tfr	Predicted Value	Residual
1	−2.198	4.28	5.8534	−1.56935
2	2.664	7.60	5.6967	1.90233
5	−2.161	4.29	5.8295	−1.54350
17	−2.349	1.26	2.9337	−1.67771

a. Dependent Variable: tfr

Residuals Statistics[a]

	Minimum	Maximum	Mean	Std. Deviation	N
Predicted Value	1.3201	5.9771	3.3925	1.26105	109
Std. Predicted Value	−1.643	2.050	.000	1.000	109
Standard Error of Predicted Value	.084	.331	.147	.043	109
Adjusted Predicted Value	1.3119	5.9677	3.3934	1.26469	109
Residual	−1.67771	1.90233	.00000	.70078	109
Std. Residual	−2.349	2.664	.000	.981	109
Stud. Residual	−2.369	2.721	−.001	1.007	109
Deleted Residual	−1.70609	1.98504	−.00085	.73832	109
Stud. Deleted Residual	−2.424	2.810	−.001	1.017	109
Mahal. Distance	.509	22.232	3.963	3.318	109
Cook's Distance	.000	.105	.011	.019	109
Centered Leverage Value	.005	.206	.037	.031	109

a. Dependent Variable: tfr

Figure 9.17 SPSS linear regression output III

errors are random) then we would expect up to five residuals of this size. We have only four and they do not seem to be cause for concern. Note that the case numbers that SPSS reports correspond to the row numbers in the **Data Editor** window **Data View** mode. The table headed **Residuals Statistics** gives us a plethora of numbers, most of which can safely be ignored until

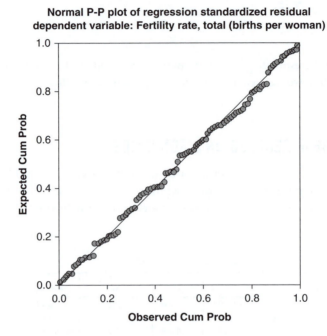

Normal P-P plot of regression standardized residual dependent variable: Fertility rate, total (births per woman)

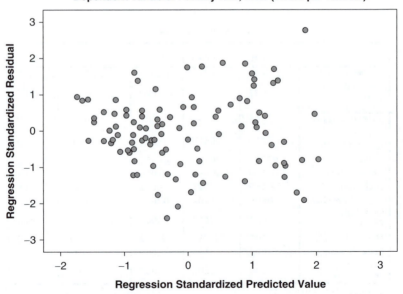

Scatterplot
Dependent variable: Fertility rate, total (births per woman)

Figure 9.18 SPSS linear regression diagnostic plots

your regression skills are more advanced. **Predicted Value**s outside the range of what would seem plausible, or large **Residual**s are a potential cause for concern. For example, predictions of a negative or very high fertility rate would be cause for concern. *Cook's distance* is a statistic that measures the influence on the regression model of individual cases. For example, an outlier or extreme value in a regression with relatively few cases can shift the slope of the regression line and affect the coefficient estimates. Cook's distance values greater than $4/n$ for a case may be worth further investigation. For our data $4/n = 4/109 = 0.037$. We can check how many cases are above this level by producing frequency statistics for a new variable that SPSS has created labelled COO_1. We have eight cases with Cook's distance larger than this; all except Montenegro and Haiti are in sub-Saharan Africa and with relatively high fertility rates. One way of responding to this might be to explore producing a distinct model for sub-Saharan African countries, or introducing a dummy variable to distinguish them. We'll return to this below. Finally, the *Durbin–Watson* statistic tests for the independence of residual terms. It can take a value between 0 and 4, with values close to 2 indicating independence. It is presented in the second group of output (Figure 9.16) under **Model Summary**, and we have a value very close to 2.

We asked SPSS to produce two plots (Figure 9.8). The *normal probability plot* plots the distribution of standardised residuals against a normal distribution by way of a cumulative plot, and gives a quick visual check of the distribution of residuals. A good model will have residuals that cluster close to a 45-degree slope. Finally, a *scatterplot* of the standardised values for **tfr** predicted by the regression model against the standardised residuals will indicate if there are problems with either nonlinearity or heteroscedasticity. The latter occurs when the absolute value of residuals increases with the predicted value of the dependent. This would mean that the model is better at predicting low values of **tfr** than high ones. This can lead to biased standard error estimates and other problems. When heteroscedasticity is a problem the plot assumes the shape of a 'funnel' lying on its side; residuals to the left of the plot cluster close to zero then spread out as we move rightwards. Mild heteroscedasticity is common and not a cause for concern. If it is severe, transforming one or more of the independents can sometimes solve the problem. Overall we can be fairly happy with the diagnostics of our model.

9 ● 15 CREATING DUMMY VARIABLES

Linear regression requires that the independent and dependent variables are all at the interval level of measurement. However, independent variables which are ordinal or nominal can be included as dummy variables which take only two values. It is convenient, but not mandatory, for these two values to be coded as 0 and 1. This makes the interpretation easier. Any variable taking N values can be recoded as a set of $N - 1$ dummy variables. One value of the original variable is chosen as a reference category to which the other values are compared. Each new dummy variable takes the value 1 for the corresponding value in the original ordinal or nominal variable, and 0 otherwise. The reference category takes the value 0 for *all* the new dummy variables. The example of turning the nominal variable **worldregion** into a set of dummies is shown in Table 9.1.

Table 9.1 Worldregion variable by dummy variables

		Corresponding dummy variable values					
Worldregion values and labels		EAP	ECA	LAC	MENA	NA	SA
1	East Asia & Pacific	1	0	0	0	0	0
2	Europe & Central Asia	0	1	0	0	0	0
3	Latin America & Caribbean	0	0	1	0	0	0
4	Middle East & North Africa	0	0	0	1	0	0
5	North America	0	0	0	0	1	0
6	South Asia	0	0	0	0	0	1
7	Sub-Saharan Africa	0	0	0	0	0	0

It is easiest to use syntax and a series of **if** statements to create the new variables. Try to do this yourself and then, as usual, compare your results to the syntax suggested below.

```
COMPUTE eap eq 0.
COMPUTE eca eq 0.
COMPUTE lac eq 0.
COMPUTE mena eq 0.
COMPUTE na eq 0.
COMPUTE sa eq 0.
IF (worldregion = 1) eap eq 1.
IF (worldregion = 2) eca eq 1.
IF (worldregion = 3) lac eq 1.
IF (worldregion = 4) mena eq 1.
IF (worldregion = 5) na eq 1.
IF (worldregion = 6) sa eq 1.
CROSS worldregion by eap to sa.
```

Some caution has to be used in interpreting the output from dummy variables to keep clear what comparisons are being made when they are used. Remember that the coefficient for each dummy variable represents the contrast with the reference category for which there is no dummy. If the dummy is coded 0 and 1, we can take the coefficient as the direct difference in the mean value of the dependent variable associated with that dummy (since the coefficient is multiplied by one of the variable's two values, 0 and 1).

Run the regression model for **tfr** again, but this time enter the set of dummy variables for region of the world as a new block in the regression. If you are using the GUI, click **Next** above the **Independent(s):** box and enter the dummy variables. If using syntax, simply repeat the **/METHOD=ENTER** subcommand with the dummy variable names. You should find that the R^2 for the model increases to 0.83 and that all the dummies for region are significant. They thus seem to be a valid addition to the model; however, this comes at the cost of pushing the tolerance statistics for two of the independents just below the 0.4 threshold. If you run the normal probability plot you'll also see that the distribution of the residuals is a little further from normal than before, and the value for the Durbin–Watson statistic has fallen to 1.9. None of these changes is a severe problem. Using the dummies, we can now make a judgement about whether there are 'regional' effects on fertility, beyond the differences we'd expect anyway based on factors such as level of economic development, education or public health. Since our reference category is sub-Saharan Africa, our comparison is with fertility there. As we might expect, given high fertility in many sub-Saharan African countries, the coefficients are all negative and quite substantial. Thus it appears that even allowing for the low GDP of most sub-Saharan African countries, fertility there is higher than we'd expect it to be, based on predictors such as per capita GDP.

9●16 EVALUATING REGRESSION MODELS

It is useful to go through a check-list of issues to consider when evaluating a regression model, whether that is one you have constructed yourself, or one that has been published and reported in an academic journal.

A good model is about more than carrying out the regression analysis and its diagnostics correctly. The most important and most difficult question is simply *are the right variables in the model?* Beyond satisfying goals such as parsimony and having independents that account for a substantial amount of variance in the dependent, identifying and choosing the correct variables is often a matter of data availability. Some things are difficult or costly to measure well, or are of minor interest to those who conduct or resource social surveys or other data capture exercises. What we'd ideally like to measure and what actually has been measured are often not the same thing. A judgement has to be made about whether missing variables are likely to bias the coefficients in the model. Keep in mind Kahneman's (2012: 86) warning about WYSIATI (What You See Is All There Is) and consider what relevant missing variables might compromise the model. Note any likely prior or intervening variables that are not included in the model. Think about how they might influence the results if you did have such information.

Be clear too about the *purpose* of a model. You may be simply trying to identify the variables associated with variation in the dependent (e.g. what are the correlates of high income among different earners; what varies with the extent of literacy across different countries). Or you may wish to discover if a strong association between two variables remains when controlling for other variables. Be clear about what you are trying to find out and how you would interpret the results, before you obtain them. Doing this will help you construct a clearer causal path diagram for your variables. Of course, once you have your results you can still modify the path diagram, or change the variables you use.

Your next concern *is how well the variables in the model have been measured*. Measurement error may be ubiquitous, but some data is of higher quality than others. Pay particular attention to data gathered in different countries; although consistency in definitions and survey procedures is improving, making precise comparisons depends upon being sure that like is really being compared with like. Check question translation procedures, definitions of concepts such as 'secondary education', 'migrant', 'urban', as well as sampling strategies. Always consider if it is reasonable to treat the dependent as an interval level variable. Although linear regression is fairly robust to the violation of its assumptions, it is rarely a good idea to use dependent variables with a limited range of values or that it might make more sense to treat as ordinal.

What is the impact of missing data? As we've seen, a model with many variables may have problems with missing data. This can be especially troublesome when the number of cases is small (e.g. when comparing countries or regions within a country). Consider alternative sources of data that might be used to estimate values for missing observations.

Is the relationship between the independents approximately linear, or made so by transformation? If transformed, does the relationship make substantive sense?

Are the causal paths in the model correctly specified? This is another quite subjective question. As we've noted above, almost any social relationship has some degree of reverse causality in it and neither good research design nor measurement strategies can always remove it altogether. Specifying all the potential direct and indirect effects of variables in a model can be challenging, but may not always be necessary if it can be safely assumed that indirect effects are small in size. Remember that OLS multiple linear regression will give you values for the *direct* effect of an independent upon the dependent controlling for all other independents in the model, whether they are prior or intervening variables.

How good are the model diagnostics? Are there problems with homoscedasticity, collinearity, residual outliers, leverage or nonlinearity? It is straightforward to check these with a model you have run yourself. Unfortunately, journal editors have an uneven record in requiring authors to report model diagnostics, and too much emphasis is typically placed on *p*-values below 0.05. In an age where there is no limitation on the supplementary online material that authors can be asked to supply, hopefully this is something that will improve.

In a good model, residuals will be normally distributed with mean zero. Residuals that are very large indicate cases that are poorly predicted by the model, and may exercise undue influence on it. Residuals that are positively associated with the value of the dependent (heteroscedasticity) can bias regression coefficients.

9 ● 17 HOW TO REPORT A LINEAR REGRESSION MODEL

When deciding how to report a regression model, follow two guiding principles: first, clear presentation of substantive conclusions and the evidence for them; and second, enough material to allow an interested reader to duplicate the model and run it. It is good practice to report:

The source of the data

Any transformations carried out on the original variables

Any steps taken to deal with missing data

A brief account of model development

Descriptives for the variables in the model, including *N*

R^2 for the model, and either the *F* statistic or associated significance

The regression coefficients and standard errors

Any potential weaknesses revealed by model diagnostics

Reporting standard errors for the regression coefficients allows readers to reach their own conclusions about significance. Depending on the purpose of the model, it may be preferable to report the unstandardised or standardised regression coefficients, or both.

9 ● 18 GOING FURTHER

There has only been space in this chapter to introduce the basics of linear regression. Hopefully, as well as giving you the skills you need to get started, it will also have given you a sense of the manifold potential applications of regression – all rooted in its ability to examine variables while controlling for the effect of others – and an appetite to delve deeper. A good place to start is Paul Allison's book *Multiple Regression: A Primer* (1999).

what you have learned

- What it means to regress a variable on another
- The relationship between regression and correlation
- Regression to the mean
- The equation for any straight line in two-dimensional space described by its slope and intercept
- The ordinary least squares method of fitting a regression line
- Residual and regression sums of squares that partition the variance in a variable
- How to identify individual cases in a scatterplot
- How to use scatterplots to check for linearity
- How to transform a variable using logarithms
- How to create dummy variables to handle nominal and ordinal independent variables
- How to draw causal path diagrams
- How to use SPSS to produce a regression equation, raw and standardised regression coefficients and diagnostic outputs for the distribution of residuals
- Multicollinearity, heteroscedasticity and leverage
- How to assess the performance of a regression model using these outputs
- How to report a model

exercises

1   Using your World Development Indicators dataset, regress women's adult literacy rate on the percentage of the population with access to electricity. Do you think that electricity has an important role to play in promoting women's literacy? If not, explore other variables that might account for the correlation between these two variables. Keep in mind that you may need to transform some variables.

2   Explore the correlates of the total fertility rate (**tfr**) and build a model to account for the variation in the fertility rate across countries.

3   Treat the variable **depress** in the ESS dataset as a dependent variable. Can you identify any social groups in Europe that appear to be at greater risk of depression?

GETTING STARTED WITH LOGISTIC REGRESSION

━━━━━ **introduction** ━━━━━

Linear regression is unsuitable when the dependent variable you want to model is categorical because a straight regression line is no longer an adequate summary of the values we want to predict. However, we can get round this problem by modelling the probability that the dependent variable will take a specific value. Since many of the variables we are interested in are categorical, logistic regression is a very useful technique. One way of approaching logistic regression is to see it as a way of representing the contents of a contingency table by relating the contents of one cell in the table, the reference category, to all other cells in the table. In this chapter we look in depth at how logistic regression works. In Chapter 11 we work through an example. We look at:

- Odds, odds ratios, logged odds and the logit
- Odds and probabilities
- Converting a contingency table into an equation
- Reference categories
- Nested models
- Running a logistic regression in IBM SPSS Statistics software
- Interpreting logistic regression output

10 ● 1   INTRODUCTION

The linear regression that we examined in Chapter 9 is designed to analyse two or more variables, when one of the variables is designated as a dependent variable and is continuous. Although it can handle categorical independent variables as dummies, it cannot be used when the dependent variable we want to explain or predict is categorical because we would not be able to fit a straight regression line. Logistic regression can be used when the dependent is categorical with either continuous or categorical predictors. Rather than being a special case of the log-linear or logit model (as it is sometimes presented), it is a hybrid between the logit model and the OLS regression model we looked at in Chapter 9 (Menard, 2010: 41). We will look at the simplest case of logistic regression when our dependent takes two values.

The essence of the logistic approach is to model the *probability* (expressed as odds) that the dependent variable will take a specified value rather than modelling these values directly. While the theory of logistic regression is a little more complex than that of linear regression, running the regression itself is straightforward. However, interpreting the output requires a little more care than with linear regression. Because most of the variables that we use to describe people rather than institutions or organisations are categorical, variants of logistic regression are very common in social science work.

10 ● 2   THE ADVANTAGES AND LIMITATIONS OF CONTINGENCY TABLES

By now you will be very familiar with contingency tables where the distribution of values for one categorical variable is shown conditional upon the values for another. I referred to it earlier as the workhorse of the social sciences, because much of what we measure is categorical, because standardisation of a table is easy by using row and column percentages, and because two-way contingency tables are fairly intuitive to understand, so that they can be used in reports with a reasonable expectation that the audience will understand them, especially if care is taken to keep the contents simple and well labelled.

However, contingency tables have four limitations. First, although they present the reader with a concise summary of the data that is intuitively understandable, this can nevertheless lead to erroneous conclusions being drawn if readers are not alert to the way in which the distribution of data in the table margins impacts upon their interpretation. Second, contingency tables rapidly become cumbersome and difficult to read if there are more than two or three variables, and if any variable takes more than three or four categories. Readers baulk at seemingly endless rows or columns of numbers. Third, by the same token, it is difficult to combine analysis of continuous with categorical variables using contingency tables, unless the continuous variable is recoded into interval ranges, which means some loss of information. Finally, when presenting data based on sampling, it is usually cumbersome to add confidence intervals or other indications of sampling variation to a table. Typically this information is just omitted, which may encourage readers to view the data as more certain or precise than it actually is.

Logistic regression deals with all of these challenges, since it allows us to use a regression approach but with a categorical dependent variable. It is possible to see logistic regression as essentially the same as the more familiar linear regression but with both sides of the equation transformed by the use of logged odds, or the *logit*. However, such an approach tends to underplay some important differences between the two forms of regression, especially when it comes to the interpretation of coefficients, and also overlooks the roots of logistic regression in log-linear and logit analysis and, ultimately, the contingency table itself. Since we have just looked at linear regression in Chapter 9, this chapter starts not from linear regression, but the contingency table.

10 3 DOWNLOADING THE WORLD VALUES SURVEY WAVE 6 DATA

As usual, we'll explore logistic regression using some concrete examples. We'll use the data for the Netherlands from the World Values Survey Wave 6 dataset, on which we did some online analysis in Chapter 3. Download the data at

🔧 http://www.worldvaluessurvey.org/WVSDocumentationWV6.jsp

You can either create a new dataset with the cases from only the Netherlands, or you can use the full dataset but filter out other countries using **Select Cases** syntax, menus or icons, using the skills you learned in Chapters 4 and 6. You'll see that no weights are supplied in the WVS dataset with the Netherlands data, so there is no need to apply weights. The WVS data comes with a weight variable **v258**, but it takes the value 1 for all respondents from the Netherlands.

First we'll create some new variables for this exercise. 🔧 The syntax for creating these variables is available on the companion website, but you should attempt to create this yourself, using the skills we've covered in earlier chapters. Remember to create new variables from your recodes rather than altering the original variables (so that you can correct any errors), and to label both the new variables and their values clearly. Be sure to keep the syntax you use, as we'll use this variable with data from other countries later on.

10 ● 4 CREATING NEW VARIABLES

The five existing WVS variables **v185** to **v189** are based on questions asking respondents if they have *ever* taken part in different forms of political activity: signing a petition, taking part in a strike, boycott or peaceful demonstration, or some other form of protest. Create a variable that records whether each respondent reports having taken part in *at least one* such activity, or reports *never* having taken part in any of these activities. I've called the new variable **polaction**. It takes two values: 0 = no for respondents reporting they have *never* taken part in any of these activities, and 1 = yes for respondents who reported taking part in *one or more* of the political activities covered by **v185** to **v189**.

v238 is based on a question asking people what social class they think they belong to ('subjective' social class) and currently takes five values. To simplify things we can collapse these categories down to two: 'middle class' (comprising all those describing themselves as 'upper class', 'upper middle class' and 'lower middle class') and 'working class' (comprising those who said they were 'lower class' or 'working class'). To remind myself where this variable came from I've called it **v238jmnl**, but you may prefer to give it another name.

v248 records people's levels of education. Again we can collapse the categories. We can group together all response categories up to and including 'complete secondary school' and form a second group from the two categories of post-school education. I've called the result **v248jmnl**.

10 ● 5 DESCRIBING THE ASSOCIATION BETWEEN POLACTION, V238JMNL AND V248JMNL

Now we can examine two two-way crosstabs between **polaction** and each of our two other variables, with column percentages to standardise the tables (Figures 10.1 and 10.2).

polaction * V238jmnl Crosstabulation

			V238jmnl		Total
			working class	middle class	
polaction	no activity	Count	369	723	1092
		% within V238jmnl	67.0%	54.2%	58.0%
	taken part	Count	182	610	792
		% within V238jmnl	33.0%	45.8%	42.0%
Total		Count	551	1333	1884
		% within V238jmnl	100.0%	100.0%	100.0%

Symmetric Measures

		Value	Asymp. Std. Error[a]	Approx. T[b]	Approx. Sig.
Nominal by Nominal	Phi	.117			.000
	Cramer's V	.117			.000
Ordinal by Ordinal	Gamma	.262	.049	5.220	.000
N of Valid Cases		1884			

a. Not assuming the null hypothesis.
b. Using the asymptotic standard error assuming the null hypothesis.

Figure 10.1 Crosstab of **polaction** by **v238jmnl**

polaction * v248jmnl Crosstabulation

			v248jmnl		
			up to secondary	post school	Total
polaction	no activity	Count	822	270	1092
		% within v248jmnl	67.4%	40.7%	58.0%
	taken part	Count	398	394	792
		% within v248jmnl	32.6%	59.3%	42.0%
Total		Count	1220	664	1884
		% within v248jmnl	100.0%	100.0%	100.0%

Symmetric Measures

		Value	Asymp. Std. Error[a]	Approx. T[b]	Approx. Sig.
Nominal by Nominal	Phi	.259			.000
	Cramer's V	.259			.000
Ordinal by Ordinal	Gamma	.502	.037	11.309	.000
N of Valid Cases		1884			

a. Not assuming the null hypothesis.

b. Using the asymptotic standard error assuming the null hypothesis.

Figure 10.2 Crosstab of **polaction** by **v248jmnl**

It's clear from the crosstabs that each of our variables has an association with political activity, although the association with education looks stronger. The problem comes when we choose how to describe and compare these associations, especially to a non-specialist audience. A chi-square test would simply tell us the probability that we'd get the results shown given that there was in fact no association between the pair of variables. In each case, we could see that the probability would be vanishingly small given the distribution of counts across the cells of the crosstab. We could use a measure of association such as *phi* or *gamma*, both of which suggest that the association is about twice as strong for education as for class, but this faces two difficulties. Non-expert audiences for our results are unlikely to know about or understand measures of association, and they might not understand just what is meant by 'twice as strong'.

Perhaps because of such difficulties, often the *differences* in percentages in the cells of the table are simply compared, treating the proportions as probabilities. Thus 59% of those with post-school education had taken part in political activity compared to only 33% without such education, a difference of 26%; similarly 46% of middle-class respondents compared to 33% of working-class ones had, a difference of 13%. However, the size of the percentage differences depends not only on the variables' effects on political action but also on the marginal distribution of cases in the table, so that comparisons across different tables can be misleading. For example, if the prevalence of political activity was lower (say, 21% rather than 42%) exactly the same strength of influence of class or education would nevertheless result in percentage differences *half* the size of those shown in our tables.

Moreover, percentage differences do not operate in a linear fashion. Suppose we find a variable that, controlling for other effects, appears to double the probability that a respondent is politically active. Imagine we have two groups of respondents, one in which 25% of people are active, and one in which 60% are. What would be the impact of this variable? We can think of the 25% doubling to 50%, but we *cannot* double 60% because we have a ceiling of 100%: even if every respondent became active the probability of activity would still not have doubled.

One way round these difficulties is to deal in ratios of percentages rather than absolute differences. We could say that the percentage of those taking part in political activity was $(593/326) - 1 = 82\%$ higher for those with post-school education or $(458/330) - 1 = 39\%$ higher for those who thought of themselves as middle class. This addresses the difficulty of the marginal distribution of the dependent variable, but doesn't address the others we've set out. Moreover, I find that non-expert audiences often get confused between absolute and relative percentage differences.

Produce a three-way crosstab of political activity by education and subjective social class for the Netherlands: you should get Figure 10.3.

polaction * V238jmnl * v248jmnl Crosstabulation

v248jmnl				V238jmnl working class	middle class	Total
up to secondary	polaction	no activity	Count	344	478	822
			% within V238jmnl	70.8%	65.1%	67.4%
		taken part	Count	142	256	398
			% within V238jmnl	29.2%	34.9%	32.6%
	Total		Count	486	734	1220
			% within V238jmnl	100.0%	100.0%	100.0%
post school	polaction	no activity	Count	25	245	270
			% within V238jmnl	38.5%	40.9%	40.7%
		taken part	Count	40	354	394
			% within V238jmnl	61.5%	59.1%	59.3%
	Total		Count	65	599	664
			% within V238jmnl	100.0%	100.0%	100.0%
Total	polaction	no activity	Count	369	723	1092
			% within V238jmnl	67.0%	54.2%	58.0%
		taken part	Count	182	610	792
			% within V238jmnl	33.0%	45.8%	42.0%
	Total		Count	551	1333	1884
			% within V238jmnl	100.0%	100.0%	100.0%

Figure 10.3   Crosstab of **polaction** by **v238jmnl** by **v248jmnl**

Even though we have only three variables with two categories each, the table is rather unwieldy: it is hard to see any pattern of relationships because the table has over 50 separate numbers in it. We could simplify it, however, by omitting the category 'no activity' (since it is simply the shadow percentage of the other category 'activity') and reporting only the total N for each combination of the class and education variables as in Table 10.1. This table is clearer. If we compare the margins to the body of the table, in order to compare the impact of each variable on its own, both level of education and class seem to have a substantial association with political activity, but controlling for education, class seems to have less impact, especially for those with some post-school education. However, it is still difficult to get a summary sense of the impact of class compared to education as the number of working-class respondents with post-school education is relatively small, and for those with post-school education, being middle class actually seems to *reduce* the probability of being politically active. There is still the possibility that readers will misunderstand the table: they might treat the percentages as column, row or total percentages unless this was very clearly labelled.

Table 10.1 Political activity by self reported class and education, Netherlands

% reporting political activity	Working class	Middle class	All
Secondary	**29.2%**	**34.9%**	32.6%
Total *N*	486	734	1,220
Post-school	**61.5%**	**59.1%**	59.3%
Total *N*	65	599	664
All	33.0%	45.8%	42.0%
Total *N*	551	1,333	1,884

Source: World Values Survey Wave 6, author's calculations, unweighted data.

10 ● 6 ODDS

One solution to some of these difficulties is to deal in *odds* rather than *probabilities* of action. This may seem like jumping from the frying pan into the fire, since readers will be unfamiliar with odds; however, it enables us to use regression as a tool to investigate categorical dependent variables, so that eventually we will be able to describe the impact of individual variables, in terms of either how they change the odds of a dependent variable taking a given value, or, so long as we are careful, how they change the probability. Getting accustomed to working with odds is very useful preparation for working with logistic regression.

Odds describe the ratio of one probability to another. Thus the *odds* of an event happening is defined as the probability that the event occurs *divided by* the probability that the event does not occur. Thus, to continue with our example above, the odds of someone being politically active (regardless of education or class) are the probability of being active (0.42), divided by the probability of not being active (0.58) = 42/58 = 0.72. We can use the term *complement* to describe the latter probability. The odds of someone being inactive would be the reciprocal of the odds we've just calculated = 58/42 = 1.38. Betting language uses odds, but confusingly, typically expresses the odds *against* something happening: 'three to one' means odds of 1/3. If I toss a fair coin the probability of it landing heads up is 0.5; the possibility of any other result is also 0.5. This thus equates to odds of 0.5/0.5 or 1, often referred to as 'evens'. The probability of my tossing a fair coin twice and getting heads both times would be 0.25. The odds would be 0.25/0.75 = 1/3. Odds of *more than* 1 thus describe situations where something is *more* probable than its complement; odds of *less than* 1 describe situations where it is *less* probable. In statistics odds are always presented either as a raw ratio (e.g. 6/19; 1/100) or more usually as that ratio expressed as a decimal, to facilitate calculation or comparison (e.g. 104/175 = 0.594; 1/100 = 0.01).

We can move between odds and probabilities using two simple formulae. Note how both simply adjust for the fact that probabilities are expressed as the ratio of the outcome of interest to *all* outcomes (including the outcome of interest) while odds are expressed as the ratio of the outcome of interest to all *other* outcomes, the complement:

$$\text{odds} = \frac{p}{1-p} .$$

Note that while the value of p can only range from 0 to 1, odds can range from 0 (when $p = 0$) up to infinity (when $p = 1$). We can rearrange this equation and express probability in terms of odds:

$$p = \frac{odds}{1 + odds} .$$

These formulae are not difficult to work out from first principles. It is easiest to think in terms of proportions of observations. If the proportion of observations in a crosstab cell is p then the cases not in that cell will be $1 - p$ (since proportions sum to 1). In that case the odds for being p compared to not being p must be $p/(1 - p)$. Odds thus express the probability that a case is in one cell of the crosstab *compared to* the probability that it is in another cell in the same row, or same column of the crosstab. Thus they are simply the ratio of the cases in the cell of interest to the other cells in the row or column of the table. Odds are actually easier to calculate than probabilities, as we only need to know the raw counts in each cell of the table, not the marginal totals.

You can check that these formulae work by using the example of the **polaction** variable we have just seen:

$$\text{odds (political action)} = \frac{792}{1092} = 0.725,$$

$$p(\text{political action}) = \frac{0.725}{1 + 0.725} = 0.420 .$$

We could reconfigure Figure 10.3 as shown in Table 10.2 (I've included the calculations to show where the odds come from).

Table 10.2 Odds of political activity by class and education

(counts)	Working class	Middle class	All
Up to secondary			
No activity	344	478	822
Taken part	142	256	398
All	486	734	1,220
Odds of activity	0.413 (142/344)	0.536 (256/478)	0.484 (398/822)
Odds ratio	1	1.297 (0.536/ 0.413)	
Post-school			
No activity	25	245	270
Taken part	40	354	394
All	65	599	664
Odds of activity	1.6 (40/25)	1.445 (354/245)	1.459 (394/270)
Odds ratio	1	0.903 (1.445/1.6)	

The rows labelled 'Odds of activity' show the odds of taking part in political activity (compared to not taking part) for each group of respondents defined by class and level of education. Thus the odds of middle-class respondents with up to secondary education taking part in political activity are 256/478 = 0.536. The odds for those of all classes and with post-school education are 394/270 = 1.459, and so on. Individual odds may be of interest, but still more useful are the comparisons of two odds, known as *odds ratios*. Odds ratios are just *odds of odds*.

10.7 USING ODDS RATIOS TO DESCRIBE THE ASSOCIATION BETWEEN VARIABLES

We can compare the odds of different groups of respondents taking part in political activity in exactly the same way as we have just used odds to compare the number of those taking part in political activity and not taking part. For example, the odds of *middle-class* respondents with no post-school education taking part in such activity are 0.536; the odds of *working-class* respondents with no post-school education taking part in political activity are 0.413; therefore, the odds of middle-class respondents with no post-school education taking part in political activity *compared to* working-class respondents with no post-school education are = 0.536/0.413 = 1.297. Note that we could also have calculated this odds ratio by comparing the product of the number of cases in the diagonals of the table (344 × 256) / (142 × 478) = 1.297.

This odds ratio can be used as a *measure of association*. Such use is widespread in epidemiology, but it is rare to find it in the social sciences. This is unfortunate, not only because odds ratios are easy to calculate (as we have just seen) but also because they have the very useful property of being less constrained by the distribution of marginals in a table. However they do have the drawback that there is no upper bound to the size of an odds ratio, unlike other measures of association which take values between 0 and 1.

With a few extra calculations we can use odds to make comparisons of the relative impact of two categorical variables on a third, and circumvent the difficulty we faced earlier of disentangling the impact of class and education on political activity. Not only is this useful in itself, it is also an excellent way of seeing how logistic regression operates.

Let's set aside our education variable for the moment, and examine the two-way association between class and political activity. Table 10.3 shows the counts, odds of activity and odds ratio.

We can choose a *reference category* against which we'll make comparisons: working-class respondents. The *odds* of their taking part in political activity are 182/369 = 0.493. The *odds ratio* of activity of middle-class respondents *compared to* working-class respondents is 1.711.

Table 10.3 Odds of political activity by class

(counts)	Working class	Middle class	All
No activity	369	723	1092
Taken part	182	610	792
All	551	1333	1884
Odds: taking part	0.493	0.844	0.725
Odds ratio		1.711	

We can think of this as the change in odds of political activity associated with being middle class as opposed to working class. It follows that we could calculate the odds of middle-class respondents being active by multiplying the odds of working-class respondents being active by the odds ratio of middle-class to working-class activity: $0.493 \times 1.711 = 0.844$.

10 8 CONVERTING A CONTINGENCY TABLE INTO AN EQUATION

We could then express this as an equation (read the '|' sign as 'conditional upon' or 'given'):

$$\text{odds of (activity | class)} = \text{odds activity | WC} \times \text{odds ratio } \frac{\text{odds activity class}}{\text{odds activity WC}}.$$

For working-class respondents we would have the result:

$$\text{odds of activity} = 0.493 \times \frac{0.493}{0.493} = 0.493 \times 1 = 0.493.$$

For middle-class respondents we would have the result:

$$\text{odds of activity} = 0.493 \times 1.711 = 0.844,$$

that is, the odds of activity for our reference category multiplied by the odds ratio for middle-class respondents.

As we have seen, odds take values from zero up to infinity. Were we to use the *logarithm* of odds, these would take values between negative infinity and positive infinity. The log of 'evens', or odds of 1, would be zero. Negative log odds would represent odds of less than 1, and positive log odds would represent odds greater than 1. The log of odds is called the *logit*, and is an extremely useful and widely used transformation. Remember that adding logs is the same as multiplying the original numbers (or *exponents* of the logs). If you are unsure about logarithms, see the quick guide in the appendix to Chapter 4.

We can now rewrite our equation as follows (keep in mind that *adding* logs has the same effect as *multiplying* their exponents):

$$\text{log odds (activity)} = \text{log odds activity WC} + \text{log odds ratio } \frac{\text{odds activity class}}{\text{odds activity WC}}.$$

For working-class respondents this would give us:

$$\text{log odds (activity)} = -0.707 + 0;$$

this is the log of the odds of working-class activity (0.493) that we saw above. For middle-class respondents it would give us:

$$\text{log odds (activity)} = -0.707 + 0.537 = -0.170;$$

this is the log of the odds of middle-class activity (0.844) that we saw above.

The right-hand side of our equation has two terms that we can think of as a *constant* and a *coefficient*. We can think of the log odds of activity for working-class respondents as a *constant* or *reference category*. If we wish to use class to explain political activity, the proportion of working-class respondents who are nevertheless politically active represents the influence of unobserved factors unaccounted for by our class model. We can now think of the log odds ratio of middle-class to working-class odds of action as a *coefficient* that describes the impact of class. If we assign the values 0 to the category working class and 1 to middle class in our class variable we can now not only describe our entire crosstab as an equation, but as a *linear* equation, that is to say, there are no power terms on the right-hand side and the components are added rather than multiplied.

10●9 LOGISTIC REGRESSION WITH A SINGLE PREDICTOR VARIABLE

We've successfully turned our contingency table into an equation! In fact, we've carried out a simple *logistic regression*. To check this, run the logistic regression procedure in SPSS. Go to **Analyze→Regression→Binary Logistic**. This brings up the **Logistic Regression** dialog box shown in Figure 10.4.

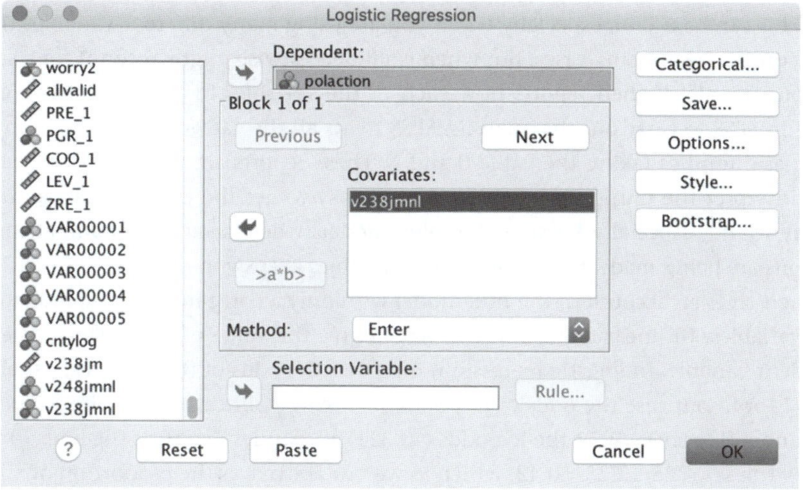

Figure 10.4   The **Logistic Regression** dialog box

Put the variable **polaction** in the **Dependent:** box and **v238jmnl** (or whatever you have called your recoded class variable) in the **Covariates:** box; then click the **Categorical…** button to open the **Logistic Regression: Define Categorical Variables** dialog. Put **v238jmnl** in the **Categorical Covariates:** box. By default SPSS will use the last (higher-value) category as the reference category. If your numerical code for working-class respondents is a higher value than that for middle-class respondents you need do nothing more. However, if it is lower (as it is for my coding of the variable with working class = 0 and middle class = 1) you will need to change the reference category to the **First** rather than **Last** category by clicking the appropriate button next to **Reference Category:** and then clicking **Change**. When you have done so the dialog box should look like Figure 10.5.

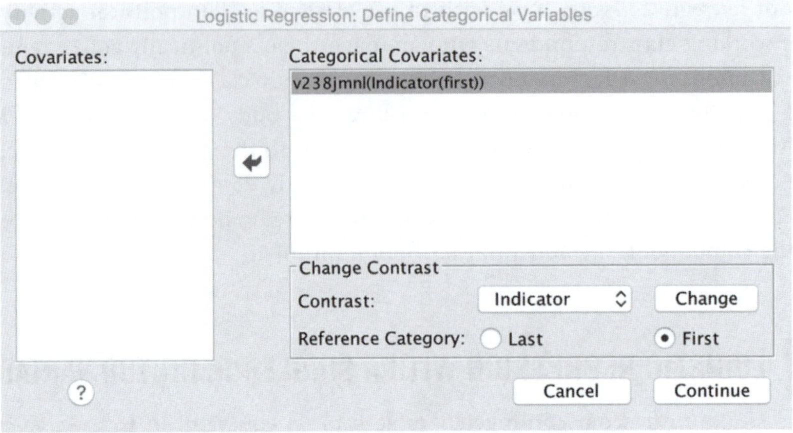

Figure 10.5   The **Logistic Regression: Define Categorical Variables** dialog box

Once back in the main dialog, click on **Continue** and then on either **Paste** or **OK** and examine the output. As usual SPSS first produces a note of how many cases were included in the analysis. This can be useful, especially when you are using many different variables that might each have only a few missing cases, but when excluded listwise might account for a substantial part of your sample. It then reports how each of the variables in the analysis were encoded internally in SPSS to carry out the analysis. SPSS treats all the categorical variables in a logistic regression as dummies taking the value 0 and 1. These reports are very useful in making sure that you interpret the output correctly. It is very easy to get the categories in a dummy the wrong way round, especially in more complex models where a range of comparisons within comparisons are being made. Checking these two tables keeps you right.

SPSS then gives an account of the null model with only a constant and no predictor or independent variables. In linear regression this would give the value of the mean of the response or dependent variable. In logistic regression, it reports the odds of the response variable taking the value 1, or in our case the odds of respondents taking political action (Figure 10.6). This is reported under **B** for beta (β) as the log odds (–0.321) and under **Exp(B)** as the odds (0.725). As a probability this is 0.725/1.725 = 0.42, which as we saw above was the proportion of all respondents who had ever taken political action. Note, however, that we now have an estimate for the *standard error* of this value (under **S.E.**).

SPSS also attempts the best prediction of the value of the response variable without any of the predictors, which is just the modal value of the variable, together with a classification table reporting the percentage of cases for which this prediction is correct (Figure 10.7). Since 58% of respondents had taken no political action (the modal value) this is also the percentage of correct predictions. SPSS also gives some useful information about the variables not yet included

Variables in the Equation

	B	S.E.	Wald	df	Sig.	Exp(B)
Step 0 Constant	–.321	.047	47.362	1	.000	.725

Figure 10.6   SPSS logistic regression output I

Classification Table[a,b]

			Predicted		
			polaction		
Observed			.00 no activity	1.00 taken part	Percentage Correct
Step 0	polaction	.00 no activity	1092	0	100.0
		1.00 taken part	792	0	.0
Overall Percentage					58.0

a. Constant is included in the model.

b. The cut value is .500

Figure 10.7 SPSS logistic regression output II

in the model. Under **Score** it reports the improvement in the model that would come about by including the variables not in the model and the associated significance level of the difference between the model and the null model.

SPSS then runs the model we specified earlier, with **v238jmnl** as the sole predictor variable. It is good practice to get into the habit of thinking of models as *nested* within one another, so that comparisons can be made between them. We can describe model X as *nested* within model Y if model Y contains all the parameters of model X, in addition to any new parameters model Y may specify. You'll sometimes see these described as the *reduced* (fewer parameters) and *full* models.

Comparing models in logistic regression is often of more interest and value than the significance or size of individual regression coefficients: an important difference from OLS regressions (see Table 10.2). The **Omnibus Test of Model Coefficients** (see Table 10.8) gives a chi-square value for the model, which is highly significant at one degree of freedom (the single predictor variable in the model), while the **Model Summary** reports the **–2 Log likelihood** for the model and the **Nagelkerke R Square** which gives an account of the proportion of variation in the dependent explained by our model and thus mimics the R^2 statistic for OLS models. Our variable accounts for only a small amount of variation. You'll also see that the **Classification Table** is unchanged: since a minority of both classes took part in any political activity the best prediction is still 'no political activity' for all cases.

Finally, in **Variables in the Equation** we get the log odds values we calculated before. Just as the constant in an OLS regression can be interpreted as the value of the dependent variable when all the predictors take the value zero, so here the constant is the value of the response variable (the log odds of political activity) for our reference category, class = 0, in other words for working-class respondents. The beta coefficient for our predictor variable is the change in log odds associated with class when it takes the value 1, in other words middle-class respondents, and is the odds ratio for our original contingency table. Indeed, if we wanted, we could reconstruct all the original cell frequencies for our contingency table from this output, since we know the total number of cases (1,884), the marginal distribution for our response variable, and the distribution of that variable contingent upon the two values of our predictor variable. This is not something that we'd ever want to do in an analysis, but it shows how the logic of logistic regression grows out of the kind of analysis of contingency tables that you will be familiar with. Shifting to odds and log odds doesn't change the analysis, but what it does do is make it possible to extend it in ways that contingency tables can't, by using greater numbers of variables and making it possible to include continuous variables.

Omnibus Tests of Model Coefficients

		Chi-square	df	Sig.
Step 1	Step	26.359	1	.000
	Block	26.359	1	.000
	Model	26.359	1	.000

Model Summary

Step	−2 Log likelihood	Cox & Snell R Square	Nagelkerke R Square
1	2537.445[a]	.014	.019

a. Estimation terminated at iteration number 3 because parameter estimates changed by less than .001.

Classification Table[a]

			Predicted		
			polaction		
	Observed		.00 no activity	1.00 taken part	Percentage Correct
Step 1	polaction	.00 no activity	1092	0	100.0
		1.00 taken part	792	0	.0
	Overall Percentage				58.0

a. The cut value is .500

Variables in the Equation

		B	S.E.	Wald	df	Sig.	Exp(B)
Step 1[a]	V238jmnl(1)	.537	.106	25.670	1	.000	1.711
	Constant	−.707	.091	60.887	1	.000	.493

a. Variable(s) entered on step 1: V238jmnl.

Figure 10.8 SPSS logistic regression output III

10.10 LOGISTIC REGRESSION WITH MORE THAN ONE PREDICTOR

Let's continue this exercise by looking again at the three-way contingency table we produced for political activity by class and education (Table 10.2), and having SPSS carry out the corresponding logistic regression. Rather than using the GUI, let's use syntax for this regression. Note that as well as entering each of our two variables (**v238jmnl** and **v248jmnl**), I have entered the *interaction* between them (**v238jmnl** × **v248jmnl**) as a predictor, and have done so as a distinct step in the model by repeating the **/METHOD=ENTER** command. Thus this syntax asks SPSS to carry out the regression in three steps: a null model with only the odds of the dependent variable itself; a model with the variables **v238jmnl** and **v248jmnl** as predictors; and finally, the model with both these variables and their interaction. (We'll discuss interactions when we examine the output.)

```
LOGISTIC REGRESSION VARIABLES polaction
/METHOD=ENTER v238jmnl v248jmnl
/METHOD=ENTER v238jmnl*v248jmnl
/CONTRAST (v238jmnl)=Indicator(1)
/CONTRAST (v248jmnl)=Indicator(1)
/CRITERIA=PIN(.05) POUT(.10) ITERATE(20) CUT(.5).
```

If you are still using the GUI, you can specify successive steps in a model by clicking the **Next** button above the **Covariates:** box before adding new variable(s) to the model. To specify an interaction, select each of the variables you wish to test for the effect of their association (using the keyboard **command** key to select the two items from the variable list) and then click the 'add interaction' button ⬚>a*b>⬚ to the left of the **Covariates:** box.

SPSS creates a lot of output, since it reports on each of the three models we requested. First it reports a null model 'Block 0', which is exactly the same as the one you have already seen when we used a single predictor. Block 1 reports the results from regressing **polaction** on both our predictor variables and Block 2 reports the results from regressing **polaction** on both our predictor variables and the interaction term. Its easiest to deal with this output by starting at the end and working backwards. From the **Variables in the Equation** output reproduced in Figure 10.9 we can see that the **Constant** represents the log odds of activity when each or our predictor variables takes the value 0, that is, working-class respondents with up to secondary education. The **beta coefficient** log odds of –0.885 corresponds to odds of 0.413. The effect of the class variable (**v238jmnl**), log odds of 0.260, corresponds to odds of 1.297, which is the value of the odds ratio for class in the reference category of our education variable and represents the change in odds of activity associated with being middle class rather than working class. The effect of the education variable (**v248jmnl**) is log odds of 1.355, corresponding to odds of 3.876, and represents the odds ratio for education in the reference category of our class variable: working class. You can calculate this from our contingency table (Table 10.4) by taking the odds of activity for working-class respondents with post-school education (1.6) and dividing by the odds for those with only secondary education (0.413).

Finally, the interaction term tells us the additional effect (if any) of the association between education and class, *beyond the impact of each of these variables acting on its own*. It tells us the effect of being *both* middle class *and* having post-school education that exists beyond the impact of each of these variables on their own. There is a small effect, but it is not significant. We can also see the weak explanatory power of the interaction term by looking at the **Omnibus Tests of Model Coefficients** and **Model Summary** for each step in the model building, shown in Figure 10.10. Against **Step** and **Block** SPSS reports the value of chi-square and the corresponding *p*-value for the test that the variables added to the model from the last step or block all have coefficients equal to zero, i.e. that they have no effect, and do not increase our ability to predict the odds of political action. For our first block, compared to the null model, our two predictor variables obviously do make a difference, so that we have a substantial value for chi-square and very low probability indeed that our model is no better than the null. However for block 2 this is not the case. Adding the interaction term produces a model that is not significantly different to the previous model with only two predictor variables and does not improve it. The

Variables in the Equation

		B	S.E.	Wald	df	Sig.	Exp(B)
Step 1[a]	V238jmnl(1)	.260	.126	4.251	1	.039	1.297
	v248jmnl(1)	1.355	.274	24.490	1	.000	3.876
	V238jmnl(1) by v248jmnl(1)	-.362	.296	1.494	1	.222	.696
	Constant	-.885	.100	78.689	1	.000	.413

a. Variable(s) entered on step 1: V238jmnl, v248jmnl, V238jmnl * v248jmnl .

Figure 10.9 SPSS logistic regression output IV

Block 1

Omnibus Tests of Model Coefficients

		Chi-square	df	Sig.
Step 1	Step	128.717	2	.000
	Block	128.717	2	.000
	Model	128.717	2	.000

Model Summary

Step	-2 Log likelihood	Cox & Snell R Square	Nagelkerke R Square
1	2435.086	.066	.089

Block 2

Omnibus Tests of Model Coefficients

		Chi-square	df	Sig.
Step 1	Step	1.515	1	.218
	Block	1.515	1	.218
	Model	130.232	3	.000

Model Summary

Step	-2 Log likelihood	Cox & Snell R Square	Nagelkerke R Square
1	2433.572	.067	.090

Figure 10.10 SPSS logistic regression output V

value for chi-square is very low. Note that you can see the same result by comparing the -2 Log likelihoods for the two models reported under model summary. In the interests of parsimony, we can safely drop this interaction term from the model.

Unlike a contingency table, logistic regression enables us to specify continuous variables as predictors. Let's examine whether taking account of respondents' age (v242) has an impact on their probability of taking political action. Again, we can add the variable as a separate step in our regression to check whether it adds to our ability to predict political action. We can also add an interaction term for age and each of our other two predictor variables. ✎ I have not shown the syntax separately, but it is available on the companion website if you need to check it. Two features of the output we obtain tell us that age does *not* add to our ability to predict political activity. The chi-square value for the step of the model in which age and its interactions are added is not significant, and neither age nor its interactions are significant when added to the model. Note, however, that when we add age it lowers the impact of the class variable. This is a common feature of logistic regression. Adding extra predictor variables typically changes the coefficient values of other variables in the model, whether or not the newly added predictors are significant. Also note that the value for our constant has changed. Since the constant estimates the odds of activity with all predictor variables taking the value zero, our new constant does not have a sensible interpretation, since people aged zero are rarely politically active!

You can also quickly check the result for the age variable by looking at the mean age of respondents by **polaction**. The difference is very small and just significant. Politically active respondents are slightly younger. Since we know that younger people are also more likely to have had post-school education, it is unsurprising that age does not add much to our model.

Let's add another variable to our model: interest in politics (**v7**). We'd expect this to have some impact. The variable takes four values and we can use the last one, 'not at all interested in politics', as our reference category, with the expectation that each of the other categories will be associated with increased odds of political activity. As before, add the interaction terms for this variable with each of the other two variables. We can also add a third interaction term specifying the effect of the three-way interaction between **v7**, **v238jmnl** and **v248jmnl**. ✎ Again, if you struggle to write the correct syntax, it's available on the website. Note that in logistic regression SPSS allows you to specify categorical predictors with several values, which it then transforms into dummies automatically, reporting how it has done so in the **Categorical Variables Codings** section of the output.

You should find that none of the interaction terms in the model are significant; however, all but one of the categories of the interest in politics variable add something to our model. Not surprisingly, there is little difference between respondents who say politics is 'not very important' in life and those who choose 'not at all important'. Since each category of our predictor variables adds a new dummy variable to the model, we could collapse these two categories of **v7** together in the interests of model parsimony. However, there is a more interesting feature of our output. Once we include this variable, the impact of social class, which was less strong than

Table 10.4 Logistic regression of **polaction** on **v7** and **v248jmnl**: main results

	B	S.E.	Sig.	Exp(B)
Politics: Not at all important (reference category **v7** = 4))			0.004	
Politics: Very important (**v7** = 1)	0.873	0.301	0.004	2.394
Politics: Rather important (**v7** = 2)	0.476	0.163	0.004	1.610
Politics: Not very important (**v7** = 3)	0.291	0.160	0.068	1.338
Post-school education (**v248** = 1)	1.068	0.101	0.000	2.911
Constant	−1.038	0.146	0.000	0.354

N = 1857. 45 (2.4%) cases were excluded because of missing values.

Model chi-sq. 136.43 with 4 d.f., −2 log likelihood 2396.4.

Source: World Values Survey, Wave 6, Netherlands, unweighted data, author's analysis.

education, falls considerably and drops out of significance. We could consider dropping it from the model. Table 10.4 shows the main results for a model with only **v7** and **v248jmnl**.

Just as with OLS regression, we can present our model as an equation. Here is the equation corresponding to the output above, with regression coefficients for the education dummy variable and each of the three **v7** variable dummies:

$$\text{log odds (activity)} = -1.038 + 1.068 \text{ v248jmnl} + 0.873 \text{ politics1} + 0.476 \text{ politics2} + 0.291 \text{ politics3}.$$

Just as with OLS regression, the coefficients are multiplied by the variable values to find the corresponding value of the dependent variable. However, in logistic regression independent variables are often 0/1 dummies, so that this process is a simple matter of counting the coefficients for the relevant dummy for a variable category, and ignoring the others, which will take the value zero. In the example above the estimated log odds of action for those who find politics 'rather interesting' (i.e. **politics2** = 1) and have no post-school education would be:

$$-1.038 + 0 + 0 + 0.476 + 0 = -0.562.$$

As odds this would be 0.57, or as a probability 0.36.

10 ● 11 DIAGNOSTICS

Just as with OLS regression, we need to evaluate how good our model is by examining the pattern of residuals, checking for multicollinearity, looking for cases with excessive influence and so on. However, we'll look at this in greater depth in the next chapter rather than here.

10 ● 12 REPORTING LOGISTIC REGRESSION OUTPUT

As with any statistical analysis, you should report enough results to allow expert readers to replicate your analysis. It is good practice to add descriptive statistics for your predictor and response variables too. Especially if you are reporting results to non-expert audiences, it is a good idea to add some illustrations of the model using probabilities. Here is how I would report the simple model we have just run.

Using the definition of political activity described above as a dependent variable, educational background and interest in politics were found to be significant predictors of adults' activity, so that the percentage of cases correctly classified by the model rose from 57.5% (for the null model) to 64.4%. Age and social class, as well as interaction terms for the variables in the model, were also explored but not found to be significant. Table 10.4 presents the log odds associated with each predictor and their standard errors, together with the associated significance values and exponentiated odds. Just over one-quarter of respondents with up to secondary education and who thought that politics was 'not at all important' in life had ever undertaken some political activity. The belief that politics is 'very important in life' more than doubled the odds of having taken some action and having some post-school education almost trebled them. Thus, according to the model, 73% of post-school educated respondents who thought politics was very important were likely to have taken some action.

what you have learned

In this chapter we've seen how the relationships between two or more variables that can be displayed as contingency tables can also be transformed into a series of odds that describe the relationship between a reference category cell and each of the other cells in the table. By taking the logarithm of these odds we can transform this series of odds into a linear equation that models the log odds of each combination of values for the dependent variable taking the chosen value of the dependent variable. To do this we've looked at:

- Probabilities and odds
- Odds ratios and log odds, the logit
- Selecting a reference category in a table and expressing its other cells as the odds of a case being in that cell compared to the reference category
- Transforming the contingency table into a linear equation using log odds
- Running the logistic regression command in SPSS
- Interpreting output from a logistic regression

exercise

1 In your **ESS6** dataset the variables **contplt**, **wrkprty**, **badge**, **sgnptit**, **pbldmn** and **bctprd** record different kinds of political activity by respondents over the last year. Use **count** to create a binary variable like **polaction** which describes whether or not a respondent has been politically active. The variable **polintr** records respondents' interest in politics. The variable **eisced** describes their educational qualifications. Recode this variable so that it divides respondents into those with up to *upper-tier secondary* education and others with higher qualifications. Produce a three-way crosstab of these variables. Then run a logistic regression of **polaction** on **polintr** and **eisced**. Do this for all countries together, then select only the Netherlands. Do you find that you can replicate the World Values Survey results using this different survey?

USING BINARY
LOGISTIC REGRESSION

━━━━━━━━━━ **introduction** ━━━━━━━━━━

In this chapter we continue our exploration of logistic regression by looking at evidence on the correlates of political activity using data from ten Arab countries covered by Round 6 of the World Values Survey. We'll look at comparing models and using diagnostics to see how well a logistic regression model performs. We will:

- Calculate population-based weights for analysing groups of countries
- Use Excel to calculate and display 'smoothed' trends
- Cope with country-specific differences in questionnaires and variables
- Understand the conditions under which logistic regression coefficients can be compared
- Build a logistic regression model
- Produce and interpret a range of model diagnostics
- Report the model comprehensively but concisely

11●1 INTRODUCTION

What came to be known as the Arab Spring was a series of both peaceful and violent demonstrations that broke out towards the end of 2010 in Tunisia and spread to many Arab countries during 2011 and 2012. The existing governments fell in Tunisia, Egypt, Libya and Yemen. Major protests, boycotts or strikes took place in Bahrain, Iraq, Kuwait, Jordan, Algeria, Morocco and elsewhere, while civil war erupted in Syria. The protests and movements were diverse in character, probably having origins in both economic and political discontent, but a common feature was thought to be both the dissatisfaction and disillusion of younger people in particular. The impression created by the events was of an Arab world in considerable turmoil, with mass civil participation in the protests.

Wave 6 of the World Values Survey (WVS) was fielded in around a dozen countries in the Middle East and North Africa between 2011 and 2014. Moreover, for some of these countries we can make comparisons over time, as they were included in Wave 4 of the WVS at the turn of the century. We'll use the IBM SPSS Statistics software datasets produced by the WVS, together with the relevant data documentation, all available from the WVS website at www.worldvaluessurvey. org. It would be possible to carry out some of these analyses online (as we saw how to do in Chapter 3), but downloading the data and working with SPSS allows us to do much more, and makes things easier, faster, more flexible and much quicker to record. Download the integrated dataset for WVS6. We'll keep this download as our 'master' copy that we can return to if we damage the file we work from by mistake, so first *make a copy* of the download.

From the data documentation you'll see that the following Arab countries participated in Wave 6 with between 1,000 and 2,000 respondents in each country.

Algeria	Lebanon
Bahrain	Libya
Egypt	Morocco
Palestine	Qatar
Iraq	Tunisia
Jordan	Yemen
Kuwait	

Looking at the source questionnaire for Wave 6 (you may like to review Chapter 5 for advice on how to deal with survey documentation), there are many promising variables. Not only is interest in politics and the respondent's view of its importance in life measured, but also participation in different forms of political activity, attitudes to government and democracy, satisfaction with various aspects of economic, social and political life, and there is information on the age, sex, religion, education, economic activity and area of residence of respondents.

We might want to focus on the questions about whether respondents had taken or might take part in political activity (Table 11.1).

Table 11.1 Questions on political activity from World Values Survey Wave 6

	Have done	Might do	Would never do
V85. Signing a petition	1	2	3
V86. Joining in boycotts	1	2	3
V87. Attending peaceful demonstrations	1	2	3
V88. Joining strikes	1	2	3
V89. Any other act of protest?	1	2	3

The WVS data should allow us to investigate what the correlates of political action might be in the countries we have chosen. However, before proceeding further it would be wise to check the fieldwork reports for the individual country surveys. Fielding a survey in stable political times, with the cooperation or indifference of the state (e.g. in the development of a sampling frame) may be a much easier affair than in times of political turbulence. Moreover, there is much less of a tradition of social survey work in Arab countries than in, for example, Europe or North America. Respondents in the latter parts of the world are used to the activities of survey companies (often doing marketing rather than social science research), unlikely to be suspicious of them, and, if they agree to respond, are unlikely to worry that their answers might reach the ears of someone they would prefer did not know about them. It is not always clear how true this would be for respondents in countries with a less established tradition of social research.

We can look at the 'methodology questionnaire' completed by those conducting the survey in each country to check how the sample was obtained, when the fieldwork was done, and so on. If you review this metadata you'll find that although sampling techniques varied from country to country, most countries were able to achieve a sample that they could expect was broadly representative of the population by age, gender or area of residence. However, you will also find that in some of our countries, one or more of the questions we are most interested in from the source questionnaire were *not* fielded. In Qatar we learn that the questions on political activity were not asked 'because the optional activities are not allowed in these countries' and that many other questions could not be asked for similar reasons. In Bahrain too we find that some of the political activity questions were not asked, but no reason is given. In Kuwait the Central Statistical Bureau 'declined' some of the questions. We shall therefore have to drop these three countries from our selection.

The methodology questionnaire also shows that response rates varied widely across countries and that in many cases substitution of households was permitted to deal with non-response. This can be a valid procedure if substitute households are chosen with care, but it does bring with it the danger that households which are harder to contact are under-represented in the survey. However, we should be able to proceed with our analysis of ten countries with some degree of confidence in the results.

11●2 WEIGHTING THE DATA

We have one further preparatory task to undertake. The WVS was aimed at the population of those aged 18+ in the relevant countries. If we want to make statements about the adult populations of all these countries together, we shall need to weight them according to their adult population sizes. The weight variable we create will play the same role as **pweight** in the European Social Survey. Population estimates are available on the UN World Population Prospects site (http://esa.un.org/unpd/wpp/DataQuery/). We can then construct a table like Table 11.2 to make our weights calculations (while you can do this in SPSS, I find Excel more convenient to work with for this kind of material).

We can now calculate the approximate population aged 18+ in each country by multiplying the third and fourth columns of the table. We can obtain the total population of the ten countries by summing the result. When you do this you should find that the total population aged 18+ was 154.8 million. Next we need to calculate the proportion of the total population 18+ of all the countries found in each country, which we do by dividing each individual country's 18+ population by this total. To calculate weights for making statements about individual respondents we now need to multiply the total sample size (the sum of column 5, which is 12,859) by this proportion to obtain the number of respondents we'd have in each country, were they to have an equal probability of selection across all countries. We then divide the result by the actual sample size to arrive at the weight that needs to be applied. If we apply this weight we can make statements about this population in the ten countries combined. Once you have completed these calculations examine the values for this weight. Egypt is by far the most populous country in the sample, accounting for over one in three of all adults in these countries. Four other countries have substantial populations: Algeria, Morocco, Iraq and Yemen. All the other countries each account for only a few per cent

Table 11.2   World Values Survey Wave 6 Arab countries, populations and sample sizes

Country	v2 code	Proportion of population 18+	Total population (millions)	Sample size (N)
Algeria	12	0.67	38.2	1,200
Egypt	818	0.62	87.6	1,523
Iraq	368	0.52	34.1	1,200
Jordan	400	0.58	7.2	1,200
Lebanon	422	0.70	5.3	1,200
Libya	434	0.655	6.3	2,131
Morocco	504	0.67	33.5	1,200
Palestine	275	0.53	4.4	1,000
Tunisia	788	0.67	11	1,205
Yemen	887	0.51	25.5	1,000

of the total population. The experience of their populations will contribute less to any picture we paint of the region as a whole, so long as we are examining the experiences of individuals.

Once you have calculated the weights you can compare your calculations with the ones shown below to check them. (Note that I have not truncated the decimal places in the intermediate calculations. Were you to be doing this without the benefit of a spreadsheet or statistics package you would not need this level of accuracy in these calculations.) In some countries in the WVS the survey organisations supplied weights for their data to correct for the differential probabilities of selection of different types of respondent within each country, recorded as **v258**. This was done for Libya and Egypt only, for the other countries all cases take the value 1 for this variable. However, this means that to use the weights we have produced here we should multiply the relevant weight (individual or country) by **v258**. For each country we now have three weights. If we are doing an analysis of an individual country we can use **v258**. If we wish to analyse all ten countries together we can treat the sample as if it had been taken across all the countries with each person having an equal probability of selection by applying the weight for region given in column E of Table 11.3, together with **v258**.

Table 11.3   Sample, population and weight data

Country	A Achieved sample size	B Population 18+ (millions)	C Proportion of total pop. 18+ in country	D Sample size for equal p selection (C × 12,859)	E Weight: region (D/A)
Algeria	1,200	25.594	0.16533324	2,126.02022	1.771683
Egypt	1,523	54.312	0.35084704	4,511.54217	2.962273
Iraq	1,200	17.732	0.11454595	1,472.94641	1.227455
Jordan	1,200	4.176	0.02697630	346.88835	0.289073
Lebanon	1,200	3.710	0.02396602	308.17906	0.256815
Libya	2,131	4.127	0.02665654	342.77652	0.160852
Morocco	1,200	22.445	0.14499119	1,864.44182	1.553701
Palestine	1,000	2.332	0.01506435	193.71255	0.193712
Tunisia	1,205	7.370	0.04760905	612.20477	0.508053
Yemen	1,000	13.005	0.08401027	1,080.28807	1.080288
All					

11 ● 3   MANAGING THE DATA

We'll use syntax for our analysis, since this will allow us to repeat and amend procedures easily as well as keeping a record we can return to in the future. Instead of working with the large file for all countries, we can delete the countries we are not interested in. Later on we might want to draw comparisons between our ten Arab countries and others, so in addition to our ten Arab countries select the United States, Germany, the Netherlands and Sweden. The quickest way to do this is to create a new variable that groups together the countries we are interested in, by recoding the existing variable for country **v2**. If you are uncertain how to do this revise

Chapter 4. ✎ A copy of the correct syntax is on the companion website as usual. Once you have done this you can use the **Select Cases** procedure to delete the countries you have not selected. Run a frequency table to check that the recode worked as you expected it to.

Next produce weight variables for the weights that we calculated earlier, using a series of **if** statements – note that I've run the means procedure to check that the weight variable has been correctly produced:

```
COMPUTE weight = 0.
IF (v2 eq 12) weight = 1.771683521.
IF (v2 eq 275) weight = 0.193712556.
IF (v2 eq 400) weight = 0.289073626.
IF (v2 eq 422) weight = 0.256815889.
IF (v2 eq 504) weight = 1.553701518.
IF (v2 eq 788) weight = 0.508053757.
IF (v2 eq 818) weight = 2.962273262*v258.
IF (v2 eq 434) weight = 0.16085243*v258.
IF (v2 eq 887) weight = 1.080288077*v258.
IF (v2 eq 368) weight = 1.227455349*v258.
MEANS weight by v2.
```

11 ● 4 DESCRIBING THE DATA

The first step in any analysis is to run some descriptive statistics to get a sense of the size and nature of the variation we want to describe and analyse. Always produce frequency tables of the categorical variables you are going to use, or descriptive summary statistics for continuous ones. This allows you to check for missing values and how they have been coded, or problems such as possible errors in coding, as well as providing a first picture of the distribution of the variables. A good start would be frequencies for **v84** to **v89** and a crosstab of **v2** by these variables on political activity. We have data for 14 countries, so our output will be easier to read if we put **v2** in the rows of our tables. To look at the distribution of the politics variables we can look at *row percentages*, but it is important also to ask for *counts* in the *cells* since we want to check what our cell sizes look like. If you are uncertain about how to do this, review Chapter 4.

Consulting the data documentation, you'll see that WVS uses a simple numbering system for naming variables. This means that you must consult either the variable labels in the **Data Editor** window, or the description of the variables in the data documentation to identify the relevant variables you wish to use, and how they were produced from the source WVS questionnaire. You'll see that WVS produces a codebook that includes frequency distributions for each variable for each individual country. This is useful to check that the results you obtain from your downloaded and edited dataset are correct, and that you have not inadvertently corrupted the data when processing it. You do not need to weight the data at this stage (although it would not be wrong to do so).

One feature of the commentary on the Arab Spring was the argument that the demonstrations and political change were driven by young people, argued to be either more disillusioned or more radical in their demands than the older generation. Another common observation was the dominance of politics by men, and although women participated in the protest movements, this participation itself was something new. A useful first exploratory step would be to look at the age and sex distribution of those who said they were interested in politics or had been involved in political and protest activity of various kinds.

Select our ten Arab countries for analysis using the **filter** procedure (if you need to review how this works, check Chapters 4 and 7) and apply the weight for the region you calculated above along with **v258**. **v84** records respondents' answers to a question about how interested they are in politics on a four-point scale. We can examine its distribution by age and sex by way of a three-way crosstab. Since we have data for single-year ages the crosstab itself will be rather unwieldy, but we can transform it into a graphic that will be more readily understandable. Produce a cross-tab of **v84** by **v240** (sex) and **v242** (age) putting **v84** in the columns of the crosstab, **v242** in the rows and **v240** as the third (control) variable and with a count of cases in the cells.

```
CROSSTABS v242 by v84 by v240
/FORMAT=AVALUE TABLES
/CELLS= COUNT
/COUNT ROUND CELL.
```

The resulting table is difficult to interpret because it contains around 1,000 numbers. While we could use SPSS to produce a graphic from the table, you will often find it easier and more flexible to copy the table across to Excel and use its graphing capabilities. **Export** the table to Excel. Select the table in the output window by clicking on it so that a small red arrow appears to the left of the table, or by selecting it in the output index in the left-hand pane of the **Statistics Viewer** window. Click the **Export** icon 📄 and choose the **Selected** option under **Objects to Export** in the dialog box (otherwise SPSS will export the entire contents of your **Viewer** window). You will also need to amend the suggested name for the output file, and perhaps also edit the file path in the **File Name:** box, so that you can locate it easily on your computer (Figure 11.1).

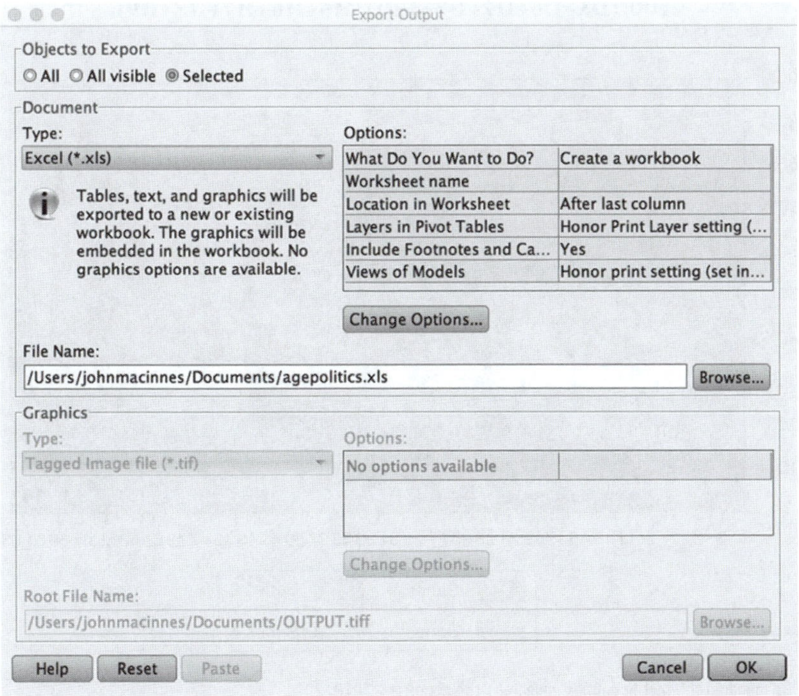

Figure 11.1 The **Export Output** dialog box

11.5 USING EXCEL TO CREATE GRAPHICS

Open the Excel file you have created. Drag across the contents of the first level of the table (that for men) from age 18 to 80, and across the four categories of interest in politics and ask Excel to produce a *100% stacked area chart*. Precisely how you do this will depend on whether you are using a PC or a Mac, and which version of Excel you are running. In the latest versions you can do this via the icons on the toolbar, or from the **Insert** menu on the main menu bar choose **Chart→Area**, and then choose the **100% Stacked Area** option. The chart that you create should look like Figure 11.2. (I have left the chart and its content without labels; we will edit these in later if necessary. Series 1 to series 4 refer to values 1 to 4 of **v84** with 1 = very interested.)

It is difficult to see the trends in this chart: the numbers fluctuate because there are relatively few respondents in each single-year age category. However, we can get around this by taking a moving five-year average of age categories to smooth out these fluctuations. This is a handy technique to master as it is often a useful way of making patterns in data based on relatively small numbers more visible. We can also stop at about age 70, since the numbers get progressively smaller above this age. Thus our first age category would be the average of those aged 18–22, the next would be that for 19–23, and so on. The average will have to be weighted by the numbers in each year category, since these fluctuate. Figure 11.3 shows how your Excel worksheet with the exported SPSS table should look.

You'll see that I've selected a cell in column J in the row corresponding to age = 20 years and entered the formula to sum the totals for ages 18–22 in the column for **v84** = very interested and divide them by the totals for all categories of **v84** for these ages and express the result as a percentage:

$$=100*(D5+D6+D7+D8+D9)/(H5+H6+H7+H8+H9)$$

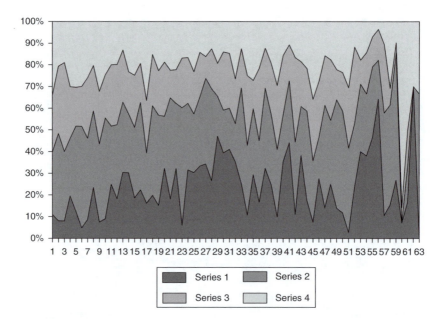

Figure 11.2   Respondent interest in politics, selected Arab countries, 2010–2014

SQRT `fx` `=100*(D5+D6+D7+D8+D9)/(H5+H6+H7+H8+H9)`

			1 Very interested	2 Somewhat interested	3 Not very interested	4 Not at all interested	Total					
Count												
				V84 Interest in politics								
V240 Sex	V242 Age											
1 Male	V242 Age	18	26	68	62	81	237					
		19	14	70	54	36	174					
		20	16	64	82	38	200	=100*(D5+D6+D7+D8+D9)/(H5+H6+H7+H8+H9)			
		21	22	30	27	34	113	9.29705	38.322	26.644	25.737
		22	18	57	26	44	145	9.38865	37.7729	26.0917	26.7467
		23	12	117	46	75	250	13.1799	38.3891	21.6527	26.7782
		24	18	78	58	54	208	11.4674	39.2614	21.8659	27.4052
		25	56	85	50	49	240	10.8676	40.6393	22.0091	26.484
		26	14	67	45	60	186	15.0476	36.4762	24.0952	24.381
		27	19	98	42	52	211	16.8388	35.9504	23.7603	23.4504
		28	51	55	58	41	205	18.7117	35.1738	24.5399	21.5746
		29	23	43	35	25	126	22.5841	33.8762	23.8871	19.6526
		30	76	81	60	33	250	25.3874	30.5125	24.9106	19.1895
		31	39	35	25	30	129	24.9677	33.2471	22.7684	19.0168
		32	24	42	31	32	129	24.933	31.7694	22.118	21.1796
		33	31	56	25	27	139	21.5926	33.8438	21.7458	22.8178
		34	16	23	24	36	99	18.5976	36.7378	21.9512	22.7134
		35	31	65	37	24	157	20.7063	35.534	21.9904	21.6693
		36	20	55	27	30	132	19.6697	37.6877	20.2703	22.3724

Figure 11.3 Excel worksheet for **v242** by **v84** by **v240**

You can then use the fill right and fill down functions of Excel (**Edit→Fill→Down**) to carry out the same operations for the other categories of **v84** and other ages. We can do this for both men and women creating 100% stacked area charts in new worksheets and then also add labels to our graphic. ✎ If you are unsure how to do this in Excel you can follow the tutorial on the website. You should obtain two graphs like Figures 11.4 and 11.5.

It looks as if interest in politics increases slowly with age for men, reaching its peak in middle age and then declining. Change with age is rather less for women. If you carry out the same analysis for our four North American and European countries you should get

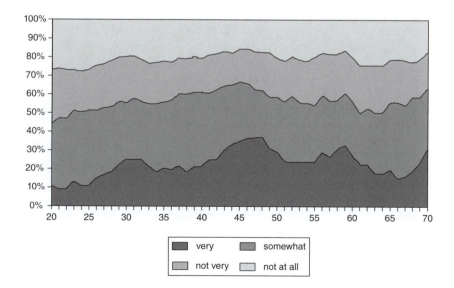

Figure 11.4 Interest in politics, Arab region, men by age (smoothed)

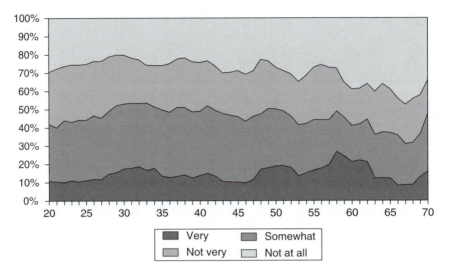

Figure 11.5 Interest in politics, Arab region, women by age (smoothed)

results similar to those in Figures 11.6 and 11.7. Interest in politics seems to increase fairly steadily with age for both men and women, and to higher levels of interest than that found in our Arab countries.

Let's now use the variable that reports respondents' political activity, **polaction**, that we created in the previous chapter, using the values of **v85** to **v89**, to create a graph of political activity by age (again using a five-year moving average) and sex for our two groups of countries. This time I've used a line chart to show a five-year moving average of the proportion

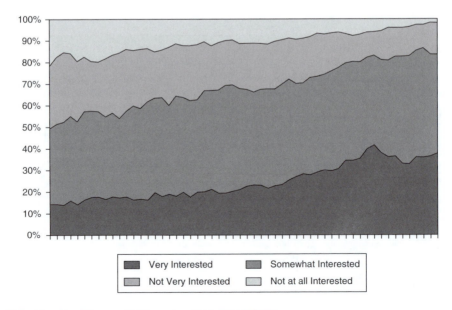

Figure 11.6 Interest in politics, men 18–75 years (smoothed), USA and Europe

of respondents reporting any political activity for our four groups of respondents. ✎ Again if you are unsure how to do this you can consult the website tutorial. The graph you produce should look like Figure 11.8.

At a glance we can see that the trends are quite different. Political activity seems to be much commoner in Europe and the USA. In contrast to media images of mass demonstrations, on average, people in Arab countries are still less likely to have taken some action than their

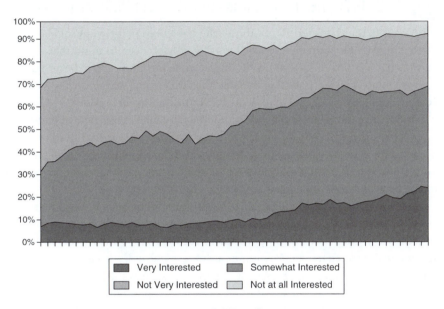

Figure 11.7 Interest in politics, women 18–75 years (smoothed), USA and Europe

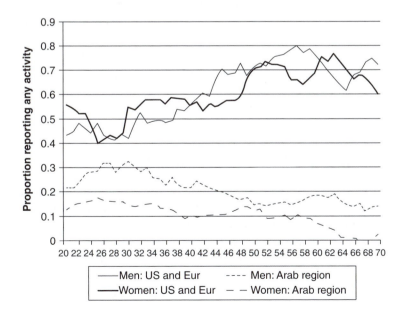

Figure 11.8 Political activity by age, sex and region

counterparts in Europe and the USA. The pattern of participation too is different. In Europe and the USA it rises with age, and there is no substantial difference between men and women, while in the Arab countries it is indeed the young who are more likely to have taken some action, and men are more likely to have done so than women.

11 ● 6 A LOGISTIC REGRESSION MODEL OF POLITICAL ACTIVITY

We can investigate the characteristics of those who have been involved in some political activity in Arab countries by building a *logistic regression* model. Keep in mind that our definition of political activity is broad, so that, for example, someone who reported ever having signed a petition is counted in the **polaction** variable that we created earlier, in the same way as a respondent who might have regularly attended demonstrations or boycotts.

You'll find that building, running and testing the model takes less time and effort than the preparation of the data that will be used. Avoid the temptation to rush. I find it is also a good idea to leave some time between data management and model building. Model building needs a clear head, and if your mind is still cluttered by any data management and preparation problems you've overcome, this will be harder to achieve.

It is also important to keep a clear sense of what your *objectives* are in building a model. Is it to examine the influence of one particular variable on a dependent, controlling for the presence of others? Or is it to model the outcome variable, selecting those variables that best predict it in order to explore the correlates of behaviour or attitudes? One objective in a model is *parsimony*: other things being equal, to use the fewest possible predictor variables. This not only makes interpretation easier and the conclusions you can draw clearer, but also guards against 'over-fitting' the data. It is possible to think of any dataset as containing both signal (the underlying social relationships or structures about which we want evidence) and noise (caused by random variation, measurement error and other background interference). A parsimonious model is more likely to capture signal, while too elaborate a model may waste information by modelling the shape of noise in the particular set of data you are exploring. Resist the temptation to use stepwise or other statistical selection procedures to build a model. Rather the selection of predictor variables ought to be driven by theory (derived from the existing literature, from other analyses or from a hypothesis you want to test) about which variables are *substantively* important, together with how well they perform in the model itself.

11 ● 7 BUILDING A LOGISTIC REGRESSION MODEL

Model construction and coefficient interpretation in logistic regression do *not* proceed in the same way as for OLS regression, because of the different assumptions logistic and linear regression make about the variables that we do not observe (i.e. that are not in our model, or not in our dataset) and the distribution of errors for those we do, known as *unobserved heterogeneity*. Comparing coefficients across models, we ought to keep in mind that the addition of a new independent variable to a model will change the existing coefficients for independent variables *even if the new variable is not correlated with them*. This means that when comparing models we need to keep in mind that the new coefficients represent not only possible effects of the new variable upon the existing independents, but also the extra information and reduction in unobserved heterogeneity we gain from adding the new variable. Comparing across groups is less problematic, since even if the values of unobserved variables differ, this can be seen as a property of the groups being compared.

A useful, but quite technical summary of the problems is given by Mood (2010). The fundamental point to grasp is that in logistic regression it can be problematic to compare the sign and size of individual regression coefficients either across *different* models applied to the *same* data, or across the *same* model applied to *different* samples. This argument has been challenged by other researchers (e.g. Buis, 2016) who argue that the impact of unobserved heterogeneity on the coefficients, inasmuch as it represents a real difference in samples, is a legitimate influence upon the coefficients rather than representing error. This discussion takes us well beyond the level of statistics knowledge I assume in this book, but if you intend to use logistic regression extensively in your work it is a debate you should review. In what follows I have adopted an approach that is perhaps closer to that of Buis than Mood but follows the general outlines of that suggested by Hosmer et al. (2013). Finally, remember that comparisons of the predictive power, as measured by the log likelihood or chi-square, across *nested* models remain a valid procedure. As we saw in Chapter 10, a nested model is one that contains all of the variables of the reduced model, plus one or more other variables.

11 ● 8 SELECTING AND PREPARING THE INDEPENDENT VARIABLES

Our first step is to select all the variables that we propose to include in our model. Reviewing the variables in the WVS and with my (sparse) background knowledge of political participation, we might select the following candidate predictor variables:

v242 (age)

v240 (sex)

v7 (how important is politics in life)

v84 (interest in politics)

v115 (confidence in the government)

v147 (whether 'a religious person')

v217–v224 (sources of information)

v181-2 (worries about job or child's education)

v188–v191 (material and physical security)

v248 (education)

v238 (social class)

Our first task is to examine our chosen independent variables and prepare them for use in our model of the correlates of political activity. First we have to check that the variables we are interested in have been fielded in all the countries we wish to study, and have been defined in the same way, or whether, if there are differences, they can nevertheless be used to create a consistent indicator across countries. We can refer to the data documentation to check that the country reports are consistent with what appears to be in the dataset itself. Then we have to look at the level of *missing data* in these variables. Remember that in any regression, cases that are missing on any one of the independent variables used will be excluded from the analysis.

There are two grounds for concern. First, there may be some variables that have been measured only for a subset of respondents: for example, those who have never worked for pay cannot sensibly be asked questions about their earnings, occupation or conditions of employment! A judgement has to be made whether a sensible value can be allocated to those not measured (so that a category 'never worked' might be added to variables about employment), or whether it might make sense to estimate two different models, one for those who have worked and one for those who have not.

Second, we have to check that modest rates of missing cases on individual variables do not lead to a high rate of cases missing overall when several variables are used in the model. To the extent that a model uses more variables, even modest rates of missing data on individual variables can lead to a substantial part of the data being lost, with not only the accompanying loss of information, but also the possibility that the selection of cases with values for all variables differs substantially in its character from other cases: there may be a *selection effect*. If missing values were spread randomly around the data this need not be a concern, but this is unlikely to be the case. Thus we need to check that the cases (with no missing values) that end up in our model are not systematically different from those we have to exclude. Again this is a matter of judgement and no hard and fast rules apply.

Finally, we need to examine whether each variable does in fact display variation. It is perfectly possible for a variable to take the same value for the overwhelmingly majority of cases. In such a situation, while the distribution itself may well be of interest, it is unlikely to help our analysis of the distributions of *other* variables, since it has so little variation to contribute. If everyone is alike in some respect, that feature cannot be used to make comparisons between groups of people, which is what we are generally interested in doing.

We could run a crosstab of our independents with **v2** to examine them separately for each country (since the details of the survey fieldwork will almost certainly have differed across countries), but this has the drawback that SPSS does not include missing values in contingency tables. One way around this is to run the crosstab from syntax and include the sub-command **/MISSING=INCLUDE** (the option is not available in the GUI). An alternative that I prefer is to use the **Split File** procedure to have SPSS produce results separately for each value of **v2** and then run frequency tables for these variables, since a frequency table includes missing values. As we saw in Chapter 6, when you split the dataset by a variable, SPSS treats cases with the same value of that variable as a separate dataset and produces results for these cases only, repeating the analysis for each group of cases defined by each of the values the variable takes. Thus if we split the file by **v2** we'll get an analysis for each individual country for whatever procedures we run. Be careful not to confuse the **Split File** icon on the toolbar ▦ with the **Select Cases** icon nearby. The **Split File** dialog asks you which variable you wish to split the file by. Choose **Organize output by groups** and always choose the option to **Sort the file by grouping variables**.

Once **Split File** is on you will see an alert at the bottom right of the **Data Editor** window, next to those for any filters or weights you are using. As usual, syntax is easier:

```
SORT CASES BY v2.
SPLIT FILE SEPARATE BY v2.
```

For **v240**, **v7** and **v84** we have no issues to address: the variables are fielded in each country, levels of missing data are low and there are no obviously redundant categories with very few responses. For **v115** missing data is potentially a problem, with over 900 missing cases, mostly 'don't know' responses. If our overall rate for missing data is unacceptably high, we could consider recoding these don't knows to the median response category.

11 ● 9 RECODING VARIABLES V217–V224

Sources of current affairs information present a challenge. Respondents were asked a variety of questions about how often they read papers or magazines, watched television, used the internet, spoke with friends, and so on, captured in variables **v217–v224**. These variables provide more detail than we probably need. We want a parsimonious model with as few variables as possible, so that we need to summarise the information from these variables. We also face the complication that a slightly different form of these questions was fielded in Morocco, captured in variables **v218_ESMA** onwards. In Morocco people were asked if they had used each of the sources in the preceding week, rather than how often they usually used them. This kind of inconsistency is common in comparative survey work: it can be very difficult to secure the agreement of diverse survey organisations to exactly the same version of the survey instrument.

First, we can drop the variable about television since it fails our variation test: almost everyone watches television news. This may well be an interesting finding, but our objective is to distinguish those who take part in political activity from others: this variable contains little variation that would help us to do this. Next, we could record how many different sources of information are ever used by individuals as captured in **v217**, **v218** and **v220–v223**, by using the **Count** command to produce a new variable. This gives us a variable with values ranging from 0 to 6 describing the number of different sources respondents use. We could then recode this to a dummy variable, splitting the responses between values 2 and 3. Once we have done this, we also need to take account of missing cases. No use of the relevant media will have been recorded under these variables for some respondents because they have not answered the question or said they didn't know: we need to distinguish these from the 'real zeros' – those who used none of these means of information. Try to work out the syntax to do this. (Hint: use the **Count** command, and then compare your syntax with what I suggest in the box. ✎ You can also copy and paste the syntax from the companion website.) Next we need to deal with Morocco, fitting the responses we have to the slightly different variables there into the new variable we have created. To do so we will have to equate 'use in the past week' with 'use ever'. This creates some measurement error, but that is hardly likely to be serious, and far better than having to drop an entire country from the analysis. I've called the variable that I've created out of these procedures **info1**.

```
COUNT information=v217 v218 v220 v221 v222 v223(1 thru 4).
FREQ information.
RECODE information (0 thru 2 = 0) (3 thru 6 = 1) into info1.
VALUE labels info1 0 "few sources" 1 "many sources".
FREQ info1.
COUNT missinfo=v217 v218 v220 v221 v222 v223(MISSING).
IF (missinfo eq 6) and (v2 ne 504) info1 = 9.
MISSING VALUES info1 (9).
FREQ info1.
COUNT morinfo=v217_ESMA v218_ESMA v220_ESMA v221_ESMA
v222_ESMA v223_ESMA (724001).
FREQ morinfo.
RECODE morinfo (0 1 = 0) (2 thru hi = 1).
COUNT missinfo1=v217_ESMA v218_ESMA v220_ESMA v221_ESMA
v222_ESMA v223_ESMA (MISSING).
FREQ missinfo1.
IF ((v2 eq 504) and (missinfo1 eq 6)) info1 = 9.
IF (v2 eq 504) info1 eq morinfo.
FREQ info1.
```

11.10 PREPARING THE DUMMY VARIABLES

Just as in linear regression, categorical predictor variables in a logistic regression are entered as dummy variables. It therefore makes sense to collapse categories as far as possible, especially if you have a large number of predictor variables, to avoid producing a cumbersome model that is difficult to interpret. There is no 'correct' way to collapse categories, other than creating categories that are meaningful and capable of interpretation, and avoiding new categories with few cases in them. Since we will have over ten predictors, we can reduce them all to two categories, so that each predictor is one dummy, rather than a set of dummies. If we wish to investigate any individual predictor variable in greater detail, we can always re-run the model later with a larger number of categories. Give your variables value labels as you recode them. This helps to keep the interpretation of the model clear and avoid confusing the direction of impact of each variable.

First I'll recode the education variable to distinguish those with higher education from all others.

```
RECODE v248 (1 thru 7 = 0) (8 9 = 1) (lo thru 0 = SYSMIS) into v248jm.
VALUE LABELS v248jm 0 "none/secondary" 1 "higher".
```

We can measure people's economic situation using the questions about different hardships in **v188–v191**. We could simply total the scores on these four variables to get a crude measure of prosperity, and look at the distribution of the raw scores to decide how we might divide up respondents into different categories. Note what assumptions we make in order to do this. We are assuming that these dimensions of hardship are all equally important and that their impact is additive. Neither of these assumptions holds much water, but our key interest is only in being able to distinguish between more and less prosperous respondents. This will probably serve us well enough. Again think about how you might create a variable that divides respondents into four groups, and compare your syntax with mine. (Hint: there are two or three equally good ways to create this variable.) I've called my variable **hardship**.

```
COMPUTE hardship = 17- (v188 + v189 + v190 + v191).
RECODE hardship (1 thru 5 = 0) (6 thru 13 = 1).
VALUE LABELS hardship 0 "little hardship" 1 "more hardship".
FREQ hardship.
```

We could combine **v181** and **v182** (worries about the future) and have the resulting variable take two categories. However, you will see that there are many respondents who did not answer these questions or said that they didn't know. We could infer that many of these respondents may be without either a job to lose or children to worry about. We could minimise our missing responses by coding as worried those who answered 'very much' to either question, and putting everyone else, including the non-responses, into an 'other' category. I've called this variable **worry1**.

```
COMPUTE worry1 = 0.
If (v181 eq 1) worry1 = 1.
If (v182 eq 1) worry1 = 1.
VALUE labels worry1 0 "other" 1  "worried" .
FREQ worry1.
```

Next we'll create dummies from **v7** (importance of politics), **v84** (interest in politics), **v115** (confidence in central government) and **v238** (social class).

```
recode v7 (1 2 = 1) (3 4 = 0) into v7dum.
VALUE LABELS v7dum 0 "not important" 1 "important".
recode v84 (1 2 = 1) (3 4 = 0) into v84dum.
VALUE LABELS v84dum 0 "not interested" 1 "interested".
recode v115 (1 2 = 0) (3 4 = 1) into v115dum.
VALUE LABELS v115dum 0 "some confidence" 1 "little confidence".
recode v238 (2 3 = 1) (4 5 =0) (ELSE = COPY) into v238dum.
missing values v238dum (-6 thru -1).
VALUE LABELS v238dum 1 "middle class" 0 "working class".
freq v7dum  v84dum v115dum v238dum.
```

11 11 CREATING A RELIGION VARIABLE

Religion faces the problem that none of the relevant variables were asked in *all* countries. Those *not asked* for **v145** all come from Morocco where the question was not asked. The NAs in **v146** and **v147** all come from Egypt where these questions were not asked. However, it is also striking that in no Arab country does any respondent report having no religious denomination (**v144** = 0). Unless you know Arabic it is not possible to tell from the questionnaires fielded if 'none' was offered as a response to the question about religious denomination, or whether it was omitted. Either way, if we are making comparisons with countries outside the region we will need to keep in mind this substantial difference in the way religion is conceived.

My solution to this is to use the simplest variable, **v147**, which was asked everywhere except Egypt, and to use the answers to **v145**, a question that *was* asked in Egypt, as a proxy for how respondents there might have answered the question for **v147**. Again this procedure is open to discussion. Unquestionably, **v147** and **v145** measure different things. However, it could also be argued that both attempt to measure some underlying propensity to religious commitment, albeit in different ways, so that combining them in some way makes sense. We can code those who answered 'Never, practically never' in answer to the question 'How often do you pray?' as not seeing themselves as a religious person in our new version of **v147**. If we are going to do this for cases in Egypt with missing values on this variable, it makes sense to follow this approach in other countries too. Again try writing the syntax to produce this new variable and compare it with the box, or the companion website ❧ (Hint: use **if** statements.)

```
RECODE v147 (2,3=0) (1 = 1) (else = copy) into v147jm.
VALUE LABELS v147jm 1 "religious" 0" non-religious".
IF ((v2 eq 818) and(v145 eq 7)) v147jm eq 0.
IF ((v2 eq 818) and(v145 le 6) and (v145 ge 1)) v147jm eq 1.
FREQ v147jm.
MISSING VALUES v147 ().
IF ((v147 lt 0) and (v145 eq 7)) v147jm eq 0.
IF ((v147 lt 0) and (v145 le 6) and (v145 ge 1)) v147jm eq 1.
FREQ v147jm.
MISSING VALUES v147jm (-6 thru -1).
```

In other countries about 5% of respondents *did not answer* **v147**. We've already imputed values for respondents in Egypt who *weren't asked* the question by assigning the value 'a religious person' on the basis of frequent attendance at religious services (**v145**), a question that *was* asked in Egypt. We could do the same for those who gave no answer or said don't know in other countries on **v147**, but *did* give an answer on **v145**. Again, try to create the syntax for this operation, and check it against my suggested syntax. I've called the variable that results from these procedures **v147JM**.

11 ● 12 DEALING WITH MISSING VALUES

Our next task is to check the pattern of missing values in our independents. For the regression procedure SPSS will exclude every case that takes a missing value on any of the independent variables. We need to ensure that this subset of cases does not differ substantially from the all the cases in our dataset. This too is a matter of judgement. Rarely are missing values distributed randomly across the data. A respondent who answers 'don't know' to one question may also be more likely to give that response to other questions.

We can check the distribution of missing values by creating a variable that describes which cases have a missing value. There is more than one way to do this, but the simplest is to create a variable that is the sum of the values taken by all the independent variables for each case. SPSS will return a **missing value** for this variable when it encounters any missing value in the sum operation. We can then recode the missing cases on this variable to take one value (e.g. 0), and all the cases with valid values to take another (e.g. 1). I've called my variable **allvalid**.

```
COMPUTE allvalid=v240 + v242 +v7dum + v84dum + v147jm + v238dum + v248jm + hardship
+ worry1 + info1 + v115dum.
RECODE allvalid (1 THRU HI = 1) (SYSMIS = 0).
FREQ allvalid.
```

Now we can use the **Split File** procedure to organise our output by the values of **allvalid** (or whatever name you have given your new variable). Produce and review frequency tables for all the variables we will use in the regression, taking notes if you notice that the distribution of each variable is substantially different between the two values of **allvalid**. The first thing to note is that we have a rather high proportion of missing cases, about 15%, and many of these seem to be caused by **v115**. The second thing to note is that the distribution of the values for the cases with missing values on one or more of our variables is not too different from those for whom we have information on all the variables. We could recode the values of don't knows on **v115** to the median for the variable, as an alternative to keeping them as missing, but first let's just accept that the number of missing cases is on the high side, but not disastrously so, and that there is not a great deal of difference between those cases with some missing values and the others.

Our next task is to turn off the **Split File** function, then select those cases without missing values (using **allvalid** and the **Select Cases** commands) and produce a contingency table of each potential predictor categorical variable by the outcome variable **polaction**, using a chi-square test to assess its significance. Hosmer et al. (2013) suggest including any variable with $p < 0.25$ on the chi-square test. However, with large samples this is not stringent enough and could lead to the inclusion of many variables with little substantive effect. I suggest that, with samples of around 1,000, $p < 0.1$ might be better. When you do this you should find that all the variables we have selected have a substantial bivariate association with **polaction** and merit inclusion in the model.

11●13 CHECKING FOR LINEARITY

Next we need to check that our continuous variable for age is approximately a linear function of the log odds of the dependent. The easiest way to do this is to use the **means** procedure to calculate the mean value of the outcome variable (coded 0/1) for a reasonably large number of interval ranges of the continuous variable. Copy this across to Excel, transform the proportions into log odds and plot the results. Figure 11.9 shows the result for 5/10 year groups of the age variable **v242**. It is not strictly linear, but neither is it very badly off. We can safely use **v242** should it perform well in the model.

As we did in the previous chapter, we'll arrange the reference category of our predictors to be the category of respondent that we expect to have the lowest probability of taking political action. We can use the crosstabs you have just produced to check what these should be. I've summarised this in Table 11.4.

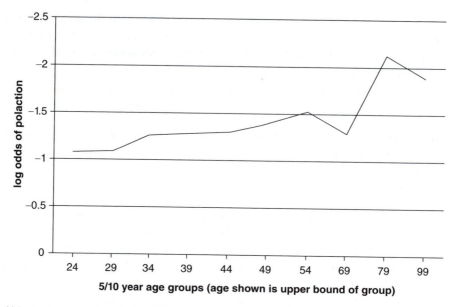

Figure 11.9   Age (grouped) by log odds of **polaction**

Table 11.4   Variable reference categories

Variable	Reference category (value)
V7dum	First (0, not important)
V84dum	First (0, not interested)
V115dum	First (1, a great deal)
V240	Last (2, female)
V147jm	Last (1, religious)
V238dum	First (0, working class)
V248jm	First (0, no higher education)
worry1	First (0, not very worried)
hardship	First (0, little hardship)
info1	First (0, few sources)

11 14 RUNNING THE MODEL

Our next step is to run a model with all of our candidate predictor variables entered at once. We can then remove variables which do not appear to contribute to the performance of the model. Since we will be running a series of models, we can save time and effort by using syntax. However, you may find it easier to run the first model from the GUI, and paste the syntax. If you do so correctly, your syntax should look like that in the box or on the companion website ✎ (note that the order of the variables is unimportant).

```
LOGISTIC REGRESSION VARIABLES polaction
/METHOD=ENTER v242 v240 v84dum v7dum v238dum v248jm hardship worry1 info1
v115dum v147jm
/CONTRAST (v7dum)=Indicator (1)
/CONTRAST (v240)=Indicator
/CONTRAST (info1)=Indicator(1)
/CONTRAST (v84dum)=Indicator (1)
/CONTRAST (v238dum)=Indicator (1)
/CONTRAST (hardship)=Indicator (1)
/CONTRAST (worry1)=Indicator(1)
/CONTRAST (v115dum)=Indicator (1)
/CONTRAST (v147jm)=Indicator
/CONTRAST (v248jm)=Indicator(1)
/CRITERIA=PIN(0.05) POUT(0.10) ITERATE(20) CUT(0.5).
```

At this stage we are less interested in the performance of the model than in the components within it. To maximise model parsimony we can drop any variable that does not appear to make a significant contribution to the model as measured by the significance value associated with the size of its coefficient in relation to its standard error in the **Variables in the Equation** output (Table 11.5).

Table 11.5 Variables in the Equation output

Variables in the Equation

		B	S.E.	Wald	df	Sig.	Exp(B)
Step 1[a]	V242	-.014	.002	50.020	1	.000	.986
	V240(1)	.666	.054	149.409	1	.000	1.946
	v84dum(1)	.684	.070	94.147	1	.000	1.981
	v7dum(1)	-.186	.069	7.282	1	.007	.830
	v238dum(1)	.123	.057	4.617	1	.032	1.131
	v248jm(1)	.436	.060	53.374	1	.000	1.547
	hardship(1)	-.286	.065	19.560	1	.000	.751
	worry1(1)	.364	.055	43.678	1	.000	1.438
	info1(1)	.866	.054	254.491	1	.000	2.378
	v115dum(1)	.284	.056	26.136	1	.000	1.329
	v147jm(1)	.200	.061	10.825	1	.001	1.222
	Constant	-2.699	.114	556.479	1	.000	.067

a. Variable(s) entered on step 1: V242, V240, v84dum, v7dum, v238dum, v248jm, hardship, worry1, info1, v115dum, v147jm.

11 ● 15 DROPPING VARIABLES FROM THE MODEL

Although we could retain all of the existing variables in our model, there are two which do not seem to add very much to its explanatory power: v7dum (importance of politics) and v238dum (class). Although they are both below the conventional 5% significance threshold, the size of their coefficients is modest, and we must keep in mind our sample size, which is large enough to make not only weak relationships but what may also be spurious noise patterns in our data significant. Let's drop these two variables, but before we do so we must consider two criteria.

One criterion is whether the deletion of a variable makes a large change to the values of the coefficients of the other variables in the model. It is possible for a variable to add little to the ability of the model to predict the outcome variable, yet influence how the other variables behave by substantially changing their coefficients. In this situation keeping such a *confounder* variable in the model improves it by giving us a better picture of how the remaining variables behave.

The other criterion is whether or not a variable makes a direct contribution to the model. The essential criterion here is the change in the **–2 Log likelihood** or *deviance* reported under **Model Summary** and the associated chi-square statistic reported under **Omnibus Test of Model Coefficients**. The deviance is analogous to the residual sum of squares in OLS, so that lower values represent an improvement in the model fit. The associated chi-square statistic and its *p*-value come from the ratio of the likelihoods of the two models (or their difference when logged).

We can check the impact of the two variables we are considering dropping from the model by entering them as a separate block in the model. This enables us to examine the effect upon the coefficients of the *other* variables when these two variables are present or absent, and also to see how much explanatory power of the model increases with their addition. To do this, drop the two variables from the first /METHOD=ENTER command line in the syntax and insert a new command line entering these two variables so that your syntax will now start:

```
LOGISTIC REGRESSION VARIABLES polaction
/METHOD=ENTER v242 v240 v84dum v248jm hardship worry1 info1 v115dum v147jm
/METHOD=ENTER v7dum v238dum
```

The rest of your syntax remains unchanged. You should find that removing these two variables has little effect on the coefficients of the other model variables, and that although their addition makes a significant difference to the model, they do little to increase its explanatory power and can be safely dropped in the interests of model parsimony. As usual, the companion website has a record of all the correct syntax.

SPSS routinely also produces a classification table of the observed values of the dependent by the values predicted by the model and two 'pseudo R^2' measures that attempt to mimic the role of R^2 in OLS regression. Common sense tells us that the classification table should surely be a good test of the goodness of fit of the model: its ability to correctly predict the values of our dependent and account for variation. At issue here is the predicted outcome (0 or 1) derived from the predicted probabilities, rather than the predicted probabilities themselves. Unfortunately, this is one of those situations where common sense can lead us astray. Classification depends heavily upon the distribution of the dependent. This can be seen by the way in which classification in the null model is simply to the modal value of the dependent.

The distribution of cases to predicted categories depends upon the cut-off point. However, a perfectly good model might nevertheless produce predicted probabilities near the cut-off point. Classification derives values of 0 and 1 from these probabilities, rather than using the information in the predicted probabilities themselves.

Hosmer et al. (2013: 171) give a hypothetical example that makes this distinction, and the way that the classification of individual cases is different from the distribution of probabilities across all cases, clearer. We could have a model in which 100 cases with a common covariate pattern produce a result for the estimated probability of the dependent taking the value 0.51. (A covariate pattern is each single combination of values of the independent variables in the model (e.g. female, aged 25 years, thinks politics is not very important, and so on).) The model therefore estimates that out of 100 cases taking this pattern of values for the independents in the model, 51 cases would be expected to take the value 1 for the dependent. However, in the classification table, with a cut-off point of 0.5, all 100 of these cases would be rounded up to the value 1 for the dependent. In other words, our model gives us information about the probability distribution for all cases, while the classification table applies this distribution to each individual case, which is rarely what we want. The moral of the story is not to pay too much attention to classification tables.

Other diagnostic statistics with debatable value are the various measures of pseudo R^2 that have been proposed, including the Cox and Snell and Nagelkerke R^2 reported by SPSS. While they have some value in comparing different models on the same data, they are *not* necessarily a good guide to model fit, nor do they give any absolute indication of the performance of the model. The values they report are typically much lower than that for R^2 in OLS regression.

11 ● 16 EXAMINING INTERACTIONS

Our next step is to consider interaction effects in the model. Since we have a large number of variables we will have a large number of interaction terms to consider. An interaction exists when the impact of one variable on the dependent differs according to the value taken by a third variable and the interaction has a coherent substantive interpretation. Within a logistic regression model it can be thought of as the combined effect of the variables in the interaction term, controlling for the individual effects of each of the individual variables. Best practice is to add interaction terms one at a time, retaining only those that lead to an significant improvement in model fit over the model with no such terms. We add the interaction term as a new block in the regression by repeating the **/METHOD=ENTER** command line in the syntax. Interaction terms are the products of the two (or more) variables involved. Again, given our large sample size, I'll include interaction terms only if they have a statistically significant effect over all categories of the two variables involved.

One interaction that appears to make a useful addition to the model is that between the variables for hardship and education. Hardship on its own *decreases* the probability of taking part in political activity. This is a finding we might expect, even if at first sight it might appear counter-intuitive. Those facing greatest hardship may have so few expectations of the existing system that they see little use in trying to change it, or see themselves as having no ability to do so. Higher education on its own increases the probability of political action. However, higher education *and* hardship together (our interaction) strongly *increases* the probability of political action. Thus the impact of hardship is strongly mediated by education. Let's retain this interaction in our model and proceed to assess its fit.

11 ● 17 ASSESSING THE MODEL FIT: THE HOSMER–LEMESHOW TEST

We can now assess the *goodness of fit* of this model. Again this is a more complex matter than with OLS. Hitherto we have essentially been investigating a series of questions asking whether one set of fitted (predicted) values is superior to another set. We now ask a different question: we compare the fitted values to the observed values *in our data*.

It is useful to think in terms of the number of covariate patterns in the data when discussing goodness of fit in logistic regression. If there are one or more continuous variables in the model the number of covariate patterns will approach the number of cases in the data, because of the large range of individual values taken by the continuous variable(s). However, if the model has only categorical variables the number of covariate patterns may be much less than N: its maximum value will be 2^x where x is the number of dummies. The number of different possible predicted values of the *logit* will be constrained by the number of covariate patterns.

A useful and straightforward test of goodness of fit that is easy to produce in SPSS and gives reasonably robust results is the *Hosmer–Lemeshow* test. It produces a ten by two contingency table of the expected and observed probabilities of cases taking the value 1 in each decile of cases ranked by the expected probabilities, or 'deciles of risk'. A Pearson chi-square test with eight (10 – 2) degrees of freedom is then applied to the table and goodness of fit is measured by the value of the chi-square statistic and associated *p*-value. If the model fits well the value for chi-square will be low and its associated *p*-value high, indicating that the observed and expected probabilities are close to each other.

This test has to be administered with a little care. If N is small, there is a risk of one or more of the cells in the 10 × 2 table containing less than 5 cases, which will affect the chi-square value (as it would in any contingency table). If the number of covariate patterns is small, there is the possibility that a common covariate pattern (and thus common predicted probabilities) will spill over more than one decile, creating the problem of how to deal with ties. With some models, a small change in the number of cells in the contingency table (e.g. dividing the data into nine or eleven risk deciles rather than ten) leads to substantial change in the value of the chi-square statistic and associated *p*-value. Finally, when N is large (more than 500 or 1,000) even small relative differences between the observed and expected values in the contingency table will produce a chi-square statistic large enough to produce a small and significant *p*-value even with a very good model fit.

━━━━━━━━━━━━━━━ **type I and type II errors** ━━━━━━━━━━━━━━━

When we accept or reject a hypothesis we can be right in two ways or wrong in two ways as the table at the bottom of this box shows. Of course we do not have definite knowledge of the truth or untruth of our hypothesis: that is why we're using statistical evidence to estimate the probabilities in the first place! An example of rejecting a hypothesis that is in fact true would be when we *reject a null hypothesis* of no association between a pair of variables that are in fact independent of each other, on the basis of a low *p*-value in a significance test. Indeed, you can interpret the *p*-value directly as the risk of committing such an error, called a *Type I* error. We could avoid committing Type I errors by insisting on more stringent standards for rejecting the null and accepting a result as 'significant'. However this lays us open to the obverse problem: accepting a hypothesis that is in fact untrue, if our more stringent standards lead us to discard as insignificant, results that were in fact evidence of some association. Note that hypotheses and Type I/II errors refer to statements about the target population, not to our sample data. For this reason we cannot usually know definitely if we are committing an error: but we can estimate the *risk* of having done so.

Accept a hypothesis that is true	Accept a hypothesis that is untrue **Type II error**
Reject a hypothesis that is true **Type I error**	Reject a hypothesis that is untrue

The chi-square statistic in the *Hosmer–Lemeshow* test is for a 'Type II error' (see box). That is to say, if $p > 0.05$ we accept the null hypothesis that the observed and expected frequencies in the table are the same. What matters is therefore the *power* of the test. High power requires both a large sample (above 500) and an outcome that is not too infrequent so that the mean value of the dependent (i.e. the proportion of cases taking the value 1) preferably lies between 0.25 and 0.75. However, *too much* power can also be a problem, which typically occurs if N is above 1,000. The absolute value of the chi-square statistic will increase directly in proportion to the sample size. Hosmer and Lemeshow emphasise the importance of careful examination of the frequencies in each cell of the decile of risk contingency table itself. Large cell frequencies with small differences in each decile between observed and modelled outcomes should be taken as evidence of good model fit, even if the *p*-value associated with the table chi-square is low. This would be an example of excessive power in the test caused by a large sample size.

To run this test you can either call it from the dialog box using the **Options** button which brings up the dialog box (Figure 11.10) and check **Hosmer-Lemeshow goodness-of-fit**, or add the line **/PRINT=GOODFIT** on a separate line of syntax before the **/CRITERIA** subcommand if you are using syntax.

Your output should include Table 11.6, which divides the data by 'deciles of risk', and you'll see that in the first decile the observed and expected probabilities of people having taken political action were 3–4%, while in the final decile they were 45–47%. The model clearly fits better in some deciles than others. The performance is relatively poor in the sixth and eighth deciles but good elsewhere. Note the contrast between this table and the classification table. When we deal in probabilities, rather than assigning individual cases to groups using a cut-off, the equivalent of less than 100 cases (1% of the total) are misclassified: a good performance. SPSS reports the Pearson chi-square for this table as 29.2 with 8 degrees of freedom, which is highly significant. This formal test indicates that the results predicted by the model are significantly different from those observed in the data: in other words, that our model is *not* a good fit. However, this is a good example of how this test must be interpreted with care. The significance of the chi-square test here is driven not by the poor model fit but by the size of the sample, so we can safely disregard the *p*-value.

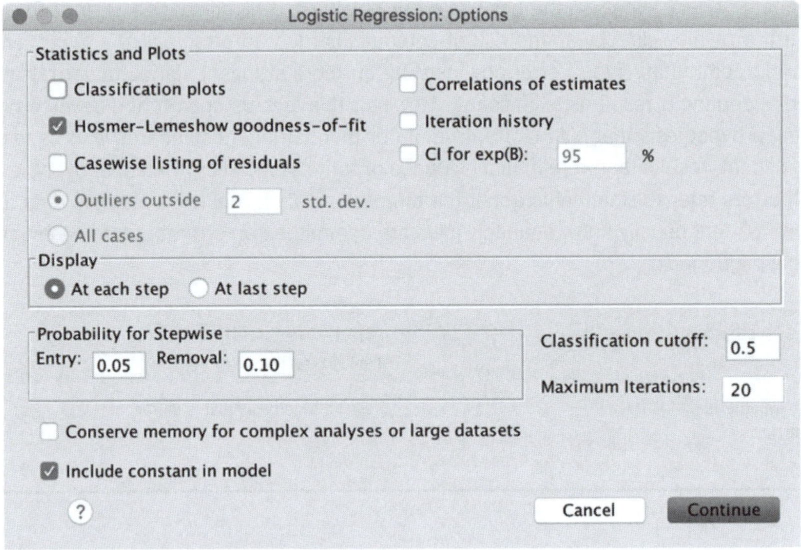

Figure 11.10   Logistic Regression: **Options** dialog box

Table 11.6   Hosmer–Lemeshow test

Contingency table for Hosmer and Lemeshow test

		polaction = .00 No activity		polaction = 1.00 some activity		
		Observed	Expected	Observed	Expected	Total
Step 1	1	1051	1071.852	66	45.335	1117
	2	1045	1041.348	68	71.704	1113
	3	1039	1022.709	78	94.226	1117
	4	986	995.562	129	119.785	1115
	5	1000	968.924	118	148.897	1118
	6	914	933.170	199	180.299	1113
	7	916	890.163	201	226.374	1117
	8	820	834.639	295	280.907	1116
	9	764	762.586	355	355.513	1118
	10	619	633.515	508	493.606	1127

11 ● 18   RESIDUAL DIAGNOSTICS

Just as with OLS regression, we can look at the distribution of residuals to check for cases that are poorly predicted by the model, and for cases that exert an undue influence on the results. SPSS offers us a range of residuals and leverage statistics to work with. The most useful to work with are shown in Table 11.7.

Table 11.7 Useful residuals and leverage statistics

	Syntax code	Created variable name
Predicted probabilities	PRED	PRE_1
Cook's distance	COOK	COO_1
Leverage values	LEVER	LEV_1
Standardised residuals	ZRESID	ZRE_1
Deviance	DEV	DEV_1

You can select these using the dialog box called by the **Save** button from the main logistic regression dialog shown in Figure 11.11 – but, as usual, it is easier to use syntax. The sub-command syntax below added to the logistic regression command will produce these statistics for each case.

/SAVE=PRED COOK LEVER ZRESID DEV

SPSS names the variables created by using the first three letters of these statistics followed by an underscore and a number that increments each time you call for them. Thus if you run a model asking for these variables, perhaps make some changes and then rerun the logistic regression procedure, that iteration will produce **PRE_2**, **COO_2** and so on. As you refine a model you may generate a very large number of such diagnostic variables, making it easy to

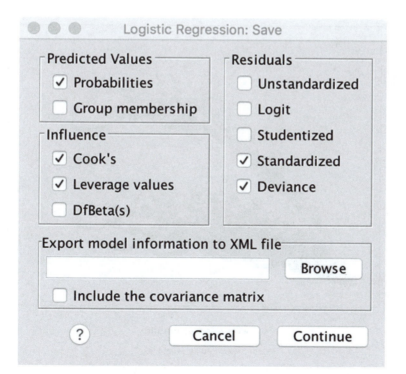

Figure 11.11 **Logistic Regression: Save** dialog box

confuse them. My advice is to delete previous iterations of diagnostic variables after producing new ones, once you have made any relevant comparisons.

First we'll produce scatterplots of the probabilities of **polaction** estimated by our model (**PRE_1**) by the leverage (**LEV_1**) and by Cook's distance (**COO_1**). As with linear regression, these look for cases or covariate patterns exerting an undue influence on the model. The patterns of the two scatterplots are typical of those produced by a successful logistic regression model. Our first plot (Figure 11.12) shows reassuringly low leverage values with no outliers, and the same is true for Cook's distance (Figure 11.13).

Next we want to create two plots that require us to calculate diagnostic variables that SPSS does not create itself. These are the *change* in chi-square and *change* in the deviance for the model produced for each case or covariate pattern. They are given by the formula below (this syntax will change depending on the iteration of the model that has produced the **ZRE_**, **LEV_** and **DEV_** diagnostic variables, so that you will need to insert the correct numbers after the underscores):

```
COMPUTE DELTACHISQ=ZRE_1**2/(1-LEV_1).
COMPUTE DELTADEV=DEV_1**2 + (ZRE_1**2 * LEV_1)/(1 - LEV_1).
```

The scatterplots for the change in the Pearson chi-square and deviance are shown in Figures 11.14 and 11.15. Large values indicate a poor fit. We have a tail of cases with low estimated probabilities for **polaction** and high **deltachisq** values that are probably worth further investigation. The 99th percentile of values for **deltachisq** begins at 13.6 (see Table 11.8). We might wish to examine these

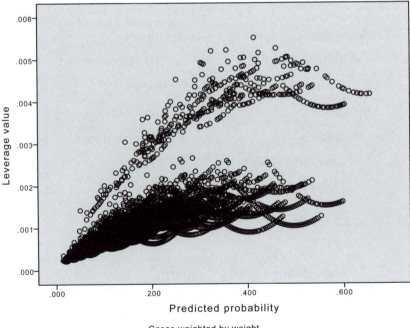

Cases weighted by weight

Figure 11.12 Plot of leverage by predicted probability

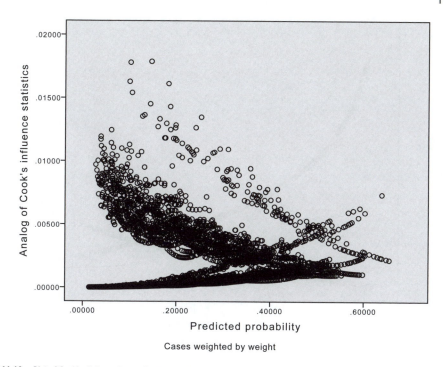

Figure 11.13 Plot of Cook's distance by predicted probability

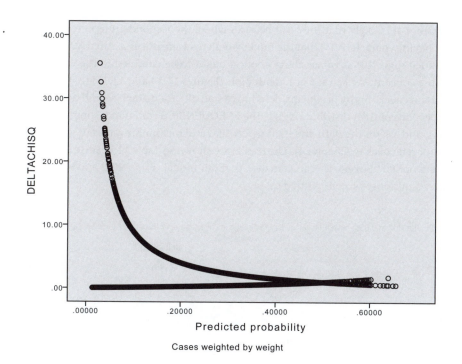

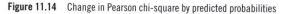

Figure 11.14 Change in Pearson chi-square by predicted probabilities

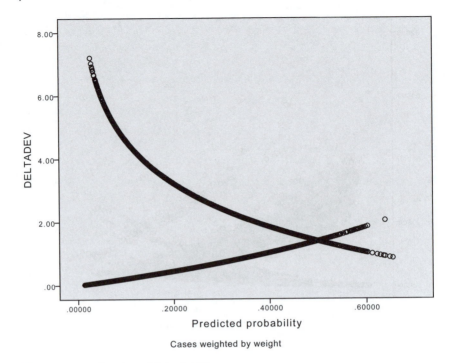

Figure 11.15 Change in deviance by predicted probabilities

cases further. It is likely that they will be cases where the respondent reported political activity, despite having characteristics that the model predicted were not associated with activity. Hosmer et al. (2013) suggest that values above about 4 ought to be confined to the 95th percentile and may cause concern. We can see from both plots (Figures 11.14 and 11.15) that we have such values and can check this by producing descriptive statistics for **deltachisq** and **deltadev** to examine the upper ends of their distribution. Use the **FREQUENCIES** command, suppress the production of tables, and ask for the 95th and 99th percentiles and maximum values (if you are unsure how to do this, refer back to Chapter 4). The results are shown in Table 11.8. Since the 95th percentile values are not far above 4, we can conclude that our model is a good fit and is not unduly influenced by a minority of poorly fitted cases.

Table 11.8 The 95th and 99th percentile values for the change in chi-square and the change in deviance

		deltachisq	deltadev
N	Valid	11171	11171
	Missing	0	0
Maximum		35.55	7.21
Percentiles	95	5.22	3.66
	99	13.70	5.39

11 ⬤ 19 INTERPRETING THE MODEL

Having undertaken these diagnostic tests, we are at last ready to interpret our model. We leave this till last since there would be little point in interpreting a poorly fitting model that is likely to be misspecified. Our attention now focuses on the **Variables in the Equation** table (Table 11.9) from the original regression output. Remember that the exponentiated coefficient in the final column gives us the change in the odds of a respondent reporting political activity associated with a one-unit change in the predictor variable, which in the case of dummy variables represents the contrast with the reference category of that variable. Our first variable, age, shows that the odds of political activity decrease slightly for each extra year of age. Thus a 10-year increase in age is associated with a *decrease* in odds of $0.986^{10} = 0.87$. To get a better feel for the magnitude of this change, we could express it in terms of typical values for our variables.

The probability of those aged 25–29 in the model reporting political activity was 0.249 (24.9%). These are odds of 0.332. Controlling for the other variables in the model, we'd expect the odds of political activity to decline to $0.332 \times 0.87 = 0.289$ or, in terms of probabilities, to 0.224 or 22.4% for respondents aged 35–39. This is just the kind of slow decline we saw back in chart 6.

The change in odds of political activity associated with being male are 1.93. We saw that around 12% of women had taken political action, or odds of 0.14. Thus, controlling for other variables in the model, the odds for men are $0.14 \times 1.93 = 0.27$ or a probability of 21%.

As we might expect, interest in politics almost doubles the odds of activity. So too does being male, while those who use several sources of information to keep up with current affairs

Table 11.9 Variables in the Equation output

Variables in the Equation

		B	S.E.	Wald	df	Sig.	Exp(B)
Step 1[a]	V242 Age	−.014	.002	51.530	1	.000	.986
	V240(1) sex	.657	.054	146.177	1	.000	1.928
	v84dum(1) interest politics	.573	.055	106.834	1	.000	1.773
	v248jm(1) education	.323	.064	25.497	1	.000	1.381
	hardship(1)	−.487	.072	45.252	1	.000	.614
	worry1(1)	.359	.055	42.839	1	.000	1.432
	info1(1)	.889	.054	270.712	1	.000	2.432
	v115dum(1) confidence	.286	.056	26.537	1	.000	1.331
	v147jm religious	−.211	.061	12.123	1	.000	.810
	v248jm(1) by hardship(1)	.717	.146	24.002	1	.000	2.048
	Constant	−2.405	.115	440.409	1	.000	.090

a. Variable(s) entered on step 1: V242, V240, v84dum, v248jm, hardship, worry1, info1, v115dum, v147jm, v248jm * hardship.

are also much more likely to have taken some political action. Higher education is associated with more activity, as are worries about material security. Conversely being religious, or suffering hardship are associated with slightly lower odds of being active. As with linear regression, the coefficients can be used to predict values of **polaction** for given values of the predictor variables. Rather than multiplying the coefficients, it is easiest to add the original logged coefficients and then convert them to odds and probabilities. Table 11.10 shows a worked example of how this can be done. Note that in this example the coefficient for being religious is omitted since the example we are examining is of respondents who do not describe themselves as being religious and is therefore in the reference category for that variable. Note too that the interaction coefficient is added to the coefficient for each of the variables in it (education and hardship). Recall that the average probability of having taken part in some political activity was 18%. Thus the type of respondent described here is just over three times as likely to have been politically active as others.

Exponentiated, this is odds of 0.744, which corresponds to a probability of 43% of being politically active, or around two and a half times the average probability for all respondents. The relevant coefficients are highlighted in Table 11.9.

Table 11.10 Logits, odds and probability of taking political action for man, aged 40, with higher education, interested in politics, worried, experiences hardship, uses many news sources, not religious, has little confidence in government.

(Constant)	-2.405
40 years old	40*-0.014= -0.56
Male	+0.657
Interested in politics	+0.573
Hardship	-0.487
Higher education	+0.323
Worried about future	+0.359
Uses many news sources	+0.889
Little confidence in government	+0.286
Hardship and higher education (interaction)	+0.717
Total	+0.352
Exponentiated odds	+1.42
Probability	0.59

11 ● 20 PRESENTING RESULTS FROM A LOGISTIC REGRESSION ANALYSIS

In the course of carrying out any analysis based on logistic regression, you inevitably create a veritable army of statistics, all of which have some importance in describing the model. These can be divided into those that describe its substantive results and the conclusions that might be drawn from it on the one hand, and the adequacy of the model on the other. You now face the difficult decision of what to report. This ought to be guided by the nature of your audience. An article in an academic journal can assume greater understanding of the more technical aspects than a piece aimed at a more general audience of policy-makers or the general public. The latter ought to focus on the substantive conclusions together with a general account of how they were reached, while the former ought to include all the material necessary for interested critics to replicate the analysis themselves. However, much of this material can be placed either in an appendix or in the supplementary online material that many journals make available. What you should try to avoid is large tables of coefficients that readers are unlikely to plough through.

Thus, were I to prepare an article based on this analysis, I'd include some information about the data used (the organisation of the WVS), basic descriptive statistics for the variables used in the analysis, the exponentiated regression coefficients and their associated significance levels, the summary statistics on the fit of the model and an illustration of its substantive results. In an appendix I'd include summaries of the main regression diagnostics and the data preparation procedures used to produce the variables used in the analysis. For a general audience it would be sufficient to give a basic idea of what regression does, which is to measure the relative impact of the predictor variables on the outcome variable, while controlling for the other variables in the model, and report some of the main findings using terminology such as 'other things equal, men were substantially more likely than women to have taken part in any political activity'.

what you have learned

If you review this chapter you'll notice that despite the large volume of material we have worked through, most of the new skills were about specific techniques of analysis, especially those concerned with logistic regression model diagnostics, rather than any fundamentally new ideas about the principles and methods of data analysis. As you go further with more advanced forms of data analysis you will find that this tends to be the case: specific techniques and procedures are developed to deal with the challenges of making the most of different configurations of data. The devil is usually in the detail.

You will almost certainly find it useful to divide your knowledge and understanding of data analysis into fundamental questions and principles on the one hand, and more specific applications of these principles on the other. It is important to acquire a secure grasp of the former, so that these principles permeate your thinking and understanding of data analysis. However, when it comes to the specific application of these ideas in this or that analysis technique or diagnostic procedure, there is no need to memorise what to do. You can always turn to guides, handbooks or manuals to take you through each step of the process. However, what cannot be stressed too much is the importance of *understanding* what you do, rather than the detail of how it is done. There is little point in running a diagnostic procedure if you do not understand why you should be running it or what the output actually means. There is no harm at all in carrying out an analysis with the data in one hand, as it were, and a technical manual in the other, so long as you can see beyond the details of the technique to the underlying purpose in applying it.

exercises

1. Run the model we have just built for our ten Arab countries on the four North American and European countries we chose. How well does it perform? Can you improve its performance by dropping some independent variables and/or adding new ones?
2. Search the ESS6 dataset for variables that are broadly similar to the ones we used with the World Values Survey. Construct a logistic regression model and compare the results for European countries with those for the Arab countries we have just examined. What differences do you find?

PRACTISING REGRESSION SKILLS WITH REPLICATION

The logistic regression skills we developed in Chapters 10 and 11 allow us to replicate the regression analyses in the articles we examined in Chapter 6. In this chapter we will:

- Identify how other analysts have set up their regression analyses
- Create sets of dummies for categorical independent variables
- Explore alternatives to the models reported in published work
- Replicate the microdata behind published contingency tables

12●1 INTRODUCTION

In Chapter 6 we looked at articles by Karlsen and Nazroo (2015) on Britishness, religion and ethnic identity and by Purdham and Tranmer (2014) on attitudes towards helping. Now that we've developed our logistic regression skills we can replicate the final analyses made in these two works. You'll find that this final part of the replication takes relatively little time: we've already done almost all the preparatory work recoding variables and so on in Chapter 6. All that remains to do is produce the dummies used as the dependent variables in the regression models and run the models themselves.

12●2 FEELING BRITISH

Return to the Home Office Citizenship Survey dataset that you worked on in Chapter 6. You'll see that you have already prepared most of the independent variables that you'll need to run the regression that Karlsen and Nazroo report in Table 2 of their article. They report running a logistic regression of each of three dependent variables, **febrit**, **sbegb** and **dualid**, on variables for age, gender, ethnicity and religion, economic activity, birthplace and perception of discrimination. We can use the original variables for age and gender in the dataset, **DVAge** and **Sex**, as they are. In addition, we will need the new economic activity variable we created in Chapter 6, **ecact**, in a version that takes only five values: those for *Employed*, *Unemployed*, *Sick*, *Retired* and *Looking after home*. Then we'll need the dummy variables we created in Chapter 6 for place of birth and whether the respondent thought they would be a victim of institutional racism. I called these variables **birth** and **discrim1**.

We now need to produce dummy versions of the three dependent variables used in the regression: **febrit**, **dualid** and **sbegb**. You'll see that the article authors chose to distinguish respondents who 'very strongly' agreed with the relevant statements from all others, including those who agreed. It looks as if they chose to do this because the distribution of these variables shows that the overwhelming majority, between 83% and 93%, of respondents agreed with them, leaving only small numbers in the other categories. However, we might want to reflect on whether the distinction between 'strong' agreement and simple agreement is one that all respondents would tend to draw in the same way. We can check this later on. Table 12.1 lists the variables to be used in the regression.

Once you have produced these three dummies, and weighted the data (use **wtfinds**) you are ready to run the regression and the relevant diagnostics. It is quickest to use the GUI to enter

Table 12.1 Variables in the regression

Variable	Reference category (0)	Other category (1)
febrit	Strongly agrees that they feel part of Britain	Agrees, disagrees or strongly disagrees
dualid	Strongly agrees that it is possible to fully belong to Britain and maintain a separate cultural or religious identity	Agrees, disagrees or strongly disagrees
sbegb	Feels that they very strongly belong to Britain	Agrees, disagrees or strongly disagrees
sex	Male	
ethrelig	Caribbean Christian	Dummy variables for other categories
ecact	Employed	Dummy variables for other categories
birth	Born in the UK	
Discrim1	Does not believe they would be a victim of institutional discrimination	Does believe they would be a victim

the details of the regression, but then **Paste** the syntax so that you can edit and change it; you'll almost certainly want to run more than one model, so that having syntax to edit is faster than the GUI. When entering the variables you will need to define the reference categories for categorical variables in the same way as the authors did, and ask for confidence intervals for the exponentiated coefficients. 🔊 As usual, the correct syntax is available on the companion website if you run into difficulties. For diagnostics, request a Hosmer–Lemeshow goodness-of-fit test, Cook's distance and leverage values, and standardised and deviance residuals (if you're unsure how to request these, you'll find this in Chapter 11). When you have run the model, produce scatterplots of the predicted probabilities by the leverage values and Cook's distance, and compute values for the change in chi-square and the change in deviance, as we did in Chapter 11, in order to produce scatterplots of the change in chi-square and the deviance by the predicted probabilities.

When you do this you should be able to replicate the results in the published paper almost perfectly. The only coefficient that you'll find comes out substantially differently is that for the economic status *Sick* for the dual-identity question.

If you look at the Hosmer–Lemeshow tables you'll see that they indicate close fits between the observed and predicted probabilities for the dependent. You should also find that the diagnostic scatterplots and distribution of the change in chi-square and change in deviance statistics look satisfactory. 🔊 They are shown on the companion website so that you can compare your results in detail. Table 12.2 compares the results reported in the article with what I obtained.

12 ● 3 ALTERNATIVES TO THE PUBLISHED MODEL

Once you have successfully replicated what the authors achieved, you can explore alternatives to some of the analytical choices made by the authors. The most obvious alternative would be to alter the definition of the dependent dummies, so that we distinguish those who strongly agreed or agreed as one group, against the smaller numbers who disagreed or disagreed strongly. If you do so you'll find that although the sizes of the individual coefficients change, as we

Table 12.2 Comparison of exponentiated regression coefficients, Karlsen and Nazroo (2015) and replication

		Dependent variable					
		Febrit		Dualid		Sbegb	
		Replication	Article	Replication	Article	Replication	Article
Independent variable	Category						
DVAge		1.02	1.02	1.01	1.02	1.03	1.04
Sex(1)	Female	0.81	0.80	1.04	1.05	0.95	0.96
ethrelig	Caribbean Christian						
	African Christian	0.92	0.92	1.43	1.44	1.19	1.20
	Asian Christian	1.02	1.02	1.31	1.31	0.90	0.90
	Hindu	1.06	1.06	1.86	1.86	1.03	1.03
	Sikh	1.22	1.22	1.68	1.69	1.32	1.32
	Indian Muslim	1.34	1.33	3.52	3.53	1.30	1.31
	Bangladeshi Muslim	1.34	1.33	2.55	2.57	1.57	1.57
	Pakistani Muslim	1.74	1.72	1.72	1.72	1.77	1.77
	African Muslim	0.86	0.82	1.86	1.93	0.86	0.89
ecact	Employed						
	Unemployed	0.98	0.98	1.01	0.98	1.09	1.15
	Sick	0.95	0.96	1.39	1.42	1.03	1.04
	Retired	0.83	0.85	0.85	1.00	0.92	1.02
	Looking after home	0.87	0.89	0.97	0.97	1.03	1.00
birth	Born elsewhere	0.80	0.79	1.13	1.12	0.76	0.75
discrim1	Discrimination: Yes	0.63	0.63	0.90	0.90	0.58	0.58

Source: Home Office Citizenship Survey, 2008–9; weighted data; author's analysis.

would expect, the substantive conclusions remain much the same, so that Karlsen and Nazroo's choice seems to have been a sound one.

Respondents' expectations of discrimination in different institutional settings were represented in the model by a dummy variable, **discrim1**. However, since this variable was based on the interval-level variable **discrim**, it could be entered in the model in this way. Does this have an impact? Another avenue to explore is the parsimony of the model. Looking across the three dependent variables, the only ethnic religious categories to have an impact were *Bangladeshi Muslim* and *Pakistani Muslim*. We could produce a variable distinguishing this group from all the other religious and ethnic categories together. We could drop the economic activity variable as it failed to produce many significant predictors. We could also compare the results for our ethnic categories and white Christian or non-religious respondents. Finally, there are many alternative variables in the survey that would be candidates for inclusion in the model.

12●4   HELPING ATTITUDES AND BEHAVIOUR

The second article we examined in Chapter 6 also went on to run and test a series of logistic regression models that you can replicate. As with the contingency tables that we reproduced, you'll find that replicating the exact numbers isn't possible, but the results are close enough to make no substantive difference.

Return to the ESS Round 3 dataset you previously downloaded. First you will need to prepare the dependent and independent variables. Recode **hlprtrn** so that expectation of help is coded as 1, no expectation of help is coded as 0, and other values, including *neither agree nor disagree*, are coded as missing; recode **gndr** so that male = 0 and female = 1; recode **edulvla** so that it becomes a dummy variable where qualifications up to and including lower secondary are coded 0 and higher qualifications 1. Convert **iphlppl, atnoact,hlpoth** and **pplahlp** into dummies where 1 corresponds to value helper, helper in practice, informal helper and area of helping/high helping.

Table 12.3   Comparison of exponentiated regression coefficients, Purdham and Tranmer's (2014) first model and replication

Predictor	Replication	Article
Age (in years)	0.98	0.98
Male (0); female (1)	0.81	0.78
Education (lower secondary qualification (0); higher qualification (1))	1.15	1.12
Main activity (reference – in paid work)		
In education	1.06	1
Unemployed, looking for job	0.96	0.82
Unemployed, not looking for job	1.66	1.38
Permanently sick or disabled	0.82	0.71
Retired	1.78	1.62
Housework, looking after children/others	1.30	1.17
Value helper (important to help the people around you and care for others' well-being (1))	0.77	0.73
Helper in practice (help with or attend local activities (1))	0.75	0.7
Informal helper of others (excluding family, work or voluntary organisations (1))	0.76	0.73
Local context of help (areas of perceived low/no levels of helping (0); areas of perceived/high levels of helping (1))	0.99	0.92
Area type – urban/suburban area (0); rural (1)	1.19	1.21
Constant	1.78	1.82

Finally, convert **domicil** to a dummy variable with urban and suburban areas coded as 0 and rural areas coded as 1.

You are now ready to run the first model reported by Purdham and Tranmer (2014) which uses age, gender, educational level, economic activity, value helper, helper in practice, informal helper, local help context and area type as predictor variables. Table 12.3 compares the results you should obtain, using a combination of **pweight** and **dweight** as weights.

Purdham and Tranmer then run a second model including the countries as a set of dummy variables. Create these dummies and then run the model with these dummies added. You'll see that including country dummies substantially increases the amount of variation that the model is able to explain. Once again you should find that the regression diagnostics look satisfactory. Table 12.4 shows the main coefficient results.

Table 12.4 Comparison of exponentiated regression coefficients, Purdham and Tranmer's (2014) second model and replication

Predictor	Replication	Article
Age (in years)	0.98	0.98
Male (0); female (1)	0.70	0.70
Education (lower secondary qualification (0); higher qualification (1))	0.69	0.71
Main activity (reference – in paid work)		
In education	0.92	
Unemployed, looking for job	1.11	1.09
Unemployed, not looking for job	1.56	1.54
Permanently sick or disabled	0.80	0.82
Retired	1.32	
Housework, looking after children/others	1.21	1.2
Value helper (important to help the people around you and care for others' well-being (1))	0.93	0.92
Helper in practice (help with or attend local activities (1))	0.98	
Informal helper of others (excluding family, work or voluntary organisations (1))	0.91	
Local context of help (areas of perceived low/no levels of helping (0); areas of perceived/high levels of helping (1))	0.91	0.9
Area type – urban/suburban area (0); rural (1)	1.19	1.18
UK		
Cyprus	0.63	0.6
Switzerland	0.76	0.72
France	0.77	0.72
Belgium	1.04	0.98

Predictor	Replication	Article
Portugal	1.04	0.99
Netherlands	1.14	1.1
Ireland	1.32	1.22
Finland	1.33	1.32
Spain	1.38	1.27
Germany	1.85	1.78
Poland	2.12	2.04
Norway	2.32	2.22
Estonia	2.95	2.88
Bulgaria	3.56	3.39
Slovakia	4.06	3.93
Hungary	4.08	3.98
Denmark	4.85	4.74
Sweden	4.91	4.78
Austria	5.52	5.26
Slovenia	6.12	5.96
Russian Federation	11.05	10.77
Ukraine	11.24	10.65
Constant	0.82	0.94

Note: The Cox–Snell (Nagelkerke) R^2 is 0.21 (0.29) for both replication and article. The model chi-square is 7.900 for the replication and 7.721 in the article.

As well as reproducing the other models that Purdham and Tranmer run, you might pursue some of your own, changing how some of the key variables were defined, or adding or dropping other variables from the model. One obvious line of investigation would be to divide countries into groups based on the coefficients in Table 12.4, and explore other correlates of helping attitudes and behaviour. Promising variables to investigate would include those on trust such as **ppltrst**, **pplfair** and **pplhlp**.

12●5 USING SPSS TO INVESTIGATE PUBLISHED CONTINGENCY TABLES

Sometimes you'll find yourself reading published work where the original microdata is not available, but you want to explore the results in a contingency table in greater detail. It is possible to replicate the microdata for the variables used in a crosstab, so long as there are no missing values.

Table 12.5 Contraceptive use by age and desire for more children

Age i	Desire j	Using y_{ij}	Not using $n_{ij} - y_{ij}$	All n_{ij}
<25	Yes	58	265	323
	No	14	60	74
25–29	Yes	68	215	283
	No	37	84	121
30–39	Yes	79	230	309
	No	158	145	303
40–49	Yes	14	43	57
	No	79	58	137
Total		507	1100	1607

Source: Rodríguez (2007: Table 3.7).

If you study the crosstab in Table 12.5 (from Rodríguez, 2007) you will see that it is based on three variables: one for age group, one for desire for more children and one for contraceptive use. This produces a crosstab with 16 cells in the body of the table. In a new IBM SPSS Statistics software **Data Editor** window in **Data View** mode, give each of these variables a name and add a *fourth* variable (call it **count** or **weight**). Then enter the 16 combinations of value categories for the three variables in successive rows of the **Data Editor** window, entering the final value for **count** as the number in the corresponding cell in the crosstab, so that your **Data Editor** window looks like Figure 12.1.

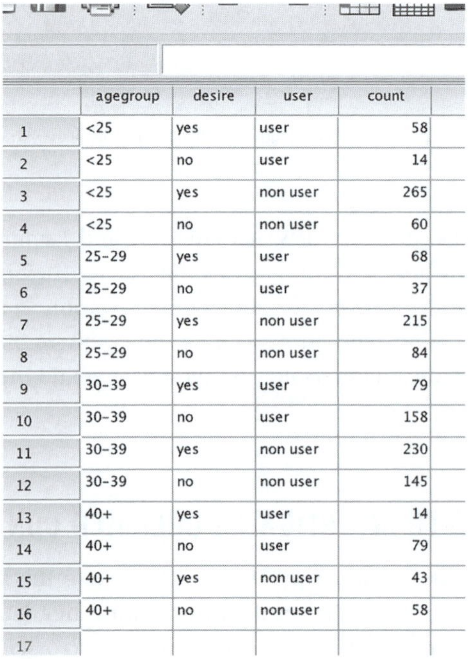

	agegroup	desire	user	count
1	<25	yes	user	58
2	<25	no	user	14
3	<25	yes	non user	265
4	<25	no	non user	60
5	25–29	yes	user	68
6	25–29	no	user	37
7	25–29	yes	non user	215
8	25–29	no	non user	84
9	30–39	yes	user	79
10	30–39	no	user	158
11	30–39	yes	non user	230
12	30–39	no	non user	145
13	40+	yes	user	14
14	40+	no	user	79
15	40+	yes	non user	43
16	40+	no	non user	58
17				

Figure 12.1 The completed Data Editor (Data View mode) window

To reproduce the original contingency table, apply the **count** variable as a weight, and run a crosstab of the three variables, which will reproduce the original table perfectly. You can then produce output such as row or column percentages, graphical output, correlation coefficients or significance tests, or run a logistic regression on the data. Of course, you've not been able to reproduce each individual case in the data, but you have been able to reproduce each of the 16 individual covariate patterns.

what you have learned

This chapter has brought together skills you've learned throughout the book to address quite a challenging task: replicating original binary logistic regression results using the information published in journal articles or other media together with the original micro data.

- How to reconsider the author's original analytical choices, and explore alternatives to them
- How to produce microdata based on covariate patterns from published contingency tables

exercises

1   Using the Home Office Citizenship Survey, construct a logistic regression model to compare how strongly 'White British' respondents feel they belong to Britain compared to other ethnic and religious groups. Control for age, gender, economic activity and place of birth. What do you find?

2   Using the regression coefficients shown in Table 12.4 as a guide, divide the countries in ESS3 into three or four groups. Produce contingency tables with the main variables used by Purdham and Tranmer. Do attitudes and helping behaviour vary between these country groups? Produce an appropriate regression model to explore one of these differences.

3   Find a contingency table from a book or journal article that you have read recently and reproduce it in SPSS using the procedure shown in Section 12.5. Produce an appropriate correlation coefficient and run a significance test for the table.

A LOOK BACK

How to Enjoy 'An Avalanche of Numbers'

13●1 THE AVALANCHE OF NUMBERS

If you have read and understood this book, and worked through the exercises in each chapter, you should now be an accomplished secondary data analyst, with a toolbox of skills that you can apply to deal with many kinds of data. However, you are also at the start of what can be a long and hopefully exciting journey. If you recall the map metaphor I used in Chapter 1, you now have an almost endless series of worlds that you can discover. The range and quality of data available for analysis is expanding and improving all the time: it is there for you to explore. Ian Hacking (1990) coined the phrase 'an avalanche of printed numbers' to describe how in the early nineteenth century there was an explosion of interest in trying to make more sense of society by measuring it, almost for the first time. In earlier ages there had been sporadic attempts to organise crude censuses, usually with a view to taxing or conscripting the population, but almost nothing in the way of systematic measurement. By the end of the century virtually every country had a population census and work began, which continues to this day, to broaden and deepen the information available through the more efficient collection of administrative data, such as vital registration data or through the activities of the local and national state, or through sample surveys. Today this avalanche of numbers is so vast that we hardly notice it and tend to take it for granted. We assume that data is almost instantly available on trends in population, employment, or education, the performance of the health service or the views of the public on almost any important matter. Yet almost all this information comes from sample surveys of various kinds and requires decisions to be made about how this survey evidence might best be interpreted. It is available for further and critical analysis that holds these decisions up to the light and questions them.

I hope too that this book will have given you a healthy scepticism about the value of this ever expanding volume of data available to those competent enough to make some sense of it. Almost any data is better than no data at all – better than ignorance. However, you should also now be able to appreciate just how crude is much of the data paraded in everyday life, and served up in political or policy debate. Rarely is there a rigorous concern with measurement or with the quality of the data used. Rarely is there much attention paid to the vital distinction between correlation and causation. Rarely is there sufficient effort made to make the most illuminating possible comparisons, to attempt to mimic in observed data the kind of control that experiments can produce. Instead there tends to be the resort to numbers to give a patina of 'scientific' respectability to any old argument arrived at by other means. The responsibility of the data analyst is to distinguish crude analyses and badly drawn comparisons from those that give us some valuable evidence about the nature and functioning of different social processes, societies and their institutions.

Just as data comes in a myriad of different forms, so the last few decades have brought the growth of many new approaches to analysing data that the proficient data analyst can master. Two examples are longitudinal data and Bayesian approaches. Longitudinal data is produced when the same subjects (people, organisations, countries, etc.) are observed on more than one occasion, giving us much more powerful information about change over time. However, such data also brings its own challenges. For example, our statistical tests will have to take into account the fact that observations from the same subject at different points in time are no longer independent of each other. Studying subjects over time requires that we can continue to observe them, so that responses rates and attrition of the sample have to be dealt with:

subjects who drop out of a study may not share the same characteristics as those who remain. As we saw in Chapter 4, significance tests tell us about the probability of getting the data we observe given that our hypothesis is correct, when what we really want is some measure of the probability of our hypothesis being correct, given the data that we've observed. Bayesian approaches tackle this problem. Until very recently such approaches were made very difficult by the volume of computation required, even with simple data. Modern computing power has overcome this obstacle, so that Bayesian approaches to probability now contend with the frequentist approach used in this book.

The brilliant statistician John Wilder Tukey once commented that 'the best thing about being a statistician is that you get to play in everyone's backyard'. Of course, reading and understanding this book has not turned you into a statistician. However, it will have given you skills that many of your colleagues will not have, whether you enter academia, or pursue a research or other career elsewhere. You'll almost certainly find your data analysis skills not only useful, but in demand from colleagues. In the last few years I've worked on subjects as diverse as development, sustainability and climate change; national identity, young people and politics; population ageing; economic recession and fertility; industrial relations; and more besides. There have been few dull moments. With every project comes the opportunity to master a new technique of analysis, or learn something genuinely new about the world.

With the foundation of the skills you've developed from this book, you are well equipped to go much further in exploring new and more complex techniques of data analysis and statistics. In any science it is the beginning that is the most difficult part, and the rewards tend to come later, as your portfolio of skills enables you to embark on more interesting and revealing analyses. To get some idea of the scope of the possibilities open to you, it is worth looking at the IBM SPSS Statistics software Syntax reference manual (accessed via the **Help** menu in SPSS). In this book we've used about 20 main commands (frequencies, crosstabs, means, descriptives, regression, logistic regression, compute, if, filter, select, weight, recode, count, sort, aggregate, split, match files, save outfile, export and a few others). However, the reference manual extends to well over 2,000 pages. I doubt that any one researcher has ever used every procedure available in SPSS. The range of possibilities is testimony to the power of statistics to get to grips with the diversity of challenges that making sense of different kinds of data throws up. However, it can be easy to lose sight of the underlying rationale of data analysis as you become immersed in the technicalities of more powerful procedures. Thus it is useful to end by thinking of some of the core principles that we've covered in this book that keep this rationale in mind.

13.2 ANY DATA IS BETTER THAN NO DATA, BUT ALL DATA CONTAINS ERROR

The first is that *all* data is socially constructed and produced; it is neither a product of 'nature' nor does it lie around, perfectly formed, waiting to be collected or harvested by the diligent social scientist. This social construction has two main elements. One is our conceptual and theoretical understanding. It would make science a lot easier if we had some guarantee that how we perceived the world was a direct function of that world itself, that the empirical facts of the external world somehow made their way into our brains without us interfering in the process. Of course we know that this is not and cannot ever be so. Since our only experience of the world is just that – our experience of it – we can never appeal to anything outside of that experience to validate it.

However, that does not mean that we cannot build up an increasingly powerful knowledge of that world if we proceed in a rigorous scientific manner. There is ample room for debate about exactly what science comprises, but there is absolutely no room for doubt that it in fact works. The proof of that is something we might do more to reflect upon: the unprecedented explosion of material progress and revolutionary change ushered in by the spread of the application of scientific ways of understanding the world since the seventeenth century, first in north-western Europe and then over the entire world. If we want to accomplish anything, in practice we turn to science, regardless of our other beliefs or of what we might think of science itself. The religiously devout may believe in prayer, but in their everyday lives they rely on technology to get things done.

Unlike the natural sciences, the social sciences are still in their infancy. In part this is because their raw material is less tractable. Unlike atoms, people can think. Societies are constantly in movement. They may even change under the impact of social scientific knowledge itself. In part this is because their raw material is inexorably infused with a moral dimension. We can neither treat people nor think about them in the way a chemist or physicist might handle a rock. In part this is because social science has yet to develop sufficient consensus about itself to allow the growth of cumulative knowledge rather than mutually contradictory perspectives. However, another reason for their failure to emulate the success and prestige of the natural sciences has been the balance between theoretical and empirical work. More energy and attention has been given to developing theories than to testing them empirically, in large part because empirical work has been unduly neglected. In short, there has not been nearly enough good empirical primary and secondary data analysis. Were there more, we'd realise just how much we do not know – the first step in producing any worthwhile knowledge.

The second element of the social construction of data is simply the ubiquity of measurement error. Measurements require classifications, categories and definitions, and these have to be capable of being practical to implement 'in the field'. This process inevitably squeezes a complex reality into something simpler and cruder. It is difficult to stress just how important it is to keep this in mind when analysing data. Unless you make a conscious effort to resist, as you work with data it will gradually tend to appear ever more real and convincing than it actually is. All data is ultimately provisional, imprecise and uncertain. It can be used more effectively and powerfully if we keep its limitations in mind, and do not convince ourselves that we have more knowledge than we in fact possess.

13●3 ALL MODELS ARE PRECISELY WRONG, BUT SOME ARE APPROXIMATELY USEFUL

There are many versions of this saying, but they all capture the idea that we can sometimes get sidetracked into getting a very clever answer to what we fail to realise is a very stupid question. Any model we use abstracts from the reality it is based upon, and reduces it to simpler, more tractable dimensions. Good models focus on what we are interested in and strip away the nuances that are less important. The focus of our interest, and what we deem important, are functions of an explicit or implicit theory, and the more empirically testable these theories are, the better.

Good models focus on comparisons or differences that are substantial, have some real implications for how we understand the world, or solve some practical problem that we have in mind and have a theoretical context that makes them meaningful. This is a better guide than simply looking out for statistical significance, or a high value for R^2 or some other key statistic. When building a model it is rather easy to get carried away by the complexity of the detailed operations involved and lose sight of the overall purpose for constructing it in the first place. Always have an answer to the question: what is my model there to do?

13●4   REPLICATION, REPLICATION, REPLICATION!

Replication is the cornerstone of science, so that it is unfortunate that there is not a lot more of it in social science research. There are two pressures that work against more extensive replication work. The first is the pressure to publish, which has increased in most higher education systems in recent years. However, journal editors are typically reluctant to publish replication studies because they are not 'original' work. Clearly replication that simply comprises exactly reproducing another analysis is of little interest, although it is nevertheless useful in checking whether some error has crept into a published study. However, showing that a result obtained from one study replicates or fails to replicate in another is extremely useful. It is much stronger evidence than any significance test of whether the result is a function of sampling fluctuation or of the particular way in which variables were defined and measured in any study. One of the reasons for editors' reluctance comes from a second pressure: which is that towards innovation and originality in research and its methods. In disciplines where science is genuinely cumulative such an approach helps drive science forward. Where, as in the social sciences, knowledge is not yet cumulative, innovation is a double-edged sword. It may bring improvements, but in the absence of much consensus about method or theory it also tends to increase the heterogeneity of chaotic and competing understandings. Were there as much emphasis on the consolidation of existing knowledge, something that replication can promote, the social sciences would be in a healthier state.

13●5   CURIOSITY TRUMPS CONVICTION

Confirmation bias is ubiquitous, and it is most pernicious when we are not aware of it, as the story of the horse Clever Hans we met in Chapter 2 makes clear. Cognitive psychologists have shown how we tend, without even being aware of it, to filter and absorb new evidence in such a way as to make it as consistent as possible with our existing beliefs. The reason why curiosity is by far the most important secondary data analysis skill is that it takes you to places you might never otherwise go, and to conclusions you might otherwise never reach. The most wonderful thing about secondary data analysis is that it wrests control of your conclusions from your own, perhaps dearly held, beliefs and hands them over to the evidence. It is, as I suggested in Chapter 2, the only alternative to 'argument from authority'.

None of this means that secondary data analysis turns you into some kind of empiricist simpleton, or strips you of your own convictions, or social or political beliefs. However, it does require you to confront these with the available empirical evidence.

13 ● 6 THE SEVEN MORTAL STATISTICAL SINS

Perhaps the best way to sum up some of the lessons in this book is to consider how to avoid what I think are some of the most pervasive mistakes made in the analysis and presentation of data, and some simple rules that help guide the presentation of clear and concise evidence based on data. Numbers can be used well or badly. Here is my list of pitfalls to avoid.

1 No measure is perfect, but some are more perfect than others

Numbers are only as good as the people who produce them. Any number depends upon the clear definition of *what* is measured and *how* it is measured. Very often it is difficult or impossible to precisely measure what is actually wanted (i.e. to obtain a *valid* measurement) in a way that will give consistent results whenever it is repeated (*reliable* measurements).

Numbers are more robust if they are based on definitions and means of measurement that are widely agreed, and whose strengths and weaknesses are well understood. Where there is controversy, the definition or measurement method used should be made clear. The source of numbers should always be provided. Never use a number if you don't know where it has been.

Comparisons over time or across different groups can only be made if the measurement method stays the same. Extra care has to be taken when information from different sources is used to make such comparisons. Definitions used by different organisations rarely coincide exactly. Even within the same survey instrument, question wording may change over time or new response categories may be added. Results can be influenced by the context within which a question is asked (including what questions have come before it). Comparisons across countries or language groups pose special problems.

Often it is sensible to report a range within which the true value of a measurement is thought to lie, but without *both* upper and lower limits, such ranges become meaningless. 'Up to 99% of people' includes the number zero; 'as few as 1%' does not rule out 99%. Robust results ought to be presented as confidence intervals within which we have a measureable degree of confidence that the true value we are trying to estimate lies.

Orders of magnitude matter. It is easy to misplace a decimal point or confuse a million with a billion, and thus get a number wildly wrong. Numbers should be presented with some readily recognisable comparison that makes their magnitude comprehensible, and also makes the detection of such errors more likely.

None of this means that measurement, quantitative methods, statistics or data analysis are futile pursuits. Almost any data is better than no data, or speculation unconstrained by empirical evidence.

2 Percentages or proportions have a base (denominator) which *must* be stated

Percentages express numbers as a fraction of 100. If what that 100 comprises is not stated, then the meaning of the percentage will be unclear or misleading. Growth rates will depend upon the base year from which growth is measured. It is easy to confuse different groups of people on which percentages are based. For example, does 'working women' refer to all women who do work, paid or unpaid; those currently in the labour force; those in employment; employees; employees working full-time hours…?

When the base is itself a percentage, as often happens when change is discussed, this presents two further problems. The first is the confusion of absolute and relative change. If the growth rate rises from 2% to 3%, that is a 50% increase *not* 1%, but better expressed as a 'one percentage point increase' in the rate of growth. In this context the absolute change probably gives a better sense of what is happening than the relative change.

The second is the multiplication of the margin of error contained in calculating relative change on the basis of small numbers that themselves have a margin of error. For example, a survey may show that over a period of time the number of people in a particular category has increased from 5% to 15%. This could, correctly, be described as a 300% increase. However, it is from such a small base that the impression created is misleading. The obverse, that the number of people not in this category has declined from 95% to 85%, suggests a much more modest change, and one that will be less influenced by error in the original data because the absolute size of the base is larger: a few percentage points either way makes much less difference to 95% than to 5%.

Incidence and prevalence are often confused. Incidence is a time-based measure, of those 'at risk' within a given time period experiencing an event: 10% of people caught a cold in 2009; 2% of motorists had an accident in 2009. Prevalence refers to a state of affairs at a point in time: on 1 December 2009, 3% of people currently had a cold; on 1 December 2009, 24% of motorists had ever been involved in an accident.

3 The average may not be the same as 'typical', and will not be universal

Averages summarise a lot of information in a single number. This makes them very useful, but their limitations should also be borne in mind. Averages may describe the most typical condition, but they *may* also describe a highly atypical mid-point between two or more very different conditions. Wherever there is variety, many cases may not be close to the 'average' and a few cases may be very far from it. This need not make such cases either 'abnormal' or unusual.

Distributions around an average may not be symmetrical. If there are a small number of cases with very high or very low values, this can drag the average up or down. When this is the case the *median*, the value of the case with the middle value when all cases are ranked, gives a better guide. Earnings are typically skewed in this way, so that substantially more than 50% of earners earn below 'average' earnings, but the level of 'median' earnings will divide earners into two equally sized groups.

4 Highly unusual events may be fairly common

The probability that an event will occur depends not only upon what the chances are of it occurring in a given situation, but also upon the number of such situations (the base). The chances of winning the lottery are very low, but since millions buy tickets each week, there are regular winners. The occurrence of an unusual or unexpected event is not, in itself, evidence that some special factor must have caused it, especially if there are many situations in which it might occur (the 'Texan sharpshooter' fallacy). Many events and states of affairs follow an approximately normal distribution in which fewer cases are found, the further one travels from the value typical of the average case. However this does not mean that outliers towards the 'tails' of such a distribution must be mistakes or should not exist. Unfortunately there have been several miscarriages of justice in which people have been convicted because it has been wrongly supposed that the chances of an event (e.g. a death) occurring by chance have been so small as to point towards the culpability of the defendant.

Repeated measures of the same phenomenon regress towards the mean, showing spurious improvement or deterioration. Because no measurement is perfect, it contains some element of random error. To the extent that results towards the extreme ends of a scale (e.g. the 'best' and 'worst' performers) contain more of such error, repeating the measurement of performance is likely to lead to results less far from the mean, even if there has been no change in the underlying value of the characteristic that is being measured. This should always be taken into account when analysing the performance of 'failing' schools, hospitals, football teams, managers or companies, accident blackspots, and so on.

5 Correlation is not causation

Natural sciences and medicine frequently use randomised controlled trials to obtain evidence about cause and effect. If, on average, two groups in the experiment are the same to start with (randomised), and only one group is subjected to the experimental condition, any difference between this experimental group and the control group *must*, on average, be *caused by* the experimental condition. Evidence of cause and effect in human affairs is much harder to produce because usually only observation is possible, not experiments. We can observe *correlations* between conditions (e.g. sex and earnings; age and religious belief; unemployment and crime; social class and voting preference) but this is not evidence, in itself, of causation. It is *stronger* (but by no means conclusive) evidence of causation if it can be shown that, aside from the characteristics under discussion, the different groups in what is thought to be the causal category (e.g. men and women; young and old; employed and unemployed) are otherwise similar in terms of any other relevant characteristic. This is what social scientists or economists mean when they refer to 'control'. In the absence of such control, correlations may simply be 'spurious': the product of another, prior, causal factor. For example, there is a high cross-country correlation between the number of mobile phones in a country and the rate of infant mortality: more phones are associated with fewer infant deaths. It would be foolish, however, to think that mobile phones saved infant lives; both are the results of a prior factor, the level of economic development.

Observational or experimental studies rarely, if ever, claim to discover *the* cause of a condition or state of affairs. Usually such claims concern the possible size of one or more contributory causes among many.

6 Surveys are a product of their samples

Sampling makes it possible to get information about populations that are usually far too large and expensive to measure directly. But it can do so *only* if the sample has been systematically selected: usually by random selection. 'Convenience' samples, especially those in which *members of the sample select themselves* in some way, describe little more than the sample itself. Many 'surveys' used to promote products or publications take this form and have no more than propaganda value.

A 'selection effect' also operates when a group of people or things apparently defined by one characteristic is also defined in whole or in part by another one, either by dint of the method of their selection, or because of a strong correlation between the two characteristics. Selection effects can be extremely powerful. A recent, prominent example is given by Ben Goldacre (2012) who has drawn attention to the way in which studies of the effect of pharmaceutical drugs are much less likely to be published if the result of the study is that the drug has no effect. Journal editors prefer to report what they think of as substantive results rather than non-results. The effect of this is to bias public knowledge of any drug towards the conclusion that the drug is effective. Studies with positive result are selected for publication, and then the assumption tends to be made that these published studies comprise all studies that have been undertaken.

The likely accuracy of estimates of the characteristics of populations obtained from random samples depends upon the relevant number in the *sample*, rather than the *population*. Thus estimates about small subsections of the population (e.g. teenagers; single mothers; widowers; the self-employed; a minority ethnic group) may be liable to large errors. Surveys may also suffer from response bias if a substantial proportion of people choose not to respond to the survey, and there is reason to think that their characteristics may differ from those who choose to respond.

7 Significance is not substance

When working with random samples, any finding is often tested by calculating the probability that it is a result of chance sampling variation rather than a pattern that actually exists in the population. Conventionally a level of 5% probability is chosen, sometimes referred to as 'statistical significance'. In this context significant means *neither* 'important' *nor* 'substantial': it just describes how unlikely it is that such a finding could have occurred randomly. It also means that up to around one in 20 'results' are due to chance sampling variation – but, of course, we cannot know *which* ones. This is why replication is an important part of both natural and social scientific research.

■■■■■■■■■■■■ **exercise** ■■■■■■■■■■■■■■■■■■■■■■■■■■■■

Find a report in a magazine or newspaper that uses numbers but commits *none* of the seven mortal sins I've identified. Happy hunting!

REFERENCES

Allison, Paul D. (1999) *Multiple Regression: A Primer*. Thousand Oaks, CA: Pine Forge Press.

Blastland, Michael and Dilnot, Andrew (2008) *The Tiger That Isn't*. London: Profile Books.

Buis, Martin (2016) 'Logistic regression: When can we do what we think we can do?' Available at http://www.maartenbuis.nl/wp/odds_ratio_2.1.pdf (accessed 14 June 2016).

Ellenberg, Jordan (2015) *How Not to Be Wrong*. Harmondsworth: Penguin.

Goldacre, Ben (2012) *Bad Pharma*. Harmondsworth: Penguin.

Hacking, Ian (1990) *The Taming of Chance*. Cambridge: Cambridge University Press.

Hacking, Ian (2002) *An Introduction to Probability and Inductive Logic*. Cambridge: Cambridge University Press.

Haseldon, Lucy and Joloza, Theodore (2009) 'Measuring sexual identity: A guide for researchers'. ONS, Newport. Technical Report.

Hosmer Jr., David W., Lemeshow, Stanley and Sturdivant, Rodney X. (2013) *Applied Logistic Regression*, 3rd edition. Hoboken, NJ: John Wiley & Sons.

Kahneman, Daniel (2012) *Thinking Fast and Slow*. Harmondsworth: Penguin.

Karlsen, Saffron and Nazroo, James Y. (2015) 'Ethnic and religious differences in the attitudes of people towards being "British"'. *Sociological Review*, 63, 759–781.

Marsh, Catherine (1988) *Exploring Data*. Cambridge: Polity Press.

Menard, Scott (2010) *Logistic Regression: From Introductory to Advanced Concepts and Applications*. Thousand Oaks, CA: Sage.

Mood, C. (2010) 'Logistic regression: Why we cannot do what we think we can do, and what we can do about it'. *European Sociological Review*, 26(1), 67–82.

Norton, Trevor (2011) *Smoking Ears and Screaming Teeth: A Celebration of Scientific Eccentricity and Self-Experimentation*. New York: Pegasus.

Porter, Theodore (1986) *The Rise of Statistical Thinking*. Princeton, NJ: Princeton University Press.

Purdham, Kingsley and Tranmer, Mark (2014) 'Expectations of being helped in return for helping – citizens, the state and the local area'. *Population, Space and Place*, 20, 66–82.

Rodríguez, Germán (2007) 'Logit models for binary data'. Lecture notes for Generalized Linear Statistical Models course. Available at http://data.princeton.edu/wws509/notes/c3.pdf (accessed 14 June 2016).

INDEX